Urban Perspectives

Books by Alan Shank

New Jersey Reapportionment Politics: Strategies and Tactics in the Legislative Process

Political Power and the Urban Crisis, First and Second Editions

Educational Investment in an Urban Society (with *Melvin R. Levin*)

American Politics, Policies, and Priorities

Books by Ralph W. Conant

The Public Library and the City

The Politics of Community Health

Problems of Research in Community Violence (with *Molly A. Levin*)

The Prospects for Revolution

The Metropolitan Library (with *Kathleen Molz*)

The Politics of Comprehensive Health Planning (with *Jonathan West*)

JOHN C. BOLLENS
Consulting Editor
University of California, Los Angeles

Urban Perspectives
POLITICS AND POLICIES

ALAN SHANK
*State University of New York
at Geneseo*

RALPH W. CONANT
*formerly Director
of the Institute for Urban Studies
and the Southwest Center
for Urban Research*

Holbrook Press, Inc.   Boston

Printed in the United States of America.

Library of Congress Cataloging in Publication Data

Shank, Alan, 1936–
    Urban perspectives.

    Includes bibliographies and index.
    1. Municipal government—United States. 2. Metropolitan government—United States. 3. Cities and towns—United States. 4. Metropolitan areas—United States. I. Conant, Ralph Wendell, 1926–   joint author. II. Title.
JS341.S53   320.9′73   74–30351
ISBN 0–205–04704–1

Contents

part two

THE URBAN CRISIS: PROBLEMS AND PROSPECTS

Causes of Riots • Rioters and the Police • Insurrection • The Police and Civil Protest • Police Training and Attitudes • Police-Community Relations • Politicalization of the Police • The Police Culture • The New Immigrants and Civil Liberties • Police Attitudes Toward the Community • Regulating the Police • Varieties of Police Behavior • Conclusions

Introduction • Origins and Developments of AFDC Policy • The Welfare Explosion • Explaining the Welfare Explosion • Problems of the Welfare System • Income Transfer Proposals • Overhauling Welfare: President Nixon's Family Assistance Plan

Introduction • Precedents for Community and Citizen Participation • Participation and Planning • Implementing the Community Action Programs • The Model Cities Program • Evaluating Citizen Participation

Introduction • The Nature and Function of Comprehensive Health Planning • Origins of Community Health Planning • Evaluating the Effectiveness of Community Health Planning • The Future of Community Health Planning

Introduction • Housing Conditions • An Overview of Housing Policy Objectives • New Deal Responses: FHA and Public Housing • Urban Renewal • Model Cities • Federal Housing Subsidies • Concluding Note

Figures

Tables

Preface

Urban Perspectives: Politics and Policies explores and analyzes some of the key political and policy problems of our cities, suburbs, and metropolitan areas. We provide the basis for understanding how urban problems evolved, developed, and came to the forefront of national attention during the 1960s. Such problems included social unrest, urban poverty, law enforcement, inner-city slums, public assistance, education, and community health. These policy dilemmas continue unresolved and unabated in the 1970s.

Governmental commitment toward urban problems has increased considerably in the past two decades. No longer are urban problems felt to be the responsibility of particular regions or sections of the country. Nor are they regarded as the sole concern of state and local governments. During the 1960s, the federal government became deeply involved by encouraging planning and providing financial assistance to cities, suburbs, and metropolitan areas. Big-city mayors and other state and local officials became lobbyists and spokesmen in Washington to gain increased support from the president, Congress, and the various administrative agencies of the federal government.

In tracing federal urban policies over the past quarter century, we observe that federal commitments are frequently modified or diluted as national priorities change. While the federal government is not solely responsible for solving all urban problems, it collects a major share of the nation's tax revenues so that decentralized state and local solutions are almost impossible without federal financial aid. Neglect of urban problems and lack of attention to urban priorities can seriously threaten the health and welfare of the nation; over time, such neglect can also produce serious political crises and unrest.

One of the goals of this book is to identify national urban priorities which should be high on the public agenda. These include:

Maintaining a stable and prosperous economy
Ending poverty in the nation's midst and helping others toward this fundamental goal

Creating a health system to which all have equal access

Providing high-quality educational opportunities for every child and every adult

Eliminating all forms of environmental pollution

Making cities livable by effectively controlling crime, creating efficient systems of transportation, eliminating slums, and encouraging thoughtful use of land and open space

Placing special emphasis on citizen involvement in planning new programs and improving established ones

Finally, encouraging and maintaining vigorous citizen initiative in governmental action at all levels.

Urban Perspectives: Politics and Policies not only provides readers with the drama of events, but also encourages social science analysis and the development of recommendations for alleviating urban problems. In applying our analyses to a wide variety of undergraduate and graduate courses such as Urban Politics, Urban Policy, Urban Administration, State and Local Government, Public Policy, City Planning, Urban Economics, and Urban Sociology, our book draws upon a rich variety of policy studies, reports, court cases, research investigations, and teaching experiences of the authors.

Shank originated the plan for the book during a 1969–1970 European teaching assignment in the Boston University Overseas Graduate Program made possible by Hubert S. Gibbs, Dean of Metropolitan College at Boston University. Outstanding graduate student participation influenced the early evolution of the book in a Brussels (Belgium) urban seminar by Sandy Anderson, Jack Boyle, Larry Daugherty, and Ed Elmendorf. The SUNY-Geneseo Faculty Research Committee generously provided a release-time grant during the spring of 1971 which assisted in completing Chapters 2 and 3. Earlier versions of Chapter 5 were presented at the Workshops on Mayoral Leadership organized by Frances Burke at the Northeastern Political Science Association meetings in Amherst, Massachusetts (1972) and in Buck Hill Falls, Pennsylvania (1973). Ed Elmendorf read, criticized, and offered helpful suggestions for Chapters 1, 2, and 3. John Bollens, Philip Coulter, Michael Lipsky, Suzanne Sebert, and Donald Zauderer reviewed the entire manuscript. Paul Conway of Holbrook Press was most patient and understanding in assisting this project from its inception to its completion. David Kerwin provided many critical and useful observations on American urban problems from a Canadian perspective. Samuel Spizer (Shank's father-in-law) offered numerous suggestions on urban education, housing, and welfare in many hours of conversation. Finally, special gratitude is extended to Shank's wife, Bernice, for her continual encouragement and support over the years it took to complete the book. The title, *Urban Perspectives: Politics and Policies,* was inspired by her. Also, his children, Steven and Naomi, provided moral support during the usual difficulties that arise during any extended writing experience.

Chapters 6 and 7 are based in part upon the previous work of Conant at the Lemberg Center at Brandeis University in his studies of social unrest which dominated the 1960s. Chapter 4 on metropolitan politics and planning grew out of Conant's work at the Joint Center for Urban Studies (with Charles Haar and others) for the U.S. Senate Subcommittee on Intergovernmental Relations, for the Greater Hartford Chamber of Commerce in the Town Meeting for Tomorrow project, and for the Connecticut Legislature Commission on the Necessity and Feasibility of Metropolitan Government. Chapter 9 on citizen participation in federal-local poverty programs and Chapter 12 on urban education are new essays written especially for this book. Chapter 10 is based upon Conant's previous and ongoing studies of the politics of health planning (*The Politics of Community Health,* Public Affairs Press, 1968 and *The Politics of Comprehensive Health Planning,* forthcoming with Jonathan West). Jonathan West of the Institute for Urban Studies, University of Houston reviewed Chapters 6, 9, 10, and 12 and provided the list of suggested readings for Chapters 10 and 12. The Southwest Center for Urban Research and the Institute for Urban Studies provided secretarial and other supporting services. Conant's wife, Audrey Karl Conant, has for many years maintained a carefully organized clipping service principally from the *New York Times,* the *Christian Science Monitor,* and the *Wall Street Journal,* materials from which lend a special vitality to the contemporary topics of this book. The case study on Lincoln, Nebraska, in Chapter 10 was prepared in part by Beverlie Elaine Conant, a former staff member of the Southwest Center for Urban Research.

Had the authors more time and space in this edition, several additional topics might have been added: an analysis of suburban communities in their new role as important economic entities in their own right; an account of the evolution of land management policy, which is the larger issue in the concern about the use and preservation of the environment; an analysis of the influence of the energy problem on the form of cities; and the problem of transportation as it relates to the energy problem and to development planning. These and other salient policy problems will be addressed in a subsequent edition.

As teachers, we seek to provide students with examples of sound policy analysis, and we also try to point out the flaws in the system and to suggest corrective action. We hope that students who use this book will come away inspired to join in the task of seeking out and implementing solutions to the problems we face in common.

introduction

Perspectives on Urban Politics and Policies

During the 1960s most Americans became more aware than ever of various problems in cities, suburbs, and metropolitan areas: racial conflict, rising crime, increasing taxes, deteriorating services, municipal employees' strikes, violence and protest demonstrations, urban sprawl, congested highways, smog, pollution, and environmental neglect, to name some of the most serious ones. The responses of different city groups and suburban dwellers were sometimes drastic and frequently divisive: "law and order," Black Power, community control, neighborhood schools and antibusing regulations, and strict zoning controls. By the 1970s the threat of an energy shortage, which some feared might immobilize or at least slow down the economy, added to the list of urban and metropolitan concerns.

The urban problems of recent years are the product of different converging forces which need to be identified and explained. This chapter discusses a variety of approaches to the study of urban politics and policies. These set the stage for understanding the origins, developments, and underlying causes of the nation's urban political and policy dilemmas. In particular, we consider the following questions:

1. What are the historical, structural, functional, and power bases of urban politics and city government?

1

2. What are the contemporary challenges to power and authority in city government and politics?
3. What are some of the key elements of the urban problems and how did they arise?
4. How can we best analyze the components of these urban problems?
5. What are some suggested solutions for urban problems, and how might these changes be achieved?
6. What are the future prospects for city politics and urban policies?

THE ANTIURBAN BIAS

At the outset, students of urban problems should be aware of a fundamental anticity or *antiurban bias* that has pervaded and conditioned American attitudes. Even today, most people prefer to live in a suburb, small town, or village rather than in a city. As the nation became urbanized with great concentrations of population, economic wealth, communications, and educational and cultural resources, there was no associated commitment or attachment to urban values. Community living was not equated with an urban way of life. Cities, suburbs, and metropolitan regions developed largely on an unplanned and pragmatic basis without any particular attention to the goals and purposes of urban living. Instead, an almost schizoid situation persisted. As urbanization intensified, urban critics ridiculed and attacked the cities. Morton and Lucia White effectively summarize the list of chronic complaints against cities throughout the course of national development:

> The American city has been thought by American intellectuals to be: too noisy, too dusty, too dirty, too smelly, too commercial, too crowded, too full of immigrants, too full of Jews, too full of Irishmen, Italians, Poles, too industrial, too pushing, too mobile, too fast, too artificial, destructive of conversation, destructive of communication, too greedy, too capitalistic, too full of automobiles, too full of smog, too full of dust, too heartless, too intellectual, too scientific, insufficiently poetic, too lacking in manners, too mechanical, destructive of family, tribal, and patriotic feeling.[1]

The antiurban bias has caused cities to be neglected by the states and the federal government. Except for the burst of industrialization and municipal construction activity after the Civil War, the temporary relief programs of the New Deal during the 1930s, and employment opportunities provided by national defense activity during two world wars, most cities languished under the constraints of rurally dominated state legislatures.

CITY POLITICS: REFORMED AND UNREFORMED INSTITUTIONS

Associated with the antiurban bias were the struggles to reform city governmental institutions and electoral processes which focused upon the procedures rather than the substance of public policies. As discussed in Chapters 1, 2, and 3, these reform efforts did not adequately take into account the kinds of leadership necessary to manage urban areas, and such reforms did not always address the needs of inner-city minority groups except to promote their voting allegiance in return for social welfare benefits.

The reformers of the Progressive era sought to replace the decentralized coalition politics of boss rule with centralized nonpartisan professional administration. In general, an "unreformed" municipal system consists of partisan ballots, ward-based councilmen, and strong executive and party leadership exercised either by a "boss" or by a mayor who controls the party machinery and city government. An unreformed system is neighborhood- or ward-oriented and is less concerned with questions of accountability than it is with dispensing favors to party workers and supporters. In contrast, a "reformed" municipal system includes nonpartisan ballots, at-large elections for councilmen, and a council-manager government. Ironically, Black Power and community control advocates of the 1960s and 1970s have pressed for "reforms" which would bring back many of the features of local government which the early "good government" reformers tried to suppress.

Students of urban politics should be aware of the underlying assumptions of both reformed and unreformed municipal structures since, as shown in Chapters 2 and 3, the benefits of reform may not always be achieved. In fact, in some communities, structure is considered to be less important than the responsiveness of government to the needs of the people. Also, in recent years, both reformed and unreformed city governments have encountered increasing difficulty in providing essential services. The policy chapters in Part II of the book show the necessity of cooperation between cities and the federal government in social welfare programs.

Structural considerations are also found in proposals for integrating city and suburban government. As discussed in Chapter 4, new forms of government and areawide planning can include a variety of approaches, ranging from informal interlocal agreements to areawide consolidation. The metropolitan government approach attempts to overcome the fragmentation and decentralization of localities which cannot deal with such areawide policy problems as pollution, transportation, taxation, parks, and recreation.

CLEAVAGES AND COMMUNITY POWER

The heterogeneity of urban communities and the lack of areawide government results in endless unresolved conflict among the numerous interests which compete for political advantage. Political scientists Edward C. Banfield and James Q. Wilson identify four such persistent divisions within metropolitan areas, including those between (1) suburbanites and the central city, (2) political parties, (3) ethnic and racial groups, and (4) haves and have nots.[2]

Socioeconomic status, economic class, and ideology strongly influenced city development in the era between the Civil War and World War I. Chapters 1, 2, and 3 discuss the demands on urban political systems resulting from extreme disagreement over which community groups should control or determine who gets what. A useful guide to understanding this conflict is provided by the historian Richard Hofstadter, who distinguished between the values of European immigrants supporting boss rule and machine politics and the businessman's upper-middle-class attachments to urban reform. The immigrants had a narrow attachment to ethnic affiliations, a neighborhood orientation, and the expectation of material gains from political participation.[3] Banfield and Wilson characterize the immigrants' attitudes as a "private-regarding" or "individualist" ethos: a view of the public interest which identifies with "the ward or neighborhood rather than the city 'as a whole,' who look to politicians for 'help' and 'favors,' . . . and who are far less interested in the efficiency, impartiality, and honesty of local officials than in its readiness to confer material benefits of one sort or another upon them."[4] In contrast, the upper-middle-class reformers had a "public-regarding" or "communitywide" view of the public interest, favoring "good government," which meant efficiency, impartiality, honesty, planning, strong executives, no favoritism, moral legal codes, and strict enforcement of laws against gambling and vice.[5]

The "public-regarding" or communitywide orientation toward urban politics and policies not only provided the foundation for attacks against boss rule, but more recently, as discussed in Chapter 4, also influenced the attitudes and objectives of academics, reformers, and professional administrators who supported various forms of inter-governmental cooperation, planning, and metropolitan govern-mental integration.

In recent years, the fundamental disagreements in urban politics and policies have focused upon *racial* conflicts. Chapters 6, 7, and 12 deal with controversies between blacks and whites in the urban arena. In the first edition of *Political Power and the Urban Crisis*, race is identified as the key to understanding the cleavage between the central city and suburbia:

> Cities have become, at an ever-increasing pace, the location of the poor, lower-class, underprivileged, unskilled, and in recent times, growing numbers of angry and militant [blacks]. On the other hand, our suburbs contain millions of white Americans who enjoy un-matched affluence. . . . Barring any dramatic reversals of current trends, the future of our metropolitan areas will be characterized by this central city-suburban cleavage, which is rooted in both racial and class differences.[6]

Community power analysis provides useful insights on the rela-tionships between local political environments, types of power struc-tures, and formal governmental institutions.* Chapter 3 indicates that middle-class suburbs are closely associated with both economic elite power arrangements and the council-manager plan. On the other hand, Chapters 3 and 5 indicate that large central cities tend to be more politically competitive, have pluralistic power systems,

---

*The community power literature provides a rich source of studies analyz-ing elitist, pluralistic, and mixed power systems in local communities. Some of the leading studies are: Robert E. Agger, Daniel Goldrich, and Bert E. Swanson, *The Rulers and the Ruled* (N.Y.: John Wiley, 1964); Peter Bachrach and Morton Baratz, "Two Faces of Power," *American Political Science Review*, Vol. 57 (December 1962), pp. 947–952; Edward C. Banfield, *Political Influence* (N.Y.: Free Press, 1961); Robert A. Dahl, *Who Governs?* (New Haven: Yale University Press, 1961); Floyd Hunter, *Community Power Structure* (N.Y.: Doubleday, Anchor Books, 1963); M. Kent Jennings, *Community Influentials* (N.Y.: Free Press, 1964); Norton E. Long, "The Local Community as an Ecology of Games," *American Journal of Sociology*, Vol. 63 (November 1958), pp. 251–261; Nelson W. Polsby, *Community Power and Political Theory* (New Haven: Yale Uni-versity Press, 1963); Robert Presthus, *Men At The Top* (N.Y.: Oxford University Press, 1964); Arnold Rose, *The Power Structure* (N.Y.: Oxford University Press, 1967); Arthur J. Vidich and Joseph Bensman, *Small Town In Mass Society* (N.Y.: Doubleday, Anchor Books, 1960) and Aaron Wildavsky, *Leadership in a Small Town* (Totowa, N.J.: Bedminster Press, 1964).

and strong mayoral leadership. Furthermore, the examination of mayoral and managerial leadership in Chapter 5 provides another view of community power and influence. This chapter deals exclusively with *formal leaders* who are elected or appointed and function within local government. Executive and administrative leaders use different kinds of roles and styles in exercising power and influence.

URBAN PUBLIC POLICIES

Urban policies, which are discussed in Chapters 7 to 12, are treated as productive outputs of government and include such activities as law enforcement, antipoverty programs, public assistance, housing, education, and community health. Unlike earlier studies of urban areas, policy is not considered exclusively as service activity occurring in specific localities. Rather, urban policy problems are linked to nationwide trends over which specific localities have little control. In recent decades, these trends have included:

Mobility and Immobility. The upwardly mobile middle class did not want to live in crowded, rundown neighborhoods and, since the end of World War II, has moved from central cities to the suburbs. Meanwhile, vast numbers of blacks, Puerto Ricans, Mexican-Americans, and rural whites moved from small towns and farms to the major cities. However, the poverty and social and economic disabilities of these minorities prevented them from escaping the deteriorating conditions of the central cities.

Affluence and Poverty. The white flight to the suburbs was associated with the increasing affluence of American society. Many cities lost a substantial source of tax revenues as people, commerce, business, and industry moved away. In contrast, the impoverished minorities placed greater demands on city governments for more social services, which they claim they could neither afford nor provide without federal and state assistance.

Political Stability and Instability. Fiscally strapped central cities encountered repeated political crises which contrasted with earlier battles over "reformed" and "unreformed" municipal arrangements. As blacks and other minorities expressed dissatisfaction with governmental inaction, neither machine-type nor reform-oriented city governments could respond to such demands. Violence, disorder, and racial clashes created a siege environment in ghetto neighborhoods. Suburbs neglected metropolitan areawide problems of pollution, transportation, land-use planning, and urban sprawl. Suburban isolation was preferred over metropolitan planning and intergovernmental cooperation. Without incentives to cooperate, suburbs continued to act as independent self-contained communities.

As discussed subsequently, most past and present urban policies have *not* dealt effectively with the underlying causes of social malaise. Other than the daily concerns with ongoing services, the cities and the federal government have been more attuned to the demands of private enterprise than to the problems of impoverished ghetto residents. For example, federal-local urban renewal and public assistance programs assisted downtown business interests and worked against the poor. Similarly, when antipoverty programs created political awareness among inner-city blacks, the federal government reduced program funding and support. Our view is that the considerable awareness and involvement of blacks and other minorities in attempting to deal with urban problems was short-circuited during the 1960s by heavy spending on the Vietnam War and in the 1970s by revelations of political corruption in President Nixon's administration.

President Johnson's Great Society resulted in many new federal programs—the War on Poverty, the 1968 Housing Act, federal aid to education and law enforcement, the Partnership for Health, etc. President Nixon came forward with the "new federalism," which changed the structure of many federal grant programs through revenue sharing. He opposed busing to achieve racial balance in public schools, but tried to achieve drastic reform of the welfare system with the Family Assistance Plan. Caught up in the post-Vietnam budget crunch and inflation, President Nixon cut federal spending for urban programs, while urging local and state governments to assume greater responsibility for dealing with their problems. Nixon's legacy from Johnson was the Vietnam War, which caused unprecedented national upheaval and led to Johnson's withdrawal from the 1968 election campaign.

In the unease that accompanied these events, national concern for solving domestic problems diminished even though the cities, suburbs, and metropolitan areas continued to experience vexing difficulties. As the decade of the 1970s opened, environmental, energy, and transportation problems loomed ominously. While we do not include an analysis of these problems in our policy chapters, we observe that concern for air and water pollution emerged as major national priorities. Environmental policy is linked with energy resource and allocation as well as to urban transportation. The October 1973 Arab-Israeli war led to an Arab oil embargo of the United States, resulting in gasoline and home heating fuel shortages, unemployment in automobile factories, and much higher fuel prices (as well as windfall profits for oil producers and distributors). As the issues of the early 1970s seemed to approach near-crisis proportions, national, state, and local leaders began to search for a more rational set of programs and policies to protect the environment, to produce efficient non-polluting automobiles, and to build better and more effective systems of urban mass transportation.

More optimistic signs are evident in metropolitan planning and intergovernmental cooperation. Federal initiatives, as discussed in Chapters 7 to 12, have brought city and suburban representatives together in establishing intergovernmental priorities. Recent attention to the environment, transportation, and the energy crisis will require further cooperative policy solutions by cities and suburbs in metropolitan areas.

In Chapters 7 to 12, we offer a number of alternative policy solutions which might reverse the persistent inability of the cities to deal with social problems, but we observe that serious resistance and governmental inaction characterize the 1970s. Consequently, future policy debates involving the cities and the federal government must consider whether or not urban problems should be a preeminent national priority. Otherwise, national urban problems will surely get worse, and the victims of urban neglect will experience greater social deprivation.

NOTES

1. Morton and Lucia White, *The Intellectual Versus the City* (New York: New American Library, Mentor Books, 1964), p. 222.
2. Edward C. Banfield and James Q. Wilson, *City Politics* (New York: Random House, Vintage Books, 1963), p. 35.
3. Richard Hofstadter, *The Age of Reform* (New York: Random House, Vintage Books, 1955), p. 9.
4. Banfield and Wilson, *City Politics*, p. 46.
5. *Ibid.*
6. Alan Shank, *Political Power and the Urban Crisis* (Boston: Holbrook Press, 1969), p. v.

SUGGESTIONS FOR FURTHER READING

Banfield, Edward C., and James Q. Wilson. *City Politics*. New York: Random House, Vintage Books, 1963.
A landmark study indicating the nature of conflict in urban politics.

Bonjean, Charles M., Terry N. Clark, and Robert L. Lineberry, eds. *Community Politics: A Behavioral Approach*. New York: Free Press, 1971.
Methodological survey of approaches to urban politics with emphasis on community power structure, elites, and leadership.

Callow, Alexander, Jr., ed. *American Urban History*. New York: Oxford University Press, 1969.
Useful collection of articles concerning urban developments from colonial to modern times.

Hawkins, Brett W. *Politics and Urban Policies*. Indianapolis, Ind.: Bobbs-Merrill, 1971.
Application of a systems approach to urban environmental, political system, and policy output variables.

Kirlin, John J., and Steven P. Erie, "The Study of City Governance and Public Policy Making," *Public Administration Review*, Vol. 32, No. 2 (March/April 1972), pp. 173–184.
Useful bibliographical essay reviewing major trends and approaches to city politics.

Morgan, David R., and Samuel A. Kirkpatrick. *Urban Political Analysis: A Systems Approach*. New York: Free Press, 1972.
Collection of articles organized around a systems approach to urban politics and policies.

Rose, Arnold M. *The Power Structure*. New York: Oxford University Press, 1967.
The definitive critique of elite analysis of American society.

Shank, Alan, ed. *Political Power and the Urban Crisis*, 1st and 2nd eds. Boston: Holbrook Press, 1969, 1973.
Wide range of articles dealing with urban politics and policies.

White, Morton and Lucia. *The Intellectual Versus the City*. New York: New American Library, Mentor Books, 1964.
Traces the underlying causes and reasons for the historical anti-urban bias in American thought.

part one

*Political Power
in Cities, Suburbs,
and Metropolitan Areas*

1

Boss Rule
and Machine Politics

INTRODUCTION

Boss rule and machine politics are two of the most colorful, best known, and harshly criticized phenomena of American cities. The rise of the city bosses paralleled the emergence of the United States as an urban nation. Students of urban politics can quickly identify many of the famous bosses—William Marcy Tweed of New York City, Frank Hague of Jersey City, Tom Pendergast of Kansas City, and Richard Daley of Chicago. These men were extraordinarily effective in mobilizing the voting power of ethnic minorities to gain control of city hall. Upon establishing their control over local parties and city government, the bosses often used graft and corruption to maintain power and influence over local affairs. Boss rule has been justifiably condemned because of its association with voting fraud, violence, and the subversion of public office for private gain. We often assume that these unsavory practices were effectively attacked by crusading law enforcement officials. In some cases they were, but more often these same officials were part and parcel of the machine and owed their appointments to the boss.

Which approaches can best explain the complex underlying causes which brought the bosses to power, which enabled them to gain control over large city populations, and which permitted them to maintain their influence and authority over long periods of time? More specifically, how did the political machines initially gain voter support? What benefits did the voters expect to receive in supporting such party organizations? Why did enterprising businessmen find it useful, necessary, and rewarding to cooperate with the bosses? These and other aspects of boss rule are explained in this chapter under the following topics:

1. A *historical view* of urban political developments from the post–Civil War period (about 1870) through the New Deal (1939) which focuses upon the rise to power and influence of the big city bosses
2. An evaluation of *institutional forms* of city government and party organizations which preceded and accompanied boss rule
3. An examination of *brokerage politics*, which traces the relationships between bosses, businessmen, and voters in terms of an exchange of favors and bartering analogous to the economic marketplace
4. A discussion of *graft and corruption*, which not only enriched the city bosses but also eventually led to the demise of many powerful city machines
5. The replacement of machine influence by city and federal *social welfare agencies* in providing goods and services
6. The *reformist* attacks on boss rule, which led to new forms of political participation and institutional innovations to establish an alternative basis for conducting city affairs (See Chapters 3 and 4)

In employing the above framework, this chapter shows how boss rule and machine politics developed, flourished, and declined in American cities. While much of our subsequent discussion reveals considerable criticisms of these old-style machines, the antimachine reformers, as discussed in Chapters 2 and 3, did not necessarily solve these problems with their electoral and institutional changes. Boss rule and machine politics, it should be emphasized, contributed to the growth and expansion of cities during an era of rapid urbanization. Also, the big city bosses had considerable political leverage which contributed to the economic advancement and upward mobility of large numbers of European immigrants.

With the demise of the powerful machines, local neighborhoods no longer reaped the rewards of municipal life. Recent city newcomers, including blacks, Puerto Ricans, Mexican-Americans, and various white ethnic groups, have experienced considerable frustration, anger, and hostility which city governments are unable to alleviate. Urban poverty, racial tensions, and social and economic disabilities persist because social welfare bureaucracies are remote, impersonal, and resistant to organized group demands which challenge ongoing policies. Racial and ethnic minorities have attempted to develop their own sense of group identity and neighborhood cohesion in their conflicts with local agencies. Such organization is necessary to have enough political clout to obtain the same kinds of benefits and opportunities which were formerly provided by the old-style political machines.

HISTORICAL BACKGROUND: JACKSONIAN DEMOCRACY AND WEAK MAYOR-COUNCIL GOVERNMENT

Machine politics flourished during an era of rapid urbanization. Following the Civil War, American cities experienced great economic expansion and physical growth. Prior to 1860, people were moving from the Atlantic seaboard to the west, building new towns and opening the frontier. The fifty years following the Civil War witnessed the development of American cities on a large scale. By 1910, sixteen cities had more than 250,000 residents, and three, Chicago, New York, and Philadelphia, had more than one million.[1] Much of the rapid growth resulted from large-scale foreign immigration. More than twenty-five million foreign-born immigrants flocked to American cities. Post–Civil War urbanization transformed the United States from a predominantly rural to an urban nation. By the end of the first decade of the twentieth century, nearly half of the total population was living in cities.

A rapidly growing population, the emergence of new cities, the movement of the population westward, and the impact of the industrial revolution all placed new pressures and demands on the governing of American cities. However, pre-industrial attitudes toward local government limited the capacity of cities to respond to social changes. American attitudes supported small-scale, limited government. The philosophy of Thomas Jefferson, "that which governs least, governs best," did not seem appropriate to an emerging urban society. Furthermore, the weak mayor-strong council structure, a product of Jacksonian Democracy, was the most typical form of city government during the post–Civil War years. The extraordinary ineffectiveness of the weak mayor-strong council structure resulted in the rise of boss rule and machine politics in many American cities. How did this occur?

Jacksonian Democracy accompanied the westward expansion of America. Urbanization and industrialization enhanced national power. The Jacksonians attacked monopoly and concentration of wealth by the propertied aristocrats. Jacksonian Democracy supported Adam Smith's notion of economic *laissez-faire:* the open marketplace where all men competed equally without governmental restraints. *Laissez-faire* principles were also applied to political affairs. The Jacksonians sought to displace the older oligarchy which had entrenched itself by restricting voting to those who owned property and refused to consult the masses or provide them with opportunities to participate in local affairs.

Government by the common man was the basic political principle of Jacksonian Democracy. Government should be open to all, not remain the monopoly of the privileged few. Egalitarianism led to a shift in power from the propertied oligarchy to the pioneers and factory workers. How was this accomplished? The Jacksonians advocated the abolition of property requirements for voting and for the holding of elective offices.

Universal manhood suffrage broadened the base of popular participation in elections and ensured access to government by all without regard to special qualifications or prior training. Additionally, the Jacksonians wanted officials to be directly responsible to the voters. Nearly all important executive, legislative, and judicial offices became elective rather than appointive. Voters selected these many officials from a "long ballot," which included the names of candidates for every office to be filled. Democratizing electoral practices directly affected city politics. Between 1822 and 1824, the office of mayor became an elective position for the first time in Boston, St. Louis, and Detroit.² Popular election of other local officials followed and included the tax collector, city treasurer, clerk, tax assessor, and city attorney.

Jacksonian Democracy also advocated popular participation in political parties. To achieve the shift of political control from the older propertied classes to the newly enfranchised frontiersmen and factory workers, the Jacksonians established broad-based party organizations. Success in elections produced rewards for the party faithful. The victorious political party appointed party workers to governmental positions. A guiding principle of the Jacksonians, the spoils system, offered the advantages of party control of the government, was a rich source of patronage to reward campaign workers, and led to party influence over personnel policies and appointments to administrative agencies. Party patronage often meant short tenure,

frequent rotation in office, and government management by amateurs. This system of rapid turnover of appointed officials permitted
increased participation by citizens in the affairs of their government.

In practice, the principles of Jacksonian Democracy were most
applicable to smaller cities and towns where the citizens knew each
other and had personal contact with public officials. But it is questionable whether Jacksonian prescriptions worked well for large
cities. For example, the long ballot, which allegedly guaranteed representative and responsive local officials, tended to confuse voters.
For example, the Chicago *Tribune* of 1932 indicated the complex
problems faced by voters in deciding how to select candidates from
long ballots in primary elections.[3]

1. First, get a list of the four or five hundred primary candidates
   and memorize their names.
2. Study the pictures and posters of all office seekers.
3. Discuss the various candidates with your friends.
4. Weigh the qualifications of each aspirant during office hours.
5. Attend all the political meetings.
6. Tune in on every political address.
7. Save and study every political pamphlet.
8. By this time you have lost your friends, your wife and your job,
   but you have the satisfaction of knowing you can vote intelli-
   gently, and you're a good citizen.

Criticisms can also be levelled against the Jacksonian objective of
government by amateurs rather than by trained experts. In smaller
communities untrained officials could manage governmental affairs.
However, as the cities grew, amateur officials found it increasingly
difficult to administer complex problems. The spoils system deprived
local administrations of expertise free from the vagaries of political
controversy. Patronage was a valuable instrument for maintaining
party loyalty, but the rapid turnover of government personnel in nonpolitical positions hindered effective solutions to the financial and
service problems of the cities.

Perhaps the most serious criticism of Jacksonian Democracy was
that broadened participation of people in party affairs did not result
in popular control of municipal government. Instead, Jacksonian
principles produced the weak mayor-strong council form of city government, an extraordinarily inept structural octopus. Such an
entangled framework of city government permitted enterprising

politicians to bring city affairs under personal control. What were the essential shortcomings of the weak mayor-strong council system?

Weak mayor-strong council city government gave a central role to the local legislature in law-making, budgeting, and administration Elected by popular vote and usually representing wards or single-member districts, the city council frequently consisted of two chambers. Councilmen controlled both policy-making and administration through extensive appointment powers to various city agencies, although the growing tendency of state legislatures after 1850 to appoint members to independent boards and commissions undercut the power of city councils to control either policy or administration.

In contrast, the mayor did not have control over his own administration. He lacked effective appointment and removal powers. He controlled neither the policies of city government nor its financial affairs. He was only one of several elected officials in the executive branch. He also lacked authority over both the members of independent boards and commissions and ward-based city councilmen. The mayor could recommend new legislation, veto bills, and preside over council meetings, but he lacked any effective means to centralize his political influence. Deprived of the powers of strong executive leadership, the mayor either became a victim of periodic city council maneuverings or acted in collusion with factions of city councilmen in their many deals and arrangements to enhance individual power and self-interest.*

Weak mayor-strong council government was not conducive to establishing political consensus in rapidly expanding urban communities. By 1860 the weak mayor-strong council system had produced near anarchy and chaos in various American cities. It was a disjointed, leaderless, and uncoordinated local governmental monster with dispersed power centers in the local legislatures and the distribution of influence among many independent administrative boards and commissions. By way of illustration, urban historian Alexander B. Callow, Jr. offers a description of the breakdown of New York City government in 1866, an analysis that could well be applied to many other American cities during post–Civil War days:

> It was a government lopsided and filled with loopholes in responsibility. Two differently constituted Boards of Councilmen had been established in succession. The affairs of the city were dominated by

---

*The lack of executive leadership encouraged the development of boss rule. However, it is also true that the bosses were effective under strong mayor regimes. As will be shown in Chapter 3, the system of ward-partisan elections facilitated boss control of city government.

a rurally oriented State legislature, and the city was forced to turn lobbyist to protect itself. . . . The city was hopelessly entangled in overlapping jurisdictions of authority concentrated in the Common Council, where Supervisors and Aldermen literally constituted a double government. Each had its own large battery of officials and high salaries, one government for the county, the other for the city. These governments were divided into sixteen departments. . . . As a fitting touch to governmental chaos, all the departments were independent and not responsible to any central authority; and, to add chaos to confusion, independence was granted to the commissioners who owed allegiance not to New York City but to Albany.[4]

City government, under the weak mayor-strong council system, resulted in dispersing and fragmenting responsibility and thereby created a power vacuum, which in the succeeding decades encouraged boss rule and machine politics. It was not surprising that a parallel structure of power and influence developed alongside such a chaotic governmental situation. Local politicians, skilled in mobilizing party workers and voters, used tightly organized party machinery to bring elected officials and appointed administrators under their influence. By doing so, city bosses seized control of municipal government. We turn next to an examination of how these political party processes developed.

PARTY ORGANIZATION: THE POLITICAL MACHINE AS A CENTRALIZING INFLUENCE

Urban political machines attained power by mobilizing reliable blocs of voters on election day to produce repetitive and predictable victories. According to Fred I. Greenstein, political machines have four distinctive organizational characteristics:

1. There is a disciplined party hierarchy led by a single executive or a unified board of directors.

2. The party exercises effective control over nomination to public office, and, through this, it controls the public officials of the municipality.

3. The party leadership—which quite often is of lower-class social origins—usually does not hold public office and sometimes does not even hold formal party office. At any rate, official position is not the primary source of the leadership's strength.

4. Rather, a cadre of loyal party officials and workers, as well as a core of voters, is maintained by a mixture of material rewards and *nonideological* psychic rewards—such as personal and ethnic recognition, camaraderie, and the like.[5]

The party leadership exercised power in the inner *ring* and in the ward-based neighborhoods. The citywide organization gained political power when it was able to obtain control over a majority of ward bosses, each of whom had their own locally based party hierarchies. As explained by Moisei Ostrogorski, machine politics functioned on both a centralized and a decentralized basis:

> Each Machine being in reality composed of a larger number of smaller and smaller Machines which form so many microcosms within it, the respective powers as well as the rank of the chief engineers and their fellow-workmen represent a sort of expanding ladder. This is the case in the first instance with the hierarchy of the Machine's staff: the title and the role of boss do not belong exclusively to the man who controls the Machine in the city or in the State; the leader is the local boss in his own district; the person in charge of the precinct is himself a little boss.[6]

The central party leadership, or ring, was comparable to a corporate board of directors. By controlling the ward bosses and coordinating election victories, the ring was in a position to distribute the rewards or "profits" to the stockholders.[7] The profits consisted of material benefits, favors, payoffs, patronage appointments, and other spoils. In his classic nineteenth-century study, Lord James C. Bryce, a British observer of American politics, concluded that the ring members "cement their dominion by combination, each placing his influence at the disposal of others, and settle all important matters in secret conclave. The power of the ring is immense, for it ramifies over the whole city."[8]

Bryce also found that machine party leadership was analogous to a military command system. Within the ring, as well as at the ward level, there was usually one man who became the most skillful political operator. As a "boss," this leader became the commander-in-chief of a loyal army of party workers.

> An army led by a council seldom conquers: it must have a commander-in-chief, who settles disputes, decides in emergencies, inspires fear or attachment. The head of the Ring is such a general. He dispenses places, rewards the loyal, punishes the mutinous, concocts schemes, negotiates treaties. He generally avoids publicity, preferring the substance to the pomp of power, and is all the more dangerous because he sits, like a spider, hidden in the midst of his web. He is a Boss.[9]

To attain citywide control of party machinery, the central party ring depended upon the reliability of the ward-based organizations to mobilize the voters on election day. City bosses and other ring leaders typically began their political careers in neighborhoods crowded with recently arrived immigrants. For example, William Mercy Tweed was leader of the seventh ward before organizing the notorious Tweed Ring in 1866; Jim Pendergast used his saloon as the center for gaining control over the first ward prior to becoming boss of Kansas City; and Frank Hague was initially the ward leader of Jersey City's horseshoe district before reigning as mayor and leader of Hudson County's Democratic party organization from 1913 to 1949.

Ward leaders attained power and influence particularly by controlling the voters and assuring predictable turnouts for designated candidates in primary elections. Frank R. Kent, a journalist for many years with the Baltimore *Sun*, provided at least three reasons why the primary elections were the key to understanding party machine power:

1. All candidates of the two great parties must be nominated as a result of the primaries.

2. In nearly all states, Republicans are barred from voting in Democratic primaries and Democrats must keep out of Republican primaries, which means that each party machine in the primaries is free from conflict with the other party machine.

3. Not only are the nominations made in the primaries, but members of the state central committee, control of which is the key to the whole machine, are elected in the primaries.[10]

Officially designated as party committeemen, the ward leaders were chosen by enrolled party voters in the primary elections. Ordinarily, however, only relatively few voters participated in electing party committeemen. The committeeman or ward boss was usually an enterprising neighborhood politician who gained his position by organizing a sufficient number of voters to get himself elected. He was especially concerned with attracting loyal voters who would obey his commands. Political scientist Harold F. Gosnell, in his classic analysis of Chicago machine politics in the 1920s and 1930s, concluded that "You can't lick a ward boss."[11] Gosnell found that most registered voters did not participate in primary elections, most ward leaders ran unopposed, and, as a result of voter apathy and confusion over the large number of offices to be filled on the primary ballot, ward bosses were practically immune from intraparty opposition challenges at the polls.[12]

Ward bosses needed energetic party workers to bring out the vote. The party faithful were mobilized by precinct captains, who formed the rank and file of ward-based machines. The ward leaders selected precinct captains from among the most loyal, hard-working, and knowledgeable local politicians. Precinct captains were expected to have direct contact with the voters, understand their problems, and to befriend them in neighborhood saloons and political clubs.

Prior to elections, the precinct captains thoroughly canvassed the neighborhoods, going from door to door ensuring that all eligibles were registered to vote. During the heyday of the old-style political machines, it was not uncommon for the precinct captains to arrange instant citizenship and voter registration for the newly arrived immigrants. On election day, party workers mobilized the entire neighborhood vote. Maximum voter turnout was assisted by assisting voters to the polls and helping them to cast their votes. All in all, these ward politicians led a "strenuous life," according to the colorful New York Tammany Hall leader George Washington Plunkitt:

> Everyone in the district knows him. Everyone knows where to find him, and nearly everyone goes to him for assistance of one sort or another, especially the poor of the tenements.
> He is always obliging. He will go to the police courts to put in a good word for the "drunks and disorderlies" or pay their fines, if a good word is not effective. He will attend christenings, weddings, and funerals. He will feed the hungry and help bury the dead. . . .
> He seeks direct contact with the people, does them good turns when he can, and relies on their not forgetting him on election day. His heart is always in his work, too, for his subsistence depends on its results.[13]

BROKERAGE POLITICS: THE POLITICIANS AND THE IMMIGRANTS

All of the activities of party politicians, ranging from the inner ring to ward bosses to precinct captains and party workers, were dependent upon the support of a particular group of voters, the recently arrived European immigrants. Described by historian Oscar Handlin as an "uprooted" population,[14] these city newcomers were confronted by the harsh realities and dangers of urban life. Crowded into unsafe and unsanitary tenements, the immigrants were poor, lacked jobs, had no economic security, frequently did not speak English, were unfamiliar with local customs, and often encountered religious and ethnic hostilities from city residents.

Their social and economic dislocation meant that the immigrants required a wide range of public services that most city governments were not prepared to offer. In addition to the chaotic arrangements of the weak mayor-strong council structure, municipal government did not have public works programs, minimum wage and maximum hour laws, social security, or unemployment compensation to ameliorate the problems of persistent and pervasive poverty. Additionally, city government did not have a broad-based tax system from which to derive revenue for new social welfare programs.

To fill the vacuum, boss rule and machine politics provided the immigrants with services to alleviate their economic and social problems which were not available from traditional governmental remedies. The voting power of the newcomers could be used to overcome their social and economic liabilities arising from crowded tenements, a flooded labor market, and other discomforts of urban existence. But the helping hand of local politicians required the solid voting support of the urban poor. Voters did not have to be bribed. Rather, the local politicians became the protectors of the poor by establishing a kind of informal exchange system. They offered the poor physical assistance in the form of jobs, food, shelter, and direct payments during times of unemployment. Local bosses provided the immigrants with protection and relief from conflicts with the police. They offered jobs to unskilled laborers on city construction projects. They encouraged the immigrants to become active in party affairs. By providing a wide range of opportunities to the immigrants, machine politicians obtained the loyalty, support, and allegiance that enabled them to win city elections.

Protection of the poor, the "helping hand," and sympathy and direct assistance for individual problems do not entirely explain why the machine politicians were so effective in gaining the immigrants' voting support. In addition, the European newcomers brought to American cities political attitudes toward government that were fulfilled by the machine. These political views differed substantially from both Jeffersonian and Jacksonian democratic principles. According to Richard Hofstadter, the immigrants had political beliefs that were:

> . . . founded upon their unfamiliarity with independent political action, their familiarity with hierarchy and authority, and upon the urgent needs that so often grew out of their migration, took for granted that the political life of the individual would arise out of family needs, interpreted political and civic relations chiefly in terms of political obligations, and placed personal loyalties above allegiance to abstract codes of law or morals.[15]

Edward C. Banfield and James Q. Wilson have characterized Hofstadter's analysis as a "private-regarding" view of the public interest.[16] According to their analysis, the immigrants came from European societies where they had little experience with democracy or representative forms of government. Rather, they were accustomed to living in ethnic or religious enclaves where political relationships were viewed in terms of personal obligations, family ties, and bonds of friendship. Machine politicians established rapport with the immigrants by offering them material rewards and opportunities for social cohesion. The local saloon and the political club gave the immigrants a meeting place for relaxation and conversation with friends and neighbors. Favors, jobs, payoffs, and a wide range of informal social services became the *raison d'etre* of local political dialogue and activity rather than citywide issues, political ideology, or the "objective" qualifications of candidates for public office. Consequently, local party politicians who appealed to the neighborhood and the private concerns of the immigrants were more likely to gain their support than civic-minded activists who stressed community service, efficiency in government, and other reformist goals.

BROKERAGE POLITICS: BUSINESSMEN AND THE MACHINE

As previously indicated, the distinguishing features of political machines were authority, discipline, loyalty, and sanctions. The party leadership needed oil and grease to keep the machine wheels working, the pulleys running, and the cogs slipping into one another.[17] Material rewards were required to maintain the smooth functioning of the political machine. Ready sources of cash were required to provide inducements for support by party workers and voters.

The old-style city bosses were not independently wealthy men. Their political careers typically began in the immigrant neighborhoods where the ethnic and religious minority groups lived. Consequently, machine politicians had to enter into alliances with co-operating businessmen who could provide the cash to keep the party organization "well oiled and greased."[18] Such arrangements were accurately described by Lincoln Steffens, the crusading muckraker journalist, at the turn of the twentieth century:

> . . . Now the typical American citizen is the business man. The typical business man is a bad citizen: he is busy. I found him buying boodlers in St. Louis, defending grafters in Minneapolis, originating corruption in Pittsburg[h], sharing with bosses in Philadelphia, deploring reform in Chicago, and beating good government with corruption funds in New York. He is a self-righteous fraud, this big business man. He is the chief source of corruption, and it were a boon if he would neglect politics. . . .[19]

Machine politicians offered enterprising businessmen rich opportunities for profitable ventures in city affairs. During the period of rapid urban expansion from 1860 to 1910, American cities required a vast number of new municipal facilities and public services. To meet the demands of a burgeoning urban population, the cities had to construct new streets, develop new transportation systems, and provide a wide range of public utilities, including waterworks, municipal lighting plants, and sewerage systems. Machine politicians provided businessmen with lucrative and virtually monopolistic municipal contracts and franchises to construct and operate these new public facilities. By 1900 the extent of private business investment in local governmental operations was considerable. Privately owned utilities, for example, had invested over $300 million in gas works, $250 million in electric lighting plants, and over $2 billion in street railway systems.[20] In return for such profitable ventures in city facilities, contractors and developers were expected to return part of their profits to the political machine.

The era of boss rule and machine politics resulted in great construction activity in American cities. New hospitals, public buildings, parks, and civic centers provided jobs for the immigrants and social services for the needy. For example, Frank Hague, the boss of Jersey City, was responsible for building a multimillion dollar medical center in the heart of the city, which prompted the slogan, "Have your baby or your operation on Mayor Hague."[21]

Alliances between machine politicians and businessmen were facilitated by the breakdown and confusion of city government and administration. The weak mayor-strong council system produced a proliferation of city councilmen who had authority to award municipal contracts and franchises. Through effective party organization, machine politicians gained control over the wards from which councilmen were elected. This gave the machine direct influence over the decisions of councilmen. Furthermore, the administrative chaos resulting from the multiplicity of boards and commissions provided machine politicians with opportunities to influence appointments. Without civil service, the spoils system flourished. City bosses gained control over local bureaucracy and, in turn, provided protection for businessmen from governmental interference and regulation.

According to sociologist Robert K. Merton, the political machine performed "latent functions" for both legitimate and illicit business activities that decentralized local government was unable to provide.[22] City bosses offered businessmen access to city council and administrative agencies, protected them from the dangers of uncontrolled competition and regulation, enhanced their profits, and facilitated market demands for goods and services.[23]

Cooperative relationships between machine politicians and businessmen did not always result in public benefits. The "latent functions" of the machine oftentimes included widespread protection of rackets, gambling, vice, and other crime, especially in the immigrant ghettos. Additionally, the bosses themselves sometimes assumed the role of entrepreneur and made wholesale raids on the public treasury. A notorious example of profit-hungry political operators was the infamous county courthouse scandal of the Tweed Ring. From 1858 to 1871 more than $13 million was spent for New York City's courthouse, but the building itself was never completed. In fact, the entire project was nothing more than an enormous boondoggle by professional "con" artists. When finally "completed," this building, according to Alexander B. Callow, Jr., had a remarkable appearance:

> . . . a waste of masonry, a gloomy maze of rooms, dark halls, and ugly walls, resembling more an ancient ruin than a new, unfinished building. In 1871, after thirteen years of construction work, one of the largest offices, the Bureau of Arrears of Taxes, had no roof. The County Clerk's office, Sheriff's office, the office of the Surrogate were not carpeted but were covered with oilcloth and grimy matting. The walls were filthy, and in many places large chunks of plaster had peeled off, leaving ugly blotches.[24]

MUNICIPAL GRAFT AND CORRUPTION*

Graft and corruption were the lifeblood of the political machine. Voting fraud, violence, and other strong-arm methods were commonly associated with elections. Bribery, blackmailing, extortion, and other methods of public thievery enabled city bosses to maintain the party treasury, discipline party workers, gain influence over public officials, and form alliances with businessmen.

Election fraud was commonplace in machine-controlled city wards. Maximum voter turnout was assured by assisting the blind, the aged, the disabled, and the illiterate to the polls. Precinct captains brought out repeaters, stuffed ballot boxes with illegal votes, and altered the

---

*In this section, we analyze the largely negative features of graft and corruption. Chapters 2 and 3 provide reform solutions to eliminate the abuses of these practices. The reader might also consider such administrative reforms as professionalization, civil service, higher salaries, and competitive bidding as other ways of reducing or eliminating graft and corruption.

vote counts. Voters frequently experienced violence and brutality. D. W. Brogan, a British observer of American politics, commented that:

> It often took real, physical courage to vote in primaries or even in elections in New York after the Civil War, at any rate in the rowdier districts. Primaries were usually held in saloons, and attempts to nominate candidates not approved of by "the lads" were foolhardy enterprises. Electoral campaigns were often marked by serious violence. The police usually took a tolerant view of physical persuasion or the intimidation of the official workers of the other party. . . .[25]

Subsequent to gaining complete political control, machine politicians took advantage of available municipal contracts and franchises to amass personal fortunes. George Washington Plunkitt, a Tammany Hall leader, coined the term "honest graft" to describe the process:

> Everybody is talkin' these days about Tammany men growin' rich on graft, but nobody thinks of drawin' the distinction between honest and dishonest graft. There's all the difference in the world between the two. Yes, many of our men have grown rich in politics. I have myself. I've made a big fortune out of the game, but I've not gone in for dishonest graft—black-mailin' gamblers, saloonkeepers, disorderly people, etc.—and neither has any of the men who made their big fortunes in politics.
>
> There's an honest graft and I'm an example of how it works. I might sum up the whole thing by sayin': "I seen my opportunities and I took 'em."
>
> Just let me explain by examples. My party's in power in the city, and it's goin' to undertake a lot of public improvements. Well, I'm tipped off, say, that they're going to lay out a new park at a certain place.
>
> I see my opportunity and I take it. I go to that place and I buy up all the land I can in the neighborhood. Then the board of this or that makes its plan public, and there is a rush to get my land, which nobody cared particular for before.
>
> Ain't it perfectly honest to charge a good price and make a profit on my investment and foresight? Of course, it is. Well, that's honest graft. . . .
>
> Now, in conclusion, I want to say that I don't own a dishonest dollar. If my own worst enemy was given the job of writin' my epitaph when I'm gone, he couldn't do more than write:
>
> "George W. Plunkitt. He seen His Opportunities, and He Took 'Em."[26]

Whether "honest" or "dishonest," the level of graft reached excessive proportions in many American cities with political machines. For example, Mayor Frank Hague, the boss of Jersey City, was able to invest $392,910.50 in real estate on a yearly salary of $7,500.[27]

In New York City, the Seabury investigations of 1932 found evidence that Tammany Hall leaders were involved in:

> . . . gambling and prostitution, with influence peddling, rigged nominations, and scandalous appointments, with bank books and canceled check stubs, with letters of credit, brokerage accounts, and safety deposit boxes: evidence, in short, having to do with municipal chicanery of the more hoggish sort.[28]

In the absence of public controls over bidding for municipal contracts and proper accounting procedures of city funds, the practices of "honest" and "dishonest graft" resulted in an enormous waste and theft of the taxpayers' money. For example, Boss Tom Pendergast's city manager juggled the Kansas City budget to give the appearance of efficiency and economy during the 1930s, when, in reality, later investigations revealed that the city was operating under a deficit of $20 million.[29]

Although it now seems obvious that graft and corruption have a damaging effect on public confidence and trust in the honesty of city officials,* James Q. Wilson has suggested that perhaps some positive benefits accrue from *centralized* (rather than decentralized) machine control over the distribution of the rewards and spoils of political victory.[30]

---

*Although this section relies on the Wilson analysis of graft and corruption, another useful approach is provided by Rogow and Lasswell in their study of the psychological roots of political behavior. They distinguish between two types of bosses, described in the excerpts below as the "game politician" and the "gain politician":

"For the *game politician* politics functioned as the principal mode of self-expression and self-realization. He enjoyed "the game" for the ego rewards it offered, which were chiefly power, prestige, adulation, and a sense of importance. The manipulation of men and events, in which he excelled, served less his convictions, which were few, than as an exercise in strategy, which he valued for its own sake. Viewing the outcome as always more important than the issue, he derived great satisfaction from political victories of large and small consequence, no matter how obtained." (p. 47)

"Although the *gain politician* was firmly attached to few principles, he thought of himself as a "friend of the people," and indeed in a sense he was. He put innumerable relatives and friends on the city payroll and befriended countless others with gifts or loans of money. . . . Radiating warmth, fellowship, and generosity, he earned a citywide following that was sufficiently large and loyal to maintain him in power through several damaging investigations of his political machine." (p. 50)

SOURCE: Arnold A. Rogow and Harold D. Lasswell, *Power Corruption, and Rectitude* (Englewood Cliffs, New Jersey: Prentice-Hall, Inc., 1963).

Wilson argues that machine control over graft in *capital formation* permitted politicians and businessmen to assemble large parcels of land for transit systems, roads, public buildings, schools, hospitals, sewers, and airports. Cities could not undertake these public works projects unless bribes and other payoffs were offered to resistant and noncomplying property-owners. City construction projects also enabled machine politicians to provide many new jobs for the party faithful and voters during times when other employment opportunities were not available.

Political machines achieved central control over city government by the use of various forms of *integrative corruption*. This was needed to overcome the extensive fragmentation of executive authority and dispersal of administrative control under the weak mayor-strong council system.[31] The political boss sought to coordinate the activities of many independent public officials and administrators who formally acted as free agents. By the skillful use of patronage appointments, payoffs, and bribes, machine politicians had the necessary inducements to ensure a minimal amount of coordination in the decision-making process of city government.

The problem with attributing benefits to graft and corruption is that machine politicians often used material rewards to subvert and undermine the public interest. In the past, it was often difficult to distinguish the public benefits of new and improved city services from the outright theft and personal greed of city politicians. Capital formation graft and integrative corruption oftentimes caused the mismanagement and inefficiency of municipal services. Such problems are still evident in modern city administrations. Edward N. Costikyan, a former Tammany Hall leader, pointed out that city officials do not act in the public interest when they sell their discretionary authority to businessmen and other special interest groups in return for support, honorific appointments, and other debts and obligations that can be redeemed in the future. Costikyan observes that the locus of corruption has changed in American cities:

> The gift of public privileges by government officials on a discretionary basis in the absence of public bidding is the greatest source of corruption, quasi-corruption, influence peddling, and demeaning of the governmental process in America today. That distribution of public largess is more and more non-political does not make it any better.[32]

When influence peddling by city administrators is combined with the activities of organized crime, the foundations of municipal government are seriously threatened. The indictment and conviction of New York City Commissioner James L. Marcus illustrates such problems. In 1967, Marcus was accused of receiving $16,000 on a $40,000 kickback from a contract to clean and repair a Bronx reservoir. Marcus was acting under the direction of Mafia loan sharks when he awarded the reservoir contract to a company without competitive bidding. His involvement with organized crime resulted from the necessity to borrow money from the Mafia to pay off personal debts arising from losses in private stock transactions. As one of Mayor Lindsay's closest friends and trusted advisors, Marcus shocked Lindsay by using his official position as Commissioner of Water Supply, Gas, and Electricity to resolve personal financial difficulties.[33]

An even more startling example of recent municipal corruption and organized crime was the conviction of Newark Mayor Hugh J. Addonizio in 1970. Addonizio, with a prior political career of twelve years in the House of Representatives and seven years as mayor of New Jersey's largest city, was found guilty of receiving payoff extortions in connection with city contracts on sewers and reservoirs. The company doing business with the city was under the control of the Mafia, which also sought protection from the police for illegal gambling activities in Newark.

Addonizio's involvement with the Mafia was the ultimate proof that a pervasive feeling of corruption existed in Newark city government. This charge had been made by a special commission appointed by Governor Hughes in a study of the underlying causes of the disastrous Newark city riots of 1967.[34] Addonizio's successor, Kenneth A. Gibson, found that previous graft and corruption was only the "tip of a vast iceberg."[35] Mayor Gibson discovered that nearly every recent city contract was inflated by 10 percent to allow for kickbacks to city officials, that numerous city officials regularly received offers from the Mafia to permit organized crime to flourish without police interference, and that, as a result of faulty financial management, the city was on the brink of bankruptcy.[36]

Graft and corruption resulting from cooperation between city officials and organized crime appears to fit a "textbook" pattern, according to the President's Commission on Law Enforcement and the Administration of Justice. The model of disintegrative corruption brings public officials under the direct influence of criminal syndicates. City government becomes an arm of organized crime; gambling flourishes openly; local officials are placed on the payroll of the syndicate, or they add to their personal incomes by accepting kickbacks on the sale or purchase of city equipment, licenses, or the awarding of zoning variances.[37]

Disintegrative corruption is a threat to honest, efficient, and responsible city government. The public loses respect for the integrity of its elected officials when criminal elements become entrenched in city politics. It is no wonder that the voters become cynical about politics and politicians. Judge George H. Barlow, who sentenced Mayor Addonizio and three others on extortion charges, commented on the extent to which public confidence is undermined by revelations of graft and corruption:

> How can we calculate the cynicism engendered in our citizens, including our young people, by these men—how does one measure the erosion of confidence in our system of government, and the diminished respect for our laws, occasioned by those men? These very men who, as government officials, inveighed against crime in the streets, while they pursued their own criminal activities in the corridors of city hall? [38]

THE DECLINE OF THE OLD-STYLE POLITICAL MACHINES

Large American cities, with the exception of Chicago,[39] are no longer ruled by powerful machine organizations of city bosses. The classic old-style city machines belong to a bygone era. What accounts for the decline and fall of boss rule and machine politics? In analyzing the demise of the city machines at least three factors are evident, including internal factional rivalries, changed attitudes of upwardly mobile city voters, and the development of federal social welfare programs during the 1930s. A fourth cause of the defeat of city machines, municipal reform efforts, will be discussed in the next two chapters.

Internal Rivalries and Exposure of Graft and Corruption

The Tweed, Pendergast, and Hague machines were defeated by the voters at the polls. This occurred when the party leadership was no longer able to deliver expected payoffs, and when direct challenges to machine leadership by ambitious political rivals were successful.

The strategy of antimachine forces was to expose excessive graft and corruption and to convince the voters that incumbent bosses were no longer responsive to the needs of the people.

The Tweed Ring fell in 1871 following public disclosure of the scandalous waste of public funds in the county courthouse scheme. This $13 million theft by the Tweed Ring and corrupt businessmen was publicized by the *New York Times* after the newspaper was given copies of city vouchers by a disgruntled sheriff who had not received his expected payoff from the Ring. A blue ribbon citizens investigating committee uncovered further evidence of graft and corruption. A reform ticket challenged the Ring in 1871, and the voters swept the Tweed gang out of office.[40]

In the late 1930s, Governor Lloyd Stark was largely responsible for the defeat of the Pendergast machine in Kansas City. Stark, whose political career began with Boss Tom Pendergast's support, wanted to eliminate vice and crime within the Kansas City police department. The governor convinced the Missouri state legislature to bring the city police department under state control. After extensive evidence of police corruption was uncovered, massive resignations by Kansas City police officials occurred. Stark then convinced the U.S. Treasury Department to investigate Pendergast's sources of income. This resulted in the discovery of an insurance swindle from which Pendergast had received $750,000. Furthermore, Pendergast had not paid income taxes on more than one million dollars he had received over eleven years. Finally, Governor Stark supported a rival candidate for the state supreme court who was victorious over a Pendergast-backed nominee in the 1939 Democratic party primary. In 1940 the Citizens' Reform ticket won all city offices and ended the reign of Boss Pendergast in Kansas City politics.[41]

During the 1940s, John V. Kenny led the assault against the Hague machine in Jersey City. As a rival ward leader seeking to replace Boss Hague, Kenny mobilized his ward organization and attacked Hague as an "evil dictator." Kenny charged that Frank Hague Eggers, Hague's hand-picked successor, was nothing more than a stooge. Hague had resigned as mayor in 1947 but continued to retain his position as state and county Democratic party chairman. Kenny's faction formed a fusion ticket with antimachine Republicans to challenge Hague in the 1947 city elections. This so-called Freedom Ticket was victorious when enough voters were apparently convinced that Boss Hague, with all of his personal wealth and absentee leadership, was no longer responsive to the needs of the people.[42]

Changing Attitudes of City Voters

The decline of boss rule and machine politics can also be attributed in part to the changing attitudes of city voters. At least two conflicting explanations, assimilation and mobilization, may account for this new direction of voter behavior. The assimilation approach argues that the European immigrants moved out of the ghettos, achieved middle-class status, and rebelled against the machine appeals for reliable and predictable support of its candidates. In contrast, the mobilization theory claims that certain ethnic groups felt ignored by the bosses and switched their votes to the rival candidates who best identified with their needs.

City voters began to rebel against boss rule when they moved out of poverty and achieved middle-class status. By offering the European immigrants social welfare services, employment in public works, and jobs in the party hierarchy, machine politicians assisted these newcomers in gaining an economic foothold and a new sense of political awareness. In time, the immigrants envisioned better opportunities in factories, labor unions, privately owned business, and white collar jobs. More financial security was available in private employment than in city patronage jobs. Ironically, the city machines contributed to the upward mobility of the immigrants by destroying the social base of boss rule.[43]

Residential and occupational mobility changed the character of ethnic bloc voting in city elections. The immigrants moved from their older ghetto neighborhoods to outlying city areas and the suburbs. Their children joined new organizations and developed new loyalties and affiliations that went beyond ethnic identities. The immigrants no longer felt obligated to the bosses and machines. The second- and third-generation offspring of the immigrants considered themselves assimilated in American political life. They could identify with antimachine candidates, rival political parties, and reform "good government" groups.

The assimilation theory of declining ethnic identity in city elections has been challenged by political scientist Raymond E. Wolfinger. Wolfinger indicates that the Italian voters of New Haven, Connecticut became solidly Republican voters from the time that William C. Celantano was first nominated as the Italian mayoral candidate in 1939. Celantano was not elected until 1945, but Italian allegiance to Republican candidates remained consistent, even though Italian wards were among the poorest in town.[14] Mobilization may account for the persistence of ethnic bloc voting in city elections:

> The strength of ethnic voting depends on both the intensity of ethnic identification and the level of ethnic relevance in the election. The most powerful and visible sign of ethnic political relevance is a fellow-ethnic's name at the head of the ticket, evident to everyone who enters the voting booth. Middle-class status is a virtual prerequisite for candidacy for major office; an ethnic group's development of sufficient political skill and influence to secure such a nomination also requires the development of a middle class. Therefore ethnic voting will be greatest when the ethnic group has produced a middle class, i.e., in the second and third generations, not in the first. Furthermore, the shifts in party identification resulting from the first major candidacy will persist beyond the election in which they occurred.[45]

Analysis of the Italian vote for Fiorello LaGuardia in the New York City mayoral election of 1933 supports Wolfinger's mobilization theory. Running on the Republican and Fusion Party tickets, the "Little Flower" campaigned heavily against the evils of the Tammany Hall Democratic machine. Italian voters responded enthusiastically to LaGuardia's appeals for group pride and recognition. Having provided Roosevelt with 87 percent of their votes in the 1932 presidential election, the Italian electorate switched to the insurgent LaGuardia in 1933 and gave him 87 percent of their votes.[46] What accounted for LaGuardia's overwhelmingly attractive responses by the Italian voters of New York City? Urban historian Arthur Mann offers this explanation:

> The enthusiasm was unprecedented because the Italo-Americans believed that their kind, the most numerous of the recent newcomers to the largest of the big cities in the United States, stood at long last on the threshold of a major breakthrough in American politics. The chief symbol of that breakthrough, LaGuardia was also the beneficiary of the self-consciousness that was making it possible.[47]

Persistent ethnic bloc voting in city elections occurs particularly among immigrant, ethnic, or racial groups that arrive on the political scene when machines are disintegrating and cannot deliver the material rewards or social welfare programs needed by the people. When the machine is under direct attack, such voters may switch to "name" candidates who best identify with their needs. Such candidates may represent reform, good government objectives, or maverick political attitudes. Without machine politics, newly aware city voters, such as blacks and Puerto Ricans, will similarly support candidates who represent their political aspirations.[48] Finally, ethnic bloc voting is encouraged when there are no other reliable guides for voter decisions, when issues are unimportant or irrelevant in city elections, and when party labels have been removed in nonpartisan ballots.[49]

Social Welfare and the Bureaucratic City-State

The temporary emergency relief and permanent social welfare programs of the federal government in the 1930s had the long-run effect of undercutting the power of boss rule and machine politics in the cities. Edwin O'Connor, in his novel *The Last Hurrah*, illustrated the effects of the New Deal on city bosses:

> Why Roosevelt? Because . . . he destroyed the old-time boss. He destroyed him by taking away his source of power. . . . If anyone wanted anything—jobs, favors, cash—he could only go to the boss, the local leader. What Roosevelt did was to take the handouts out of local hands. A few little things like Social Security, Unemployment Insurance, and the like—that's what shifted gears. . . . No need to depend on the boss for everything; the Federal Government was getting into the act. Otherwise known as a social revolution . . .[50]

In attacking the serious social crisis of the 1930s, President Roosevelt initiated numerous domestic programs that had the effect of "nationalizing" welfare services. Temporary emergency relief measures such as the Works Progress Administration (WPA) were followed by federal laws dealing with social security, maximum hour and minimum wage requirements, unemployment compensation, and guarantees of collective bargaining for labor unions. New federal agencies were established to administer these programs in cooperation with state and local governments. The "helping hand to the poor" approach of the old-style machines was replaced by the administrative rules and regulations of federal bureaucracies.

However, the long-range impact of federal social welfare programs and bureaucratic intervention in city politics was not immediately perceived by either President Roosevelt or the city bosses. Initially, the President needed the support of the Democratic party bosses to win elections. It seemed that Roosevelt was involved in the same kind of voter exchange system with the city bosses as the ward leaders had with the immigrants. As the bosses mobilized large and predictable bloc votes to swing cities and entire states into the Democratic column, Roosevelt returned favors by giving the bosses control over patronage jobs in the temporary emergency relief programs such as the WPA.

For example, President Roosevelt cooperated very closely with two of the most powerful city bosses of the 1930s, Tom Pendergast and Frank Hague. The reward for solid Democratic majorities in Missouri was Pendergast machine control over county directors and employees of the WPA. This enabled Boss Pendergast to consolidate his power and control over the statewide Democratic party in Missouri. Similarly, Roosevelt rewarded Frank Hague with thousands of patronage appointments and control over $47 million of WPA funds in return for the solid Democratic bloc votes in New Jersey.[51]

Roosevelt's alliances with the city bosses disintegrated when the machines could no longer deliver their predictable votes and when the President supported candidates that threatened statewide machine control of the Democratic party. The President broke with Boss Pendergast when Governor Stark launched his attack on police corruption in Kansas City, and the machine lost a battle with Stark over the Democratic nominee for the state supreme court in 1938. Roosevelt clashed with Hague when he tried to convince the boss to support Charles Edison for governor of New Jersey in 1940. Edison vowed his independence of the machine that threatened Hague's control over state patronage.

In the long run, New Deal programs changed the character of local politics. Poverty-stricken groups began to turn their attention to social welfare agencies for assistance rather than to seek help from machine politicians. As the power and influences of the old-style city machines waned, the social welfare agencies became dominant in the provision of city services. In a perceptive analysis, Theodore J. Lowi characterizes the shift of power from the party machines to the social welfare agencies in terms of an emerging "bureaucratic city-state."[52] City bureaucracies have replaced party machines and, in doing so, have become the new machine-type organizations. These new-style machines are "islands of functional power," organized around specific social welfare services and clientele.[53]

The new-style administrative machines are not centralized to the extent of the old-style party machines. Rather, each large agency functions to provide specific services. Formal legal authority and bureaucratic management characterize the operation of these power centers rather than a voter mobilization and material reward exchange system. Leadership is relatively self-perpetuating and not subject to higher authority. Power and influence are maintained by the cohesion of influential groups such as the press, the educated public, dedicated civic groups, and organized clientele groups. In recent years, the bureaucratic inflexibility and rigidity of the administrative machines made them unable to adjust to the increasing dissatisfaction of the poor. If Lowi's analysis is accurate, social welfare agencies have become less responsive to the needs of the poor than were the old-style political machines. Our later chapters indicate that tensions in city politics are frequently caused by clashes between social welfare agencies and organized recipient groups, particularly in such federally funded and locally administered programs as anti-poverty, Model Cities, public assistance, and public housing.

CONCLUSIONS

The demise of the city machines has left a power vacuum in city politics, especially in the relationships between the poor and the bureaucracies that administer social welfare services. While many changes have occurred in the composition of city populations since the heyday of the old-style machines, it is evident that untold thousands of poor and dependent people continue to reside in the central cities. No longer can the political machines provide assistance to the impoverished. Blacks, Puerto Ricans, poor whites, and others frequently turn to city hall and city agencies for help. The responsiveness of city government is tested when the goals of the bureaucracies and the needs of the recipients sharply diverge. This appears especially to be the case in public welfare, public housing, health services, and law enforcement. Hostility between social welfare agencies and their clientele has led to many tense relationships and crises in our cities. Ghetto residents have demanded an increasing measure of participation and control over the policies of social welfare services. At the same time, officials at the city and federal levels are trying to change both the substance and administration of many city services. These trends will continue to dominate city politics in the future. Attempts to reform, modernize, and revitalize city services will continue along with protest activities by organized recipient groups. Both trends suggest an increasingly unstable period in American city politics.

NOTES

1. Charles N. Glaab and A. Theodore Brown, *A History of Urban America* (New York: Macmillan, 1967), pp. 133–139.
2. *Ibid.*, p. 170.
3. Harold F. Gosnell, *Machine Politics: Chicago Model*, 2nd ed. (Chicago: University of Chicago Press, Phoenix Books, 1968), p. 182.

4. Alexander B. Callow, Jr., *The Tweed Ring* (New York: Oxford University Press, Galaxy Books, 1969), p. 82.
5. Fred I. Greenstein, "The Changing Pattern of Urban Party Politics," *The Annals*, Vol. UR353 (May 1964), p. 3.
6. Moisei Ostrogorski, *Democracy and the Organization of Political Parties*, Vol. II: *The United States* (New York: Doubleday, Anchor Books, 1964), p. 184.
7. James C. Scott, "Corruption, Machine Politics, and Political Change," *American Political Science Review*, Vol. 63, No. 4 (December 1969), p. 1144. See also: Scott Greer, *Governing the Metropolis* (New York: John Wiley and Sons, 1962), pp. 62–63.
8. James Bryce, *The American Commonwealth*, Vol. II (New York: Macmillan, 1889), p. 75.
9. *Ibid.*, p. 76.
10. Frank R. Kent, "How the Boss Runs the Organization," in *Urban Government*, rev. ed., ed. Edward C. Banfield (New York: Macmillan, 1969), pp. 202–203.
11. Gosnell, *Machine Politics: Chicago Model*, p. 27.
12. *Ibid.*, pp. 33–35.
13. William L. Riordon, *Plunkitt of Tammany Hall* (New York: E. P. Dutton, paperback ed., 1963), pp. 90–91.
14. Oscar Handlin, *The Uprooted* (New York: Grosset & Dunlap, Universal Library, 1951), pp. 144–169, 201–226.
15. Richard Hofstadter, *The Age of Reform* (New York: Alfred A. Knopf, 1955), p. 9.
16. James Q. Wilson and Edward C. Banfield, "Public Regardingness As A Value Premise In Voting Behavior." *American Political Science Review*, Vol. 58, No. 4 (December 1964), p. 876.
17. Callow, *The Tweed Ring*, p. 111.
18. *Ibid.*
19. Lincoln Steffens, *The Shame of the Cities* (New York: Hill and Wang, American Century Series Paperback, 1966), p. 3.
20. Glaab and Brown, *A History of Urban America*, p. 183.
21. Thomas J. Fleming, "The Political Machine II: A Case History—'I Am The Law'," *American Heritage*, Vol. 20, No. 4 (June 1969), p. 34.
22. Robert K. Merton, "The Latent Functions of the Machine," in *Urban Government*, rev. ed., ed. Edward C. Banfield (New York: Macmillan, 1969), pp. 223–225.
23. *Ibid.*, pp. 225–233.
24. Callow, *The Tweed Ring*, p. 205.
25. D. W. Brogan, *Politics In America* (New York: Harper & Brothers, 1954), p. 136.
26. Riordon, *Plunkitt of Tammany Hall*, pp. 3–6.
27. Fleming, *American Heritage*, Vol. 20, No. 4, p. 40.
28. Arthur Mann, *LaGuardia Comes To Power: 1933* (Chicago: University of Chicago Press, Phoenix Books, 1965), p. 47.
29. Lyle W. Dorsett, *The Pendergast Machine* (New York: Oxford University Press, 1968), pp. 118–119, 135.
30. James Q. Wilson, "Corruption Is Not Always Scandalous," *The New York Times Magazine* (April 28, 1968), p. 67.
31. *Ibid.*, p. 59.
32. Edward W. Costikyan, *Behind Closed Doors* (New York: Harcourt, Brace & World, Harvest Books, 1966), p. 302.
33. *The New York Times*, December 19, 1967, p. 1, col. 8.

34. Governor's Select Commission on Civil Disorder, *Report For Action* (Trenton, N.J.: February 1968), pp. 20–21.
35. *The New York Times,* September 20, 1970, p. 68, col. 1.
36. *Ibid.,* p. 1, col. 1–4.
37. *Ibid.,* December 21, 1969, p. 1, col. 1–2.
38. *Ibid.,* September 23, 1970, p. 52, col. 1.
39. The most notable exception is Mayor Richard J. Daley of Chicago, who will be discussed in Chapter 5.
40. Callow, *The Tweed Ring,* pp. 253–278.
41. Dorsett, *The Pendergast Machine,* pp. 118–137.
42. Fleming, *American Heritage,* Vol. 20, No. 4, pp. 44–46.
43. Scott, *American Political Science Review,* Vol. 63, No. 4, p. 1157.
44. Raymond E. Wolfinger, "The Development and Persistence of Ethnic Voting," *American Political Science Review,* Vol. 59, No. 4 (December 1965), pp. 901–902.
45. *Ibid.,* p. 905.
46. Arthur Mann, *LaGuardia Comes to Power: 1933* (Chicago: University of Chicago Press, Phoenix Books, 1965), p. 134.
47. *Ibid.,* p. 137.
48. See discussion in Chapter 6.
49. Wolfinger, *American Political Science Review,* Vol. 59, No. 4, p. 908.
50. Edwin O'Connor, *The Last Hurrah* (New York: Bantam Books, 1957), p. 330.
51. Fleming, *American Heritage,* Vol. 20, No. 4, p. 42.
52. Theodore J. Lowi, "Machine Politics—Old and New," *The Public Interest,* No. 9 (Fall 1967), p. 86.
53. *Ibid.,* p. 87.

SUGGESTIONS FOR FURTHER READING

Adrian, Charles R., and Charles Press. *Governing Urban America,* 3rd ed. New York: McGraw-Hill, 1968, pp. 72–75, 148–152. Jacksonian principles of local democracy and analysis of boss rule and machine politics.

Banfield, Edward C., and James Q. Wilson. *City Politics.* New York: Random House, Vintage Books, 1963. Ch. 9, "The Machine," pp. 115–127. Centralization features and political strategies of machine politics.

Brogan, D. W. *Politics In America.* New York: Harper & Brothers, 1954. Ch. 4, "Machines and Bosses," pp. 123–173. Colorful description and analysis of rise and fall of boss rule and machine politics.

Bryce, James. *The American Commonwealth,* Vol. 2. New York: Macmillan, 1889. Ch. 63, "Rings and Bosses," pp. 74–86. Classical nineteenth-century interpretation of old-style machine organization.

Callow, Alexander B., Jr. *The Tweed Ring.* New York: Oxford University Press, Galaxy Books, 1969.

Colorful, interesting, and humorous study of the first famous big-city machine.

Cornwell, Elmer E., Jr. "Bosses, Machines, and Ethnic Groups," *The Annals*, Vol. 353 (May 1964), pp. 27–39.
Analyzes rise and fall of old-style city machines and the lack of responsiveness of present urban parties to the needs of blacks and Puerto Ricans.

Costikyan, Edward N. *Behind Closed Doors.* New York: Harcourt, Brace & World, Harvest Books, 1966. Ch. 26, "The Locus of Corruption," pp. 296–307.
Former Tammany Hall leader indicates that bureaucracies are now responsible for more corruption than party organizations.

Dorsett, Lyle W. *The Pendergast Machine.* New York: Oxford University Press, 1968.
Case study of the powerful Kansas City machine.

Fleming, Thomas J. "The Political Machine II: A Case History—'I Am The Law'," *American Heritage,* Vol. 20, No. 4 (June 1969), pp. 33–48.
Description of the political career of Frank Hague, boss of Jersey City.

Glaab, Charles N., and A. Theodore Brown. *A History of Urban America.* New York: Macmillan, 1967. Chs. 7–8, pp. 167–227.
Analysis of nineteenth century urban political environment.

Goodnow, Frank J. "The Tweed Ring in New York City," in *The American Commonwealth,* by James Bryce. New York: Macmillan, 1889. Vol. 2, pp. 335–353.
Lively description of the successes and demise of the notorious nineteenth century New York City machine.

Gosnell, Harold F. *Machine Politics: Chicago Style,* 2nd ed. Chicago: University of Chicago Press, Phoenix Books, 1968.
Excellent analysis of machine politics during the 1920s and 1930s, particularly in discussing the roles of ward bosses and precinct captains.

Governor's Select Commission on Civil Disorder. *Report for Action.* Trenton, N.J. (February 1968). pp. 20–21.
Official state report on the city riots of 1967 with commentary that a cause of the disorders was "a pervasive feeling of corruption" in city hall.

Greenstein, Fred I. "The Changing Pattern of Urban Party Politics," *The Annals,* Vol. 353 (May 1964), pp. 2–13.
Useful survey of organizational features of old-style city machines.

Greer, Scott. *Governing the Metropolis.* New York: John Wiley and Sons, 1962. Ch. 4, "The Governance of the Central City," pp. 59–82.
Economic aspects of old-style machine politics.

Handlin, Oscar. *The Uprooted.* New York: Grosset & Dunlap, Universal Library, 1951. Ch. 8, "Democracy and Power," pp. 201–226.
Relationships between the city machines and the immigrants.

Lockard, Duane. *The Politics of State and Local Government,* 2nd ed. New York: Macmillan, 1969. pp. 207–214.
Analysis of bossism in American city politics.

Lowi, Theodore J. "Machine Politics—Old and New," *The Public Interest,* No. 9 (Fall 1967), pp. 83–92.
Argues that the legacy of the reform movement in destroying the old-style machine is the bureaucratic city-state which has become a new kind of political machine.

Mann, Arthur. *LaGuardia Comes To Power: 1933.* Chicago: University of Chicago Press, Phoenix Books, 1965.
Colorful, interesting, and humorous account of the "Little Flower's" successful campaign for mayor of New York City in opposing Tammany Hall.

McKean, Dayton D. *The Boss: The Hague Machine in Action.* Boston: Houghton Mifflin, 1940.
One of the best studies of a boss and machine politics. Hague's control of Jersey City extended to statewide politics and the courts.

McKelvey, Blake. *The Urbanization of America, 1860–1915.* New Brunswick, N.J.: Rutgers University Press, 1963. Ch. 6, "The Shame of the Cities," pp. 86–98.
Historical review of the rise of machine politics.

Merton, Robert K. "The Latent Functions of the Machine," in *Urban Government,* ed. Edward C. Banfield. New York: Free Press, 1969. pp. 223–233.
Argues that the old-style machines established important alliances with business interests.

Miller, Zane L. *Boss Cox's Cincinnati.* New York: Oxford University Press, 1969.
Case study of an accommodating city boss during the Progressive era of American political development.

O'Connor, Edwin. *The Last Hurrah.* New York: Bantam Books, 1957.
Fictional and somewhat sentimental account of Boston Mayor James M. Curley.

Ostrogorski, Moisei. *Democracy and the Organization of Political Parties,* Vol. 2: *The United States.* New York: Doubleday, Anchor Books, 1964. Ch. 6, "The Politicians and the Machine," pp. 179–227.
Classical interpretation of old-style machine politics.

Reeves, Richard. "Newark Corruption Held a 'Textbook Case' for U.S.," *The New York Times,* December 21, 1969, p. 1, col. 1–2.
Useful report concerning the stages of disintegrative graft and corruption resulting from activities of organized crime in city government.

Riordon, William L. *Plunkitt of Tammany Hall.* New York: E. P. Dutton, paperback ed., 1963.
Colorful and humorous account of machine politics by a successful practitioner.

Schlesinger, Arthur M., Jr. *The Age of Jackson.* Boston: Little, Brown, 1945. Ch. 24, "Jacksonian Democracy As An Intellectual Movement," pp. 306–321.
    Philosophical and intellectual roots of Jacksonian democratic principles as applied to local government.

Schumach, Murray. "Bosses and Bamboozlers: A Glimpse at City's Corruption Over the Last Century," *The New York Times,* December 19, 1967, p. 53, col. 1–3.
    The Marcus scandal of 1967 placed in a historical perspective of graft and corruption in New York City.

Scott, James C. "Corruption, Machine Politics, and Political Change," *American Political Science Review,* Vol. 63, No. 4 (December 1969), pp. 1142–1158.
    Important comparative analysis of old-style American machine politics with urban problems in developing countries.

Scott, James C. *Comparative Political Corruption.* Englewood Cliffs, N.J.: Prentice-Hall, 1972.
    Comparative analysis of political corruption, tracing historical roots, and indicating its incidence in Western and developing nations.

Shipler, David K. "Gibson Finds Graft Worse Than Expected," *The New York Times,* September 20, 1970, p. 1, col. 1–4.
    Mayor of Newark, New Jersey finds pervasive graft in city government upon succeeding Hugh J. Addonizio who was convicted of extortion charges.

Steffens, Lincoln. *The Shame of the Cities.* New York: Hill and Wang, American Century Series Paperback, 1966.
    Classic muckraker attack on the evils of graft and corruption in American cities at the turn of the twentieth century.

Steinberg, Alfred. *The Bosses.* New York: Macmillan, 1972. Descriptive study of six city bosses, who exercised power during the 1920s and 1930s.

Wilson, James Q. "Corruption Is Not Always Scandalous," *The New York Times Magazine* (April 28, 1968), pp. 54–74.
    Useful classification and evaluation of honest and dishonest graft.

Wolfinger, Raymond E. "The Development and Persistence of Ethnic Voting," *American Political Science Review,* Vol. 59, No. 4 (December 1965), pp. 896–908.
    Claims that ethnic bloc voting continues when middle-class status is attained by attractive ethnic candidates.

————. "Why Political Machines Have Not Withered Away and Other Revisionist Thoughts," *Journal of Politics,* Vol. 34, No. 2 (May 1972), pp. 365–398.
    Suggests that the persistence of machine politics is not directly correlated with needs of present-day impoverished groups. Also, that regional variations in political style may be a better explanation to the incidence of machine politics rather than socioeconomic composition of urban populations.

2

Municipal Reform: Democratic Participation

INTRODUCTION

American municipal reform, a product of the Progressive era (1900 to 1920), introduced most of the major political and structural innovations which characterize city government in the United States. Both democratic aspirations and business-oriented objectives motivated reform efforts to change the style and performance of local government. This chapter will deal with the democratizing aspects of municipal reform, while Chapter 3 will analyze the major structural changes that were brought about by the reformers.

The *democratic* side of reform emphasized the importance of popular participation in civic affairs. In their desire to return government to the people and to ensure effective grass-roots democracy, the reformers attacked corrupt political machines, incompetent elected officials, and obstructive local legislatures. While numerous assaults were made on the local party system, the reformers often achieved only mixed success in the electoral arena because they usually lacked the professional organizing skills and persistence of the machine politicians. Two alternatives to party reform were direct democracy and proportional representation. The initiative, referendum, and recall were intended to maximize citizen involvement in both the legislative and electoral processes by checking the actions of unresponsive and dishonest councilmen and mayors. Proportional representation provided a means of ensuring maximum minority group participation in local government without the guiding hand of the political machine. Table 2–1 summarizes these major democratic reform innovations.

HISTORICAL OVERVIEW: THE CITY
AS THE HOPE OF DEMOCRACY

The reform goals of the Progressive era were firmly rooted in Yankee-Protestant attachments to democratic values. The reformers were primarily Americans who had migrated from the farms and small towns to the burgeoning cities. They were shocked by the debilitating effects of urban life and industrialization which produced poverty, slums, and crime. Local self-government, they believed, was undermined by economic privilege and irresponsible political power. Democratic ideals were threatened by political bosses and conniving businessmen who shared the spoils of municipal franchises and city construction contracts. The reformers believed that campaigns against graft and corruption were necessary to rid the cities of "evil" men whose greed for personal power and material wealth prevented popular control of city government. Josiah Strong typified such attitudes when he warned:

> . . . It is chiefly in the city that the enormous powers of organization and of centralized wealth are wielded; and it is there that these powers must feel the wholesome restraint of righteous laws and of an enlightened popular conscience. It is in the city that the unprecedented increase of wealth affords unprecedented opportunities for self-gratification; and, without a corresponding increase of self-

TABLE 2–1   Municipal Reform Objectives: Democratic Participation

Political Party Reforms		Direct Popular Democracy	Representation Reform
Extraparty	*Intraparty*		
Citizens' Leagues	Blue Ribbon Factions	Initiative Referendum Recall	Proportional Representation
Candidate Appraisal Committees	Amateur Democrats		
Independent Local Parties			

control, we shall become enervated and demoralized in the lap of luxury. As the city grows populous and rich, the administration of its vast interests affords increasing opportunities for the corrupt use of money. There is, therefore, an increasing need of officials whose moral character is absolutely incorruptible—those who accept office for the public good, not those who seek it for private gain.[1]

Led by the clergy and muckraking journalists, the democratic reformers unleashed moral crusades against graft and corruption. For example, in 1894 the Rev. Charles Parkhurst led a successful attack on Tammany Hall by linking it with prostitution, gambling, and bootlegging. His exposés of police connivance with vice resulted in an electoral victory over the political machine and the appointment of Theodore Roosevelt as a reform police commissioner in New York City.[2] Similarly, Lincoln Steffens' muckraking assaults against political machines in a variety of cities aroused public ardor and became a monument of righteous indignation for the reform movement.[3]

Political Party Reform

Reform victories in the electoral arena were usually short-lived and did not permanently displace machine power. The antimachine forces were hostile to the local party system. In their view, machine domination of the party system resulted in control of city government. Consequently, the reformers shied away from the "dirty politics" required to compete with the bosses on their own terms. The reformers could not arouse mass voter support to build a viable base of political power. Rather, they were more concerned with pointing out the excesses of boss rule, such as the exorbitant waste of public funds, the dishonesty and incompetence of elected officials, and the maladministration of city government. Their long-range goal was to improve the efficiency and economy of local administration by instituting structural changes in city government. For these reasons, George Washington Plunkitt, a master practitioner of Tammany Hall politics, correctly labelled the antimachine forces as "mornin' glories":

> They were mornin' glories—looked lovely in the mornin' and withered up in a short time, while the regular machines went on flourishin' forever, like fine old oaks. . . .
> The fact is a reformer can't last in politics. He can make a show for a while, but he always comes down like a rocket. Politics is as much a regular business as the grocery or the dry goods or the drug business. You've got to be trained up to it or you're sure to fail . . .[4]

James Q. Wilson's discussion of local party reform generally supports Boss Plunkitt's criticism of the antimachine forces.[5] Wilson classifies two types of reform efforts: *extraparty* activities that supplement or supersede the regular parties and *intraparty* challenges by competitive groups or factions to provide voter alternatives to machine-dominated candidates. In evaluating the effectiveness of the party reformers, it becomes clear that their ranks consisted primarily of upper-class business, civic, and professional groups that shied away from building a base of mass voter support. Additionally, these "good government" forces did not employ long-range electoral strategies to bring about fundamental change in the local party structure. Rather, the party reformers generally assumed a "nonpolitical" (or nonprofessional politician) stance toward the functioning of the party system. They were hostile to using patronage and other material inducements to reward party workers and strengthen the organization. Consequently, party reformers had only minimal success in changing local parties. They enjoyed only short-run victories in the electoral arena. At best, reform was a cyclical phenomenon in American cities with strong local parties. As Theodore Lowi indicates, traditional party politics was the norm, while reform politics was the sporadic exception.[6]

Extraparty Reform

Antimachine organizations operating outside the regular party structure seek two major objectives. Citizens' leagues, candidates appraisal committees, and independent local parties attempt to recommend improvements in city government structure and to promote "good government" candidates for local offices.

Citizens' leagues such as the League of Women Voters and the Chicago Better Government Association are nonpartisan voluntary organizations that enlist voter participation and serve as guides to improve local government performance. In recent years, the Chicago Better Government Association has modified its approach from advising changes to conducting investigations of alleged inefficiency in city administration, incompetence and dishonesty of local officials, and questionable practices in election procedures. In 1969, for example, it disclosed the results of twenty-six separate investigations ranging from charges of illegal voter registration to loafing by city employees in the Department of Forestry. Democratic Mayor Richard

J. Daley was so irritated by these allegations that he criticized the nonpartisan group as an arm of the Republican party.[7]

Candidate appraisal committees screen, evaluate, recommend, support, and promote "good government" candidates as alternatives to machine-controlled nominees in local elections. In cities with weak parties and nonpartisan elections, these committees may also raise funds and campaign actively for their candidates. Alternatively, in cities with strong parties (New York, for example), the appraisal committees simply offer the voters the results of their preferences by listing candidates as "endorsed," "preferred," "qualified," or "unqualified."[8]

Independent local parties are frequently formed after citizen investigating committees disclose the results of exorbitant graft and corruption practiced by political machines. Spurred by citizen outrage and moral indignation, the "good government" forces put together antimachine tickets to "throw out the rascals" from city hall. For example, the New York City Citizens' Union opposed Tammany Hall in 1897 (unsuccessfully) and in 1901 (successfully) with reformer Seth Low as their candidate for mayor.

In analyzing the defeat of the New York City Citizens' Union in 1897, Moisei Ostrogorski argued that successful direct electoral competition with political machines required persistence and effective voter organization by independent local parties:

> . . . The result of the election showed that the struggle undertaken against the Machine was not a desperate one, but it also proved—for the hundredth time, it is true, or for the thousandth—that it was not by sudden attacks culminating in a furious assault that the enemy could be overcome; that to lead the electors away from the Machine it was necessary to make efforts just as persistent as the Machine itself makes to win and to retain them.[9]

The continuing success of the New York Liberal party offers a useful contrast to the short-lived victories of reform-based independent parties. Formed in 1944 by labor leaders of the International Ladies' Garment Workers' Union and the Hatters' Union, the Liberal party has a strong organizational and financial base of support. The Liberal party does not attempt to eliminate party machines from city politics. The major objective, according to Alex Rose, the party's chief political strategist, is to unite Democratic, Republican, and independent voters who support "liberal" candidates for good government.[10] The Liberal party attracts voting support by providing separate ballot lines for preferred candidates in local, state, and national elections.

The party leaders contend that such endorsements make the difference in electing Liberal candidates in close elections.

The Liberal party scored a major success in the hotly contested New York City mayoral race of 1969 by supporting John V. Lindsay for reelection. Rejected by the Republican party in the primary, Mayor Lindsay faced an uphill struggle to overcome the early leads of both Republican-Conservative John J. Marchi and Democrat Mario Procaccino. By combining the Liberal party nomination with his own specially created bipartisan Independent party, Mayor Lindsay received approximately 42 percent of the popular vote and won a close victory over both Marchi and Procaccino. There was little doubt that Lindsay's success depended upon the 844,023 Liberal party votes he received. This vote represented the largest ever received by the Liberal party in a city, state, or national election during its twenty-five-year history.[11] Lindsay's victory also indicated that the regular base of electoral support for the city's two major parties was temporarily shattered.[12]

Intraparty Reform

Two very different strategies are employed by reformers who use existing party machinery to achieve their goals. First, "blue ribbon" leadership factions try to convince the professional politicians of a dormant party machine to nominate "good government" candidates. Their objective is to defeat an entrenched machine that has not adapted to critical needs faced by the city. The reform factions seek men of "unassailable integrity," "high professional competence," and with records of "complete devotion to public service."[13] By gaining electoral support from the party machine, the reformers hope to bring about new changes in the direction of city government. However, leadership factions cannot expect to win control of the party, and, in fact, lack the necessary power, influence, and resources to do so.

In contrast, the intraparty reformers want to revitalize and restructure the internal party machinery. They seek to transform the local Democratic party by eliminating the power of the "old-style" professional politicians. Intraparty reform goals include the democratization of party rules and procedures, promotion of candidates who show commitment to critical issues, and employment of electoral techniques used by the old-style machines (face-to-face contact with the voters, canvassing, voter registration campaigns, and turning out the vote on election day).

The best example of a mutually acceptable accommodation between "blue ribbon" leadership factions and regular party bosses is found in Philadelphia. Between 1949 and 1962, reformers Richardson Dilworth and Joseph S. Clark, both of whom were members of Philadelphia's old "Main Line" families, brought about extensive changes in city government. Their election successes depended upon the political support of Congressman William J. Green who exercised substantial power as the city's Democratic party boss. Clark and Dilworth first opposed the city's entrenched and unresponsive Republican machine in 1947. Unsuccessful in their initial efforts, the two reformers won victory in 1949 by gaining pluralities of more than 100,000 votes for city treasurer (Dilworth) and city comptroller (Clark). Two years later, Clark was elected mayor and Dilworth became district attorney. When Clark ran successfully for United States senator in 1955, Dilworth began his tenure as mayor. Dilworth won reelection in 1959 and resigned from office in 1962 when he made an unsuccessful attempt to become governor of Pennsylvania.[14]

Clark and Dilworth had a unique political relationship with Congressman Green. During the thirteen years of reform leadership in city hall, Clark and Dilworth controlled all high-level administrative appointments and instituted an effective civil service system. They were also quite successful in starting important program innovations such as urban renewal.[15] At the same time, Green maintained virtually complete control over all party patronage and jobs that were independent of mayoral appointments and civil service. Furthermore, Green had influence over city councilmen who owed their elections to machine control of Democratic wards.

In summary, Philadelphia's reform mayors were able to bring about numerous governmental improvements and program innovations for more than a decade, while, at the same time, the Democratic party machine consolidated its power and control. The strategy of a mutual accommodation of conflicting interests between the reformers ("good government" gains and programmatic achievements) and the party professionals (control of patronage and other material inducements for party workers) proved to be a winning formula. The problem, of course, was that without reform mayors, Philadelphia faced the distinct possibility of machine retrenchment in the future.[16]

Intraparty reform represents the most recent effort to change the internal structure of state and local parties. In his comprehensive study, James Q. Wilson characterizes the intraparty activists as "amateur Democrats."[17] These reformers, who represented a younger generation of college-educated, middle- and upper-class professionals, found their inspiration in allegiance to the ideals expressed by Adlai Stevenson, the twice-defeated Democratic presidential candidate of 1952 and 1956. For them, Stevenson was a man of principle rather than of expediency. He was considered a new "liberal" who had broken away from the control of the party professionals.

The amateur Democrats turned their attention to local politics and attempted to build a genuine base of grass-roots support for Stevenson's ideals. They sought to eliminate the "old-style" politics based on ethnic ties, patronage rewards, and blind loyalty to party leaders. The new reformers hoped to democratize party rules and procedures to permit the broadest possible popular participation. They wanted to transform local parties into forums of discussion on critical issues. The goal was to discover the best-qualified candidates and to campaign actively on their behalf.

Wilson found important differences in the approaches used by the reform clubs in New York, Chicago, and California.[18] New York's amateur Democrats were supported by the Committee for Democratic Voters (CDV), an organization founded in 1958 by Mrs. Eleanor Roosevelt and Herbert Lehman, a former governor and United States senator. By 1960, the New York City reformers had made significant gains by displacing several of the old Tammany Hall district leaders, including Tammany chairman Carmine DeSapio. The central objective of the New York City reformers was to democratize the party rules and to install leaders from their own ranks. By controlling the district organizations, they would have party leaders responsible to the rank and file membership. This would lead to the development of party policy upon which selected candidates would campaign for office.

Chicago reformers faced difficult obstacles in transforming the internal structure of the Democratic party. Neither the Independent Voters of Illinois (IVI) nor the Democratic Federation of Illinois (DFI) could break the control of Mayor Richard J. Daley over the local and state party machinery. Formed in 1944, the IVI was a liberal faction of the Democratic party that sought to convince the party professionals to promote "good government" candidates in city elections. In this regard, the IVI closely resembled both the candidate appraisal committees and "blue ribbon" leadership factions previously discussed. On the other hand, the DFI was a statewide organization created in 1957 which attempted to work within the existing structure of the Democratic party. The DFI sought a voice in candidate selection, issue discussion, and party democratization. But Mayor Daley and the other party leaders thwarted both organizations by maintaining a very tight control over the internal party structure and by resisting all efforts to change party rules and procedures. Mayor Daley resisted reform efforts effectively by shrewd concessions made to Cook County suburban voters and downtown business interests. He convinced them that the party favored its own "good government" candidates. Since the machine could turn out a predictable vote for such "reformers," there was little opportunity for either the IVI or DFI to claim success. Both groups tended to dissolve into impotent factions without any real power or influence over either Mayor Daley or the Democratic party.

The efforts of California's amateur Democrats represented a third variation of intraparty reform goals. Functioning within a statewide nonpartisan political system which lacked both a strong central party organization and patronage rewards for party workers, the California Democratic Council (CDC) was formed in 1953 to make pre-primary endorsements of liberal-reform candidates running for state elective offices. But the CDC had less success in claiming victories for independent candidates than it had in gaining a reputation for taking controversial positions on public issues such as welfare, foreign policy, and civil rights.

In overall perspective, the intraparty reformers had several liabilities that prevented them from achieving their goals. Their antipathy to party professionals and patronage led to an uncompromising situation within the Democratic party. Democratization of rules and procedures oftentimes resulted in time-consuming debates which prevented the rank and file from taking stands on social issues. The reformers made little progress in attracting to their ranks working-class white ethnic groups, blacks, Puerto Ricans, and Mexican-Americans. Their emphasis on idealism, civic duty, and programmatic goals prevented the formation of a viable coalition politics. The amateur Democrats appealed primarily to white middle-class liberals who were moving out of the central cities to the suburbs. For this reason, they had to broaden their base of support to institute a new-style politics.

Reform efforts to change the style and substance of local parties produced, at best, only temporary gains. In cities with strong party systems, reform was usually a cyclical phenomenon with the traditional parties maintaining long-term control. Lowi, in his study of New York City, indicates that the real impact of party reform is to generate "anticipated reactions" among the party professionals.[19] Traditional parties slowly accept change in response to the threat that unified reform coalitions can defeat the machines at the polls. The regular party organizations therefore agree to some innovations in order to minimize electoral defeats.[20]

DIRECT DEMOCRACY

The Progressive reformers were never fully convinced that they could bring about fundamental changes in local parties. They were essentially ambivalent about using party politics as the instrument for achieving responsive city government. Consequently, municipal reformers sought alternative approaches to arouse citizen interest, involvement, and participation. They introduced devices of direct popular democracy—the initiative, referendum, and recall—to achieve their goals. Richard Hofstadter, in his examination of the Progressive era, commented that:

> . . . The movement for direct popular democracy was, in effect, an attempt to realize the Yankee-Protestant ideals of personal responsibility; and the Progressive notion of good citizenship was the culmination of the Yankee-Mugwump ethos of political participation without self-interest.[21]

The Progressive reformers hoped that the instruments of direct democracy would permit "good citizens" to check the actions of unresponsive, incompetent, and dishonest city councils and elected officials. The concerned citizen or "Man of Good Will," as described by Hofstadter, "needed to be protected from unjust taxation, spared the high cost of living, relieved of the exactions of the monopolies and the grafting of the bosses."[22] Accordingly, direct legislation (initiative and referendum) would provide the voters with weapons to overcome machine control of city councilmen who engaged in "crooked deals" behind closed doors. The initiative and referendum represented the people's "gun behind the door."[23] Recall would serve as the people's "sword of Damocles" ready to fall on the necks of dishonest elected officials who violated the public trust.

Initiative, referendum, and recall first appeared in California cities around the turn of the twentieth century. San Francisco's city charter of 1898 provided for direct legislation, while the recall originated in the Los Angeles charter of 1903. By 1930 most cities were using the initiative and referendum, while recall had much less widespread acceptance outside of California.[24]

Initiative and Referendum

Direct legislation has two aspects. The *initiative* is a method of *proposing* laws, while the *referendum* permits *voter approval* or *rejection* of measures appearing on the ballot. Ordinarily, an initiative procedure requires that a specified number of registered voters sign a petition which requests changes in the city charter or local ordinances. After the petition is validated, the proposed change is submitted to the electorate for approval.

Generally, there are three alternative methods for placing referendums on the ballot. First, city charters or state law may require certain matters, such as bond issues or structural changes in municipal government, to be approved by the voters (compulsory referendums). Second, city councils may become deadlocked over controversial issues that they wish the electorate to decide (advisory referendums). Third, voters may challenge city council actions by requesting that particular enactments be reviewed for final approval or veto (petition or protest referendums).[25]

Evaluating Direct Legislation: The California Fair Housing Controversy

The 1964 campaign to repeal California's fair housing law (the Rumford Act) provides an important contemporary case study to examine the alleged claims and counterclaims made for direct legislation. In evaluating the role of real estate interests in the repeal effort and voter attitudes toward racial discrimination in housing, political scientists Raymond Wolfinger and Fred Greenstein focus on the four key issues of direct legislation which have been debated by defenders and critics.[26] These issues include: *citizen participation, rational voter choice, the role of special interest groups,* and *legislative responsiveness.*

Background. In 1964 California real estate interests sought to nullify the state's Rumford Act, a 1963 law which prohibited racial discrimination in private housing by realtors, home builders, and apartment house owners. The state's Real Estate Association and Apartment Owners' Association formed the Committee for Home Protection to obtain the necessary petition signatures to place an initiative-referendum proposal on the ballot to amend the state constitution. The repeal measure, known as Proposition 14, contained the following provisions:

> SALES AND RENTAL OF RESIDENTIAL REAL PROPERTY. Initiative constitutional amendment. Prohibits State, subdivision, or agency thereof from denying, limiting, or abridging right of any person to decline to sell, lease, or rent residential real property to any person he chooses. Prohibition not applicable to property owned by State or its subdivisions; property acquired by eminent domain; or transient accommodations by hotels, motels, and similar public places.[27]

The California electorate overwhelmingly approved Proposition 14 in the November 1964 election. Of the nearly 7 million voters who participated, about 4.5 million favored repeal of fair housing while approximately 2.4 million voted against Proposition 14, a majority of two to one.[28]

Issue 1: Citizen Participation. Proponents of direct legislation claim that citizen participation in the legislative process encourages awareness, interest, and concern about community issues. Also, since most communities lack a competitive two-party system, it is necessary to broaden citizen access to public decisions. When state and local governments have either narrowly based political parties or a pervasive system of nonpartisanship, city councils and state legislatures do not represent a broad cross-section of all community groups. Direct legislation, it is argued, provides for greater expression of diverse voter concerns in a pluralistic political system. However, critics charge that voter interest is less apparent for ballot proposals than for elective offices. In general, more than half of the electorate can be expected to ignore referendum measures. This means that direct popular legislation is frequently approved or rejected by less than a majority of voters participating in an election.

Claims for citizen participation in direct legislation were convincingly shown in the vote for Proposition 14. Of those who turned out for the 1964 election, 96 percent voted on the anti–fair housing measure.[29] Except for a right to work ballot proposition in 1958, fewer California voters abstained on Proposition 14 than on any initiative-referendum measure in the twentieth century.[30]

The high level of voter participation for Proposition 14 can be explained by two factors. First, residential integration and the corresponding concern for protecting individual property rights are politically explosive issues that stimulate widespread voter interest. Second, California voters are probably more accustomed to direct legislation than any other group in the country. Since the initiative and referendum were first introduced in 1911, the statewide electorate has been asked to decide an average of twenty-two ballot propositions in each California election.[31]

Issue 2: Rational Voter Choice. A second defense of direct legislation is that voters will carefully study the issues to acquire the necessary information in making rational decisions on various ballot proposals. Direct legislation is therefore viewed as an important ingredient in promoting citizen understanding of important community issues. In contrast, opponents argue that initiative and referendum measures are often poorly drafted and deal with highly complex issues that are exceedingly difficult to understand. Thus, there is no assurance that the electorate has the necessary expertise to make intelligent decisions.

The wording of Proposition 14 resulted in some initial confusion for the California electorate, since a "yes" vote signified repeal of fair housing (although the language of the measure emphasized individual control and "free choice" over one's private property), while a "no" vote indicated preference for continuation of residential integration (a civil rights issue that was avoided by the real estate interests supporting Proposition 14).

Wolfinger and Greenstein's analysis of California voter attitudes indicates that early public misconceptions about the meaning of Proposition 14 were overcome by election day. Their most important finding was that Republican party affiliation, middle-income status, and moderate educational achievement were highly correlated with consistent opposition to fair housing. While the California Republican party took no official stand on Proposition 14, the state's Democratic party strongly opposed the measure. In the actual voting, Democrats were 30 to 50 percent more likely than Republicans to reject Proposition 14.[32]

The correlation between California voter attitudes and socioeconomic status was strikingly similar to that of Detroit where a fair housing measure was similarly rejected by the electorate in 1964. Harlan Hahn's comparative study of the two referendums indicates that white voter opposition to fair housing is associated strongly with a Republican party affiliation, middle-income status, and moderate educational achievement.[33]

TABLE 2-2   Characteristics of White Voters and Positions on the Home Owners' Ordinance in Detroit and Proposition 14 in California, 1964

	Home Owners Ordinance Support (Detroit)		Proposition 14 Support (California)	
	Per Cent	No.	Per Cent	No.
Age				
21–29 years	66.7	21	63.6	154
30–39 years	62.1	29	59.9	192
40–49 years	73.7	38	58.3	199
50–59 years	63.2	38	57.5	134
60 or more years	70.2	47	61.9	126
Home Ownership				
Owns	67.9	134	57.5	574
Rents	76.7	30	67.1	231
Party Identification				
Democrat	63.6	121	56.7	333
Republican	82.1	39	64.9	450
Education				
0–8 grades	62.8	43	67.1	84
Some high school	66.7	39	64.8	105
High school graduate	76.9	39	61.9	265
Work beyond high school	71.7	46	60.5	286
College degree	50.0	12	48.4	64
Income				
Lower and lower middle	68.0	46	60.7	135
Middle	78.7	47	63.1	520
Upper middle	75.6	45	52.1	119
Upper	48.0	25	40.6	32

Source: Harlan Hahn, "Northern Referenda on Fair Housing: The Response of White Voters," *Western Political Quarterly*, Vol. 21, No. 3 (September 1968), p. 489. Reproduced by permission of the University of Utah, Copyright Holder.

The comparative findings offered in Table 2–2 raise an important question about rational voter choice in fair housing referendums. Can white voter support for the sanctity of private property values be considered separately from an electoral decision that, in effect, results in a policy of discrimination against minority groups? More specifically, can the opposition to fair housing be equated with a rational voting choice? In using Gunnar Myrdal's concept of "rank order of discrimination,"[34] Wolfinger and Greenstein suggest that California voting attitudes toward Proposition 14 reflected a conscious rating of more or less discriminatory preferences among the white middle class. Preferences for racial equality could be ranked on a descending scale of popularity. While whites may favor equal treatment for blacks in public accommodations, job training programs, and in the public schools, they invariably oppose living in the same neighborhoods with blacks. Residential integration raises a threatening specter of personal association with blacks that many white homeowners and renters wish to avoid.[35] Proposition 14 offered California voters an opportunity to express these discriminatory choices. It is questionable whether claims for voter participation in direct legislation can be justified when the result is to approve a statewide policy of racial discrimination.

House Divided

Reprinted with permission from *The Herblock Gallery* (Simon & Schuster, 1968).

Issue 3: The Role of Special Interest Groups. Proponents of direct legislation argue that the initiative and referendum serve as a deterrent to crooked deals and benefits offered by dishonest legislators to special interest groups. When the voters have the opportunity to rectify the errors of the legislature, the elected lawmakers will be less likely to engage in such corrupt practices with self-serving private interests. In response, critics claim that the influence of interest groups is enhanced rather than limited by direct legislation. Organized community groups oftentimes sponsor and promote initiative and referendum campaigns, from which they derive special benefits.

There was no doubt that the campaign to repeal California's fair housing law was led by statewide organized real estate interests. These groups viewed the Rumford Act as a restriction on the so-called "free" housing market for individual sellers, buyers, and renters. They promoted adoption of Proposition 14 by emphasizing personal freedom over private property. Supporters of fair housing had to deal with the more politically polarizing issue of civil liberty protections for minority groups. Both sides used extensive publicity comparable to electing a candidate to statewide office, including billboards, newspaper advertisements, mass media, leaflets, and automobile bumper stickers. The large voting turnout was largely the result of a hard-fought, well-publicized, and effectively financed campaign.

Issue 4: Legislative Responsiveness. A final claim for direct legislation is that citizen participation and rational voter choice will make legislatures more responsive to citizen demands. Direct legislation, it is argued, improves legislative performance by encouraging the consideration of laws that serve the public interest. Opponents argue that there is no proven correlation between direct legislation and legislative responsiveness. The initiative and referendum serve as devices to bypass the elected legislature. The goal is to correct alleged "sins of omission" or other mistaken policies of the legislature by giving the voter only the single choice of approving or rejecting the ballot proposition. There can be no compromises in the final voting decision. Furthermore, the voters can, at best, only deal with a very small proportion of all important public policy issues. The preponderance of policy decisions will always be dealt with by elected legislatures. Therefore, direct legislation may serve as a check to maintain public accountability, but the more effective channel of power and influence will remain in the legislative chambers.

The overwhelming voter support of Proposition 14 provoked a flurry of political, judicial, and legislative activities in California. Some observers found a connection between the racial disorders in the Watts section of Los Angeles (1965) and black dissatisfaction with the repeal of fair housing. Others viewed Ronald Reagan's Republican gubernatorial victory in 1966 as resulting from a voter reaction to the Democratic party's endorsement of the Rumford Act.

The federal government responded to the 1964 vote by freezing $120 million of urban renewal funds for the state. The state courts abandoned or delayed several cases of alleged racial discrimination in housing as a result of the favorable vote for Proposition 14.[36]

The United States Supreme Court provided a landmark constitutional ruling on the California referendum. For the first time, the nation's highest tribunal nullified voter approval of a ballot proposition. In the case of *Reitman* v. *Mulkey* (1967),[37] Justice Byron White, speaking for a 5–4 majority, upheld a prior ruling by the California State Supreme Court which overturned the popular vote for Proposition 14 as a denial of equal protection of the laws. Justice White claimed that the state had permitted the voters to endorse a policy of private discrimination by allowing Proposition 14 to appear on the ballot. While the state was not required to have an antidiscriminatory housing law, there was no corresponding constitutional basis that permitted the state to encourage the electorate to repeal fair housing. Why? The ultimate impact of Proposition 14 was the creation by the voters of a constitutional right to discriminate. This right was a violation of the Equal Protection clause of the Fourteenth Amendment to the United States Constitution.

The Supreme Court decision reinstated the Rumford Act. By inference, Justice White's opinion suggested that the fair housing law could be repealed by the California state legislature. Two such efforts were made in 1967, but a senate-passed bill was defeated in the assembly, and an assembly modification of the law was similarly rejected by the senate. Since then, neither the legislature nor Governor Reagan have taken any further actions to change the Rumford Act.[38]

It seems clear that intensely politically polarizing issues such as fair housing are probably better considered by legislatures rather than by the general electorate. In recent years, eight out of eleven northern cities have rejected civil rights measures offered in ballot propositions.[39] Democratic ideals are not achieved when majority will is used to override the protection of minority rights. Even with the admitted limitations and deficiencies of the legislative process, elected legislatures are usually more representative than special interest groups which mobilize referendum campaigns. The legislative process offers opportunities to consider, debate, and balance competing community interests. It also permits compromise and modification of positions on particularly inflammatory public issues. When these arguments are balanced with the use of referendums to decide civil liberty issues, we can begin to see the potential dangers and limitations of direct popular democracy. Wolfinger and Greenstein conclude their analysis of the California fair housing controversy with the following observation:

> . . . If, as seems likely, the next several years of civil rights politics in the North are characterized by confrontations between angry, demanding Negroes and intransigent whites, with violence a common recourse of disappointed Negroes, then the referendum will become an increasingly inappropriate political tool and processes leaving room for calculation and compromise will be more necessary than ever. But we have no doubt also that the referendum will continue to be a tempting opportunity.[40]

Recall

Recall, a third instrument of direct democracy, is a type of "reverse election." Under this procedure, voters may challenge the right of elected officials to remain in office. Such contests take place after a specified percentage of registered voters sign a recall petition and request that a special election be held. The special election determines if the voters approve or disapprove the completion of the officeholder's tenure.

Recall is defended on the grounds that the electorate should have continuous control over their officials. Reformers argue that the voters can effectively combat corrupt machine politics by removing incompetent and dishonest officials who do not act in the public interest. But critics point out that recall is not aimed at proving charges of poor performance. Recall is not comparable to a courtroom trial or an impeachment proceeding. Rather, such challenges may actually lead to undue harassment of elected officials by well-organized vocal minorities seeking political recrimination. Such groups may force public officials to spend inordinate amounts of time and funds to overcome charges made against them.

The suggested claims and counterclaims made for recall are difficult to evaluate. Unlike the initiative and referendum, recall has not been used very much in American cities. There have been a few cases where mayors and city councilmen were ousted by the voters. Mayors have been recalled in Los Angeles (1909 and 1938), Seattle (1910 and 1938), and Detroit (1929). All of the city councilmen in Pasadena and Long Beach, California were removed in 1932 and 1934, while six councilmen in Ft. Worth, Texas were recalled in 1938.[41] In other cities, local officials overcame recall charges by gaining victories in special elections. However, there is a notable lack of social science evidence to determine the overall effectiveness and political impact of recall. As Duane Lockard indicates, "While it is probably true that recall has little ultimate importance there have been too few systematic studies to warrant any great confidence in the conclusion."[42]

Proportional Representation

Proportional representation (PR) is an important electoral innovation to ensure minority group representation on local governing bodies. Although PR was endorsed as early as 1899 by the National Municipal League and encouraged by such municipal reformers as Richard S. Childs (the founder of the council-manager plan), PR is now advocated by some urban observers as an answer to voter apathy and alienation in central city ghettos. Blacks, Puerto Ricans, Mexican-Americans, and other minorities are often antagonistic toward electoral systems which prevent the representation of neighborhood leaders on city councils and school boards. They become hostile toward city government when their leaders are denied access to important policy-making positions. By understanding the functions and purposes of PR, it might be possible to overcome minority group dissatisfaction and frustration toward government by making it more responsive to neighborhood problems and demands.

As employed in American cities, PR is a system of preferential voting that was devised in 1857 by an Englishman, Thomas Hare. The Hare PR system requires that voters mark their ballots by ranking candidates according to first, second, third, etc., choices according to the number of elected positions to be filled. Ballots are counted by sorting them according to first choices to determine the number of valid ballots cast. To be elected, a candidate must receive a certain "quota" of the total vote. The quota is calculated by dividing the total number of votes cast in the election by the number of positions to be filled, according to the following formula:

$$\frac{\text{Total Votes Cast}}{\text{Number of Seats to be Filled}} = \text{Single Seat Quota}$$
$$\text{Plus}$$
$$1$$

Example: If 100,000 votes are cast for five positions, the minimum winning quota would be 20,001 votes.

TABLE 2-3 PR and New York City Council: Voter Strength and Representation by Parties*

	1937			1939			1941			1943			1945		
	No. Seats	% Seats	% Votes	No. Seats	% Seats	% Votes	No. Seats	% Seats	% Votes	No. Seats	% Seats	% Votes	No. Seats	% Seats	% Votes
Democratic	13	50.0	47.0	14	66.5	65.5	17	65.5	64.0	10	59.0	53.0	14	60.0	59.0
Republican	3	11.5	8.5	2	9.5	8.0	2	7.5	6.5	3	17.0	22.0	3	13.0	15.0
Insurgent Democratic	2	8.0	7.0	1	5.0	4.0	—	—	—	—	—	—	—	—	—
American Labor	5	19.0	21.0	2	9.5	11.5	3	11.5	11.5	2	12.0	11.0	2	9.0	10.0
Fusion	3	11.5	10.5	2	9.5	11.0	3	11.5	12.5	—	—	—	—	—	—
Liberal	—	—	—	—	—	—	—	—	—	—	—	—	2	9.0	7.0
Communist	—	—	2.5	—	—	—	1	4.0	5.5	2	12.0	14.0	2	9.0	9.0
Other	—	—	3.5	—	—	—	—	—	—	—	—	—	—	—	—
Total	26			21			26			17			23		

*The figures used in the third column for each election represent the votes cast for persons on the deciding count, i.e., the elimination of hopeless candidates and the transfer of their votes.

SOURCE: Belle Zeller and Hugh A. Bone, "The Repeal of P.R. In New York City—Ten Years In Retrospect," *American Political Science Review*, Vol. 42, No. 6 (December 1948), p. 1132. Reproduced by permission.

The second phase of the Hare PR system involves the "single-transferable vote." All surplus votes of winning candidates (that is, any votes in excess of the minimum quota) are transferred to the voters' second choices until the required quota is achieved. Counting continues until all votes are transferred to other choices to fill all of the elected positions. During this process, candidates who are at the bottom of the list are dropped and their votes are transferred to second, third, and fourth, etc., choices.

Unlike either the ward system or at-large elections, PR cannot result in an overwhelming monopoly of elected positions for either one party or for white middle-class groups. PR is the only electoral system that fulfills the promise of "one man, one vote," if, as one observer concludes, it means that each vote will be as *effective* as possible for the candidates supported by the voters.[43] In contrast, ward elections may serve neighborhood needs through the party machine, but without focusing attention on the fundamental causes of racial discrimination, poverty, slum housing, and inadequate education. Also, the at-large system may eradicate machine power, but it frequently results in overrepresenting middle-class, business, civic, and reform groups. At-large representation makes it difficult for indigenous community leaders to extend their base of support to a citywide constituency.

How well does PR facilitate minority group representation in comparison with ward or at-large elections? Belle Zeller and Hugh A. Bone's analysis of New York City Council elections held under PR (1937–1945) and the preexisting aldermanic (ward) system convincingly proves the greater access of minority groups to the city council under PR. As shown in Table 2–3, the five PR elections revealed a very close relationship between voting strength and actual representation of various groups on the council. While it was evident that the Democrats were the dominant majority during these eight years, it was also clear that the Republicans, insurgent Democrats, American Labor, Fusion, Liberals, and even Communists gained a few seats. In contrast, under the last ward election Democratic candidates won 66.5 percent of the total votes and 95.3 percent of the council seats.[44] Under PR, the New York City Council Democrats were confronted by a more representative opposition than under the ward system. The same situation was evident during thirty-one years of experience with PR in Cincinnati. In the last election held before PR was introduced, thirty-one of thirty-two Cincinnati councilmen were Republicans, while during PR, numerous independents, reformers, and blacks were elected.[45]

TABLE 2–4   Adoption and Repeal of Proportional Representation For American City Councils* 1915–1964

City	Date Adopted	Date Repealed	Method of Repeal		
			By Local Referendum	By State Court	By State Legislature
Ashtabula, Ohio	1915	1929	X		
Boulder, Colorado	1918	1947	X		
Kalamazoo, Mich.	1919	1920		X	
Sacramento, Cal.	1922	1922		X	
W. Hartford, Conn.	1921	1923			X
Cleveland, Ohio	1924	1931	X		
Cincinnati, Ohio	1926	1957	X		
Hamilton, Ohio	1928	1960	X		
Toledo, Ohio	1936	1949	X		
Wheeling, W. Va.	1936	1950	X		
Yonkers, N.Y.	1940	1948	X		
New York, N.Y.	1938	1947	X		
Cambridge, Mass.	1940	—	Not Applicable		
Lowell, Mass.	1944	1957	X		
Long Beach, N.Y.	1946	1947	X		
Coos Bay, Oregon	1947	1948	X		
Worcester, Mass.	1950	1959	X		
Medford, Mass.	1950	1952	X		
Quincy, Mass.	1950	1952	X		
Revere, Mass.	1950	1952	X		
Saugus, Mass.	1948	1951	X		
Hopkins, Minn.	1949	1959	X		

*SOURCE: Adopted from Richard S. Childs, *The First 50 Years of the Council Manager Plan of Municipal Government*. New York: National Municipal League, 1965. p. 67.

PR has had a stormy and controversial experience in American cities. First introduced in Ashtabula, Ohio in 1915, PR has been employed in twenty-two cities, all of which also had the council-manager form of government (except New York City). With the lone exception of Cambridge, Massachusetts, all of these cities have long since dropped PR in favor of the at-large, ward, or combination ward and at-large elections. According to Richard S. Childs' analysis (Table 2–4), PR was used most frequently in cities located in Massachusetts (7), Ohio (5), and New York (3). PR was employed over five decades, with eleven cities having it before 1940 and eleven cities during the 1940s and 1950s. Aside from Cambridge, Massachusetts, which has had PR since 1940, other cities having the longest experiences with PR were Hamilton, Ohio (32 years), Cincinnati (31 years), and Boulder, Colorado (29 years). Finally, eighteen of the twenty-one cities repealed PR by local referendum votes, two systems were declared unconstitutional by state courts in California and Michigan, and the Connecticut state legislature banned PR in West Hartford.

PR has been criticized as an electoral system that is too difficult for most voters to understand. But aside from the simple requirement that voters mark their ballots according to preferred choices, there is no conclusive evidence to prove that as an electoral system PR is any more or less confusing than the ward or at-large methods. In his analysis of PR experiences in Cincinnati, Ralph A. Straetz observes that "with perhaps the exception of the surplus distribution, experience has shown that it is not very difficult to go into the average high school classroom and carry on a PR election and count."[46] Additionally, Straetz describes the continuous voter education efforts conducted for PR in Cincinnati. Educational materials were distributed by civic groups to schools, clubs, and other community organizations. Newspapers carried sample ballots with instructions to the voters about the use of PR. Also, voters did not take more than a few minutes to make their decisions with PR ballots in the voting booths on election day.

The more serious objections to PR relate to alleged threats to majority rule and the two-party system. Opponents charge that PR results in fragmented coalition governments containing overrepresented and dangerous anti-American minorities. The evidence shows that PR does effectively reduce party control over nominations, since primary elections are unnecessary. However, this does not mean that dominant political parties will lose control over a majority of city council seats. It has already been shown in Table 2–3 that the New York City Democrats maintained firm city council control when PR was in effect.

The kind of minorities elected under PR raises a critical issue concerning the purposes of representation in city government. There is no doubt that popular hostility toward radical political parties (the Communist party) and racial discrimination toward blacks are the central reasons for the successful PR repeal campaigns in New York and Cincinnati. To what extent is the majority willing to tolerate and permit political expression and election of unpopular groups professing radical ideologies? Did the election of one or two Communists to the New York City Council constitute a threat to the American political system? If the majority of voters reject the principle of full participation by *all* minorities, then they must accept the possibility that such groups will act elsewhere, either clandestinely or subversively, perhaps resorting to street demonstrations and riots. In any event, it is highly unlikely that any Communists could be elected to American city councils today. However, there is considerable political activism among militant spokesmen for disenfranchised community groups. The militancy of ghetto leaders might be channeled into constructive political action if they had an opportunity to be elected to important policy-making positions under a PR system.

The first elections held in March 1970 under the New York City school decentralization plan are the most recent examples of the ability of PR to encourage the participation of minorities in neighborhood government.[47] State law provided that nine-member school boards be elected in twenty-five community districts located in the four boroughs of Brooklyn, Queens, the Bronx, and Staten Island. (Manhattan elections were delayed due to a legal dispute over proposed boundaries.)

About 880 candidates sought the 225 available positions on the twenty-five school boards. Prior to the elections, there was strong evidence that local coalitions of slate-making groups were formed by local chapters of the teachers' union, parents' associations, political clubs, and church-sponsored groups. These groups, along with former members of appointed school boards, were much more successful in winning office than were the independent candidates.

The voter turnout was quite low, although it compared favorably with other New York communities that conduct school elections separately from other municipal contests. The final vote tally indicated that only 359,190 of the 2,402,000 eligibles participated, representing a 15 percent turnout.[48] What was the extent of minority group participation in these twenty-five separate school board elections? Apparently, many blacks and Puerto Ricans were not convinced that PR was the answer to their problems. Many of these two minorities did not *want* to vote because their leaders argued that the state's decentralization plan was inadequate and would not achieve closer community control of the schools. Several black and Puerto Rican leaders urged a boycott of the elections. As a result, many of the neighborhood school boards did not accurately represent the ethnic composition of the school population. In districts containing sizable numbers of black and Puerto Rican students, the community school boards had a dominant majority of white representatives.

On the basis of the New York City school election experience, it appears that PR can not and will not serve as an instant panacea to the ghetto residents' hostility toward local government. Rather, ghetto leaders must understand the purposes of PR and believe that PR will in fact achieve what it promises. Political scientist Joseph F. Zimmerman argues that electoral and representation reforms will succeed only when they are a part of an overall educational effort in ghetto communities:

> . . . PR will not maximize citizen participation and end alienation overnight, and voter registration and the number of votes cast will not increase sharply in ghetto areas following its initial use. To many ghetto residents the substitution of PR for the existing system may appear to be another middle-class scheme to keep them politically suppressed. Only when the minority group leaders perceive that PR will perform as promised will political participation increase significantly.[49]

NOTES

1. Josiah Strong, "The Challenge of the City," cited in *The Urban Vision*, eds. Jack Tager and Park Goist (Homewood, Ill.: Dorsey Press, 1970), pp. 24–25.
2. Arthur M. Schlesinger, Jr., *The Rise of the City: 1878–1898* (New York: Macmillan, 1933), pp. 115–116.
3. See, especially: Lincoln Steffens, *The Shame of the Cities* (New York: Hill and Wang, American Century Series Paperback, 1966). Also, see: Richard Hofstadter, *The Age of Reform* (New York: Random House, Vintage Books, 1955), pp. 186–214.
4. William L. Riordon, *Plunkitt of Tammany Hall* (New York: E. P. Dutton, 1963), pp. 17, 19.
5. James Q. Wilson, "Politics and Reform In American Cities," *American Government Annual, 1962–1963* (New York: Holt, Rinehart and Winston, 1962), pp. 37–52.
6. Theodore J. Lowi, *At the Pleasure of the Mayor* (New York: Free Press of Glencoe, 1964), p. 178.
7. *The New York Times*, January 4, 1970, p. 43, cols. 1–4.
8. Wilson, "Politics," p. 42.
9. Moisei Ostrogorski, *Democracy and the Organization of Political Parties, Vol. II: The United States* (New York: Doubleday, Anchor Books, 1964), p. 245.
10. *The New York Times*, November 7, 1969, p. 50, col. 1.
11. *Ibid.*, November 6, 1969, p. 40.
12. *Ibid.*, September 29, 1969, p. 41, col. 1–2; and *Ibid.*, November 6, 1969, p. 1. col. 5.
13. Edward C. Banfield and James Q. Wilson, *City Politics* (New York: Random House, Vintage Books, 1963), p. 144.
14. Edward C. Banfield, *Big City Politics* (New York: Random House, Studies in Political Science, 1965), pp. 110–111.

15. Jeanne R. Lowe, *Cities in a Race With Time* (New York: Random House, Vintage Books, 1968), pp. 313–404.
16. Banfield, *Big City Politics,* p. 107.
17. James Q. Wilson, *The Amateur Democrat* (Chicago: University of Chicago Press, 1966), pp. 2–10.
18. *Ibid.,* Chs. 2, 3, 4. The following comparative discussion of the three reform efforts in New York, Chicago, and California represents a summary of Wilson's findings.
19. Lowi, *At the Pleasure of the Mayor,* p. 207.
20. *Ibid.*
21. Hofstadter, *The Age of Reform,* p. 261.
22. *Ibid.,* p. 260.
23. Charles R. Adrian and Charles Press, *Governing Urban America,* 3rd ed. (New York: McGraw-Hill, 1968), p. 108.
24. Charles N. Glaab and A. Theodore Brown, *A History of Urban America* (New York: Macmillan, 1967), p. 192.
25. Benjamin Baker, *Urban Government* (Princeton, N.J.: D. Van Nostrand, 1957), p. 201.
26. Raymond E. Wolfinger and Fred I. Greenstein, "The Repeal of Fair Housing in California: An Analysis of Referendum Voting," *American Political Science Review,* Vol. 62, No. 3 (September 1968), pp. 753–769.
27. *Ibid.,* p. 755.
28. Thomas W. Casstevens, "California's Rumford Act and Proposition 14," in *The Politics of Fair Housing Legislation,* eds. Lynn W. Eley and Thomas W. Casstevens (San Francisco: Chandler, 1968), p. 273.
29. Wolfinger and Greenstein, *American Political Science Review,* Vol. 62, No. 3, p. 753.
30. John E. Mueller, "Voting on the Propositions: Ballot Patterns and Historical Trends in California," *American Political Science Review,* Vol. 63, No. 4 (December 1969), pp. 1202–1203.
31. Wolfinger and Greenstein, *American Political Science Review,* Vol. 62, No. 3, p. 767.
32. Mueller, *American Political Science Review,* Vol. 63, No. 4, p. 1206.
33. Harlan Hahn, "Northern Referenda on Fair Housing: The Response of White Voters," *Western Political Quarterly,* Vol. 21, No. 3 (September 1968), pp. 488–489.
34. Wolfinger and Greenstein, *American Political Science Review,* Vol. 62, No. 3, p. 765.
35. *Ibid.*
36. *Ibid.,* p. 753; and Casstevens, *The Politics of Fair Housing,* pp. 281–284.
37. 387 U. S. 369 (1967). Cited in Norman Dorsen, *Discrimination and Civil Rights* (Boston: Little, Brown, 1969), pp. 373–377. Also, see: *The New York Times,* June 4, 1967, Section 4, p. 14, col. 1–2.
38. Wolfinger and Greenstein, *American Political Science Review,* Vol. 62, No. 3, p. 768.
39. Hahn, *Western Political Quarterly,* Vol. 21, No. 3, p. 483.
40. Wolfinger and Greenstein, *American Political Science Review,* Vol. 62, No. 3, p. 769.
41. Russell W. Maddox and Robert F. Fuquay, *State and Local Government,* 2nd ed. (Princeton, N.J.: D. Van Nostrand, 1966), p. 333.
42. Duane Lockard, *The Politics of State and Local Government,* 2nd ed. (New York: Macmillan, 1969), p. 254.
43. Robert G. Dixon, Jr., *Democratic Representation: Reapportionment in*

Law and Politics (New York: Oxford University Press, 1968), p. 525.

44. Belle Zeller and Hugh A. Bone, "The Repeal of P.R. in New York City—Ten Years in Retrospect," *American Political Science Review,* Vol. 42, No. 6 (December 1948), p. 1136.

45. Ralph A. Straetz, *PR Politics in Cincinnati* (New York: New York University Press, 1958), p. 43.

46. *Ibid.,* p. 283.

47. *The New York Times,* March 19, 1970, p. 50, col. 1–3.

48. *Ibid.,* March 28, 1970, p. 20, col. 5–8.

49. Joseph F. Zimmerman, "Electoral Reform Needed to End Political Alienation," *National Civic Review,* Vol. 60, No. 1 (January 1971), pp. 11, 21.

SUGGESTIONS FOR FURTHER READING

Historical Overview

Glaab, Charles N., and A. Theodore Brown. *A History of Urban America.* New York: Macmillan, 1967. pp. 211–220.
Historical account of reformer attacks on political machines and lack of mass base of voter support as party reformers were "mornin' glories."

Hofstadter, Richard. *The Age of Reform.* New York: Random House, Vintage Books, 1955. pp. 257–271.
Discussion of democratic reform attacks against the party machines by empowering the voters with the instruments of direct popular democracy during the Progressive era.

Howe, Frederick C. *The City: The Hope of Democracy.* Seattle: University of Washington Press, Americana Library Paperback, 1967.
Classic attack on the excesses of economic self-interest in the cities at the turn of the twentieth century.

Mowry, George E. *The Era of Theodore Roosevelt and the Birth of Modern America: 1900–1912.* New York: Harper & Row, Harper Torchbooks, 1962. pp. 59–84.
Social democracy in the cities during the Progressive era.

Richards, Allan R. "Half of Our Century," in *The 50 States and Their Local Governments,* ed. James W. Fesler. New York: Alfred A. Knopf, 1967. pp. 71–103.
Review of democratic and structural reforms in American cities.

Sayre, Wallace S., and Nelson W. Polsby. "American Political Science and the Study of Urbanization," in *The Study of Urbanization,* eds. Philip M. Hauser and Leo F. Schnore. New York: John Wiley and Sons, 1965. pp. 115–156.
Comprehensive overview of political science analysis and prescriptions for change in American cities.

Steffens, Lincoln. *The Shame of the Cities.* New York: Hill and Wang, American Century Series Paperback, 1966.
Classic muckraker attack on graft and corruption in the cities.

Tager, Jack, and Park D. Goist, eds. *The Urban Vision.* Homewood,

Ill.: Dorsey Press, 1970. Part I: "The Challenge of the City, 1890–1915."
Selected essays by the leading social reformers of the Progressive era.

Political Party Reform

Banfield, Edward C. *Big City Politics.* New York: Random House, Studies in Political Science, 1965. pp. 107–120.
Discussion of reform mayor accommodation with party boss in Philadelphia, 1947–1962.

————, and James Q. Wilson. *City Politics.* New York: Random House, Vintage Books, 1963. pp. 138–150.
Analysis of extraparty and intraparty reform efforts.

Costikyan, Edward N. *Behind Closed Doors.* New York: Harcourt, Brace & World, Harvest Books, 1966.
Evaluation of intraparty reform in New York City by a former Tammany Hall "reform" leader.

Lowi, Theodore J. *At the Pleasure of the Mayor.* New York: Free Press of Glencoe, 1964. Ch. 8, "The Reform Cycle," pp. 175–214.
Very useful analysis of party reform v. professional politician efforts in New York City. Author questions the long-range effectiveness of party reform.

Ostrogorski, Moisei. *Democracy and the Organization of Political Parties,* Vol. 2: *The United States.* New York: Doubleday, Anchor Books, 1964, pp. 238–252.
Criticism of party reform ineffectiveness in building an effective base of voter support to combat the machines at the turn of the twentieth century.

Reeves, Richard. "The Six-Party System," *The New York Times,* September 29, 1969, p. 41, col. 1–2.
Argues that major parties in New York City were splintering as a result of conflict over Mayor Lindsay's 1969 reelection campaign.

Reichley, James. *The Art of Government: Reform and Organization Politics in Philadelphia.* New York: The Fund for the Republic, 1958.
Discussion of Democratic party reform efforts to oust entrenched Republicans and elect "blue ribbon" mayors Clark and Dilworth to city hall in the late 1940s and early 1950s.

Wilson, James Q. *The Amateur Democrat.* Chicago: University of Chicago Press, Phoenix Books, 1966.
Intraparty reform efforts in New York, Chicago, and Los Angeles during the 1950s.

————. "Politics and Reform in American Cities," in *American Government Annual, 1962–1963.* New York: Holt, Rinehart and Winston, 1963. pp. 37–52.
Classification and evaluation of various intraparty and extraparty municipal reform efforts.

Direct Democracy: Initiative, Referendum, and Recall

Adrian, Charles R., and Charles Press. *Governing Urban America,* 3d ed. New York: McGraw-Hill, 1968. pp. 81–83, 106–113.
Historical review of municipal reform and appraisal of instruments of direct democracy.

Baker, Benjamin. *Urban Government.* Princeton, N.J.: D. Van Nostrand, 1957. pp. 199–208.
Procedures and evaluation of direct democracy.

Crouch, Winston W. "The Initiative and Referendum in Action," in *Capitol, Courthouse and City Hall,* 3rd ed., ed. Robert L. Morlan. Boston: Houghton Mifflin, 1966. pp. 308–312.
Discussion of direct democracy in California.

Lockard, Duane. *The Politics of State and Local Government,* 2nd ed. New York: Macmillan, 1969. pp. 247–254.
Evaluation of direct democracy and referendum campaigns.

Fair Housing Referenda

Blume, Norman. "Open Housing Referenda," *Public Opinion Quarterly.* Vol. 35, No. 4 (Winter 1971), pp. 563–570.
Analysis of 1967–1968 fair housing referenda in five cities—Toledo, Ohio and four Michigan cities—indicates that race (black) and high socioeconomic status correlate most strongly with favorable voting to open housing.

Casstevens, Thomas W. "California's Rumford Act and Proposition 14," in *The Politics of Fair Housing Legislation,* eds. Lynn W. Eley and Thomas W. Casstevens. San Francisco: Chandler, 1968. pp. 237–284.
Case study of 1964 fair housing campaign in California.

Hahn, Harlan. "Northern Referenda on Fair Housing: The Response of White Voters," *Western Political Quarterly,* Vol. 21, No. 3 September 1968), pp. 483–495.
Comparative analysis of fair housing campaigns in California and Detroit in 1964.

Hamilton, Howard. "Direct Legislation: Some Implications of Open Housing Referenda," *American Political Science Review,* Vol. 64, No. 1 (March 1970), pp. 124–137.
In testing several hypotheses regarding referendum voting, the author identifies voter efficacy, low turnout, correlation with concurrent elections, and entrenchment of minority rule as the key variables to explain opposition to fair housing referendums.

Mueller, John E. "Voting on the Propositions: Ballot Patterns and Historical Trends in California," *American Political Science Review,* Vol. 63, No. 4 (December 1969), pp. 1197–1212.
Comparison of 1964 voter response to fair housing referendums with a variety of other ballot propositions.

Wolfinger, Raymond E., and Fred I. Greenstein. "The Repeal of Fair Housing in California: An Analysis of Referendum Voting," *Ameri-*

can Political Science Review, Vol. 62, No. 3 (September 1968), pp. 753–769.
Comprehensive analysis of voter attitudes regarding the repeal of fair housing in California. Authors argue that it may be dangerous to permit the voters to act on civil rights issues by the referendum process.

Proportional Representation

Banfield, Edward C., and James Q. Wilson. *City Politics.* New York: Random House, Vintage Books, 1963. pp. 96–98.
Effects of P.R. in American cities.

Childs, Richard S. *The First 50 Years of the Council-Manager Plan of Municipal Government.* New York: National Municipal League, 1965. pp. 65–68.
History of development and attacks on P.R.

Dixon, Robert G., Jr. *Democratic Representation: Reapportionment in Law and Politics.* New York: Oxford University Press, 1968. pp. 525–527.
Analysis of techniques of P.R. elections.

Gans, Herbert J. "We Won't End The Urban Crisis Until We End 'Majority Rule'," *The New York Times Magazine* (August 3, 1969), pp. 12–14, 20, 24, 28.
Author argues that political minorities are alienated unless they are provided opportunities for participation in democratic government.

Hechinger, Fred M. "New York's School Vote Is a Start, But Toward What?" *The New York Times,* March 29, 1970, Section 4, p. 1, col. 1–3.
Use of P.R. in New York City school decentralization plan has mixed results for representation of blacks and Puerto Ricans on community school boards.

Straetz, Ralph A. *PR Politics in Cincinnati.* New York: New York University Press, 1958.
History of thirty-two years of P.R. elections in Cincinnati together with its demise in 1957.

Zeller, Belle, and Hugh A. Bone. "The Repeal of P.R. in New York City—Ten Years in Retrospect," *American Political Science Review,* Vol. 42, No. 6 (December 1948), pp. 1127–1148.
Authors argue that P.R. was repealed in the nation's largest city because of representation of the wrong kinds of minorities on city council, particularly Communists.

Zimmerman, Joseph F. "Electoral Reform Needed to End Political Alienation," *National Civic Review,* Vol. 60, No. 1 (January 1971), pp. 6–11, 21.
P.R., while not a panacea, can assist disadvantaged minorities if they take full advantage of it in city elections.

————. *The Federated City: Community Control in Large Cities.* New York: St. Martin's Press, 1972. Ch. 4, "The Electoral System."
Discusses proportional representation and other alternatives to at-large election systems in attempting to broaden minority group representation.

3

Municipal Reform: Institutional Innovations

INTRODUCTION

Many municipal reformers of the Progressive era were doubtful that the goals of civic participation and grass-roots democracy would be achieved through political party changes, the instruments of direct democracy, or proportional representation. They believed that democratic reforms did not attack the central sources of machine power. Consequently, various civic, business, and good government associations turned their attention to the institutional bases of elections, representation, and governmental organization. They were less concerned about the plight of the urban poor than they were with applying good business practices of efficiency and economy to city government. One of the earliest proponents of this viewpoint was James Bryce who, upon observing the conditions of American cities in 1889, concluded:

> There is no denying that the government of cities is the one conspicuous failure of the United States. The deficiencies of the National government tell but little for evil on the welfare of the people. The faults of the State governments are insignificant compared with the extravagance, corruption, and mismanagement which mark the administration of the great cities.[1]

The Progressive reformers believed in a "public-regarding" view of the public interest which was opposed to the "private-regarding" outlook of the immigrant-based machines.[2] Historian Richard Hofstadter defines this public-oriented philosophy in terms of Yankee-Protestant attitudes that:

> . . . assumed and demanded the constant, disinterested activity of the citizen in public affairs, argued that political life ought to be run, to a greater degree than it was, in accordance with general principles and abstract laws apart from and superior to personal needs, and expressed a common feeling that government should be in good part an effort to moralize the lives of individuals while the economic life should be intimately related to the stimulation of individual character.[3]

Accordingly, the "public-regarding" structural reformers argued that local officials should serve citywide needs rather than catering to the special interests of particular neighborhoods. This would be achieved by electoral and representation innovations such as the short ballot and at-large elections. Also, they wanted to remove all party labels from local elections. Nonpartisanship, they hoped, would attract the most qualified and civic-minded candidates to public office—persons who were not motivated by desires for material rewards and personal aggrandizement. "Reformed" city councilmen and mayors would then be in a position to enact enlightened public programs by applying modern business techniques and principles of public administration to city affairs. Efficiency and economy in government would be facilitated by instituting local government reorganization plans such as the strong mayor-council plan, the commission plan, and the council-manager plan. The goal was efficient and effective management of city policy by professionally qualified experts whose administrative competence (policy-implementation) would be judged by capable elected officials (policy-making). Table 3–1 summarizes the institutional innovations promoted by the structural reformers. Throughout this chapter, it should become quite clear that the structural reformers sought a desired "package" of changes for the cities. This interrelated system included short ballots, nonpartisan elections, at-large representation, and the council-manager form of government.

SHORT BALLOTS

The short ballot was envisioned by the structural reformers as a way of eliminating machine control over the electoral process. City bosses were considered as the product of the long ballot and weak mayor-

TABLE 3-1   Municipal Reform Objectives: Structural Innovations

Electoral Reforms	Representation Reforms	Governmental Reorganization Plans
Short Ballot	At-Large (rather than by wards for councilmen)	Strong Mayor-Council
Nonpartisan Elections		Commission
		Council-Manager

council government—two legacies of Jacksonian Democracy.[4] The weak mayor-council system required the popular election of numerous executive, legislative, and administrative officials. Voter confusion was readily apparent without the guidance of machine politicians who urged electoral support of political party slates. The ward bosses sought to mobilize blocs of voters for the party, rather than to encourage individual voter selection among the various candidates. The structural reformers were highly critical of voter manipulation by the machines. In their view, the long ballot was the "politicians' ballot."[5] The short ballot was crucial to restoring citizen effectiveness in city elections. Woodrow Wilson, who became the first president of the National Short Ballot Association, supported this view in 1909 when he declared: "I believe that the short ballot is *the key* to the whole question of the restoration of government by the people."[6]

By reducing the number of elective offices on the ballot, the structural reformers hoped to achieve more discriminating voter participation, which, in turn, would reduce the "blind" support of party machine candidates. This would have several beneficial aspects. First, individual voters would be able to identify only the most important elective officials among a relatively few positions on the ballot. Second, the smaller number of officials elected would be in a better position to control the bureaucracy by appointing top-level administrators. Third, the complexity, confusion, and chaos of weak mayor-council government would be overcome. In 1909, Richard S. Childs, the nation's leading promoter of the short ballot, summarized the two basic objectives of this reform:

> First—that only those offices should be elective which are important enough to attract and *deserve* public scrutiny. Second—that very few offices should be filled by election at one time, so as to permit adequate and unconfused scrutiny of the candidates by the public, and *so as to facilitate the full and intelligent making of original tickets by any voter for himself unaided by political specialists.*[7]

The short ballot movement was so closely related to several other structural reforms that separate evaluation is best deferred until later discussion. During the life of the National Short Ballot Association (1911 to 1920), Richard S. Childs also sponsored nonpartisan elec- / tions, at-large representation, and the commission and council-manager plans for city government. He was highly successful in gaining widespread support for the nearly universal adoption of short ballots in American cities. The short ballot became a catalyst for reducing the size of city councils, replacing bicameral councils with unicameral local legislatures and separating local elections from state and national elections. John Porter East, the biographer of Childs, summarizes the short ballot movement by placing it within the context of the Progressive era of municipal reform: "Progressivism—with its yearning for a return to 'democracy,' with its scorn for 'the politician,' with its trust in the proper mechanical device to return government to 'the people'—is also manifested in the struggle for the short ballot principle."[8]

NONPARTISAN ELECTIONS

Nonpartisan city elections constituted a second major structural reform effort to reduce the power and influence of political party organizations in local affairs. Municipal reformers believed that by prohibiting party labels for candidates on election ballots, neither the local machines nor the state and national parties would interfere with citizen selection of municipal officials. Two basic arguments for nonpartisanship were: (1) Formal party organizations are more concerned with state and national issues that have no bearing on the conduct of city affairs; (2) City problems are basically "non-political" and involve questions of effective public administration equivalent to "good" business practices of private corporations. These views were expressed as early as 1877 by a New York State commission appointed by Governor Samuel J. Tilden to recommend improvements for city government:

> There is no more just reason why the control of the public works of a great city should be in the hands of a Democrat or a Republican than there is why an adherent of one or the other great parties should be made the superintendent of a business corporation.[9]

Nonpartisanship has gained widespread acceptance in American cities. Following the suggestions of the National Municipal League in 1894, party labels were removed from city elections in Dallas

(1907) and Boston (1909), and in all California cities and counties in 1913.[10] By 1929, more than half of the nation's 282 cities had nonpartisan elections. As shown in Table 3–2, the most noteworthy nationwide trends in municipal nonpartisan elections by 1968 included: (1) Nearly 65 percent of all cities over 5,000 population used nonpartisanship; (2) The removal of party labels was closely related to the council-manager form of government, with slightly more than 82 percent of council-manager cities also nonpartisan; and (3) Nonpartisan city elections have been almost universally adopted in the western states, although they are also extensively used in the north central and southern regions. The Northeast continues to use partisan labels in city elections. Finally, although not indicated in Table 3–2, nonpartisanship is correlated with at-large representation for city councilmen. A 1960 survey by political scientist Eugene C.

TABLE 3–2   Ballot Affiliation for General City Elections

Classification	No. of Cities Reporting	% of Reporting Cities Nat'l Party On Ballot	% of Reporting Cities Nat'l Party Not On Ballot	No. of Cities Reporting	% of Reporting Cities Group Affiliation On Ballot	% of Reporting Cities Group Affiliation Not On Ballot
Population Group						
Over 500,000	24	41.7%	58.3%	17	5.9%	94.1%
250,000 to 500,000	25	24.0	76.0	19	...	100.0
100,000 to 250,000	90	41.1	58.9	57	3.5	96.5
50,000 to 100,000	208	31.7	68.3	148	6.1	93.9
25,000 to 50,000	427	33.3	66.7	300	9.7	90.3
10,000 to 25,000	1,057	34.4	65.6	692	10.8	89.2
5,000 to 10,000	1,049	36.9	63.1	685	12.4	87.6
Under 5,000	514	11.9	88.1	388	5.2	94.8
Form of Government [1]						
Mayor-Council	1,387	50.8	49.2	667	6.7	93.3
Council-Manager	1,229	17.7	82.3	982	5.0	95.0
Commission	174	30.5	69.5	118	2.5	97.5
Town Meeting	62	43.5	56.5	35	8.6	91.4
Representative Town Meeting	28	39.3	60.7	16	6.3	93.8
City Type [1]						
Central	252	37.3	62.7	171	4.1	95.9
Suburban	1,348	36.9	63.1	925	15.2	84.8
Independent	1,280	32.8	67.2	822	6.4	93.6
Geographic Region [1]						
Northeast	767	75.7	24.3	338	21.6	78.4
North Central	901	26.2	73.8	661	13.9	86.1
South	768	21.9	78.1	529	2.6	97.4
West	444	6.1	93.9	300	5.6	94.4
All Cities over 5,000	2,880	35.1	64.9	1,918	10.5	89.5

[1] Includes only cities over 5,000.

SOURCE: *The Municipal Year Book,* 1968. Washington, D.C.: The International City Managers' Association, p. 58. Reproduced by permission.

Lee disclosed that "83 per cent of the at-large cities are nonpartisan as contrasted with only 50 per cent of the cities using the ward system. . . . Regardless of the size of city, nonpartisan communities are more likely to use the at-large system exclusively whereas partisan cities are far more likely to elect at least some of the council by wards."[11]

Municipal reformers believed that nonpartisanship would achieve three central objectives. First, local elections would be *insulated* from the influences of city machines and state and national party organizations. Second, *better candidates* would come forward to run for city elective offices under a nonpartisan system. Third, nonpartisan elections would encourage more responsive city council candidates who, if elected, would be more *accountable* for their actions while in office.

Over the last decade, political scientists have tested the alleged claims for nonpartisan elections by examining the political and social environments of American cities. They have attempted to discover if the alleged benefits of nonpartisanship—insulation, better candidates, and accountability—do in fact occur when party labels are removed from city elections.

The Insulation Argument

The insulation claim for nonpartisanship assumes that the individual's voting choice is enhanced when party organizations are prohibited from "dictating" their decisions to the electorate. By conducting city elections at a different time from the state and national elections, voters can decide on the merits of the candidates without interference by political parties. Removal of party labels also promotes discussion of local issues. Robert Wood summarizes these arguments in his analysis of nonpartisanship in American suburbs:

> Inescapably, there is a belief that the individual can and should arrive at his political convictions untutored and unled; an expectation that in the formal process of election and decision-making a consensus will emerge through the process of right reason and by the higher call to the common good. Gone is the notion of partisan groups, leaders and followers, and in its place is the conscious assumption that the citizen, on his own, knows best.[12]

Are voter decisions in nonpartisan elections less affected by Republican or Democratic party influences than in cities with partisan ballots? Separate studies of election results in the nation's twenty-four largest cities, four Michigan cities, and Des Moines, Iowa all confirm the persistence of partisan voting preferences in nonpartisan city contests. These three surveys indicate that as local candidates pursue issues more vigorously in their campaign efforts, there is a greater likelihood that city voting results will conform more to partisan divisions in state and national elections.[13]

Not only are voter attachments to the two major parties maintained in local nonpartisan elections, but the Republican party appears to have a distinct advantage over the Democratic party. Williams and Adrian indicate that "in cities closely divided between Democrats and Republicans, a nonpartisan and at-large election leads to an increased voice in local affairs for persons who normally vote Republican."[14] Republicans tend to participate more and vote more than Democrats in nonpartisan elections. Charles Gilbert observes that in the absence of party labels and party activity, Republicans enjoy a " 'natural' edge in organization, communication, and prestige."[15]

Another criticism of the insulation argument is that a lower voting turnout results from reduced party activity and the separation of local elections from state and national elections. Eugene C. Lee's nationwide analysis reveals that the median voting participation in cities conducting nonconcurrent local contests was 29 percent, while in cities holding local elections at the same time as state or national elections, the median voter turnout was 50 percent.[16] Furthermore, regardless of whether the city election is held independently or concurrently with other contests, voting participation in nonpartisan elections is substantially lower than in partisan cities. Lee indicates that "in one-half of the partisan cities, the turnout was 50 per cent or less, while in three-fourths of the nonpartisan cities, the per cent of adults voting was 43 per cent or less."[17]

Reduced voting participation works to the disadvantage of groups that normally identify with organized labor, "bread-and-butter" issues, and civil rights. Ethnic, racial, or religious minority blocs are least likely to come to the polls without the normal voter mobilizing activities usually performed by the Democratic party. These groups are much more active in cities with partisan elections. According to Alford and Lee's voter turnout study, there is less participation in cities with nonpartisanship, council-manager government, low ethnicity, high education, high mobility, and far western location than in cities with partisan elections, mayor-council government, high ethnicity, low education, low mobility, and eastern location.[18]

A further modification of the insulation claim for nonpartisanship is the continuing role of formal political party activity in certain kinds of cities. Charles R. Adrian's classification of nonpartisanship provides two types of situations where parties continue to function and two other categories where Republican and Democratic party activity is effectively reduced:[19]

> *Type 1.* Elections where the only candidates who normally have any chance of being elected are those supported directly by a major party organization.

Chicago is the best example of a city with formally nonpartisan elections where the Democratic party machine, under the leadership of Mayor Richard J. Daley, effectively controls the selection of candidates for the fifty-member board of aldermen (Chicago's city council). In the 1971 aldermanic elections, the Daley machine overcame challenges by political independents and Republicans by retaining thirty-seven of the fifty council seats. The antimachine forces had hoped to win at least seventeen seats so they could combine their votes to block "emergency" measures under the suspension of council rules.[20]

> *Type 2.* Elections where slates of candidates are supported by various groups, including political party organizations.

In the second type of nonpartisan cities, the power and influence of the regular parties are modified to the extent that they must compete with locally based candidate appraisal committees, independent local parties, and other slate-making groups. Examples of such competitive situations are found in Denver, Seattle, Cincinnati, and Kansas City.

> *Type 3.* Elections where slates of candidates are supported by various interest groups, but political party organizations have little or no part in campaigns, or are active only sporadically.

When the regular Democratic and Republican party organizations are inactive in nonpartisan elections, various slate-making groups assume the functions of parties by promoting candidates, raising funds, and managing campaigns. Labor groups, business interests, or the press become actively involved in such electoral efforts. Nonpartisan groups in this category are found in San Francisco; Detroit; Dallas; Fort Worth; Flint, Michigan; and Cambridge, Massachusetts.

> *Type 4.* Elections where neither political parties nor slates of candidates are important in campaigns.

"Pure" types of nonpartisan communities are those where individual candidates must develop their own organizations, support, and campaign funds. Voters are presumably freed from all formal organizational influences and make their electoral selections on a "friends-and-neighbors" basis. Robert Woods's description of the conscious nonpartisan ideal in American suburbs appears to result in attracting such "independent" candidates who are elected by independent-minded voters. This situation takes place most typically in small communities of less than 5,000 population. But even in villages and small towns, there may be other informal social pressures and influences which determine voter selections of individual candidates.[21]

The "Better Candidates" Claim

Nonpartisan elections are also defended on the grounds that civic-minded candidates, who might otherwise be restrained by regular party organizations, will run for local office. However, political scientist Duane Lockard challenges the notion that nonpartisanship results in "raising the caliber of candidates."[22] He argues that it is almost impossible to evaluate the quality of candidates objectively under either a partisan or a nonpartisan system, and, furthermore, "there does not seem to be much clear evidence that a change in election system does dramatically change the quality of candidates offered."[23]

The "better candidates" claim is further modified as a result of extensive voter confusion that is apparent in nonpartisan contests. One of the major reasons for reduced voter turnout is that candidates frequently avoid controversial public issues of direct community concern. Instead, they prefer to take ambiguous positions, or no stands at all, or they emphasize such irrelevancies as ethnic identity or associations with famous political names. An extreme case of a candidate taking advantage of his name to confuse the voters occurred during the 1954 Massachusetts primary election. This candidate was a "gentleman whose prior qualifications consisted of 18 years of employment by a safety razor company, culminating as head of the firm's stock room, [who] won his party's nomination (and later the election) for state treasurer. His name was John F. (for Francis) Kennedy."[24]

It is not surprising that voters in nonpartisan elections will base their decisions on considerations other than party or civic issues. If the candidates stress ethnicity, the voters will respond accordingly.

Political scientist Gerald Pomper concluded that Newark city voters decide among the nonpartisan municipal candidates primarily in response to ethnic considerations:

> In making their choices, voters seem particularly inclined to vote for candidates of their own groups. Considerations of party, electoral alliances, and policy are apparently subordinated. The goal of non-partisanship is fulfilled, as party identification does not determine the outcome. In place of party, ethnic identification is emphasized, and the result is "to enhance the effect of basic social cleavages." [25]

The Accountability Argument

The third alleged advantage of nonpartisan elections is that the voters will be able to hold elected officials accountable for their actions when they are not obligated to party machines for electoral support. However, the evidence offered by Gilbert and Clague in their analysis of electoral systems in large cities suggests that "nonparti-san, and especially at-large elections tend to increase the security of incumbent councilmen." [26] The removal of party labels actually ob-scures voter accountability, since there are fewer opportunities to judge the merits of candidates who challenge tenured councilmen. The absence of party considerations also frustrates protest voting in nonpartisan cities. Since incumbent councilmen cannot be identified with an "in-group," the voters have no way of uniting behind an "out-group" that seeks to sweep out unresponsive and incompetent legislators. The electorate therefore has little opportunity to hear and evaluate organized protests and criticisms of elected officials.

AT-LARGE REPRESENTATION

In addition to short ballots and nonpartisan elections, municipal re-formers also advocated at-large representation for city councilmen. By replacing ward elections with citywide representation, the re-formers hoped to undercut the power of the neighborhood bosses and to achieve collective responsibility for local legislatures. Table 3–3 indicates that the at-large system has been adopted particularly in the smaller to medium-sized cities with reformed governmental structures. In 1968, slightly more than 60 percent of cities over 5,000 population nominated and elected councilmen on the at-large basis. Council-manager cities, commission cities, and New England towns

TABLE 3–3   Combinations of Nomination and Election of Councilmen

Classification	No. of Cities Reporting	Nominate At Large, Elect At Large		Nominate by Wards, Elect At Large		Nominate by Wards, Elect by Wards		Nominate by Wards and At Large, Elect At Large		Nominate by Wards and At Large, Elect by Wards and At Large		Other [1]	
		No.	%	No.	%	No.	%	No.	%	No.	%	No.	%
Population Group													
Over 500,000 ...	25	9	36.0	2	8.0	6	24.0	1	4.0	7	28.0	—	—
250,000 to 500,000	26	15	57.7	3	11.5	2	7.7	1	3.9	5	19.2	—	—
100,000 to 250,000	87	47	54.0	8	9.2	17	19.5	1	1.2	14	16.1	—	—
50,000 to 100,000	207	106	51.2	17	8.2	38	18.4	4	1.9	41	19.8	1	.5
25,000 to 50,000 .	393	239	60.8	22	5.6	73	18.6	6	1.5	53	13.5	—	—
10,000 to 25,000	999	615	61.6	54	5.4	195	19.5	17	1.7	113	11.3	5	.5
5,000 to 10,000	1,005	617	61.4	38	3.8	231	23.0	13	1.3	100	10.0	6	.6
Under 5,000	506	423	83.6	12	2.4	38	7.5	7	1.4	23	4.5	3	.6
Form of Government [2]													
Mayor-Council ..	1,327	599	45.1	57	4.3	380	28.6	20	1.5	261	19.7	10	.8
Council-Manager	1,185	848	71.6	84	7.1	158	13.3	23	1.9	70	5.9	2	.2
Commission	160	140	87.5	2	1.3	18	11.3	—	—	—	—	—	—
Town Meeting ..	48	44	91.7	1	2.1	2	4.2	—	—	1	2.1	—	—
Rep. Town Meeting	22	17	77.3	—	—	4	18.2	—	—	1	4.5	—	—
City Type [2]													
Central	248	126	50.8	24	9.7	48	19.4	5	2.0	45	18.1	—	—
Suburban	1,220	673	55.2	77	6.3	272	22.3	29	2.4	162	13.3	7	.6
Independent ...	1,274	849	66.6	43	3.4	242	19.0	9	.7	126	9.9	5	.4
All Cities over 5,000	2,742	1,648	60.1	144	5.3	562	20.5	43	1.6	333	12.1	12	.4

[1] Includes various combinations of nomination and election procedures.
[2] Includes only cities over 5,000.

SOURCE: *The Municipal Year Book*, 1968. Washington, D.C.: The International City Managers' Association, p. 59. Reproduced by permission.

were also more likely to nominate and elect councilmen at-large than mayor-council cities.

Among the larger cities, ward elections for councilmen are still used quite extensively. In 1968, 52 percent of all cities over 500,000 population employed either ward elections or a combination of wards and the at-large system for councilmanic representation. By 1974, as shown in Table 3–4, the at-large system was combined with nonpartisan elections in eight of the twenty-seven largest cities (about 30 percent) while five others (19 percent) elected councilmen from wards on nonpartisan ballots. Table 3–4 also shows that twelve of the largest cities (or 44 percent) use a combination of district and at-large representation with either partisan or nonpartisan ballots.

TABLE 3–4   Electoral Systems in Large Cities

Election At Large	Election by Wards	Combination District & At-Large Election
Partisan Ballot		
Pittsburgh	St. Louis	Baltimore Indianapolis Jacksonville New Orleans New York Philadelphia Washington, D.C.
Nonpartisan Ballot		
Boston Columbus Detroit Phoenix San Antonio San Diego San Francisco Seattle	Chicago Cleveland Denver Los Angeles Milwaukee	Atlanta Dallas Houston Kansas City Memphis

SOURCE: International City Management Association. Data includes estimated 1972 population of 27 largest cities ranging from 7,895,000 for New York to 498,000 for Atlanta. ICMA survey was made in Spring 1974 and final results will appear in 1975 *Municipal Year Book*.

The first goal of the at-large reform was to eradicate the influence of party bosses whose geographic base of operations was frequently the same as the electoral districts of councilmen. (This situation is still found in two large cities, Chicago and Cleveland.) Structural reformers argued that councilmen running on citywide tickets would not be controlled by party leaders from particular ethnic neighborhoods. Ward bosses could no longer use material rewards to influence the nomination and election of local legislators, particularly in primary contests.

On the other hand, there is evidence to show that at-large elections tend to reduce minority group representation in many cities. Distinct ethnic, racial, or religious voting blocs find that their concentrated neighborhood votes are diluted in at-large elections. For example, blacks were excluded from council representation until the late 1950s and 1960s in at-large and nonpartisan cities such as Boston and Detroit.

Boston offers an unusually strong case of simultaneous minority group representation and exclusion from city council. The at-large system has produced an overwhelming monopoly for Irish and Italian Democrats. Between 1949 and 1966, no candidate was elected to the Boston City Council who was not of Irish or Italian ancestry. In contrast, under the preexisting ward system, which was in effect for twenty-five years, eighty-four Irishmen, four Italians, twelve Jews, and nine Yankees were elected to the council.[27] Not only has the Boston at-large system excluded nearly all political independents and Republicans, but several of the city's neighborhoods have never been represented. Over a seventeen-year period (1949–1966), nine of Boston's twenty-two wards (used for state elections) had not produced a winning council candidate, while two others had not done so for ten years.[28]

The second objective of at-large representation was to promote a citywide view of community problems among councilmen. Reformers claimed that the ward system resulted in electing legislators who defended neighborhood interests and became "errand boys" for their constituents. This limited the effectiveness of the council to deal collectively with overall community concerns. Furthermore, ward-elected councilmen tended to engage in extensive bargaining, trading, and logrolling with each other. Council sessions were characterized by a mutual deference to special district interests. Such a "hands-off" policy resulted in a legislative system which overlooked graft, corruption, and special advantages as long as individual interests were protected. The at-large system would presumably overcome these limitations by electing councilmen who paid more attention to the "public interest" of the entire community rather than being concerned with collections of "private-regarding" deals for particular neighborhoods.

City councils elected at-large do not necessarily find it advantageous to restrict their attention to community problems. The nine-member Boston council, for example, finds that it is necessary to balance constituent demands for solutions to individual problems with the citizens' desires for closer contact with city hall and overall city responsibilities. In fact, the most prevalent pattern in large cities with strong mayors is councils that are relatively powerless to deal with overall city priorities and budgetary matters. The council is nearly powerless in the face of vigorous mayoral leadership. Council sessions dealing with citywide legislative programs tend to degenerate into empty debating, backbiting, and negativism. The following description of Boston council sessions appears applicable to many other large cities: "a wild, shrill theater of the absurd, where visitors are more likely to hear a string of invectives than a deliberate probing of administrative policies."[29] Under such conditions, it is important that councilmen do more than become mere rubber stamps for mayoral programs. Councilmen could enhance their roles by turning their attention to the critical neighborhood problems that cause such dissatisfaction among the community residents. This might serve to overcome the depth of citizen hostility and alienation toward city hall and the bureaucracy.

INSTITUTIONAL REFORM: STRONG MAYOR-COUNCIL, COMMISSION, AND COUNCIL-MANAGER PLANS

Municipal reformers of the Progressive era sought to link electoral and representation changes with a complete reorganization of city government. In their view, boss rule and machine politics could not be defeated merely by effective political challenges. Electoral victories over the machine had to be connected with new governmental mechanisms that supplanted the deficiencies of the weak mayor-council system. As noted in Chapter 1, boss rule was the political response to the dispersed, chaotic, and decentralized governmental authority manifested in the weak mayor-council form—a legacy of Jacksonian Democracy. Professional politicians successfully central-ized power and influence by establishing formidable party organiza-tions alongside the nearly impotent city governmental institutions. To replace machine control over city government, the reformers developed an alternate set of objectives that would achieve the re-organization of local government. These included: (1) the strength-ening of executive authority; (2) the elimination of bicameral councils by unicameral councils of reduced membership; (3) the fusion of executive and legislative powers; (4) the centralization of control over administration; (5) the separation of policy-making from administration; and (6) the institutionalization of modern methods of efficiency and economy in the management of city affairs, as modelled after the practices of private business enterprise.

Origins and Development of the Three Reorganization Plans

The three major reorganization plans evolved approximately between 1890 and 1915. In promoting these schemes, structural reformers emphasized the elimination of "politics" from city affairs. According to this view, local problems were basically administrative matters which could be solved most efficiently and effectively by professionally trained public management experts. As the structural reformers became increasingly convinced that city government should be patterned after the private corporate model, they gradually changed their support from the strong mayor-council plan to the commission plan and, finally, to the council-manager plan. Thus, the council-manager plan, along with the short ballot and nonpartisan at-large elections, became the most desirable "package" of structural innovations advocated by the municipal reformers.

The strong mayor-council plan was promoted by the National Municipal League's model charter of 1900, although earlier efforts to strengthen the mayor had been made by the Brooklyn and Boston city charters of 1882 and 1885.[30] Early reform support for the strong mayor was based on the provision of centralized authority for a single chief executive who would be in a position to effect change throughout city government. If elected on a nonpartisan ballot, the mayor could take a citywide view of issues that was favorable to the middle and upper classes. This would free the mayor from the political control of the local ward bosses, unless, of course, the machine politicians united behind his candidacy. Once in office, the mayor was empowered to centralize his authority over the administration by the appointment and removal of key department heads. This integrated administrative structure provided the chief executive with control over the formerly dispersed bureaucracy of the weak mayor-council system, which had a variety of council-administration committees, independently appointed boards and commissions, and elected administrative officials.

The commission plan was an effort to place more business expertise in city government. It was first used in Galveston, Texas in 1901 when the state legislature decided that the existing local government was incapable of dealing with a hurricane and flood disaster. A five-member commission of businessmen was appointed by the state to govern Galveston. The new commission structure achieved popularity following its adoption in Des Moines, Iowa in 1908. The Des Moines charter made the commissioners full-time officials, and instituted direct democracy (initiative, referendum, and recall), a civil service commission, and nonpartisan ballots. By 1917 some 500 cities were using the plan, the largest of which were Jersey City and Memphis.[31] Also, Richard S. Childs and his Short Ballot Association initially viewed the commission plan as a vehicle for implementing the principle of electing a few officers for a small governing body. But as the inherent defects of the plan became clear (see next section), the reformers soon shifted their support to the council-manager plan as the most favored form of local government organization.

The municipal reformers were convinced that the council-manager plan, as developed by Richard S. Childs, represented a marked improvement over the commission form. In 1908, Staunton, Virginia became the first city to experiment with the "general manager" concept. Operating under a mayor-bicameral council system, city officials decided that the solution to numerous internal jurisdictional conflicts was to hire a manager to take charge of administrative coordination. The Staunton city manager was superimposed on an "unreformed" governmental structure. Childs took the manager idea and applied it to a modified form of the commission plan. Instead of requiring that commissioners assume both legislative and administrative responsibilities, the commission-manager proposal would formally separate these two functions. The council would be responsible for policy-making, and a council-appointed manager would be in charge of administration. Childs offered this proposal to the Lockport Board of Trade which was about to request a new city charter before the New York state legislature. While the state rejected Childs' plan in 1911, Sumter, South Carolina became the first American community to adopt the council-manager plan in 1912. The new governmental form began to receive widespread attention when the first large city, Dayton, Ohio, adopted it in 1914. When the model charter of the National Municipal League included the plan in 1915, the council-manager system gained popularity. Between 1918 and 1923 more than 150 cities were governed by the council-manager system. By 1926 large cities such as Cleveland, Kansas City, and Cincinnati were using the plan.

Formal Structural Comparisons and Contrasts

It cannot be emphasized too strongly that the municipal reformers believed that structural reorganization would permit city officials to govern effectively in the "public interest." This section will deal with the formal descriptive features of the strong mayor-council, commission, and council-manager plans. However, it should be noted that the following comparisons and contrasts focus upon "ideal types," or models, rather than on actual political systems. A fuller understanding of the achievements and limitations of the three structural plans requires analysis of other important considerations such as local political environments, community power, and executive leadership roles and styles.

Strong Mayor-Council Plan. The strong mayor-council plan (Figure 3–1) sought to implement the early reform goal of shifting the locus of power from the legislative branch to the executive branch. The plan incorporates the principles of the short ballot with visible public officials, preferably a single chief executive and a small council elected at-large on nonpartisan ballots. Patterned after the national government, the system has a clear separation of powers and checks and balances between the executive and legislative branches. The mayor controls administration by appointing and removing department heads with or without council approval. He coordinates departmental activities which the council may criticize through investigations of the bureaucracy. The mayor also determines departmental

Figure 3–1   Mayor-Council Form

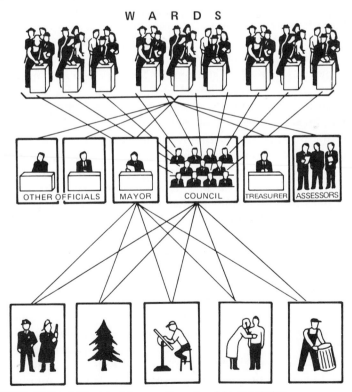

SOURCE: National Municipal League. Reproduced by permission.

allocations by preparing the budget for submission to the council. In legislative policy, the mayor shares authority with the council. He proposes major legislative programs for council consideration and approval. If the council challenges the mayor on budgetary matters or legislative bills, he can exercise a veto power which can be over-ridden only by an extraordinary council majority. Thus, the mayor clearly dominates the council. As the acknowledged ceremonial head, political leader, legislative initiator, and administrative coordinator, he is the central focus of authority and decision-making. This means that aspiring mayoral candidates must face the prospect of assuming rather burdensome responsibilities for which they are seldom adequately prepared.

In recognition of the great demands placed upon big city mayors, several large cities authorize the mayor to hire a chief administrative officer (CAO). The mayor-CAO plan was first permitted by the 1931 San Francisco charter and is now used in large cities such as Boston, Los Angeles, Louisville, Newark, New Orleans, New York, and Philadelphia. The plan represents a modification and adaptation of the council-manager system for large cities. In contrast to the council-manager form, there is neither a separation of policy-making and administration nor a fusion of executive and legislative powers. Instead, the mayor remains the central focus of political leadership and administrative coordination. The CAO is the mayor's manager of the municipal bureaucracy. His major responsibilities usually include the appointment and removal of department heads (with mayoral approval), the preparation of the budget, the supervision of personnel, and the provision of technical advice and assistance to the mayor. Thus, the mayor-CAO plan permits continued strong executive leadership by the mayor while incorporating municipal reform values for city administration such as integration, hierarchy, and professional management.[32]

Commission Plan. The commission plan (Figure 3–2), patterned after the corporate board of directors, usually has a small governing body (from three to seven members) elected at-large on nonpartisan ballots. The mayor, who is either designated as the highest vote-getter or selected by the commissioners, acts as the commission's presiding officer and the ceremonial head of the city. Otherwise, the commissioners function as equals. The plan completely abandons the strong mayor-council principles of separation of powers and checks and balances between the executive and legislative branches. Instead, there is a fusion of governmental responsibilities. Collec-

Figure 3–2 Commission Form

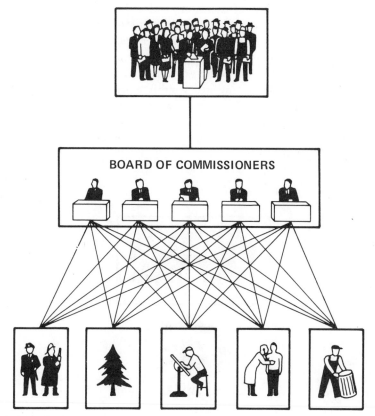

BOARD OF COMMISSIONERS

SOURCE: National Municipal League. Reproduced by permission.

tively, the commissioners make overall legislative policy. Individually, each commissioner is placed in charge of a particular city department. For example, the 1907 charter for Des Moines, one of the first cities to use the commission plan, created five departments for each of the commissioners to lead, including public affairs, accounts and finance, public safety, streets and public improvements, and parks and public property.[33]

While initially attracted to this plan, municipal reformers soon noted several defects. First, as a result of the dual responsibilities imposed on the commissioners, they frequently have divided loyalties and face difficulties in reconciling their policy-making and administrative functions. Departmental responsibilities conflict with the development of a citywide view of public policy. This tends to create a fragmented governmental system in which commission meetings result in a policy of mutual noninterference. Because commissioners function as equals, there is no central focus of political leadership. Commissioners oftentimes hesitate to criticize and review each other's activities for fear of budgetary restrictions and investigations of departmental operations. Thus, commissioners frequently engage in vote-trading, logrolling, and other similar arrangements to protect individual self-interests. Also, the reformers criticize the lack of expertise in managing city departments. The commission plan brings to city government amateurs who are not prepared for full-time administrative responsibilities.

Figure 3–3   Council-Manager Form

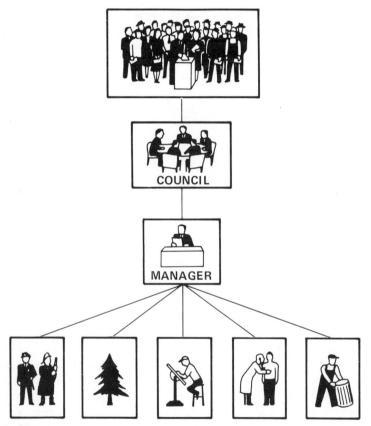

SOURCE: National Municipal League. Reproduced by permission.

Council-Manager Plan. The council-manager plan employs the short ballot principle by providing for a small governing body of five to nine members elected at-large on nonpartisan ballots. The mayor is generally chosen by the council as its presiding officer and ceremonial head of the city. In addition to this relatively simple structural framework, the council-manager plan, as shown in Figure 3–3, is favored by municipal reformers because it achieves the goals of *unification of council powers* and the *concentration of administrative authority.*[34]

As with the commission plan, the council-manager form abolishes all separation of powers and checks and balances by giving the council complete authority over legislative policy-making and administration. The council passes all ordinances and resolutions to govern the city, *but,* unlike the commission plan, individual councilmen are *not* given responsibility for administering particular departments. Instead, policy-making is formally separated from administrative implementation. The centralization of administrative responsibility is achieved by the council hiring a professionally trained manager to supervise the daily operations of municipal departments. The manager's tenure is completely dependent upon the council. His formal duties usually include the appointment and removal of department heads, the preparation of the budget for council consideration, and the provision of technical advice and assistance to the council.

Aside from the question of actual leadership styles and roles assumed by city managers (discussed in Chapter 5), the council-manager form has at least two structural limitations. First, municipal reformers such as Richard S. Childs did not recognize the artificial distinction made in formally separating policy from administration. Because the manager is usually the only full-time governmental official who oversees all departmental activities, while the councilmen are part-time amateurs, the manager's advice to the council often is crucial in the formulation of policy. If the manager does not assume policy leadership, there is the danger of creating a political vacuum under the council-manager plan. Secondly, since the council is considered a governing body of coequals, affirmative governmental action cannot be achieved unless there is a fairly high level of community consensus on public issues. Thus, the council-manager plan seems more adaptable to communities with relatively homogeneous populations rather than to cities with relatively diverse ethnic groups and considerable cleavage over issues.

GOVERNMENT STRUCTURE
AND POLITICAL ENVIRONMENT

In several recent surveys, social scientists have discovered that important community variables are associated with the mayor-council, commission, and council-manager plans. The use of socioeconomic data to analyze local government structure represents a departure from the value judgments made by earlier municipal reformers concerning alleged administrative advantages and disadvantages of the three reorganization plans. The three most important findings relating to political environment and governmental form are: (1) The strong executive and political leadership associated with the mayor-council form is particularly found in large central cities which face serious racial and ethnic cleavages and the wide range of issues related to the urban crisis; (2) The council-manager plan is highly correlated with upwardly mobile white middle-class suburbs where there is a relatively high level of community agreement on public issues; and (3) The commission plan is not only the least popular of the three plans, but it is also found most frequently in relatively "declining" communities.

The mayor-council form, which is used in 50.6 percent of all cities over 5,000 population (Table 3–5), is found especially in large central cities of metropolitan areas located primarily in the northeastern and midwestern sections of the country. All of the nation's most populous urban centers (those with more than one million persons) employ either strong mayor-council government (New York, Philadelphia, Detroit, and Houston) or the weak mayor-council form (Chicago and Los Angeles). According to the 1970 census, twenty of the nation's twenty-five largest cities over 500,000 population have mayor-council government.[35] Only four of these large cities—Dallas, San Diego, San Antonio, and Phoenix—use the council-manager plan, and Memphis, which ranks seventeenth, stands alone as a commission city. Large central cities not only have considerable racial, ethnic, and religious groupings, as well as diversified manufacturing and industrial complexes, but they also face the full range of public policy issues related to the urban crisis, including slum housing, segregated education, and unemployment among disadvantaged minority groups. Strong mayoral leadership is required to manage community conflict and to establish effective links with the national and state governments for financial and program assistance at the local level. Large cities need strong mayors because, as political scientist John H. Kessel observes, "there are so many competing interests . . . that a premium is placed

TABLE 3–5   Form of Government in Cities over 5,000 Population

Classification	No. of Cities Reporting	Mayor-Council		Council-Manager		Commission	
		Number	Percent	Number	Percent	Number	Percent
Population Group							
Over 500,000 ...	27	22 [1]	81.5	5	18.5	...	...
250,000 to 500,000	27	11	40.7	13	48.2	3	11.1
100,000 to 250,000	93	33	35.5	50	53.8	10	10.7
50,000 to 100,000	215	83	38.6	116	54.0	16	7.4
25,000 to 50,000 .	439	166	38.2	233	53.6	40	9.2
10,000 to 25,000 .	1,072	511	47.7	488	45.5	73	6.8
5,000 to 10,000 ..	1,112	686	61.7	378	34.0	48	4.3
Type of City							
Central	266	111 [1]	41.7	126	47.4	29	10.9
Suburban	1,385	717	51.8	605	43.7	63	4.5
Independent ...	1,334	684	51.3	552	41.4	98	7.3
Geographic Divsion							
New England ..	138	80	58.0	56	40.6	2	1.4
Middle Atlantic .	598	387	64.7	155	25.9	56	9.4
East North Central	647	432	66.8	190	29.4	25	3.8
West North Central	308	175	56.8	100	32.5	33	10.7
South Atlantic ..	352	117 [1]	33.2	225	63.9	10	2.9
East South Central	170	108	63.5	29	17.1	33	19.4
West South Central	305	109	35.7	180	59.0	16	5.3
Mountain	137	62	45.3	70	51.1	5	3.3
Pacific	330	42	12.7	278	84.3	10	3.0
All cities over 5,000	2,985 [2]	1,513 [1]	50.6	1,283	43.0	190	6.4

[1] Includes the District of Columbia.
[2] Not included in this table are 89 places with town meeting government, and 38 with representative town meeting government.

SOURCE: *The Municipal Year Book*, 1968. Washington, D.C.: The International City Managers' Association, p. 54.

on political leadership which can arbitrate the contest for the stakes of power in the city, and be held responsible by the electorate for its success in doing so."[36]

Council-manager government, as shown in Table 3–5, predominates in medium-sized cities ranging from 10,000 to 250,000 population, while the commission plan is used in only 6.4 percent of all cities over 5,000 population. Geographically, the council-manager plan is found in a majority of cities located in the south, southwestern, and western states, regions characterized by one-party control or weak party organization. Moreover, the two "reformed" governmental systems are associated with significantly different kinds of socioeconomic components. Schnore and Alford's analysis of 300 suburbs located in the twenty-five largest urbanized areas disclosed that council-manager communities rank consistently high in terms of proportions of younger persons with preschool age children, educational attainment, income, mobility, and new housing.[37] Additionally, Kessel's study found that council-manager cities tend to have high concentrations of local businessmen whose principal activities are conducted within the immediate area of their own city.[38] In contrast, commission suburbs are associated with communities losing population, low mobility, low white-collar composition, and low educational levels.[39]

Thus, the council-manager plan is clearly related to the suburban preferences of upwardly mobile, white middle-class Americans. In such relatively homogeneous communities, residents can agree on approaches to solving local problems by delegating responsibility to a manager. Suburban political problems can be managed by professional administrators when the level of community consensus is relatively high. In contrast, large central cities (as discussed in Chapter 5) require dynamic political leadership by strong mayors to resolve the critical urban problems associated with a complex racial and ethnic diversity.

NOTES

1. James Bryce, *The American Commonwealth*, Vol. I (New York: Macmillan, 1889), p. 608.
2. Edward C. Banfield and James Q. Wilson, *City Politics* (New York: Random House, Vintage Books, 1963), pp. 46, 138–140. Also, see: James Q. Wilson and Edward C. Banfield, "Public Regardingness As A Value Premise In Voting Behavior," *American Political Science Review*, Vol. 58, No. 4 (December 1964), p. 876; and Ch. II, *supra*, p. 14.
3. Richard Hofstadter, *The Age of Reform* (New York: Random House, Vintage Books, 1955), p. 9.
4. See: Ch. II, *supra*, pp. 2–8.
5. Richard S. Childs, *Civic Victories* (New York: Harper & Brothers, 1952), p. 11.
6. John Porter East, *Council-Manager Government: The Political Thought of Its Founder, Richard S. Childs* (Chapel Hill: University of North Carolina Press, 1965), p. 48.
7. Childs, *Civic Victories*, p. 84.
8. East, *Council-Manager Government*, pp. 54–55.
9. Charles N. Glaab and A. Theodore Brown, *A History of Urban America* (New York: Macmillan, 1967), p. 190.
10. See: Phillips Cutright, "Nonpartisan Electoral Systems in American Cities," in *Politics in the Metropolis*, eds. Thomas R. Dye and Brett W. Hawkins (Columbus, Ohio: Charles E. Merrill Books, 1967), p. 302; and Eugene C. Lee, *The Politics of Nonpartisanship* (Berkeley: University of California Press, 1960), p. 22.
11. Lee, *The Politics of Nonpartisanship*, pp. 26–27.

12. Robert C. Wood, *Suburbia: Its People and Their Politics* (Boston: Houghton Mifflin, 1958), p. 157.
13. See: Charles E. Gilbert, "Some Aspects of Nonpartisan Elections in Large Cities," *Midwest Journal of Political Science*, Vol. 6, No. 4 (December 1962), pp. 361–362; Oliver P. Williams and Charles R. Adrian, "The Insulation of Local Politics Under the Nonpartisan Ballot," *American Political Science Review*, Vol. 53, No. 4 (December 1959), p. 1058; and Robert H. Salisbury and Gordon Black, "Class and Party in Partisan and Non-Partisan Elections: The Case of Des Moines," *American Political Science Review*, Vol. 57, No. 3 (September 1963), p. 589.
14. Williams and Adrian, *American Political Science Review*, Vol. 53, No. 4, p. 1063.
15. Gilbert, *Midwest Journal of Political Science*, Vol. 6, No. 4, p. 346.
16. Eugene C. Lee, "City Elections: A Statistical Profile," *The National Municipal Yearbook, 1963* (Chicago: International City Managers' Association, 1963), p. 82.
17. *Ibid.*, p. 83.
18. Robert R. Alford and Eugene C. Lee, "Voting Turnout in American Cities," *American Political Science Review*, Vol. 62, No. 3 (September 1968), p. 809.
19. Charles R. Adrian, "A Typology for Nonpartisan Elections," *Western Political Quarterly*, Vol. 12, No. 2 (June 1959), pp. 449–458.
20. *The New York Times*, February 28, 1971, p. 27, col. 1.
21. One of the classic studies of village politics is found in: Arthur J. Vidich and Joseph Bensman, *Small Town in Mass Society* (New York: Doubleday, Anchor Books, 1960), Chs. 5–6.
22. Duane Lockard, *The Politics of State and Local Government*, 2d ed. (New York: Macmillan, 1969), p. 218.
23. *Ibid.*
24. Fred I. Greenstein, *The American Party System and the American People* (Englewood Cliffs, N.J.: Prentice-Hall, 1963), p. 58.
25. Gerald Pomper, "Ethnic and Group Voting in Nonpartisan Municipal Elections," *Public Opinion Quarterly*, Vol. 30 (Spring 1966), p. 90.
26. Charles E. Gilbert and Christopher Clague, "Electoral Competition and Electoral Systems in Large Cities," *Journal of Politics*, Vol. 24, No. 2 (May 1962), p. 344.
27. Banfield and Wilson, *City Politics*, p. 95.
28. George E. Berkley, "Flaws in At-Large Voting," *National Civic Review*, Vol. 55, No. 7 (July 1966), p. 372.
29. *The Boston Sunday Globe*, April 16, 1967, p. 24, col. 1.
30. Glaab and Brown, *A History of Urban America*, p. 190.
31. *Ibid.*, p. 195.
32. Wallace S. Sayre, "The General Manager Idea for Large Cities," *Public Administration Review*, Vol. 14, No. 4 (Autumn 1954), p. 254.
33. Benjamin Baker, *Urban Government* (Princeton, N.J.: D. Van Nostrand, 1957), p. 137.
34. Harold A. Stone, Don K. Price, and Kathryn H. Stone, *Council Manager Government in the United States* (Chicago: Public Administration Service, 1940), pp. 14–17.
35. *The New York Times*, September 2, 1970, p. 27, col. 2–3.
36. John H. Kessel, "Governmental Structure and Political Environment: A Statistical Note About American Cities," *American Political Science Review*, Vol. 56, No. 3 (September 1962), p. 616.
37. Leo F. Schnore and Robert R. Alford, "Forms of Government and

Socioeconomic Characteristics of Suburbs," *Administrative Science Quarterly*, Vol. 8, No. 1 (June 1963), pp. 11–15.

38. Kessel, *American Political Science Review*, Vol. 56, No. 3, p. 619.
39. Robert R. Alford and Harry M. Scoble, "Political and Socioeconomic Characteristics of American Cities," *The Municipal Year Book, 1965* (Chicago: International City Managers' Association, 1965), p. 95.

SUGGESTIONS FOR FURTHER READING

Historical Overview

Bryce, James. *The American Commonwealth*, Vol. I. New York: Macmillan, 1889. Ch. 51, "The Working of City Governments," pp. 606–619.
Classic indictment of city problems and suggested structural remedies.

Glaab, Charles N., and A. Theodore Brown. *A History of Urban America*. New York: Macmillan, 1967. pp. 187–199.
Historical development of late nineteenth and early twentieth century municipal reforms.

Hofstadter, Richard. *The Age of Reform*. New York: Random House, Vintage Books, 1955. pp. 3–22, 174–214.
Excellent analysis of Progressive reform attitudes toward the cities.

Low, Seth. "An American View of Municipal Government in the United States," in James Bryce, *The American Commonwealth*, Vol. 1. New York: Macmillan, 1889. pp. 620–635.
New York reform mayor discusses inadequacies of immigrants to govern themselves and the poor quality of city services together with duties and responsibilities of a big city chief executive.

The "Public-Regarding" Ethos

Banfield, Edward C., and James Q. Wilson. "Public Regardingness as a Value Premise in Voting Behavior," *American Political Science Review*, Vol. 58, No. 4 (December 1964), pp. 876–887.
Application of "public-regarding" view in local bond issues in Cleveland.

————. "Political Ethos Revisited," *American Political Science Review*, Vol. 65, No. 4 (December 1971), pp. 1048–1062.
In redefining the "public-" and "private-" regarding ethos, the authors discuss findings of a Boston homeowners' survey relating to "unitary" and "individualist" ethos as applied to conceptions of local politics (community v. neighborhood); government expenditures (community-serving v. people-helping); and attitudes toward the behavior of local leaders (good government v. benefit-minded). They discover less correlation among the three variables than might be expected, but conclude that the ethos orientations might be pervasive among influential community actors.

Hays, Samuel P. "The Politics of Reform in Municipal Government in the Progressive Era," in *American Urban History*, ed. Alexander B. Callow, Jr. New York: Oxford University Press, 1969., pp. 421–439.
Argues that middle-class basis for municipal reform is largely a myth since Progressive reformers were primarily upper-class people who wanted to shift power from bosses to their own scope of influence in the cities.

Lineberry, Robert L., and Edmund P. Fowler. "Reformism and Public Policies in American Cities," *American Political Science Review*, Vol. 61, No. 3 (September 1967), pp. 701–716.
In examining reformed institutions, nonpartisan ballots, and at-large elections, authors find less responsiveness to community cleavages than in cities with unreformed institutions.

Wolfinger, Raymond E., and John O. Field. "Political Ethos and the Structure of City Government," *American Political Science Review*, Vol. 60, No. 2 (June 1966), pp. 306–326.
In testing "public regardingness," the authors do not find sufficient evidence to support a relationship between attitudes of city residents and form of local government.

Short Ballots

Childs, Richard S. *Civic Victories*. New York: Harper & Brothers, 1952. pp. 22–47.
Criticisms of long ballot as the "politicians' ballot," and praise for the short ballot as the "people's ballot."

Childs, Richard S. *The First 50 Years of the Council-Manager Plan of Municipal Government*. New York: National Municipal League, 1965. pp. 30–34.
Application of short ballot in council-manager cities.

East, John P. *Council-Manager Government: The Political Thought of Its Founder, Richard S. Childs*. Chapel Hill: University of North Carolina Press, 1965. pp. 43–55.
Useful description of short ballot movement as a spur to municipal reform.

Nonpartisan Elections

Adrian, Charles R. "A Typology For Nonpartisan Elections," *Western Political Quarterly*, Vol. 12, No. 2 (June 1959), pp. 449–458.
Fourfold classification of nonpartisan systems where party activity is more or less influential.

Adrian, Charles R. "Some General Characteristics of Nonpartisan Elections," in *Democracy in Urban America*, eds. Oliver P. Williams and Charles Press. Chicago: Rand McNally, 1961. pp. 251–262.
Analysis of nonpartisan state legislatures in Nebraska and Minnesota and city councils of Minneapolis and Detroit reveals eleven specific consequences of nonpartisan elections.

Alford, Robert R., and Eugene C. Lee. "Voting Turnout in American Cities," *American Political Science Review*, Vol. 62, No. 3 (September 1968), pp. 796–813.
Cities with "unreformed" structures and partisan elections have higher voting turnouts than cities with "reformed" structures and nonpartisan elections.

Banfield, Edward C., and James Q. Wilson. *City Politics*. New York: Random House, Vintage Books, 1963. Ch. 12, "Nonpartisanship," pp. 151–167.
Relationship of nonpartisan elections to politicians, voters, parties, and government.

Cutright, Phillips. "Nonpartisan Electoral Systems in American Cities," in *Politics in the Metropolis*, eds. Thomas R. Dye, and Brett W. Hawkins. Columbus, Ohio: Charles E. Merrill Books, 1967. pp. 298–314.
Relationship of nonpartisan elections to community cleavages.

Gilbert, Charles E. "Some Aspects of Nonpartisan Elections in Large Cities," *Midwest Journal of Political Science*, Vol. 6, No. 4 (November 1962), pp. 345–362.
Nonpartisanship generally favors Republicans over Democrats in local communities.

—————, and Christopher Clague. "Electoral Competition and Electoral Systems in Large Cities," *Journal of Politics*, Vol. 24, No. 2 (May 1962), pp. 323–349.
Nonpartisan elections generally favor incumbents on city councils.

Greenstein, Fred I. *The American Party System and the American People*. Englewood Cliffs, N.J.: Prentice-Hall, 1963. pp. 57–60.
Irrelevant influences affect voter choices in communities where neither parties nor slate-making groups are active in nonpartisan contests.

Lee, Eugene C. "City Elections: A Statistical Profile," in *The Municipal Year Book, 1963*. Chicago: The International City Managers' Association, 1963. pp. 74–84.
Voter participation in cities with nonpartisan elections is substantially lower than in cities with partisan elections.

—————. *The Politics of Nonpartisanship: A Study of California Elections*. Berkeley: University of California Press, 1960.
After a comprehensive analysis of nonpartisanship, the author challenges the principles of nonpartisanship in terms of actual performance.

Lockard, Duane. *The Politics of State and Local Government*, 2nd ed. New York: Macmillan, 1969. pp. 214–224.
Author challenges premises of nonpartisanship by comparing it with results.

Pomper, Gerald. "Ethnic and Group Voting in Nonpartisan Municipal Elections," *Public Opinion Quarterly*, Vol. 30 (Spring 1966), pp. 79–97.
Analysis of Newark, New Jersey nonpartisan city contests in com-

parison with partisan elections for New Jersey legislature finds that ethnic cleavages replace party cues in absence of party labels.

Salisbury, Robert H., and Gordon Black. "Class and Party in Partisan and Non-partisan Elections: The Case of Des Moines," *American Political Science Review*, Vol. 57, No. 3 (September 1963), pp. 584–592.
Finds a persistence of party divisions in nonpartisan local elections.

Sanders, Heywood T. "Cities, Politics, and Elections: Partisanship in Nonpartisan Elections," in *The Municipal Yearbook, 1971.* Washington, D.C.: The International City Management Association, 1971. pp. 16–20.
Research findings for forty-nine cities test a "partisanship" score in nonpartisan electoral systems with several variables, including governmental structure, mayoral elections, region, several socio-economic characteristics, and various public policies.

Williams, Oliver P., and Charles R. Adrian. "The Insulation of Local Politics Under the Nonpartisan Ballot," *American Political Science Review*, Vol. 53, No. 4 (September 1959), pp. 1052–1063.
Analysis of voting in four Michigan cities discloses the persistence of party influences in local nonpartisan contests.

At-Large Representation

Banfield, Edward C., and James Q. Wilson. *City Politics.* New York: Random House, Vintage Books, 1963. Ch. 7, "Electoral Systems," pp. 87–100.
Comparison of at-large and ward representation together with consequences in terms of representing particular groups on city councils.

Berkley, George E. "Flaws in At-Large Voting," *National Civic Review*, Vol. 55, No. 7 (July 1966), pp. 370–373, 379.
Criticism of at-large system in Boston.

City Government Structure and Political Environment

Adrian, Charles R., and Charles Press. *Governing Urban America*, 3rd ed. New York: McGraw-Hill, 1968. Ch. 8, "Forms of Government," pp. 183–216.
Comparison of major structural plans for American cities.

Alford, Robert R., and Harry M. Scoble. "Political and Socioeconomic Characteristics of American Cities," in *The Municipal Year Book, 1965.* Chicago: The International City Managers' Association, 1965. pp. 82–97.
Council-manager cities are likely to have upwardly mobile white middle-class populations.

Childs, Richard S. *Civic Victories.* New York: Harper & Brothers, 1952. Chs. 14 and 15.
Development of strong mayor-council, commission, and council-manager plans.

————. *The First 50 Years of the Council-Manager Plan of Munici-pal Government.* New York: National Municipal League, 1965.
Progress of council manager plan as explained by its founder.

East, John P. *Council-Manager Government: The Political Thought of Its Founder, Richard S. Childs.* Chapel Hill: University of North Carolina Press, 1965.
Comprehensive political analysis of municipal reformer Childs in developing the council-manager plan.

Kessel, John H. "Governmental Structure and Political Environment: A Statistical Note About American Cities," *American Political Science Review*, Vol. 56, No. 3 (September 1962), pp. 615–620.
Council-manager plan is associated with weak party competition, absence of ethnic diversity, and a predominance of local businessmen.

Klevit, Alan. "City Councils and Their Functions in Local Government," in *The Municipal Yearbook, 1972.* Washington, D.C.: The International City Management Association, 1972. pp. 15–26.
Results of an ICMA city council survey provide data on such variables as government structure, council membership, age, length of service, organization and procedures, and election systems.

Sayre, Wallace S. "The General Manager Idea for Large Cities," *Public Administration Reveiw*, Vol. 14, No. 4 (Autumn 1954), pp. 253–258.
Development of strong mayor-CAO plan in large cities.

Stone, Harold A., Don K. Price, and Kathryn H. Stone. *City Manager Government in the United States.* Chicago: Public Administration Service, 1940.
Rationale and development of council-manager plan after twenty-five years of existence.

4

Metropolitics and Regional Planning

INTRODUCTION

Chapters 1, 2, and 3 analyzed boss rule and machine politics and the various efforts of reformers to change the political climate and the structure of city government. We turn next to the problems and prospects of metropolitan areas. The study of urban problems is not confined to the older central cities, which developed during the eighteenth and nineteenth centuries. Urban politics and policies now embrace the suburbs, many of which grew at a rapid rate during the 1950s and 1960s.

The proponents of metropolitan reform include some of the same groups as the municipal reformers. In their efforts to restructure city government, the antimachine forces succeeded in obtaining home rule charters from many state legislatures. Such charters were necessary to institute the strong mayor-council, commission, or council-manager plans. The municipal reformers wanted to eliminate excessive control of local affairs by the states, which had resulted from the weak mayor-council structure, political and patronage disputes between cities and rurally dominated state legislatures, and from the lack of city financial resources to pay for new municipal public works facilities. Home rule was intended to restore local governmental control over its own affairs, but, in the long run, such charters contributed to the proliferation and fragmentation of governments in metropolitan areas. Many suburban municipalities became virtually sovereign in a legal sense and resisted central city pressures to metropolitanize services, jurisdiction, and administration. Consequently, the metropolitan reformers sought to overcome city and suburban claims for independence. They argued that policy solutions for urban problems required a regional or metropolitan approach.

This chapter discusses the parallel development of locally initiated metropolitan governmental reform and federally sponsored planning and cooperation. We examine some of the political obstacles which have hampered both metropolitan reorganization and regional planning and trace the success of the latter to incentives provided by the federal government. We then indicate how revenue sharing in its present form affects local and regional cooperation and what the future prospects are for metropolitan planning.

METROPOLITAN REFORM IN HISTORICAL PERSPECTIVE

American society, though constitutionally a democracy, has traditionally been segregated by racial and ethnic differences and economic class. Metropolitan areas reflect these distinctions. Cities have grown from villages that were originally organized around one or more basic industries. Workers lived in the shadow of the mill, often in company-built housing. The middle classes (the mill foreman, the skilled craftsmen, and the merchants) occupied larger dwellings away from their places of business. The mill owners, the financiers, and other persons of wealth had estates and often a second residence in the country or at the seashore. Immigrants and newcomers looking for employment took the oldest, least costly housing. Particularly after the Civil War, these older areas of cheap housing became the staging areas for new immigrants in the big coastal cities. We call them slums, but they served (and continue to serve) a vital purpose in the cycle of in-migration and mobility into the economic mainstream. In the latter decades of the nineteenth century, as the older cities filled up with newcomers, new suburbs were opened not only to the upper and middle classes but also to the prosperous working classes, once streetcar lines were extended beyond the city line.[1]

Around 1920, the automobile commenced to play its now-familiar role in providing access to the suburbs. In the period of explosive population growth following World War II, the federal government helped to accelerate the development of the suburbs by providing highways and housing subsidies. The new migration to the suburbs had both an economic and a racial basis. Although blacks began moving to the cities during World War I, their migration from the rural areas of the South greatly accelerated during and after World War II when an urgent demand for unskilled labor pushed wages to record levels. Also, farm mechanization during this period removed much of the demand for manpower in rural areas. As blacks moved to the central cities, whites moved out to the suburbs. For the first time, the exodus from the central cities was as much an escape as it was a step up the social ladder. Many of the movers sought comparable housing in other white neighborhoods at a distance from the older neighborhoods which were becoming populated by black residents.[2] At the same time, other minorities were moving into the central cities: Puerto Ricans on the East Coast, Mexicans in the Southwest, Appalachians in the Midwest.*

As poverty spread, the central cities gradually became infested with crime, family disruptions, poor health, and unemployment. The suburbanites, content to make their living in the city so long as they could come and go in relative convenience, were also content with minimal services: a good school system for their children; zoning for the protection of property values; a benevolent police department; water, sewer, and refuse service; good roads; perhaps a commuter train; and some assurance that "incompatible" elements would not move into their neighborhoods.

RECENT SUBURBAN PROBLEMS AND TRENDS

White migration into the suburbs took on a new dimension in the latter 1960s and early 1970s in the wake of court-ordered plans involving citywide busing of schoolchildren. Previous attempts at school integration in cities failed because of the rapid in-migration and high birth rate among poor blacks. In the big industrial cities, especially in the North, school segregation and racially imbalanced student populations increased rather than decreased during the fifties and sixties. Moreover, the public schools invariably had proportionately larger percentages of blacks in the school district due to transfers of white children to parochial and private schools. (For further discussion, see Chapter 12.)

*Edward C. Banfield has an excellent discussion of this process in Chapter 1 of *The Unheavenly City* (Boston: Little, Brown and Co., 1970).

Meanwhile, as conditions in the inner-city ghettos worsened, sub-urbanites became increasingly wary of merger schemes.[3] At the same time, as black populations in several cities approached majorities, the blacks also resisted merger proposals, for fear that they never would gain a controlling voice in city affairs.[4]

Shifts in the economic base of cities have exacerbated the problems of the central cities. Once annexation went out of style, cities found opportunities for expansion gradually foreclosed. Eventually most of the older cities were ringed by communities that owed them no allegiance. By the middle of the 1950s, industries were migrating out of the central cities, and many new industries were choosing the suburbs. These shifts were influenced by the availability of truck transportation and by the need for cheap land on which to construct single-story plants that could take advantage of automated production lines and inventory storage and access.[5] Many industries which depended upon female office labor and skilled professionals found both available in the suburbs.

One sparsely used solution to the financial plight of cities is area-wide taxation. An areawide sales tax was approved by referendum in Denver in the early 1960s but was declared unconstitutional by the Colorado State Supreme Court. Special purpose districts operating at the metropolitan level have an independent tax base but, in general, broad-based areawide tax schemes are unpopular in the suburbs.

CITY REPRESENTATION IN STATE LEGISLATURES

A 1962 decision of the U.S. Supreme Court declaring malapportionment in state legislative districts to be unconstitutional[6] was expected to shift power in legislatures from rural to urban interests. As *Baker v. Carr* and the 1964 *Reynolds* v. *Sims* decisions were implemented in state after state, it became apparent that the main beneficiaries were to be the suburbs. Although the central cities got additional seats in reapportioned legislatures, the suburbs, whose populations were growing faster, also got more. It then developed that suburban and rural interests often formed coalitions against city interests on issues which vitally affected the latter. Thus, programs to benefit the poor and the politically disadvantaged of the cities stood no better chance in the reapportioned legislatures than they had in the old rurally dominated legislatures. As a result, the cities had to look to the federal government for assistance.[7]

METROPOLITAN GOVERNMENT
REORGANIZATION PROPOSALS

The principal target of metropolitan government advocates is the so-called "fragmentation" of governmental units in these areas. What bothers the reformers is that most of these units are relatively small in population and geographical size, and because some are largely residential, their services are minimal. Some contain an abundance of high-value commerce and industry, while others have little or none. As we point out in Chapter 12, this pattern of local government, coupled with the property tax as the principal fiscal base, can result in gross inequities among localities in services such as schools.

The reformers are also bothered by the fact that most metropolitan residents are served by a minimum of four local governmental units: the county, the municipality, the school district, and one or several special districts. They argue that this situation results in inefficiency and confusion, that most governmental units are too small to provide economical services, that popular control over local government is rendered ineffective by long ballots, that policy leadership is weak or nonexistent, and that the administrations are generally unprofessional and inadequate to meet many of the demands made upon them.[8]

Some basic facts about governmental "fragmentation" in metropolitan areas include the following: By 1972, there were over 22,000 general and special local units of governments in the 264 standard metropolitan statistical areas (SMSAs) of the United States. These include cities, towns (or townships), counties, school districts, and special districts, each with its own corporate powers, set of officials, authority to provide services, and power to raise resources through taxes or service charges. About 58 percent of these units are school districts and special districts.

The proliferation of governments in metropolitan areas has led to many proposals for reorganizations ranging from simple interlocal agreements for cooperation and contracts for services to transfer of functions to special districts and to county, regional, and state levels. (See Figure 4-1.) More comprehensive proposals involve areawide federations and large-scale annexation or consolidation. Figure 4-1 indicates that the larger the scale and complexity of the proposed change, the less willing the voters have been to accept it. The more

Figure 4-1   Metropolitan Government Reform: Continuum of Voter Acceptability

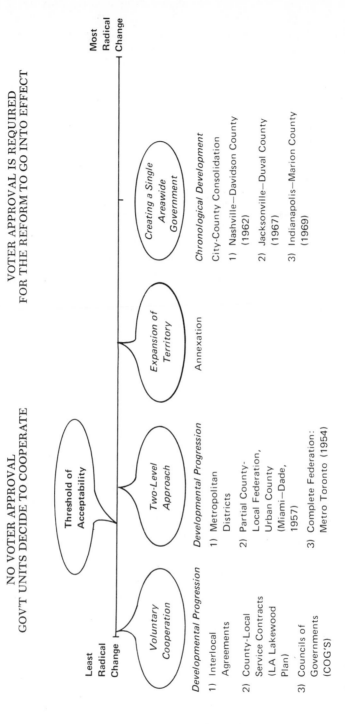

NO VOTER APPROVAL
GOV'T UNITS DECIDE TO COOPERATE

VOTER APPROVAL IS REQUIRED
FOR THE REFORM TO GO INTO EFFECT

Least
Radical
Change

Most
Radical
Change

*Threshold of
Acceptability*

*Voluntary
Cooperation*

*Two-Level
Approach*

*Expansion of
Territory*

*Creating a Single
Areawide
Government*

Developmental Progression

1) Interlocal
Agreements

2) County-Local
Service Contracts
(LA Lakewood
Plan)

3) Councils of
Governments
(COG'S)

Developmental Progression

1) Metropolitan
Districts

2) Partial County–
Local Federation,
Urban County
(Miami–Dade,
1957)

3) Complete Federation:
Metro Toronto (1954)

Annexation

Chronological Development

City-County Consolidation

1) Nashville–Davidson County
(1962)

2) Jacksonville–Duval County
(1967)

3) Indianapolis–Marion County
(1969)

SOURCE: Adopted from Figure 1, "Continuum of Radicalness of Metropolitan Governmental Change," p. 254 in Thomas M. Scott, "Metropolitan Governmental Reorganization Proposals," *Western Political Quarterly* 21 (June 1968). Reproduced by Permission of the University of Utah, Copyright Holder.

drastic the change, the more likely it will affect established interests of elected, appointed, and civil service positions. Also, people tend to resist realignment of familiar governmental services and tax structures when they are uncertain of the system that is to replace them. Suburban cities and towns have shown great reluctance to give up the community identity and the autonomy of their local units, valuing especially their control over zoning and planning, police, and schools.

Voluntary Cooperation: Interlocal Agreements

These range from informal "gentlemen's agreements" in exchanging information between administrators to formal written agreements between local units that wish to share a public service. In these agreements either one government unit performs a service or provides a facility for other local units, or two or more units act jointly to perform a function or to share a service, or several units assist one another during an emergency. These agreements do not ordinarily involve voter approval.

Services provided through interlocal agreements fall into three categories: (1) direct services to the public such as libraries, public health, and welfare; (2) services provided to governments such as personnel examinations, joint purchasing, data processing, tax collection, and assessment; and (3) cooperative assistance in emergencies such as multi-alarm fires and police action to apprehend law violators.

Most interlocal agreements are made between two governments for a single activity; most involve services rather than facilities; very few are intended to be permanent; many are stand-by arrangements for emergency or temporary conditions; and practically all are based upon state legislative authorizations for specific functions.

The Advantages and Disadvantages. Interlocal agreements broaden the geographic base for planning and administering governmental services. By enlarging the scale of administration, the agreements make possible the lowering of unit costs. Boundaries of the service area are flexible since they can be enlarged as additional governments join in the agreement. The agreements are politically flexible in that they do not require voter approval or changes in government structure. They involve little or no long-range planning. Moreover, each community which is party to an agreement can withdraw when its interests are adversely affected.

The Special Districts. These units have been widely utilized to provide particular services, many of which are normal functions of municipal government: fire protection, natural resources, water supply, sewerage systems, public housing, parks and recreation, and others. The number of special districts increased in the United States from 9,000 in 1952 to 21,000 in 1967.* They are created one-by-one in local areas under state law, usually for a single function. Their revenue is generally derived from service charges or benefit assessments. Half of the special districts have elected boards; the other half have appointed boards.

Special districts have been especially popular in states which have restrictive tax and debt limits on municipalities. In many states the counties are limited in the services they can provide, thus, when urban population spreads beyond city limits, the special district is in some places the only means of providing the needed services.

The advantages of special districts are substantial. From the standpoint of local politicians, they often take on difficult service problems. They can usually be created by an act of the state legislature, and they usually do not require approval by a local referendum. They can deal with areawide problems and therefore perform functions without the restrictions of existing local boundaries. The result is a consolidated administration and larger-scale operation than is possible through a municipality.

The disadvantages of special districts are also substantial: They constitute a "single-minded" approach to complex and related service problems of metropolitan areas. The proliferation of special districts diffuses the authority of local government and makes it difficult for the public to hold the government accountable for the services it performs. Generally, the average citizen has little control over the policy and administration of special districts because of their composition, method of selecting governing bodies, and methods of financing. Once established, a special district is hard to abolish, reorganize or consolidate.

Urban Service Contracts: Los Angeles County "Lakewood Plan"

Los Angeles County is unique in having cooperative agreements with municipalities under which agreements the county performs

---

*School districts over that same period, however, decreased substantially through consolidations, although mostly in rural areas.

specific services for them. This arrangement, known as the "Lakewood Plan," was established in 1954 when the local community of Lakewood was incorporated and entered into an agreement with the county to receive a group of urban-related services. The county now performs fifty-eight types of services under more than 1600 agreements with thirty municipalities. The "Lakewood Plan" has avoided the metropolitanization of all urban services within the county. Not all the cities purchase the same services, and over time they may terminate contracts as they develop the administrative and fiscal capacity to operate services on their own.

The advantages of the "Lakewood Plan" are similar to those of the more limited forms of interlocal agreements. A disadvantage is that the cities give up local control over service policies. Because withdrawal is expensive, most of the participating cities have to stay with the county contracts. Moreover, the county uses an inflexible pricing system for services and has complete control over allocations of services to the contracting units.

Metropolitan Councils of Governments (COGs)

The COGs are the newest form of institutionalized intergovernmental cooperation in metropolitan areas. They are not governments which pass laws or make binding decisions by their own authority. They are voluntary associations of local governments designed to advise their members on matters affecting the metropolitan region. The COGs also provide a regional forum for studies and discussions on common problems. Most COGs have taken over the planning function in their regions. The COGs are established by a specific state enabling law, by a state interlocal agreement act, or by nonprofit corporation legislation.

The first COG, the six-county voluntary association in the Detroit area called the Supervisor's Inter-County Committee, was established in 1954. Between 1956 and 1964 eight others were established in the New York City area; Washington, D.C.; Seattle; Salem, Oregon; San Francisco; Philadelphia; Des Moines; and Atlanta. Between 1965 and 1969, ninety-one more came into existence. By the early 1970s, 140 had been organized. The rapid increase after 1965 was stimulated by federal actions aimed at relieving tensions that had built up in planning regions between the professional planners in the RPAs and the elected politicians who were not ordinarily involved in these agencies. Federal officials concluded that effective regional planning had to involve the local politicians.

The first step was taken in the Housing and Urban Development Act of 1965 which declared that organizations of public officials in metropolitan areas could receive federal grants to prepare comprehensive metropolitan plans. Also, the Metropolitan Development and Demonstration Cities Act of 1966 provided that all applications for federal grants and loans in support of local and regional projects had to be submitted for review to an authorized regional planning agency composed of elected officials of local governments. A section of the 1968 Inter-governmental Cooperation Act requiring a majority of elected officials on the COGs gave them a boost in prestige and prompted the establishment of COGs in some areas where no regional planning agency had previously existed.

Organization of COGs. The typical COG membership consists of cities, counties, and certain other local units such as school districts, some special districts, state government, and in a few instances private citizens and civic groups. The COG policy boards are made up of officials designated by participating local government members. These policy boards, or general assemblies, meet once or twice a year. In practice, an executive committee does most of the work supervising staff, preparing policy recommendations for the general membership, making budget decisions, assigning projects to committees, and reviewing their work.

Functions and Activities. The major activity of COGs is development planning at the regional level for sewer and water, waste disposal, and law enforcement. The latter planning function stemmed from the Omnibus Crime Control and Safe Streets Act of 1968. As we noted earlier, the COGs have the responsibility for regional review of plans seeking federal support of physical facilities. COGs arrange training programs for officials and employees of member governments. They also sponsor joint purchasing programs and some other interlocal technical and service arrangements. They lobby for metropolitan and regional needs at the local, state, and national levels, and conduct research on regional problems.

The Advantages and Disadvantages of COGs. The very presence of a COG in a metropolitan region encourages regular discussion of areawide problems among local officials. Such discussions inevitably lead to a recognition of the value and necessity of long-range comprehensive planning as well as short-term cooperative management of problems. The discussions also tend to reduce suspicion and hostility among local communities. The planning efforts of COGs facilitate the identification and understanding of areawide problems. The voluntary nature of the COGs makes them politically acceptable, and their lack of decision-making authority permits them to function without threatening existing governmental and political structures. Contrary to initial fears, the COGs are not necessarily a step toward metropolitan government, although they provide the planning base for areas that take that step. In most states the COGs have flexible boundaries which can be expanded to add governmental units; however, in some states (for example, Texas) COG boundaries are fixed. The stronger and more vigorous COGs serve as a coordinating mechanism for local governments.

On the other hand, the COGs suffer from the United Nations approach to resolution of problems in that they lack the authority to make binding decisions. They cannot overcome city-suburban animosity and the tendency thereof to avoid cooperative relations. They have no authority to levy taxes, pass laws, or regulate local governments. They tend to focus on noncontroversial problems and to avoid social problems such as low-income housing, racial discrimination, job training for minorities, education, and the difficult issues of health planning. The presence of COGs may in some places actually delay the formation of general purpose metropolitan government by providing a facade of planning and problem-solving.

Metropolitan Reorganization: The Two-Level Approach

Where metropolitan reorganization has succeeded, two principal approaches have been predominant: (1) the two-tier form, which preserves existing local governments and adds a metropolitan government to perform areawide functions, and (2) a general-purpose metropolitan government which replaces existing ones.

The two-tier arrangement is similar to metropolitan areas which have strong COG organizations. The Minneapolis–St. Paul council, which has taxing authority and areawide service functions, is an example of a "matured" COG which is, however, not a full-fledged two-tier metropolitan government. The council was created by the state legislature, and the members are appointed by the governor. The council serves a 3,000-square-mile metropolitan area containing 320 units of local government in a seven-county region of nearly two million people. In 1967, the Minnesota state legislature gave the

Minneapolis–St. Paul council independent taxing authority and functions which include sewage and solid waste disposal, highway planning, parks, mass transit, and air pollution control. Furthermore, all zoning changes and plans of local governments must be reviewed by the council which can delay them for public hearings. At the end of sixty days, the local unit may proceed as it sees fit. The council also reviews the plans of special districts and suspends these plans if they are found to be inconsistent with the objectives of the area-wide planning.

The two-tier approach involves a division of responsibilities between local units and a metropolitan governing body which takes the form of a multipurpose district (Seattle is an example), or a full-scale metropolitan government (Unigov in Indianapolis is an example).

The multipurpose metropolitan districts usually are set up to perform a number of services in all or most of the area. They are formed (1) when established districts are given additional services to perform, (2) through consolidation of established districts, and (3) through state enabling legislation which allows new or expanded services to be performed by areawide special districts. Usually the creation of a multipurpose district requires approval of local governing bodies or of the voters of affected localities. Although frequently proposed, the only example of the multipurpose district is in the Seattle–King County metropolitan area.

The Municipality of Metropolitan Seattle, as the district is called, was established in 1958 under a 1957 state law enabling the cities and towns of Washington to act jointly to arrange for services not adequately provided for by individual local governments. The services could include planning, sewage and waste disposal, public transportation, water supply, and parks. An initially unsuccessful referendum proposed three services: sewage, transportation, and comprehensive planning. A second referendum the same year (1958) limited the district to sewage disposal and was approved. Subsequent efforts to add public transportation were defeated.

The Seattle district has a governing council of sixteen members representing the city of Seattle, thirteen suburbs, and King County. A chairman is chosen by the council. The district has no direct taxing powers, but it may accept federal grants, borrow from other local governments, issue revenue bonds, and impose service charges to finance operations and debts. Although begun on a single-purpose basis, the district has a multipurpose potential. As such, it is a threat to the established local governments. Any new functions require separate majority votes in each of the member localities, and so each one has a veto over the expansion of functions.

The Urban County. The only fully operative two-tier metropolitan government is Miami–Dade County in Florida. The Miami–Dade County reorganization was intended to convert a traditional county government into one suitable for attending to the public needs of a growing urban area. There are, in fact, several hundred counties in the United States with populations of over 100,000, and many metropolitan areas lie wholly or mostly within a single county.

Miami–Dade metropolitan government was created in two stages. In 1956 Florida voters approved a constitutional amendment to give Dade County authority to draft a new charter containing provisions for reorganization—for transferring functions to the county and for altering local boundaries. In 1957 Dade County voters approved the charter by a bare majority (44,404 to 42,620). The victory was a rare one and has been explained by the high mobility rate in the local population which overcame community traditions. Also, there were very few municipalities in the area (27) at the time of the charter proposal.

The charter gave broad powers to Dade County and to all twenty-six municipalities. The county was enabled to provide a wide range of services.[10] Also, the county could set minimum service standards for municipalities and take over local activities that failed to meet those standards. Several functions were to be jointly conducted by the county and the municipalities. A municipality could request the county to take over a service with the approval of two-thirds of the members of its governing body. The charter created a new form of county government with a professional manager and a legislative-executive board of commissioners elected on a nonpartisan ballot.

The major problems encountered in Miami–Dade may be summarized briefly. The county government (popularly known as Miami Metro) was for several years subjected to harassment by municipal officials and former county officeholders. These groups attempted repeatedly to reduce county powers and to replace the manager system with a commission. Efforts were also made to return some functions to the municipalities. The 1956 constitutional amendment gave Dade County no additional taxing powers to assume metropolitan functions. Also, a problem of equity existed between incorporated and unincorporated areas, in that the county was required to provide urban services in the latter areas which the municipalities provided for themselves.

The Metropolitan Federation: Toronto. The federated form of metropolitan government presumes a clear-cut division of responsibilities between the metropolitan and local levels. Miami–Dade was not a true federation because of extensive areas of unincorporated territory for which the county was directly responsible. Also, federation requires local representation on the metropolitan governing board. Toronto, Canada has the best example of the matured form of two-tier federated metropolitan government. There are no urban areas in the United States which have as yet developed this form of metropolitan government.

Following an extensive commission study of city and suburban problems, Toronto Metro was created in 1954 by an act of the Ontario provincial legislature without local voter participation. The division of the functions was in three categories. Those exclusively the responsibility of Metro were: assessment and taxation of property, arterial roads, mass transit, parks, health and welfare for the aged and for neglected children, administration of justice, police, licensing of trades, housing and redevelopment, planning, air pollution control, and civil defense. Some examples of the exclusive functions of the local governments include: fire protection, water supply to consumers, sewage and waste disposal, local streets, local planning and zoning, education, traffic controls, and recreation and community services. Shared functions included water supply, sewage disposal, and education.

The original Metro governing board had twelve representatives from Toronto and twelve from the suburbs (one from each town). All members were elected officials of their local governments. In 1967 several changes were made in Toronto Metro by the Ontario legislature: the thirteen local municipalities were consolidated into six; Toronto was subdivided into five boroughs; and eleven school districts were consolidated into six with the same boundaries as the municipalities. The Metro Council was increased from twenty-four to thirty-two. Toronto's representation was unchanged, and the six municipalities varied from two to six, apportioned by population. The major functional change was in education: a metropolitan school board now provides all funds through an areawide tax, thus eliminating fiscal disparities among districts.

Three factors appear to explain the political acceptance and stability of Toronto Metro: leadership, program priorities, and the federal and representational characteristics of the original design.

Leadership. The Metro Council's first chairman exercised vigorous popular leadership in working with an executive committee to secure

approval of policy proposals. He also worked closely with department heads on plans and policy before submitting proposals to the
council.

Program Priorities. There was an early emphasis on highly visible public works projects to symbolize results of the new metropolitan unity, particularly in construction of schools, water supply,
sewage disposal facilities, expressways, and subway and bus line
extensions. Regional parks, public housing, and houses for the aged
were also built.

The Federal Concept. By designating heads of local governments
to sit on the original Metro Council, fears of constituent units were
reduced. The present council is even stronger since the 1967 reforms
with the number of municipalities reduced and additional functions
assigned to Metro.

Annexation

Enlarging city boundaries by annexing contiguous, usually unincorporated territory, has been a common practice throughout the
history of American local government. Most large cities have achieved
their present size through this process. As suburbs developed between
1920 and 1950, their residents succeeded in amending state constitutions to limit annexation. In some states, suburban residents have
exclusive authority to initiate annexations; others require separate
majority votes in both the annexing city and the territory to be
annexed; in all states, incorporated suburbs are excluded from involuntary annexation. After World War II, large-scale annexations
were carried out in Kansas City, Missouri: 187 square miles, and in
Oklahoma City: 193 square miles in 1959, and 149 more in 1960.
In Texas, annexations by Houston and Dallas over the past two
decades have contributed greatly to their growth. Houston by the
end of 1974 was the fifth largest city in population in the nation, and
although its SMSA was fifteenth, Dallas has more land area than
Chicago.

In states where suburbs must agree to annexations (which includes most of them), central cities with manager governments are
more successful in annexations than those with mayors. Suburbs
tend to favor nonpartisan local politics and favor the manager form
as professional and nonpolitical. (For further discussion, see Chapters 3 and 5.) Central cities with larger proportions of middle-class
populations, with high education levels, and "white-collar" occupa-

tions are also more successful in annexations than the less middle-class cities. Thus, where social differences are minimal, political integration is more acceptable. The older the central city, the more resistance there is to changing boundaries.

Metropolitan Reorganization: The Single Level

Consolidation is the merger of two or more units of government of equal legal status. The result is a single new government, examples of which are Indianapolis–Marion County, Jacksonville–Duval County and Nashville–Davdison County. Consolidation takes three forms: (1) the merger of a county and the cities within it; (2) the merger of a county and its cities, with the county retaining some of its functions; and (3) the unification of some, but not all of the municipal governments with the county.

Three Recent Consolidations. Voters in Nashville and Davidson County had rejected a consolidation proposal in 1958 due primarily to the opposition in the suburbs. But in 1962, county government leaders struck up an alliance with business and civic leaders to overcome the opposition. The county judge, an elected official, ran for mayor, won, and led the consolidation campaign. In Jacksonville, voters were prepared for consolidation by previous efforts at metropolitan reorganization, but it took a massive scandal in which both city and county officials were involved to get a consolidation referendum approved. In Indianapolis a consensus of local and state Republican leaders paved the way for the city-county consolidation. A Republican mayor was elected to office at the same time as a Republican governor, county commissioners, and a majority of the state legislature. The party consensus for consolidation was supported by the business community which endorsed reorganization in the name of sound management. The consolidation was promulgated by the state legislature without a local referendum.

The Organization of the Consolidated Government. The Nashville–Davidson consolidation involved a two-zone taxation arrangement. One zone is an expandable urban services district, mainly the old central city. The other zone is a general services district for the entire county. An elected mayor heads the consolidated government and has the authority to appoint department heads and school board members. An elected council has forty-one members: six elected at-large and thirty-five from single-member districts.

Jacksonville also has an urban services district and a general services district. As in Nashville, the tax rate is higher in the former. A full-time mayor appoints department heads with council approval and is supported by a professional administrative officer (similar to a manager). A nineteen-member council has five members elected at-large and fourteen members elected from districts.

The Indianapolis–Marion County consolidation, known as Unigov, is headed by an elected city-county mayor and has a twenty-nine-member council. Unigov embraces some twenty-odd towns and villages but excludes services such as schools, police, and fire departments. The plan also provides options for future mergers. It has broadened the city's tax base by including new suburban industrial and commercial development.

The major opposition to metropolitan consolidation in Nashville, Jacksonville, and Indianapolis occurred in the black community, which was approaching a majority in two of them. The consolidations reduced the percentage of black influence in the metropolitan area as compared to the central city: in Nashville from 40 to 25, in Jacksonville from 43 to 23, in Indianapolis from 25 to 15. Prior to the consolidations, the blacks in Nashville and Jacksonville were close to the point where they could have taken political control of the central city. A majority of the black vote went against consolidation in Nashville and Jacksonville; in Indianapolis, the blacks got slightly more council representation under Unigov.

Voters who are dissatisfied with the scope and quality of services are more likely to support consolidation than those who are satisfied. In a survey of Nashville voters by Brett Hawkins,[9] 54 percent felt services were inadequate and of those, 81.1 percent voted for reorganization. Another factor was the expectation that taxes would not be increased as a result of the consolidation. Hawkins' survey showed that 86 percent of those who did not anticipate higher taxes supported reorganization. Also, the better educated the voter, the more likely he was to support the consolidation proposal.

The common characteristics of the three consolidations were their similar areawide problems; the strong support for consolidation by ambitious, innovative mayors; the enthusiastic support of business and civic leaders; the inconsequential opposition of county and suburban interests; and the cooperation of state legislatures.

SUMMARY OBSERVATIONS ON
METROPOLITAN GOVERNMENT

No one solution to the problem of governance of metropolitan communities in the United States can be set forth as workable everywhere. Edward C. Banfield and Martin Grodzins long ago urged that interjurisdictional conflicts at the local level may be best managed through barter and bargaining among jurisdictions through their local leaders and interest groups. Putting all the local interests together in a single jurisdiction, especially a very large and diverse one, can greatly complicate the public bargaining process and can worsen intransigent problems such as housing and racial frictions. According to Banfield and Grodzins, the intelligent use of power and negotiation, exercised through the leadership of the big city mayors and governors, can move local government toward a form of metropolitan political organization (short of governmental consolidation) which is capable of effective conflict resolution.

At the current pace of urbanization, intelligent efforts at metropolitan, regional, and "substate" planning are essential to the maintenance of a reasonable standard of quality in development. The experience of the past two decades shows that efforts at comprehensive planning in urban areas encourage positive cooperation among local jurisdictions and among the federal, state, and local levels of government. These efforts have also provided the rudimentary mechanisms of conflict resolution and as such have laid the foundations for regional governing mechanisms in the future, whether they evolve from the councils of governments, or from the emerging state administrative and planning districts, or both.

STATE RESPONSIBILITIES IN METROPOLITAN AREAS

The states have a responsibility to see that their urban regions are structured to serve national goals, to serve the shared needs of local communities, to relieve the state and national governments of unnecessary burdens, and to provide citizens with appropriate opportunities to participate in decisions affecting the region.

The states determine the conditions under which local programs can be undertaken in housing, urban renewal, new communities, open space, poverty, transportation, employment, and environmental health, regardless of whether these programs are national, state, or local in their origins. The legal context of these programs, as established by the states, includes the regulation of land use, economic development, home building, ownership and tenancy, waste disposal, employment and business practices, utilities, and forms and levels of taxation. Moreover, the states establish most of the machinery of the political process.

The concept of a cooperative partnership among the several levels of government is the basis of the American federal system, and the proper working of the system requires a strong state role. Otherwise, the power to make decisions for the local communities gravitates to the national government, thus threatening the erosion of local control and the democratic system.

At the present time in most states, neither the executive nor the legislative branch is equipped to guide local institutions in their responsibilities. The federal government, in the work of the Advisory Commission on Intergovernmental Relations, the Senate and House Committees on Government Operations, HUD, and other federal agencies, has shown more concern for the competence of local government than do many of the states. Reports of the ACIR and the congressional committees suggest specific ways in which the states could alter their constitutional, statutory, administrative, fiscal, and structural arrangements so as to make the local government better fit for the roles that both national and state policy require it to perform.

A brief review of the substantive areas of state responsibilities for local and regional development affords a perspective on the range and depth of the states' role.

Education. Education (which will be discussed in Chapter 12) is the responsibility of the state, although this function has largely been passed on to local government. The exceptions are services which require cooperative action among local jurisdictions, for example, special education for the handicapped and exceptionally talented. Education as a tool of economic development requires the establishment of vocational and technical institutes and special training and retraining programs. State economic planning must be concerned with regional educational development and its relation to regional social and economic goals.

Health. The planning and development of adequate public health services and facilities is beyond the fiscal competence of many communities, and some health problems are regional in their impact. Unlike education, the states have done very little to see to it that this function is locally well performed. Nothing was done regionally until the advent of the federal Partnership for Health Program (see Chapter 10). State health plans sponsored by this federal program are supposed to encourage regional cooperation through local cooperative efforts. An example is the New York system, which, through regional and subregional planning bodies, oversees the coordination of the health facilities development. Regional health planning and operations need to be coordinated with education, welfare, housing code standards, sanitation, mental health, and preventive medicine. State planning should provide guidance to regional planning and operations in order to bring about effective coordination among presently isolated functions.

Public Safety. The state has a basic responsibility to see that adequate public safety is provided within the state. At the regional level, cooperation is needed, especially in communications and technical services and in training for the mutual benefit of local communities. Crime control and fire, natural catastrophes, and traffic planning and control are among the priorities.

Water and Waste Disposal. The provision of water and the disposal of wastes have traditionally been the responsibility of local government, the subdivision, or the individual household. In areas of rapid and extensive urbanization, the state has the responsibility to make state or regional arrangements to insure the adequacy of water supplies and waste disposal. The disposal of solid wastes by land fill and incineration has created problems of increasing severity in land and air pollution.

Since water is a major resource in economic development and land use, state capability in controlling water supplies can provide powerful leverage in state development planning. The siting of main line sewers can also be a major tool in development planning. The greater the responsibility the state accepts for refuse disposal systems (and siting), the more sophisticated the solutions can be.

Transportation. A state role in transportation planning in the urban states can result in balanced decisions bearing upon the development of major highways, rail, port, and air facilities which have a major influence in how metropolitan areas develop and how well they work as economic systems. State-planned regional transportation authorities supervised by a state department of transportation are one approach. Direct state planning and operation is another.

Regional Planning. As we have seen, regional planning is a major goal of metropolitan governmental reform. We have also seen a growing determination in federal government to foster effective planning at the metropolitan and regional levels. The purpose is to bring about improved coordination of federal programs within the metropolitan areas.

FEDERAL COORDINATION OF METROPOLITAN PLANNING

Ever since the passage of the Housing Act of 1954, which provided assistance for local and regional planning (section 701), the federal government has encouraged governmental planning and coordination at the metropolitan and regional levels. Support for regional planning resulted in the establishment of regional planning agencies in most of the Standard Metropolitan Statistical Areas after 1954. Inclusion in the Highway Act of 1964 and the Demonstration Cities and Metropolitan Development Act of 1966 (section 204) of the requirement of mandatory referral for review and comment of federally sponsored local projects to the regional planning agencies strengthened the planning effectiveness of these agencies. We noted earlier that the Intergovernmental Cooperation Act of 1968 strengthened regional planning by bringing local officials into the process.

A 1966 report of the Advisory Commission on Intergovernmental Relations[10] recommended that states create multipurpose regional planning agencies and that federal agencies use the same areas. This report led to a presidential directive requiring federal agencies to coordinate federal efforts in regional planning. This directive was promulgated in Bureau of the Budget Circular A-80. In 1968 the Department of Housing and Urban Development made "701" planning funds available to the states to assist them in establishing the state planning districts. In 1969 the Office of Management and Budget (successor to the Bureau of the Budget) issued Circular A-95 which encouraged the establishment of state and substate or regional clearinghouses to assist in the coordination of federally sponsored projects.

The Values of Metropolitan Planning

The federal government uses metropolitan planning agencies in official review of local federally supported projects and in determining their practical and political feasibility as well as their usefulness to the regional community. Metropolitan planning agencies also serve as clearinghouses in bringing about improved coordination of federal programs within an area. Without such coordination, different federal agencies may work at cross-purposes in metropolitan development. For example, federal housing programs that promote suburban growth may also overload federally aided highways or, if badly located, create premature demands for additional federal highway aid.

Metropolitan planning can help bring about the coordination of federally aided projects with local actions. One aspect of this coordination is to assure that locally sponsored projects do not work at cross-purposes with federally aided undertakings. Improper planning of local streets, for example, can clog the interchanges of federally aided highways. Local regulatory action may be desirable to protect the investment in new facilities; special zoning may be required to keep tall structures out of approach zones to airports, or to regulate new development close to federal highway interchanges. In such cases, metropolitan planning agencies can serve as channels of communication between the federal agencies and local governments, by assisting in the review of locally proposed projects, and by suggesting appropriate local action to accompany federal investment in community facilities.

The work program of metropolitan planning agencies generally includes a coordinating role in bringing local policies affecting land development into harmony with one another within a metropolitan area, and in promoting agreement with federal policies affecting development of the same area. Effective coordination requires a consensus on the desired pattern of development, and this consensus should ultimately be reflected in a regional plan. In the absence of a metropolitan planning agency, consultations leading to a consensus among local, state, and federal officials are likely to be haphazard and deal mainly with single programs rather than the entire range of relevant policies. Both the comprehensiveness of metropolitan planning and the clear assignment of responsibility for initiating consultations to the metropolitan agencies provide the means for making federal policies more effective by relating them to the shared objectives of all levels of government in shaping the growth of metropolitan areas.

In practice, metropolitan planning focuses mainly on facilities that serve large segments of the metropolitan population: major highways, transit lines, airports, flood and pollution controls, regional water and sewerage systems, large parks, regional shopping centers, and large industrial centers. Metropolitan plans for such facilities are guided by considerations of efficiency, consistency between the location of population and the location of major service facilities, economy in the extension of utilities and services, the adequacy of transportation and other facilities to meet regional demands, and the reservation of sites to meet future metropolitan needs. Thus, metropolitan planning takes into account the compatibility of specific developments with surrounding activities, the provision of adequate services, and the programming of public investments with a view to fiscal capacity.

The concerns of metropolitan planning are typically those which require action beyond the local level, either by a number of local governments or by levels of government other than the local community alone. Other areas of concern require not only interlocal cooperation but also joint action by higher levels of government. Highways, for example, are usually designed and built by state highway departments but must meet federal standards if they are to receive federal aid. Large parks and land reserves are generally acquired and managed by state agencies or special district commissions. Effective guidance of metropolitan development almost always depends both upon an intricate coordination of action by local and state governments, often involving federal agencies as well, and upon the sensitive adjustments of governmental policies to meet changing conditions of private development. Metropolitan planning can be an instrument for bringing about this kind of coordination within metropolitan areas.

In short, metropolitan planning can be a potent means of coordinating independent decisions which affect metropolitan growth and of promoting joint action to deal with areawide problems. Its most important functions are to present the issues of metropolitan growth to governmental bodies, to stimulate public discussion of alternative patterns of development, and to bring the entire subject of urban growth within the scope of public policy decisions. Such planning can give citizens of a metropolitan area a fuller voice in development decisions as their governmental representatives come to grips with the choices they can exercise through joint governmental action. Nongovernmental interest groups such as chambers of commerce, citizens environmental associations, and the many civic groups that attempt to influence government can have improved access to areawide issues through metropolitan and regional planning.

The Clients of Metropolitan Planning

The studies and recommendations of metropolitan planning are generally addressed to three levels of government—local, state, and federal—and to the citizens of the metropolitan area. These four "clients" of metropolitan planning each use planning services in different ways and derive different benefits from them. Local governments get technical assistance, metropolitan studies and projections as background for local decisions, and an opportunity to participate in decisions affecting both the region and the local community, especially in those made at the state level. The state governments derive benefits from metropolitan planning from both the technical studies and the interlocal cooperation that planning fosters. Moreover, metropolitan planning agencies can serve as staff extensions of state executive agencies and of the state legislature, giving them advice on the probable effects of state level policy decisions. Aside from providing improved information to guide state decisions, metropolitan planning agencies can also promote an informed resolution of conflict between state and local points of view in matters relating to metropolitan development.

Metropolitan planning assists the federal government in establishing project feasibility at the local level, in judging the usefulness of projects to the local community, and in coordinating federal programs with related regional and local projects.

The contributions of metropolitan planning to the metropolitan area itself consist of three major activities. First, the planning agency can work to make public action more effective in influencing the development of the urban area. Planners take the lead in setting up consultation between governments and public agencies whose coordinated policies would influence the direction and quality of regional growth. Second, metropolitan planning can provide an informed basis for decisions in studies and forecasts about the region's potentialities in relation to particular actions and policies. Third, metropolitan planning can help bring private citizens into the decision-making process by making them aware of regional problems and by soliciting their views on possible solutions. An effective metropolitan planning operation can give the citizen opportunities to make choices about the future environment rather than leaving these choices to the separate decisions of local governments and public agencies that typically focus on their own immediate objectives.

In view of their lack of authority to make binding decisions in local municipalities, metropolitan planning agencies seek the negotiator's role in most situations which require resolution of differences among conflicting interests in their areas. There are several ways in which the work of a metropolitan planning agency can use negotiation and bargaining in the interest of areawide development goals. The planning agency can demonstrate when and where local interests are *not* in conflict and how mutual benefits can result from cooperation. It can head off some potential conflicts by proposing a larger number of alternatives in given situations than might be otherwise apparent to local officials. By bringing to light new alternatives, metropolitan planning agencies broaden the choices of local officials and their constituencies. At the same time, the power to propose new alternatives improves the bargaining power of the area interest (one's chances of success in bargaining depend in part on the number of alternatives one identifies as acceptable). Also, the chances for achieving stable solutions are improved if the parties to the bargaining agree *on the desirability of maintaining a viable planning agency* and thus work to identify solutions to problems which divide them.

REGIONAL PLANNING IN OPERATION

Regional planning, as it has developed in the United States, places less emphasis upon comprehensiveness and concerted action and much more upon planning as a communications process, mainly among the leaders of the local governments it serves and among local, state, and federal agencies which have interests in regional development.

As matters now stand, federal, state, and local governments have worked out fairly stable relationships, in large part due to the strong leadership of the federal government in insisting upon planning and coordination at the metropolitan and regional levels where large-scale development makes its impact.

One important area in which federal leadership is needed is in the invention of procedures for coordinating the relationships among complex, multipurpose social service programs aimed at the alleviation of poverty.

For example, the Model Cities program sought to achieve substantial coordination among related federal aid programs at both the federal and local levels with the assistance and cooperation of the states. By 1974, few participant cities were beginning to work out the "umbrella agency" concept in which selected agencies of city government were to improve and broaden their management capacities. In some cities new agencies are being created to manage clusters of related services which had not previously existed or had been scattered among city or private agencies.

In addition, a few participating cities were chosen to experiment with "planned variations" from the basic Model Cities program. Houston and a few other cities have begun to experiment with chief executive review and comment, a program intended to give mayors the planning capability to review federally sponsored projects originating within the jurisdiction of the city.

As we have observed, the federal government has been the principal instigator of regional planning, but it was not until the implementation of the mandatory referral program in the Metropolitan Development Act of 1966 and the strengthening of the COGs that metropolitan planning was accorded any degree of authority. That "authority," however, is very limited. The mandatory review procedure requires that comments and recommendations of the COG include information on the extent to which the project under consideration is consistent with comprehensive planning for the metropolitan area.

By 1968, various federal programs contained scores of planning requirements, some in conflict with others. The Intergovernmental Cooperation Act attempted to consolidate these requirements and to provide a consistent approach to regional planning. The act required that national, state, regional, and local viewpoints be taken into account in regional planning, and that state, regional, and local planning should seek consistency in their objectives. The act also required federal agencies to consult with each other on projects of mutual interest. Section 204 of the act required that federal agencies, upon request, notify governors and legislatures of grants being made in their states.

The 1968 act also defined comprehensive planning (for the first time in federal law) as follows:

Preparation, as a guide for governmental policies and action, of general plans with respect to:

1. Pattern and intensity of land use

2. Provision of public facilities (including transportation facilities) and other government services

3. Effective development and utilization of human and natural resources.

Preparation of long-range physical and fiscal plans for such action.

Programming of capital improvements and other major expenditures based on a determination of relative urgency, together with definitive financing plans for such expenditures in the earlier years of the program.

Coordination of all related plans and activities of the State and local governments and agencies concerned.

Preparation of regulatory and administrative measures in support of the foregoing.

The States' Responsibility for Regional Planning

Most of the tasks and objectives of state planning can only be given reality at the regional and local levels. Recognizing this point, most of the states have created a regional system of state administrative and planning districts. Should these districts become fully operative, they will enable the states to carry out their planning and development responsibilities with far greater effectiveness than they can at the present time. Substate administrative and planning districts could give local communities relief from the responsibilities that are properly regional in scope. Such a system could replace the concept of metropolitan government in that local communities would have the option of maintaining their identity and local functions without bearing the strain of services that they are unable to administer.

A carefully designed set of substate planning and operating districts could be a locus for cooperative federal-state-local programs in major programs such as planned new communities, housing for low-income people within cities, state-local fiscal reform, housing code standards and enforcement, and relocation in connection with re-development of deteriorated sections of metropolitan areas.

Local Responsibilities in Regional Planning

John Bebout once summed up the principal "goods" upon which the ancient doctrine of local self-government rests: (1) the presumed superior capacity of local people to understand and conduct their own local affairs; (2) the value of local self-government as a hedge against undue centralization which might endanger liberty; (3) the utility of local government as an instrument of political education or school for citizenship; (4) the vigor and support that local government can bring to national purpose and strength; and (5) the capacity for innovation and experimentation that is potentially useful to other jurisdictions.[11] The well-meaning efforts of the federal government to set standards and to provide leadership in the development of experimental programs to improve physical and social conditions in urban communities has had mixed results, partly because of the political and administrative incapacity of both state and local government to play the implementing role.

We have suggested how the states could improve their capacities both as implementors of national goals and programs and as initiators in their own right. The effectiveness of the system also requires vigorous local partners, because it is local government that provides, or should provide, the most numerous opportunities for citizen participation. Without these opportunities, the citizen's role atrophies, and control passes to political and professional elites. The chief responsibility of local government in a system in which national and state leadership is strongly asserted is to foster the participation of citizens and local interest groups in planning and development decisions at all levels of government. In achieving this aim, a variety of approaches, some experimental, need to be tried in order to discover which approach is appropriate to each situation. A system of community control or neighborhood government requires careful planning and clear delineation of responsibilities, none of which should be regarded as immutable. Bebout cautions that "in no case should decentralization within the city destroy the integrity or ultimate authority of the whole city."[12]

Local government should retain a central role in planning by direct representation in the councils of the proposed substate districts, in state government through the legislature, through citizen participation in agency advisory councils, and in the federal government by similar representation. Local governments should be, to the maximum feasible extent, the implementing agencies of national and state programs which directly affect local communities.

EVALUATING INTERGOVERNMENTAL PLANNING AND COOPERATION

As we have indicated, the movement toward achieving effective intergovernmental planning and cooperation at the regional and metropolitan levels has focused primarily in the COGs (before them in the regional planning agencies) and in special state planning and development districts. The baffling pattern that has emerged is described in a report of the Advisory Commission on Intergovernmental Relations:

> At the state level [there are] five types of planning districts or bodies in addition to official substate districts: (1) regional planning commissions with strong economic orientations; (2) metropolitan and nonmetropolitan COGs; (3) state functional districts, such as districts established by state highway and welfare departments; (4) special purpose districts such as transportation or solid waste functions, created in response to federal programs. . . . The states' purpose in creating [these] districts was to try to bring these various organizations together on a coordinated and geographically sound basis . . . to perform A-95 reviews and coordinate federal programs at the regional level. From a state viewpoint, they were an attempt to coordinate state and local plans with federal and state programs. . . .[13]

The resulting confusion is likely to be resolved as the states sort out planning and development priorities and attempt to match these with the different forms of districting that have been brought into being in response to specific purposes. Some of the federal districts may disappear as programs are phased out. However, the federal and state governments should try to create a network of regional planning districts which are capable of coordinating federal, state, and local programs dealing with metropolitan development. In the short term, the COGs come closest to possessing the political, planning, and administrative potential for the task.

FEDERAL AID TO METROPOLITAN AREAS

The responsibility of the federal government for current problems of planning and coordination in metropolitan areas stems from the past neglect of coordination among its local aid programs. The gradual proliferation of federal categorical aid programs over a long period of time has tended to encourage fragmentation of local (and state) administration. One reason for this fragmentation is that each new federal program originating in a different agency of the national government has usually required a new state or local agency for its administration. Until review by a comprehensive metropolitan planning agency became a standard requirement of federal programs, little or no attention was paid to coordination among these programs. As a consequence, the intended beneficiaries were often confronted with competing or narrowly focused agencies. No federal agency and no local, regional, or state agency had the effective responsibility for coordination. Lacking such oversight, local bureaucracies tended toward self-serving activities with correspondingly less emphasis on client service. They also tended toward self-protective rather than cooperative relations with other agencies whose functions were complementary or parallel to their own. Obviously, the system of categorical grants-in-aid to the localities was functioning less and less efficiently as the cities grew larger and the metropolitan areas sprouted scores of new municipalities. A new scheme of local aid had to be devised that would reinforce rather than run counter to federal efforts to encourage metropolitan planning.

Concern for this situation in the early and mid-1960s paralleled a concern in the federal government for "fiscal drag," which results from federal revenues outpacing expenditures during periods of prosperity. When this happens, an uninvested surplus in the federal treasury tends to drag down the economy. As the economy passed through a boom period in the 1960s, the threat of fiscal drag impelled the president's economic advisors to develop a plan for sharing revenue surpluses with state and local governments. Actually, by 1965, it was apparent that the Vietnam War would not only soak up any surpluses but would create deficits. Nevertheless, the war would end, and surpluses would again be a problem. So the planning for revenue sharing went forward.

In due course, President Johnson's economic advisors, chief among them Professor Walter Heller and Dr. Joseph Pechman of the Brookings Institution, came up with a scheme which bears their names. The Heller-Pechman plan proposed unconditional block grants to the states on the theory that such grants would relieve the federal treasury of undesirable surpluses and provide the states with badly needed funds. The block grant plan had the administrative advantage of relieving the federal government of the responsibility for the close supervision and control which had characterized the categorical grants-in-aid program. It also would allow the states to set their own priorities and develop and carry out their own programs.

The Fiscal Plight of the States

The case for block grants to the states seemed justified in view of the fact that state taxes had increased from $4.9 billion in 1946 to $24.2 billion in 1964. Since, it was argued, the federal government had virtually preempted the income tax, the states had to obtain their resources from other less flexible and more politically sensitive sources: the property and sales taxes, the business franchise tax, the excise tax, and many others.

The Heller-Pechman plan proposed the establishment of a federal trust fund in which 1 or 2 percent of the federal individual income tax base would be deposited annually. Funds would be distributed to the states on a per capita basis to insure equity. The plan further suggested that a portion of the funds (perhaps 10 percent) be allocated to the seventeen states with the lowest per capita income as an equalization device. The trust fund would plan the revenue-sharing program outside the normal budgeting processes of Congress and the administration and thereby protect it from short-range changes in political policy-making. The block grants would be in addition to grants-in-aid, and at least 50 percent of the grants would pass through the states to local governments. The Heller-Pechman Plan urged that state and local governments be left free to use the funds as they saw fit, subject only to normal accounting, auditing, and reporting procedures. These proposals were considered by the Johnson administration and then set aside as the Vietnam War was expanded.

President Nixon revived the concept, and in a special message to Congress on August 13, 1969, he outlined a plan which incorporated some of the features of the Heller-Pechman proposal, but departed from it on several crucial points. He proposed a formula under which states, cities, towns, villages, and counties (but not special districts) would receive funds according to their population and their current tax effort. The funds were to be derived from two-twelfths of 1 percent of the federal personal income tax base in 1971 (yielding about $500 million) and from five-twelfths of 1 percent in 1972, rising to 1 percent in 1976 (yielding an estimated $5.1 billion) where it would remain. The dollars allocated by this formula would rise by an estimated $500 million a year after 1976. The tax effort under the plan is the ratio of total general revenues collected by state and local governments from their own resources to total personal income reported for the state. The Nixon program in substantially revised form was signed into law on October 20, 1972, as the State and Local Assistance Act.

The act provided for the distribution of $30.2 billion of funds derived from federal income tax revenues over a five-year period beginning in 1972. All general-purpose state and local governments qualify (more than 38,000 in 1972). The state government receives one-third of the amount allocated to the state; the remaining two-thirds is divided among local units of government. The local share is based upon population, the general tax effort, and the relative income of these units—two formulas are used to determine the state allocation, and the allocation is the higher of the two amounts. In one formula, the amount received bears the same ratio to the total available federal funds ($5 billion in 1972) as the population of the state multiplied by the relative income factor of the state, multiplied by the general tax effort factor of the state, bears to the sum of these products for all states. The other formula is based on general population, urban population, per capita income, state income tax collection, and the general tax effort of the state. An important feature of the program is that the funds must be used only for "priority expenditures," meaning maintenance and operating expenses for: public safety, environmental protection, public transportation, health, recreation, libraries, social services for the poor or aged, and financial administration.

A Critique of Revenue Sharing

As we have indicated, the present revenue-sharing program was originally based on the assumption that a federal surplus was in the making that would create a drag on the economy. At the time of its conception in the early 1960s, federal revenues were surging ahead in the wake of a strong upswing in the national economy, and state and local revenues were lagging behind demands for new and improved services.

By 1972, when the State and Local Assistance Act became law, the picture had changed drastically. The federal budget was running a $10-billion to $15-billion deficit as a result of the heavy costs of the Vietnam War, expanding commitments to domestic programs, and inflation. Meanwhile, state and local governments were levying higher taxes, which in 1970 raised $130.76 million as opposed to $46 million a decade earlier. The Tax Foundation has estimated that state and local revenues will rise to $323.55 million by 1980. In effect, the fiscal "imbalance" between the federal government on the one hand and the state and local units on the other appeared to have reversed itself during the late 1960s and early 1970s. Thus, the federal surplus had disappeared while state and local governments seemed to have found their way out of a "crisis."

The present federal revenue-sharing program gives a share of federally collected funds to every unit of general government at the state and local levels, whether they need it or not. It also bypasses the federal bureaucracy in that there is minimal "second-guessing" regarding the purposes to which the funds are put. It neither encourages nor discourages local governmental reorganization in that the local units get a share no matter what their size, governing capacity, or needs.

Some observers who oppose or have reservations about the present revenue-sharing program point out several problems which, they argue, are not touched by the program. Lyle Fitch, an economist and former administrator of New York City lists the following problems: the incapacities of many state and local governments, the concentration of the poor in large cities, and the increasing concentration of political and economic strength in the suburbs.

If anything, Fitch argues, the federal revenue-sharing program in its present form makes these problems worse in that it makes no demands upon state or local government to increase the efficiency of their organization or administrative procedures; nor does it attempt to encourage joint planning and cooperation among functions which could be performed on a metropolitan scale. The program strengthens rural and suburban governments while leaving the big cities relatively weakened. Moreover, the program appears to ignore the nation's most pressing domestic problems. It does nothing to encourage the improvement of the state and local capacity to deliver services (which refers to organization and administrative processes as well as planning and decision-making). Also, Fitch argues, it does nothing about the problem of inflation in the governmental sector, which, he points out, is more severe than in the private sector. (Inflation in the governmental sector over the past decade has been more than twice the rate of that in the private sector.) Outright grants are made to states and provide only that "prevailing" wages and salaries be followed when applying the funds to payrolls adds to inflationary pressures that are already great. Fitch suggests that in jurisdictions where unions are strong, revenue-sharing grants may be "one more chip tossed into the collective bargaining pot and that 'sharing' would be chiefly between the federal government and the employees."*

Further, its critics charge, the program ignores the need to overhaul dysfunctional systems, such as the welfare system and public schools. Indeed, in making unconditional funds available to these institutions through established local governments, the program in-

*Lyle Fitch, "Alternatives to General Revenue Sharing," unpublished MS, p. 44.

creases their capacity to resist reform. Furthermore, it provides no incentives for improving state and local tax structures which, with few exceptions, are regressive and, therefore, disproportionately burdensome to the poor.

Finally, by allocating funds to governmental units which have little need for them, the federal government decreases its own capacity to concentrate funds in urban areas where problems are the most severe: the intractible problems of the poor, the disadvantaged minorities, the incapacitated, and the elderly, which until recently the federal government has not attempted to solve on a scale comparable to their intensity. The states and localities have borne the burden but have failed to provide the solutions. Their welfare functions have been caretaking operations at best, dehumanizing at worst. The social dynamite that such neglect creates was dramatically demonstrated in the urban ghetto riots of the 1960s.

In a mobile, affluent society with an uneven incidence of wealth and poverty, the problems of the poor and the incapacitated are, or should be, a national responsibility. Experience teaches that solutions will not be widely adopted or equitable if left to state and local governments. What is needed, as we shall demonstrate in the following chapters, is strong action by the federal government, not in administering solutions, but in experimenting with and sorting out workable solutions which it then induces the state and local governments to administer. The chief trouble with the present system of revenue sharing is that the states and localities are not likely to do any better in solving these problems than they have in the past. Thus, the program dissipates the federal government's capacity to lend the weight of its influence (bolstered by dollars) to devise and implement solutions.

In place of revenue sharing, the federal government should consider strengthening programs that reward good planning and implementation. It should insist on state and local organization that is adequate to administer programs. It should take over public assistance and eliminate the dysfunctional incentives which are now built into most state and local welfare programs. It should encourage the reform of state-local tax systems, especially the property tax. For example, a national value-added sales tax has been suggested as a substitute for the local property tax as a basis for support of public schools (see chapter 12). Federal aid to education should be broadened to give special advantages to low-income families and perhaps bonuses for state assumption of support for public education. The federal government would do well to increase substantially its support of training for public service in state and local government; nothing could make a greater contribution to the improved capacity of state and local governments than such a program.

Is there any justification for some form of block grant sharing of federal revenues? Professor Lester C. Thurow, an MIT economist, has suggested three purposes that would justify revenue sharing: to establish minimum standards of services and facilities in states and communities; to further equalize financial disparities among states; and to encourage spending on programs that have spill-over effects among states and communities, as for example, pollution control by upstream communities which benefit downstream communities. Such purposes would require conditional grants, thus preserving the federal government's leverage to encourage social and governmental improvements that the other levels of government are prone to avoid.

The Nixon administration's efforts to "turn power back to the states and localities" coupled with revenue sharing seemed to critics to be an attempt to win over the big city mayors and in doing so to aid them in their efforts to free themselves from the influence that poverty and ghetto leaders had begun to gain from the anti-poverty and Model Cities programs. The Democratic administrations of the sixties had also used these programs for political gain and to force reluctant city administrations to come to deal with the problems of poverty and racial injustice. These efforts by the federal government made life difficult for many city administrations because they were put in the position, especially with respect to working-class constitutents, of appearing to help the poor while neglecting others who felt equally hard pressed but who were paying their own way. A Democratic administration can help the urban poor (and get their votes) and still provide sufficient compensation to city administrations to hold their support. A Republican administration can only hope for the support of city hall interests, and hence its strategy of local option regarding the use of federal aid.

NOTES

1. Sam Bass Warner, *Streetcar Suburbs* (Cambridge: Harvard University Press, 1962).
2. Edward C. Banfield has an excellent summary of this process in Ch. 1 of *The Unheavenly City* (Boston: Little, Brown, 1968).
3. Anthony Downs, "The Future of American Ghettos," in *Political Power and the Urban Crisis*, 2nd ed., ed. Alan Shank (Boston: Holbrook Press, 1973), pp. 86–90.

4. Francis Fox Piven and Richard A. Cloward, "Black Control of Cities," in *Political Power and the Urban Crisis*, ed. Alan Shank (Boston: Holbrook Press, 1969), pp. 315–329.
5. Raymond Vernon, *The Changing Economic Function of the Central City* (New York: Committee for Economic Development, 1959). Also, see: David L. Birch, "The Changing Economic Function," in *Political Power and the Urban Crisis*, 2nd ed., ed. Alan Shank (Boston: Holbrook Press, 1973), pp. 91–101.
6. *Baker* v. *Carr*, 369 U.S. 186 (1962); *Reynolds* v. *Sims*, 377 U.S. 533 (1964); and *Wesberry* v. *Sanders*, 376 U.S. 1 (1964).
7. See: A. James Reichley, "The Political Containment of the Cities," in *The States and the Urban Crisis*, ed. Alan K. Campbell (Englewood Cliffs, N.J.: Prentice-Hall, 1970), pp. 169–195.
8. John C. Bollens and Henry J. Schmandt, *The Metropolis*, 2nd ed. (New York: Harper & Row, 1970), p. 328.
9. Brett W. Hawkins, "Public Opinion and Metropolitan Reorganization in Nashville," in *Politics in the Metropolis*, 2nd ed., eds. Thomas R. Dye and Brett W. Hawkins (Columbus, Ohio: Charles E. Merrill, 1971), pp. 515–525.
10. Advisory Commission on Intergovernmental Relations, *Metropolitan America: Challenge To Federalism*, A Study Submitted to the Intergovernmental Relations Subcommittee of the Committee on Government Operations, U.S. House of Representatives, 89th Congress, 2nd Session, October 1966.
11. John E. Bebout, *An Ancient Partnership: Local Government, Magna Carta, and the National Interest* (Charlottesville: University Press of Virginia, 1966), pp. 35, 92.
12. ————, "Centralization and Decentralization" (Institute for Urban Studies, University of Houston, May 1973), pp. 20–21.
13. George W. Strong, "Substitute Planning Districts—A Planner's Dream," (A paper prepared for the 1973 Workshop on Government for Metropolitan Areas sponsored by the Southern Newspaper Publisher's Association and the Institute for Urban Studies, University of Houston, May 20–23, 1973), p. 9.

SUGGESTIONS FOR FURTHER READING

Advisory Commission on Intergovernmental Relations. *Alternative Approaches to Governmental Reorganization in Metropolitan Areas*. Washington, D.C.: U.S. Government Printing Office, June 1962.
Institutional alternatives for metropolitan government.
————. *Factors Affecting Voter Reactions to Governmental Reorganization in Metropolitan Areas*. Washington, D.C.: U.S. Government Printing Office, May 1962.
The record of consistent rejection of metropolitan government.
————. *Metropolitan America: Challenge to Federalism*. A study submitted to the Intergovernmental Relations Subcommittee of the Committee on Government Operations. U.S. House of Representatives, 89th Congress, 2nd Session. Washington, D.C.: U.S. Govern-

ment Printing Office, October 1966.
A useful analysis of metropolitan areawide problems and prospects.

———. *Metropolitan Councils of Government*. Washington, D.C.:
U.S. Government Printing Office, August 1966.
An analysis of a voluntary approach to interlocal cooperation.

———. *Multistate Regionalism*. Washington, D.C.: U.S. Government
Printing Office, April 1972.
Federal participation and programs in regional intergovernmental
cooperation.

———. *Regional Decision Making: New Strategies for Substate Districts*. Washington, D.C.: U.S. Government Printing Office, October
1973.
Outlines ACIR's recommendations for Councils of Government and
other methods of interlocal cooperation.

———. *Regional Governance: Promise and Performance*. Washington, D.C.: U.S. Government Printing Office, May 1973.
Case studies of metropolitan government.

———. *Urban America and the Federal System*. Washington, D.C.:
U.S. Government Printing Office, October 1969.
An analysis of metropolitan areawide governmental, fiscal, and
planning problems together with the commission's recommendations for solutions.

Altshuler, Alan. *The City Planning Process: A Political Analysis*.
Ithaca: Cornell University Press, 1965.
A view of planning as a political process growing out of case
studies in Minneapolis and St. Paul.

Bish, Robert L. *The Public Economy of Metropolitan Areas*. Chicago:
Markham, 1971.
An attempt to explain the structure and functioning of metropolitan economies.

Bollens, John C., and Henry J. Schmandt. *The Metropolis*, 2nd ed.
New York: Harper & Row, 1970.
Comprehensive text on metropolitan problems and cooperation.

Campbell, Alan K., ed. *The States and the Urban Crisis*. Englewood
Cliffs, N.J.: Prentice-Hall, Spectrum Books, 1970.
Original essays on the state response to urban fiscal, governmental,
and planning problems.

Committee for Economic Development. *Reshaping Government in
Metropolitan Areas*. New York: Committee for Economic Development, 1970.
Proposals for metro governments plus a useful essay on the metropolitan Toronto (Canada) experience.

Coulter, Philip B., ed. *Politics of Metropolitan Areas*. New York:
Thomas Y. Crowell, 1967.
Essays on government and politics of cities, suburbs, and metropolitan areas.

Danielson, Michael N., ed. *Metropolitan Politics*, 2nd ed. Boston: Little, Brown, 1971.
Selected essays on the government and politics of the metropolis.

Downes, Bryan T., ed. *Cities and Suburbs*. Belmont, Calif.: Wadsworth, 1971.
A useful collection of essays on the politics and policies of cities and suburbs.

Dye, Thomas R., and Brett W. Hawkins, eds. *Politics in the Metropolis*, 2nd ed. Columbus, Ohio: Charles E. Merrill, 1971.
Selected essays on metropolitan government, politics, and public policy conflicts.

Eldredge, H. Wentworth, ed. *Taming Megalopolis*, 2 Vols. Garden City, N.Y.: Doubleday, Anchor Books, 1967.
Comprehensive collection of articles on metropolitan problems, planning, and solutions.

Feld, Richard D., and Carl Grafton, eds. *The Uneasy Partnership*. Palo Alto, Calif.: National Press Books, 1973.
Collected articles on the dynamics of federal, state, and urban relations.

Fox, Douglas M., ed. *The New Urban Politics*. Pacific Palisades, Calif.: Goodyear, 1972.
Selected articles on federal programs toward urban areas.

Friesma, H. P. "The Metropolis and the Maze of Local Government," *Urban Affairs Quarterly*, Vol. 2 (December 1966), pp. 68–90.
Criticism of metro government reform proposals.

Gans, Herbert J. *The Levittowners*. New York: Random House, Vintage Books, 1967.
Analysis of life and politics in a suburban community.

Grant, Daniel R. "Metro's Three Faces," *National Civic Review*, Vol. 55, No. 6 (June 1966), pp. 317–324.
Indicates that metro government solutions may not be applicable to all metropolitan areas.

————. "The Metropolitan Government Approach: Should, Can, and Will It Prevail?" *Urban Affairs Quarterly*, Vol. 3 (March 1968), pp. 103–110.
Suggests that intergovernmental cooperation rather than metro government will be the norm for the future.

Greer, Scott. *Governing the Metropolis*. New York: John Wiley & Sons, 1962.
This small book is one of the most cogent analytical accounts in print on the politics and government in metropolitan areas.

Heller, Walter W. *New Dimensions of Political Economy*. New York: W. W. Norton, 1967, Ch. 3.
Discussion of revenue sharing by one of its originators.

Macmahon, Arthur W. *Administering Federalism in a Democracy*. New York: Oxford University Press, 1972.
Fiscal relationships in the federal system.

Martin, Roscoe C. *The Cities and the Federal System*. New York: Atherton Press, 1965.
Problems and programs of intergovernmental and metropolitan development.

Meyerson, Martin, and Edward C. Banfield. *Politics, Planning, and the Public Interest*. Glencoe, Ill.: Free Press, 1955.
The theory and practice of planning as policy-making is discussed in the context of decisions about public housing in Chicago in the period following the passage of the 1949 Housing Act.

Piven, Francis Fox, and Richard A. Cloward. "Black Control of Cities," *The New Republic* (September 30 and October 7, 1967), pp. 19–21, 15–19.
Argues that blacks may not benefit from metro reform proposals.

Rabinowitz, Francine F. *City Politics and Planning*. New York: Atherton Press, 1969.
A study of the role of the physical planner in urban political and developmental decision-making.

Reagan, Michael D. *The New Federalism*. New York: Oxford University Press, 1972.
Analyzes fiscal crisis of urban areas and possible solutions through revenue sharing.

Reuss, Henry S. *Revenue-Sharing*. New York: Praeger, 1970.
Democratic congressman from Wisconsin urges enactment of revenue sharing together with tax reforms and administrative reorganization.

Rodwin, Lloyd. *Nations and Cities*. Boston: Houghton Mifflin, 1970.
Urban growth and planning strategies in selected foreign nations and in the United States.

Sanford, Terry. *Storm Over The States*. New York: McGraw-Hill, 1967.
Role of the states in urban and federal policies.

Scott, Thomas M. "Metropolitan Governmental Reorganization Proposals," *Western Political Quarterly*, Vol. 21, No. 2 (June 1968), pp. 252–261.
Suggests a framework for analyzing prospects of voter acceptance of metro government reforms.

Sharkansky, Ira. *The Maligned States*. New York: McGraw-Hill, 1972.
A defense of the states against detractors and suggestions for expanded activities.

Wirt, Frederick M., et al. *On The City's Rim*. Lexington, Mass.: D. C. Heath, 1972.
Useful examination of suburban politics and policies.

Wood, Robert. *1400 Governments*. Garden City, N.Y.: Doubleday, Anchor Books, 1964.
The maze of local governments in the New York City metropolitan region.

————. *Suburbia.* Boston: Houghton Mifflin, 1958.
Landmark study of suburban population, politics, and political outlooks.

Wingo, Lowdon, ed. *Reform of Metropolitan Governments.* Baltimore: Johns Hopkins University Press, Resources for the Future, 1972. Essays on metropolitan institutions, decentralization, and the federal role.

5

Community Leadership: Mayors and Managers

INTRODUCTION

In attacking boss rule and machine politics, the municipal reformers, as discussed in Chapters 2 and 3, focused upon changing local parties, electoral systems, and governmental structures. The "community-minded" or "public-regarding" outlook of the reformers sought to transfer the principles, objectives, and goals of corporate enterprise to city government and politics. They were concerned with "good government" and administrative efficiency, including moral crusades against graft and corruption, "proper" organizational mechanisms for broader participation in party activities and elections, and centralized lines of authority and effective management in the strong mayor and council-manager plans.

Before the reformers fought machine politics, the bosses themselves, as described in Chapter 1, rose to power in the political vacuum and dispersal of formal governmental authority created under the weak mayor-strong council system. The "good government" reforms were an attempt to reinvigorate executive authority in the institutional framework of city government by replacing the party bosses and their "stooges" with mayors and managers who were directly responsible either to the electorate or to the city council. By doing this, the reformers expected that the narrow, personal, and neighborhood interests of the party machine would be superseded by the broader, civic-minded, and communitywide orientations of strong mayors and city councilmen.

What happened after most American cities established either the strong mayor or council-manager forms of local government? Did the emphasis upon institutional change produce more responsive, efficient, and effective government? Do mayors and managers have sufficient formal authority, political resources, and policy instruments to exercise local leadership? How can leadership roles be defined, and which varieties of local leadership are most likely to achieve the goals of the mayor or the city manager?

MAYORAL LEADERSHIP QUALITIES

The "good government" reformers considered mayor leadership an integral feature of effective municipal government, but, until recently, the actual performance of big city chief executives was conspicuously ignored by social scientists. In fact, the mayor's office has usually been viewed as a political dead end. As long as the mayor's position lacked prestige, visibility, and upward mobility, politically ambitious leaders were not attracted to city hall. In a study conducted in 1963, political scientist Marilyn Gittell found that only ten of ninety-six mayors in the nation's twenty-four largest cities were elected to higher office during the preceding two decades.[1] She observed that "mayors throughout the United States have little in common but the lack of a political future—that they are, as a profession, predestined to political oblivion is a historical fact."[2]

Today, big city mayors face one of the toughest public jobs in America. The complex problems associated with party politics, local government, social conflict, and policy implementation have brought increasing attention to mayoral leadership capacities. In suggesting solutions to prevent urban riots, the National Advisory Commission on Civil Disorders emphasized the need for strong mayoral leadership:

> . . . Now, as never before, the American city has need for the personal qualities of strong democratic leadership. Given the difficulties and delays involved in administrative reorganization or institutional change, the best hope for the city in the short run lies in this powerful instrument. In most cities, the mayor will have the prime responsibility.[3]

In confronting community disorder, racial problems, and other social malaise, the mayors require sufficient *resources* to exercise effective leadership. During the 1960s the men in city hall often found it difficult to resolve conflicting demands from fragmented, hostile, and politically polarized constituencies. Political scientist James Q. Wilson observed that the mayors were constrained by "a simultaneous growth in the problems of the central cities and a decline in the authority of the mayor to handle those problems."[4]

The quality and performance of mayoral leadership reflects how well resources are employed to mobilize politically effective *constituencies*, to seek out and maximize *fiscal assistance* and *available programs* from the federal government, and to overcome formal restraints on *executive authority* and *municipal powers* in dealing with urban problems. More specifically, as indicated by political scientist Jeffrey Pressman, big city mayors require the following seven resources to exercise effective community leadership:

1. Sufficient financial and staff resources on the part of the city government
2. City jurisdiction in social program areas—such as education, housing, redevelopment, job training, etc.
3. Mayoral jurisdiction within the city government in these policy fields
4. A salary for the mayor which would enable him to spend full time on the job
5. Sufficient staff support for the mayor—for policy planning, speech-writing, intergovernmental relations, and political work
6. Ready vehicles for publicity, such as friendly newspapers or television stations
7. Politically oriented groups, including a political party, which the mayor could mobilize to help him achieve particular goals[5]

Big city mayors employ different leadership roles and styles in applying their resources to the solution of urban problems. Table 5–1 shows that mayoral leadership ranges from "active" to "passive" approaches and includes either "positive" or "negative" orientations toward party politics and public policies. These leadership classifications are adopted from James D. Barber's identification of varieties of presidential leadership:

1. "Active-Positives" seek to achieve results, are productive, and use their styles of leadership flexibly.
2. "Active-Negatives" aim to get and keep power, are aggressive, ambitious, and energetic.

3. "Passive-Positives" are receptive, compliant, agreeable, and cooperative.
4. "Passive-Negatives" emphasize their civic virtue, tend to withdraw from conflict, and lack experience and flexibility to act as effective political leaders.[6]

TABLE 5–1 A Typology of Mayoral Leadership Styles and Roles

Active Leadership		Passive Leadership	
Positive	Negative	Positive	Negative
Program-Politician	Boss-Politician	Caretaker	Figurehead or
Cosmopolitan	Renegade		Evader
Maverick-Independent	Polarizing		

ACTIVE-POSITIVE MAYORS

As indicated previously, "active-positive" leadership styles emphasize program and policy results. Such mayors attempt to use available resources to deal directly with urban problems, either through downtown reconstruction (urban renewal) or social welfare programs (antipoverty, model cities, manpower, educational, etc.). Politically, these mayors are "liberal" in supporting governmental intervention which promotes broader allocation of social goods. Within the local party structure, the "active-positives" either develop authority and control over existing machinery, work cooperatively with established party leaders or local influentials, or try to organize new coalitions to challenge entrenched party organizations. Unlike presidents, active-positive mayors are not always successful in achieving accommodation between their policy goals and their political party and constituency support. Except for the program-politicians, they frequently fail to achieve program objectives, either because they are dependent upon Washington for financial assistance or because the goals of social welfare policy may alienate crucial groups within their political constituencies. As it will be shown in the subsequent discussion, the most effective active-positive mayors were the *program-politicians* who combined civic entrepreneurship with party authority and control. In contrast, the *mavericks* and the *cosmopolitans* encountered serious conflicts between their policy goals and their political party authority.

Program-Politician Mayors

Program-politician mayors are "civic and political entrepreneurs" who use their resources to centralize authority in pluralistic communities characterized by dispersed and decentralized political power. Civic entrepreneurs, according to political scientists Charles Levine and Clifford Kaufman, are mayors who seek "to build a centrally directed coalition that mobilizes and incorporates those groups who control the resources to make innovations feasible. Thus, the civic entrepreneur has been defined by his high scores on such personality traits as originality, risk-taking, initiative, energy, openness, organizational ability, and promotional ingenuity."[7] In other words, the program-politician mayoral leadership style combines political party and/or community influential support (political entrepreneurship) with the achievement of program results in particular policies (civic entrepreneurship).

During the 1950s and early 1960s, a new breed of aggressive and energetic mayors developed innovative urban renewal programs to revitalize the economic health of their cities. They believed that the physical rebuilding of the urban core would not only provide an attractive environment, but would also restore business confidence, revive the tax base, and reverse the flight of the white middle class to the suburbs. According to political scientist Duane Lockard, the mayors who promoted urban renewal were "program-oriented in order to attract support, ready to work with a political organization and to use patronage and other traditional tools to get and hold office but unready to depend upon these alone."[8]

Among the program-politician leaders highly instrumental in developing extensive urban renewal programs were William B. Hartsfield (1937–1939, 1941–1961) and Ivan C. Allen, Jr. (1961–1969) of Atlanta; Philadelphia's two reform mayors, Joseph S. Clark, Jr. (1951–1955) and Richardson Dilworth (1955–1962); and Richard C. Lee (1953–1969) of New Haven, Connecticut. Their leadership reflected effective mobilization of their political base of electoral support and their ability to organize the business community to endorse urban renewal goals and objectives.

Although the five program-politician mayors were Democrats, the distinctive local party conditions in Atlanta, Philadelphia, and New Haven required each of them to use quite a different approach to win and maintain public office. These included (1) the development of a business-oriented, "good government" reform and a racially moderate coalition to offset attacks by antiblack extremists in Atlanta;[9] (2) the sharing of local party influence between the mayor and other "boss-politician" leaders in New Haven; and (3) the politically independent "blue-ribbon" status of Philadelphia's two mayors, which was previously analyzed in Chapter 2. Each of the program-politician leaders appeared equally successful in accommodating their party influence (or lack of it) with their civic improvement goals. However, after these men left office, they were succeeded by mayors who had different sources of political strength. In Philadelphia and New Haven, boss-politician leaders reasserted control over city hall, while in Atlanta a liberal-reform "maverick" was elected over the opposition of entrenched community influentials.

The program-politician mayors also recognized the crucial importance of business support for their city rebuilding efforts. Business endorsement was essential because most of the urban renewal programs were aimed at central city economic revival rather than at providing low-income housing for the poor. (See Chapter 11 for further discussion of federal urban renewal policies.) In Atlanta, Mayors Hartsfield and Allen effectively transferred the electoral support of the business influentials to their backing of central city policy objectives. Under their combined leadership, Atlanta became the Southeast's leading commercial and industrial center with new expressways, a prosperous downtown shopping district, an exhibition hall for trade fairs, and a municipal sports stadium for professional football and baseball. Allen had closer ties to business than Hartsfield. When he first ran for office in 1961, Allen was not only one of Atlanta's wealthiest businessmen, but he was also the president of the local chamber of commerce. On the other hand, Philadelphia's and New Haven's mayors used different approaches to attract business support, because in these two cities the business leadership was not a part of the electoral coalition. In Philadelphia, the direct involvement and participation of the most influential business elite was enlisted in key urban renewal projects, while in New Haven the business community was convinced to endorse and support the mayor's major redevelopment programs.

Philadelphia's urban renewal efforts achieved notable success because Mayors Clark and Dilworth had the substantial backing and direct participation of key business leaders. Accompanying the city's political reform efforts was the Greater Philadelphia Movement, representing thirty-five of the most influential business, civic, and educational leaders concerned wtih reviving the city's economic strength.

Among its notable accomplishments, the GPM was instrumental in organizing and financing a new $100-million Food Distribution Center. Additionally, Mayor Dilworth worked closely with Albert M. Greenfield, the city's most powerful real estate broker, to bring about downtown commercial and residential redevelopment. After Dilworth appointed him as Planning Commission Chairman, Greenfield organized the Old Philadelphia Corporation to promote the Washington Square East–Society Hill project. Together with the Redevelopment Authority, the Planning Commission, and the Development Coordinator, the OPD launched Philadelphia's "showcase" restoration of its oldest neighborhood along the Delaware River by combining a privately financed rehabilitation of historic homes with a selective clearance for walkways, parks, and recreation areas, and construction of modern high-rise apartments and attractive new townhouses.[10]

Of all the program-politician leaders, Mayor Lee probably achieved the most remarkable transformation of his city's central commercial area, including a downtown expressway connection to the Connecticut turnpike and a multilevel parking garage adjacent to new office buildings, shopping plaza, hotels, and luxury high-rise apartments. Lee's massive urban renewal efforts followed his 1953 campaign promises to reverse New Haven's economic deterioration:

> . . . By the end of 1958, New Haven had spent more federal funds per capita for planning its redevelopment projects than any of the country's largest cities, more than any other city in New England, and more than any other city of comparable size except one. Only one city, the nation's capital, had received more per person in capital grants, and no other city had so much reserved for its projects. By 1959 much of the center of the city was razed to the ground.[11]

Lee skillfully mobilized community support for his urban renewal programs by organizing New Haven's "biggest muscles" into the Citizens Action Commission.[12] Between 1954 and 1958, the CAC, which included twenty-five leaders representing Yale University, large utilities, manufacturing firms, businesses, banks, labor unions, and important ethnic groups (Yankees, Jews, Italians, and Irish), gave Mayor Lee the necessary broad-based consensus to put across his programs.

In retrospect, the program-politician mayors of Atlanta, Philadelphia, and New Haven provided effective leadership in initiating, promoting, and implementing large-scale city rebuilding programs. However, various critics have argued that such urban renewal "progress" resulted in "black and minority group" removal.[13] The considerable residential displacement caused by slum clearance reflected federal and local priorities during the 1950s and early 1960s. The social welfare needs of the impoverished black population and other racial and ethnic minorities were largely ignored. The program-politicians were not unaware of these problems, but until the ghetto riots of the 1960s, neither federal nor local governments provided adequate financial and program assistance for the black and the poor. These new priorities required modifications of the political and civic entrepreneurship which had been employed with such success by the program-politicians in attracting electoral support, business endorsement, and federal funds for the economic revival of the central cities.

Cosmopolitan Mayors

A second variety of "active-positive" leadership is found in the cosmopolitan mayors, who have strengths and disabilities which are different from the program-politicians. They comprise the articulate spokesmen of the urban crisis during the 1960s and 1970s. Through skillful use of the mass media and various public forums, the cosmopolitans focus nationwide attention on both the general causes of urban malaise and the particular difficulties of their respective cities. However, in broadening their appeals for public awareness toward the cities, the cosmopolitans run the risk of antagonizing various local groups that provide them with electoral support. Local party leaders are suspicious of their national reputations and oftentimes express outright hostility toward their programs and administrations.

James Q. Wilson pinpoints the key dilemma of the cosmopolitans by indicating the differences between their "constituency" and their "audience."[14] The constituency includes the local parties and the voters who elect the mayor. He needs their support to attain public office. However, after election day, the cosmopolitan mayor conducts his administration independently without having very much concern for local party battles. Instead, such a mayor seeks endorsement and support for his new urban agenda from an "audience" that does not vote in local elections.

The audience is a coalition of powerful interests which offers the mayor sympathetic and substantive support for tackling urban problems, providing him with new approaches to city administration, and giving him access to influential opinion-makers and voting groups outside the city. The audience includes various *federal agencies* that fund urban programs, such as the Office of Economic Opportunity, Model Cities, and the Department of Health, Education, and Welfare; the large *foundations*, including the Ford Foundation and the RAND Corporation, which provide grants, advice, and consultation for city programs; the *mass media*, which give the mayor publicity, attention, and access to influential groups; and affluent *suburban residents*, who will judge the mayor's accomplishments and provide him with important voting support if and when he decides to run for higher office.

Three recent city hall incumbents—John V. Lindsay (New York), Kevin H. White (Boston), and Jerome P. Cavanagh (Detroit)—exhibit many of the characteristics of cosmopolitan leadership. During the 1960s, all of them expressed concern for the lack of economic, social, and political opportunities among blacks and other minorities who had migrated to inner-city ghettos in vast numbers. They became associated with the new social welfare objectives of President Johnson's Great Society programs, including the War on Poverty, Job Corps, Head Start, and Model Cities. Following the intensification of American involvement in Vietnam during the mid-1960s, the cosmopolitan mayors became concerned that Washington's commitment to assist the cities was diminishing at the very time when ghetto riots, violence, and racial polarization were causing extreme urban distress. They began to argue that the seriously disruptive local urban crises should be recognized as part of overall domestic policy problems that required a reordering of national priorities.

However, at the same time that the cosmopolitans were articulating the dire consequences of urban neglect, they were encountering serious local political difficulties. The voters turned against Cavanagh, Lindsay, and White when they sought local reelection or higher state or national offices. What were the causes of these political defeats? Apparently, none of these mayors were able to overcome the "constituency-audience" conflict. Ironically, as the cosmopolitans dramatized the urban plight and sought more funds and program assistance from Washington, they were blamed for failing to resolve these problems in their own cities. They became the targets of disaffected voters who believed that violence and riots required stronger local leadership to prevent a total breakdown of community order. In sum, the cosmopolitans were the victims of a political situation resulting from the very urban conditions which they recognized as the root causes of voter fear and distrust.

Maverick-Independents

A third type of active-positive mayoral leadership includes "mavericks" who assert their personal independence from entrenched political machines or local ruling elites. Unlike either the program-politicians or the cosmopolitans, they are less concerned with political and civic entrepreneurship, which seeks to centralize political and policy influence among various influential groups. Rather, the mavericks reject traditional local alliances as irrelevant to the needs of unrepresented and relatively powerless groups. Mavericks seek office upon their own personal appeals and claims of independence. They try to convince the voters that they are "unbossed" men.

Political independents need charismatic leadership qualities to lure the electorate away from traditional voting attachments. Maverick candidates must develop their own campaign organizations and sources of financial support. Their electoral appeals are based less on substantive issues than on distinctive personalities, individual idiosyncrasies, television imagery, and emotionally charged attacks on opponents.

After assuming office, maverick-style mayors frequently find it difficult to transfer their electoral coalitions into new courses of public policy. Desired program alternatives may be opposed by party leaders, the business community, ethnic and minority groups, or the city council. Until such mayors develop broad-based community support for substantive proposals, their range of accomplishment may be seriously constrained. Thus, maverick mayors run the risk of becoming "do-nothing" executives who are politically isolated from other important interest groups. Their independence may only be transitional until it becomes clear that the chief executive desires nothing more than to preside over a caretaker administration, or unless he begins to develop a community consensus toward solving the urban crises of his city.

Peter F. Flaherty of Pittsburgh and Sam H. Massell, Jr. of Atlanta, two self-styled independent liberals, both won mayoral elections in 1969 by defeating entrenched ruling forces that had completely dominated the political life of those cities for more than three decades. Prior to 1969, Atlanta's "three-legged" coalition of business influentials, "good government" groups, and blacks had provided electoral support for program-politicians Hartsfield and Allen, enabling them to carry out massive city construction projects and to endorse civil rights programs. In Pittsburgh, the Democratic machine was unchallenged in local politics from the New Deal until the 1960s.[15] The late governor and mayor, David L. Lawrence, and his successor, Mayor Joseph M. Barr, centralized their control and influence as party leaders over the city's ward system in a manner quite similar to that employed by Mayor Daley in Chicago. Both Lawrence and Barr had close ties with the business community and particularly with the Mellon family whose leadership resulted in Pittsburgh's impressive Golden Triangle downtown renewal project in the 1950s. The two party leaders also had substantial influence with organized labor leaders who represented the Steel City's blue-collar and heavily ethnic working class.

How did Flaherty and Massell triumph over such powerful local forces? As party mavericks, both men had no ties with the local ruling coalitions. For one thing, they gained elective office without support of the Democratic machine or community influentials. After campaigning as independents, Flaherty served one term on the Pittsburgh City Council (1965–1969), while Massell was elected as Atlanta's vice-mayor and served from 1961 to 1969 without the endorsement of either Mayor Allen or the business community.

Second, the two incumbent mayors, Barr and Allen, who had both decided to retire in 1969, tried to designate successors whom Flaherty and Massell accused of representing the "establishment." Both mavericks gained reputations as underdogs who were unfairly attacked by the ruling coalitions. The Pittsburgh machine associated Flaherty with the "evil forces" of the "new left and the Students for a Democratic Society" who were determined to destroy society.[16] Responding to a demand by outgoing Mayor Allen that he withdraw from the Atlanta mayoral contest a few days before the election, Massell, a Jew, charged that "five angry adversaries," including Allen; the Republican candidate, Rodney Cook; and the presidents of the chamber of commerce, a bank, and the city's largest newspaper, were all motivated by anti-Semitic bigotry.[17]

Fourth, both independents won electoral victories by forging new coalitions that differed from the traditional political alignments in Pittsburgh and Atlanta. Flaherty's campaign represented a uniquely successful one-man battle against the machine. He developed an organization of students and independents that was completely disassociated from the Democratic machine. He relied neither on ward leaders nor on large financial contributions to bring out the vote. Although the Democratic machine successfully mobilized the electorate for all of its city council candidates, Flaherty not only won by more than 56,000 votes, but he also carried thirty-one of the city's thirty-two wards and showed substantial strength in all white ethnic and black neighborhoods.[18] On the other hand, Massell developed an alliance of white liberals and blacks to defeat Cook and the business leaders. While Cook received 73 percent of the white vote, Massell got 92 percent of the black vote, which together with white liberal backing, gave him an overall 55 percent plurality.[19] Thus, Massell's personal triumph was largely due to the tremendous bloc voting support he received from the black community.

Finally, both mayors had only limited records of accomplishment during the early months of their new administrations. Mayor Flaherty, although maintaining his steadfast independence from the Democratic machine, appeared increasingly isolated from Pittsburgh's business, labor, and party leaders. By the end of 1970, Flaherty was constantly engaged in bitter battles with the machine-controlled city council, the police, and the press over several of his controversial policies. In contrast, Mayor Massell seemed to regain some of the lost confidence from the business community by taking a firm position against the predominantly black employees public works strike. Although proclaiming that he was a friend of both organized labor and the blacks, Massell rejected the strikers' demands for a pay increase which he said the city could not afford. Massell held out until the union rank and file voted to accept the city's terms. Business leaders generally praised Massell's tough stand, while the black community did not criticize him.[20]

ACTIVE-NEGATIVE MAYORS

Unless a big city mayor is able to accommodate his party influence with his policy objectives, he may become only a political entrepreneur, an independent, or a polarizing figure. The success of the program-politicians, as previously noted, was based upon the accommodation of their partisan and program goals, particularly in attracting support for urban renewal. In effect, the attempts of the program-politicians to gain and develop party control characterize an antireform or "negative" style of mayoral leadership. For example, Mayor Lee of New Haven and Mayor Daley of Chicago saw no necessity to change the party machinery in order to mobilize city rebuilding programs. As described below, Daley of Chicago exercised nearly autocratic power over the city and county Democratic party, but he also enlisted substantial business support for downtown construction programs. Thus, boss-politicians operating within "unreformed" local parties may have "positive" leadership views toward particular community improvement policies. In contrast, the "polarizing" and "renegade" leadership styles are characterized by negative political campaigning, which exploits racial and community fear and antagonism. Such mayors either deny their municipal powers and blame others for local policy ineffectiveness, or they use inflammatory rhetoric in exploiting "law and order" demands as a reaction to the failures of previous programs which were not specifically designed for white ethnic constituencies.

Modern Boss-Politicians

As indicated in Chapter 1, the classic model of old-style boss rule and machine politics has largely disappeared from American cities. However, there are still a few mayors whose formal authority as weak or strong executives is less important than their skillful centralization of influence as party leaders. Such boss-politicians may provide the appearance and even the substance of modern, efficient executive management, but their real power is based upon ironclad control of the local party apparatus. As described by political scientists Edward C. Banfield and James O. Wilson, such boss-politicians assume the role of "brokers" to enhance and maintain their party influence:

> As a rule, the boss gets his initial stock of influence by virtue of holding a party or public office. He uses the authority of the office to acquire power, and then he uses the power to acquire more power and ultimately more authority. By "buying" bits of authority here and there . . . the boss accumulates a "working capital" of influence. Those who "sell" it to him receive in return jobs, party preferment, police protection, other bits of influence, and other considerations of value. The boss, like any investor, has to increase his influence if he is to maintain and increase it.[21]

Mayor Richard J. Daley of Chicago is not only the single best example of an incumbent boss-politician leader, but he is also perhaps the most powerful Democratic party mayor in the United States. Daley has served longer than any other mayor in Chicago's 134-year history.[22] In 1971, he was elected to his fifth four-year term with 70 percent of the popular vote, a victory margin that was only slightly below his 74 percent plurality in 1967.

What is the source of Daley's considerable political power and influence? A casual observer examining the formal governmental structure of Chicago might well conclude that the mayor is only one relatively unimportant actor in an extremely fragmented and de-centralized system. In theory, the "weak" mayor shares power with a host of elected and appointed city and Cook County officials, none of whom are responsible to each other, including the fifty-member city board of aldermen (councilmen elected from individual wards), the county board, the city and county clerks, the city and county treasurers, the city school board, the housing authority, the transit commission, and the county sheriff and coroner.

However, Mayor Daley has overcome the formal limits on vigorous executive leadership. His substantial power and influence emanate from his unchallenged supremacy as chairman of the Cook County Democratic Party Committee. As the party leader, Daley has imposed extensive centralization on the extremely decentralized governmental system. By skillfully building his influence as the master party "broker," Daley "slates" (designates) all Democratic party candidates for city and county elective offices, controls a sizeable bloc of state legislators (which all Illinois governors must reckon with), and leads the Illinois delegation to the quadrennial national Democratic party conventions (where Daley frequently plays the role of "king-maker" for aspiring presidential hopefuls).

The Cook County party organization, which consists of fifty city and thirty suburban township committeemen, mobilizes the neces-sary votes to elect Daley's handpicked candidates in the primaries and the general elections. If the expected voting margins for these candidates are not delivered, the party leaders not only face Daley's wrath, but even more importantly, the mayor can withhold favors and patronage jobs, which include some 12,000 city and 30,000 county government positions. Thus, Daley maintains a close scrutiny of the party rank and file, which can often prove to be intimidating for laggards:

> . . . One of the most withering experiences in a ward boss's life comes on election night. . . . Somewhat in the manner of a school-boy presenting his report card to a stern father, each of the 50 meets alone with Daley to submit his precinct-by-precinct vote. According to one insider who has observed the ritual, Daley sits at a desk and silently studies the tallies. If they please him, he rises and vigorously pumps both of the successful committeeman's hands. If they displease him, Daley gives the miscreant a blistering tongue-lashing. On one such occasion, the mayor was so incensed with a non-producer that he reached across his desk and began shaking him by his necktie.[23]

Daley's *role* as party boss should be distinguished from his mayoral leadership *style*, which has encompassed the urban renewal objectives of the program-politician mayors and the efficiency and economy goals of the municipal reform movement. Chicago's governing coalition includes the Democratic party machine, organized labor, the downtown business community, and suburban voters in Cook County. In return for noninterference in party affairs (other than backing the mayor for reelection), Mayor Daley provides each part of the coalition with enthusiastic endorsement for their particular objectives. Labor union leaders, many of whom are Daley's boyhood friends, are rewarded with high city construction wage rates, generous overtime pay, and appointments to prestigious boards and commissions. The predominantly Republican commercial, banking, and real estate interests support Daley's massive downtown urban renewal projects and multilane expressways, which have restored confidence in the city's economic base. Finally, Daley has catered to the "good government" reformers and the Cook County suburban constituency by preventing corruption in city hall (until recent charges of scandal), providing efficient municipal services with balanced budgets, and establishing an informal metropolitan system of government by offering the suburbs planning and technical assistance to help solve regionwide problems.

In recent years, Daley has assumed a tough "law and order" stance toward the black community. The governing coalition has generally refused to respond to demands for racial justice and minority group participation in the political process. Chicago's black community, which comprises about one-third of the population, is nearly totally isolated from the white power structure. Blacks suffer from inadequate social welfare services, high unemployment rates, and poor public schools. The black community cannot bring about meaningful change unless it accepts the old-style machine rules of the game. However, entrenched boss-politician leadership and the ruling elite are paying a price for perpetuating black powerlessness and the politically alienated anti-Daley forces. By fostering distrust, hostility, and despair among his political opponents, Daley and the ruling coalition encourage extremist and radical leaders to gain support for their revolutionary assaults on the political and social structure. Thus, while Chicago's political future under Mayor Daley's leadership is undebatable, the key problems for the future are: Can the hard line on social and political change be maintained indefinitely? And, what happens to Chicago's political life after Mayor Daley leaves office?

Renegades

The "renegade" leadership style is a variation of the previously described "maverick-independent" approach. After establishing party independence or gaining office in cities with nonpartisan elections, such mayors continue a highly personalized role in city hall. Such a leadership style is "active" because of electoral success, but it is also "negative" because the renegade mayor refuses to extend or denies his formal and informal leadership authority and influence to achieve tangible program benefits for his city. Instead of assuming direct responsibility for urban problems, he blames others for the management difficulties and social ills of his city.

If the electoral campaign themes of Peter Flaherty in Pittsburgh and Sam Massell of Atlanta emphasized "liberal" antiestablishment independence, former Mayor Samuel W. Yorty of Los Angeles provides the best example of an antiparty *conservative renegade*.[24] During his three terms as chief executive of California's largest sprawling metropolis, Yorty consistently exploited voters' fears of the allegedly threatening forces in American society while maintaining a personally flamboyant leadership style unmatched by most other big city mayors. While generally ignoring the normal daily burdens of the mayor's office, Yorty took active foreign policy positions in favor of the Vietnam War, conducted his own television "talk show," regularly visited many foreign countries, and campaigned for the presidential nomination in 1972.

As mayor of Los Angeles, Yorty's formal executive powers were extensively limited by the city charter and the extremely decentralized and fragmented local governmental system. The charter requires the chief executive to share authority with the city council and a host of independent administrative boards and commissions. Also, the county government performs a number of local and metropolitan areawide functions. The uncoordinated governmental framework of Los Angeles is somewhat similar to Chicago–Cook County, but it lacks Mayor Daley's politically centralizing influences. Unlike Chicago, Los Angeles has neither partisan elections nor a strong ward-based party organization. Not only do all California municipalities have nonpartisan elections, but there is also considerable use of direct democracy—the initiative, referendum, and recall. The "good government" reformers prevented the Los Angeles mayor from becoming a boss-politician by eliminating nearly all patronage and instituting a municipal civil service. Finally, political scientist Francis

M. Carney observes that the highly mobile, rootless California electorate is not very concerned about local politics:

> . . . Los Angeles has a low quotient of civic feeling. As a political community, it is highly attenuated. As a body politic, it is gangling and loose, and the nervous system which coordinates that sprawling body is haphazard and feeble. . . . Politics simply has a low visibility in Los Angeles. . . .[25]

Under such considerably decentralized and dispersed political and governmental conditions, it was not very surprising that Mayor Yorty built his reputation as a party maverick. He effectively employed a "devil theory" of politics by denying his formal powers and finding fault with others. Unlike the political and civic entrepreneurs who sought positive municipal objectives, Yorty took pride in doing as little as he could, dragging his feet, and blaming everyone else for his inaction.[26] In addition to the formal restrictions on his authority, Mayor Yorty blamed his alleged powerlessness on certain "anti-American" forces that were, in his view, dangerously undermining society. At various times, Yorty attacked "sinister" groups such as the Communist party, the Black Panthers, the Students for a Democratic Society, black rioters, student protesters, and black candidates for mayor. If his opponents disagreed with him, Yorty quickly charged them with character assassination, vilification, and hidden and discredited motives.[27] Such tactics were particularly dramatized in the 1969 and 1973 Los Angeles mayoral campaigns, when Yorty's chief opponent was Thomas Bradley, a black city councilman and former policeman. Both campaigns focused on the issues of race, "law and order," and Yorty's attempts to link Bradley with politically extremist groups.[28] After defeating Bradley in 1969, Yorty lost in 1973, apparently because Los Angeles voters were finally convinced that the flamboyant renegade leadership style of Yorty should be replaced by the more moderate political and civic entrepreneurship objectives articulated by Bradley, whose electoral victory made him the first black mayor of the nation's third largest city.

Polarizing Leadership

Polarizing leadership, a third variety of "active-negative" mayoral styles, occurs in cities reacting to the racial disorders and community conflicts of the 1960s. Instead of the *consensus* sought by the program-politicians and the cosmopolitans on urban renewal and social welfare objectives, the polarizing mayors try to exploit *dissensus,* or the local cleavages which drive apart different constituency groups. According to Levine and Kaufman, such conflict situations occur when "two or more groups are separated from one another by territory, class, caste, social position, race or religion. . . . [G]roups are crystallized and conscious of their separateness and distinctiveness."[29] Black demands for more political participation and influence (as described in Chapter 6) frequently cause a counter-reaction among white ethnic groups, who oppose integrated neighborhoods, busing to achieve racial balance in the public schools, and higher taxes to pay for social welfare programs from which no direct or tangible benefits are apparent. Within such cities, polarizing candidates, preaching "law and order," appeal directly to the "white resistance and hostility to black advances . . . in white-dominated, racially polarized communities."[30]

Frank L. Rizzo, the former police commissioner who was elected mayor of Philadelphia in 1971, illustrates the "partisan" style of polarizing leadership.[31] Without any previous experience in city politics, he developed an effective campaign organization with his own managers who cooperated directly with the remnants of Philadelphia's Democratic party machine. The campaign organization was a combination of the approaches used by political entrepreneurs and maverick-independents. Rizzo's popularity and reputation as Philadelphia's toughest "cop" transcended the local political organization, which had been previously run by Mayor James Tate, but Rizzo needed the voter mobilization efforts of the machine to transfer his personal popularity into an electoral victory. Secondly, Rizzo's primary and general campaign efforts were rather curiously muted. His personal flamboyance (somewhat similar to Yorty's reputation in Los Angeles) and well-known outspokenness and anger toward law-breakers were not dramatically emphasized. Instead, Rizzo ran a low-key campaign, trying to maintain the existing support of the city's large Italian, Irish, and Jewish populations. In contrast, Thatcher Longstreth, the Republican opponent, conducted a citywide "cosmopolitan"-style campaign, attempting to debate Rizzo, to accuse him of racism and antiblack antagonism, and to show his (Rizzo's) lack of understanding of municipal problems. However, Longstreth's efforts failed because of Rizzo's strong personal appeal to white ethnic voters and middle- and working-class homeowners. The white electorate knew what to expect from Rizzo, despite Longstreth's vigorous campaign efforts.

Upon assuming office, Rizzo reasserted his personal flamboyance by attacking the Democratic machine, hostile newspaper reporters, and opposing bureaucrats and other city officials. His "partisan" leadership style was no more effective than the cosmopolitans, even though his constituency remained united behind him. Philadelphia had tremendous budgetary difficulties, federal funds for various programs were reduced, and the school teachers led a long and costly strike. Also, the city's crime rate was not substantially reduced under Rizzo's leadership. Thus, by 1973, Mayor Rizzo had not achieved many tangible program innovations. He confronted local conflicts with much energy, but his "partisan" style represented more of the appearance of action than the achievement of substantive policy results.[32]

PASSIVE-POSITIVE LEADERSHIP: CARETAKERS

Unlike that of the activist mayors, the passive leadership style avoids conscious efforts to centralize party influence or to exercise civic entrepreneurship. Rather, local conflict is diffused by asserting likeable, comfortable, and unthreatening community images. Local campaigns frequently deal with "community service" and the reelection of reliable officials, who pledge to maintain low tax rates. Caretaker government is found most frequently in small or medium-sized communities, with relatively homogeneous populations, having few threatening or ominous local problems, and a traditional or nonpartisan attachment to maintain the status quo. According to political scientist Charles Adrian, caretaker leadership de-emphasizes program innovations so that "governments should perform only traditional functions at a minimum level of service."[33] In such localities, the mayor is usually only one among several officials on the council who make noncontroversial decisions. Clerks or council-appointed managers are more likely to deal with daily administrative matters. Most governmental actions reflect the needs of local retail businessmen, real estate operators, or long-time community residents.

PASSIVE-NEGATIVE LEADERSHIP:
FIGUREHEADS OR EVADERS

In contrast to the caretaker, who promotes community service and stability by defending the status quo, the evader remains in the background, permitting others to assume major political, governmental, and policy responsibilities. Such mayors dislike publicity, avoid politi-

cal conflict, and apply moralistic standards to governmental problems. As defined by Duane Lockard, evaders consciously avoid
"notoriety or excessive publicity as pushers of anything notable. . . .
To assure their tenure they avoid commitments, seek zealously to
placate disputes, and follow the lead set by councilmen or other
actors."[34]

While many mayors find it useful to evade or delay action on some
issues, there are some who adopt a consciously nonpolitical or figure-
head leadership style. Jeffrey Pressman's portrait of Oakland's Mayor
John Reading is a good example of such passive-negative leadership.[35]
Oakland, a California city of approximately 362,000 population, has
a council-manager government with the mayor presiding over the
council, responsible for leading public opinion, and initiating legislation, while the council formulates policy and the manager imple-
ments it. However, in practice, Mayor Reading, who has served four
two-year terms, defers most of his formal policy leadership to the
council and to Manager Jerome Keithley, who "has gained . . . the
solid and enthusiastic support of the council . . ." and is "unusually
adept at dealing with the internal environment of city government."[36]
With the manager's administrative leadership and cooperation with
the council, Mayor Reading, unlike his predecessor, underutilizes his
formal and informal political resources. He neither lobbies for proposals nor uses pressure to persuade the council. Instead, Reading
avoids direct intervention and remains in the background. He is "a
political leader who does not like politics," a man who "deals with
political problems in a moralistic way," and who "finds it difficult to
deal with conflict in politics."[37]

Thus, the passive-negative evader does not agonize over social conflict like the cosmopolitan mayor, does not provide conflict and
confrontation as do the maverick-independents and the polarizing
mayors, underutilizes his political and civic entrepreneurship in contrast to the program and boss-politicians, and does not even blame
others for his powerlessness, as do the renegades. Instead, his inactivity and passivity permit a nonpolitical perception of urban conflict. The mayor remains noncommittal as problems and solutions are
deferred to other actors. The evader becomes a non–decision-maker
as others decide upon the priorities of the urban agenda.

LEADERSHIP IN COUNCIL-MANAGER SYSTEMS

Chapter 3 reviewed the basic components of the council-manager
plan, which was proposed by the reformers as the most desirable

structural innovation for local government. The reform sought a council, elected at-large on nonpartisan ballots, responsible for making policy and hiring a full-time professional manager to handle administrative matters. In assuming a separation between policy and administration, the reformers viewed the manager as an engineer or technician carrying out the will of the council by dealing with such routine housekeeping matters as physical construction and maintenance, balanced budgets, and daily supervision of city departments.

Council-manager government is now widespread throughout the country. By 1970, the plan included 47 percent of all cities over 5,000 population, a majority of all cities over 10,000 population, and covered all states except Hawaii and Indiana.[38] What are the relationships between the original design of council-manager government and present-day realities? Do managers, councilmen, and mayors view their roles as different from those of the early reformers? What are the policy and administrative perceptions of managers, mayors, and councilmen?

The council-manager plan can best be understood through an examination of leadership roles assumed by the major actors in the political and policy environment. Such an analysis provides useful insights on the varieties of managerial, council, and mayoral leadership in medium- and smaller-sized cities outside of the central core of metropolitan areas which retain the strong mayor system.

First, the artificial separation between policy-making and administration cannot be applied to the crucial advisory role of the manager in informing the council. Modern city managers play important political and policy roles despite myths concerning their administrative neutrality. According to Karl Bosworth, "the manager *is* a politician" because he reports nearly all issues which the council wishes to consider, brings policy ideas to the council, makes proposals, initiates policy studies, and even argues with its members.[39]

Second, city managers have resources which can be used to enhance their influence with the council. According to political scientists John C. Bollens and John C. Ries, these resources include:

Expertise: The manager views himself as a professional because of his college training, association with other managers, and membership in the International City Management Association. His background and full-time capacity provide knowledge of the *rules* about city government procedures, including the charter, court decisions, agency functions, county, state, and federal laws. Expertise is also evident in the manager's ability to gather *information* and facts regarding governmental services and functions.

Budget Control: Managers can influence the council on budget requests and allocations because they are chiefly responsible for collecting departmental estimates, adjusting them, and presenting proposals to the council, which is more concerned with tax rates and revenue sources than with allocations.

Administrative Supervision: Since the manager is a full-time administrator, while most councilmen are part-time elected officials, he has daily oversight of ongoing departmental activities, which enables access to information and discretionary authority in applying ordinances, granting licenses, etc.[40]

Obviously, the manager's personality will determine his use of resources in playing either an active or passive role in attempting to influence the council and becoming an innovator in policy matters. Political scientist Ronald Loveridge, in analyzing questionnaire responses from fifty-nine managers and 338 councilmen in the San Francisco Bay Area region, provides valuable insights on the policy role perceptions of managers and councilmen.[41] First, most managers reject the old-style administrative neutrality (or politics-administration dichotomy) role and believe strongly that they should be *innovators* and *advocates* in municipal policy. Second, managers are less certain about their *political* roles. They divided 55–45 percent regarding whether or not managers should support controversial or divisive community policies, and they agreed only by 53–47 percent that managers should work through the most powerful members of the community to achieve policy goals. Third, most managers strongly opposed involvement in partisan politics, rejecting roles as *political recruiters* for council candidates and as *campaigners* for incumbent councilmen seeking reelection.

Loveridge then applied these findings to a manager leadership classification, as shown in Table 5–2. Using the categories of *political* and *administrative* orientations, Loveridge found that activist managers are either *political leaders* or *political executives* and have the broadest view of the policy advocacy role. These are the innovators, who participate in resolving conflict but reject partisan political activity. The political orientation is distinguished by executive styles, which are more pragmatic and less moralistic than political styles. In contrast, the *administrative* role perception is closer to the reformers' original views of the manager. *Directors* or *technicians* avoid policy innovation by narrowly defining their roles. Such managers are more advisory, show more restraint, and support the status quo by remaining subordinate to the council and confining themselves to routine, housekeeping administrative functions.

In contrast to the managers' emphasis on policy advocacy, Loveridge found that most councilmen view managers as *adminis-*

TABLE 5–2   A Typology of Manager Leadership Styles
                                Policy Orientation

Political (more positive)	*Administrative (more negative)*
Leader	Director
Executive	Technician
	Assistant

trators (directors, technicians, or assistants) who should merely carry out policy, be advisers, inform councilmen, and avoid activism and advocacy in the policy and political processes. What accounts for this divergence in policy role perceptions? Since councilmen are elected, they have political constituencies, while managers are appointed professional administrators. Councilmen are part-time officials; managers are full-time operatives. Managers and councilmen have different policy orientations and frames of reference. Managers have common socioeconomic backgrounds and are trained toward a cosmopolitan policy view, while councilmen have diverse origins and respond to local and particularistic concerns.

How are these contrasting policy role perceptions resolved? Can activist managers function effectively in communities where councilmen consider managers as directors, technicians, or assistants? Loveridge suggests that, notwithstanding most councilmen's responses, the council usually expects managers to participate in policy. The concern of most councilmen is the style of manager advocacy and involvement. This results in a high degree of frustration for activist managers. They must adopt compromise strategies to facilitate good working relations with councilmen. These include (1) camouflaging advocacy by avoiding open conflict and resorting to private or informal channels to influence councilmen, (2) promoting change in relatively safe areas, and (3) advising solutions in relatively controversial areas.

LEADERSHIP PATTERNS AND COMMUNITY VALUES

Council-manager relations are also related to a community's political values. The environment of local government affects the policy role perceptions of managers, mayors, and councilmen. In this regard, political scientists Oliver Williams and Charles Adrian have developed a typology to classify cities by major functional orientations.[42] While each of the four functions may represent an "ideal type" or an abstraction of reality, nevertheless they are useful in relating political, policy, and administrative leadership to particular community situations. The four major community types are:

(1) *The city as an instrument of economic growth.* Usually located in rapidly expanding suburban sections of metropolitan areas, such communities are experiencing population expansion, industrial and commercial development, and housing construction. Government and business promote the local "boom" by actively supporting economic activities. Local merchants, businessmen, bankers, newspaper editors, and government officials and bureaucrats become local "boosters." They seek zoning ordinances, reduced property taxes, and other subsidies to benefit commerce, to develop industrial parks, and to provide utilities and improve transportation.

(2) *The city as a provider of life's amenities.* These are usually middle- and upper-income suburbs which seek to preserve an agreed-upon and valued way of life. Characterized by homogeneous populations, retired people and young families, such communities emphasize consumption and services rather than industries. Education, public safety, beautification, and recreation are highly valued. Government services are maximized for given tax rates.

(3) *The city as maintainer of traditional services or "caretaker government."* Usually located outside of the central core and away from expanding or "bedroom" suburbs, such localities de-emphasize governmental activity and rely on local market decisions. Government reflects the interests of local merchants, businessmen, and property owners. Services, taxes, and government costs are kept at minimum levels. Zoning, planning, and other land-use regulations are opposed.

(4) *The city as arbiter of conflicting interests.* Central cities of metropolitan areas are so large and contain so many diverse interests that government emphasizes the process rather than the substance of community action. Neighborhood and welfare-oriented groups, including ethnics and racial minorities, compete for political influence, seek access, and make claims for special representation. Government tries to find satisfactory accommodations in arbitrating between competing interests.

Council-mayoral-manager relationships vary according to the different kinds of functional emphases found in these four types of communities. Loveridge discovered that economic growth (Type 1) and amenities (Type 2) predominated in three out of four Bay Area cities, but that there was no significant difference in the political or administrative orientations of the managers (see Table 5–2) even though it might have been expected that strong, activist managers would be most adaptable to these kinds of communities. Passive or administrative managers with director, technician, or assistant roles were associated with caretaker communities. Finally, activist managers were most likely to be found in arbiter governments even though the levels and degrees of community conflict might be highly dangerous and untenable for managers who cannot effectively accommodate such controversy.

The survival of activist managers in larger cities characterized by political conflict appears to depend upon their skills in developing effective alliances with the ruling factions on the city council. Banfield and Wilson suggest four patterns of conflict resolution for managers in larger cities.[43] First, the manager can *lead* the council in cities characterized by an approximately equal division between different factions when he has a strong personality to play off one side against the other. Second, the manager may become the *servant* of the council in cities where the factions are divided equally and the manager avoids antagonizing either side. Third, the manager may have confidence of a stable majority or a faction holding the balance of power. In such cases, the manager becomes the *informal leader of the majority faction.* Finally, the city may have an *unstable majority*, and the manager is required to develop a majority consensus on each issue by persuading councilmen to go along with him. Unless he is unusually skillful in such situations, the manager cannot resolve conflict and his tenure is brief.

The manager's success in any of the large city cleavage or conflict situations is also related to his alliances with active-positive mayors. In their study of forty-five council-manager cities with populations of greater than 100,000, political scientists Robert Boynton and Deil Wright found that the most typical pattern of policy-initiating and policy-making is a "team pattern" between managers and mayors.[44] In the *policy-initiating* team, the mayor and selected councilmen develop public support, and the manager gathers and distributes information for public officials. In the *policy-making* team, the mayor, the councilmen, and the manager are actively involved in gaining public support for governmental action. Finally, the *governing team* includes a frankly political role for the manager, whose tenure is directly linked with the mayor or the stability of community leadership.

These leadership patterns imply a linkage between council-manager and strong mayor cities. The institutional structure of cities and suburbs may be less important than the styles of community leadership employed for policy and political purposes. Boynton and Wright suggest that "active-positive" leadership is associated with the mayor-manager team patterns. The previous discussion of mayoral leadership indicated that the program-politicians and the cosmopolitans were political and civic entrepreneurs emphasizing policy action and program results. Also, active-positive mayors and managers are not always assured of success, particularly because of the lack of resources and opposition within the local political constituencies. Therefore, critical city and suburban problems may not be solved even with active-positive mayors and managers, although the other local leadership styles may not be any more successful. In any event, the study of community leadership, as Boynton and Wright observe, can provide a convergence of approaches used by mayors and managers and a linkage between "reformed" and "unreformed" government structures:

> If our judgment concerning the existence of explicitly political "executive" teams is correct, then it would appear that the division between council-manager systems as they are found in larger urban communities and the so-called strong-mayor systems is not as great as has formerly been suggested. . . . To the extent that the "unreformed" systems use professional skills, they approximate one of the executive team patterns found in the adaptive council-manager cities. To the extent that the council-manager systems provide mechanisms for the articulation and transference of community demands, they draw closer to the unreformed forms.[45]

NOTES

1. Marilyn Gittell, "Metropolitan Mayors: Dead End," *Public Administration Review*, Vol. 23, No. 1 (March 1963), pp. 20–21.
2. *Ibid.,* p. 20.
3. *Report of the National Advisory Commission on Civil Disorders* (Washington, D.C.: U.S. Government Printing Office, 1968), p. 155.
4. James Q. Wilson, "The Mayors vs. The Cities," *The Public Interest*, No. 16 (Summer 1969), p. 36.
5. Jeffrey L. Pressman, "Preconditions of Mayoral Leadership," *American Political Science Review*, Vol. 66, No. 2 (June 1972), p. 512.
6. James D. Barber, *The Presidential Character* (Englewood Cliffs, N.J.: Prentice-Hall, 1972), pp. 11–13.
7. Charles H. Levine and Clifford Kaufman, "Urban Conflict As A Constraint on Mayoral Leadership: Lessons From Gary and Cleveland," (Paper delivered at annual meeting of Northeast Political Science Association, Amherst, Mass., November 1972), p. 4.
8. Duane Lockard, *The Politics of State and Local Government*, 2nd ed. (New York: Macmillan, 1969), p. 390.
9. M. Kent Jennings, *Community Influentials* (New York: Free Press of Glencoe, 1964), pp. 199–201.

10. Jeanne R. Lowe, *Cities in a Race With Time* (New York: Random House, Vintage Books, 1967), Ch. 8, "Survival Through Planning: Philadelphia's Style."
11. Robert A. Dahl, *Who Governs?* (New Haven, Conn.: Yale University Press, 1961), pp. 121–122.
12. *Ibid.*, p. 130.
13. Herbert J. Gans, "The Failure of Urban Renewal," in *Urban Renewal: The Record and the Controversy*, ed. James Q. Wilson (Cambridge, Mass.: M.I.T. Press, 1966), p. 539.
14. Wilson, "The Mayors," pp. 25–37.
15. Bruce M. Stave, *The New Deal and the Last Hurrah: Pittsburgh Machine Politics* (Pittsburgh: University of Pittsburgh Press, 1970).
16. Bruce W. Gibbons, "Bye-bye Machine," *Commonweal* (June 20, 1969), p. 383.
17. *The New York Times*, October 22, 1969, p. 25, col. 5–6.
18. *Ibid.*, November 9, 1969, p. 53, col. 1.
19. Reese Cleghorn, "Nixon's Southern Strategy: Shooting an Elephant," *The Nation* (March 30, 1970), p. 359.
20. *The New York Times*, March 30, 1970, p. 49, col. 6–8.
21. Edward C. Banfield and James Q. Wilson, *City Politics* (New York: Random House, Vintage Books, 1963), pp. 104–105. For a more thorough analysis of decision-making and political power in Chicago's decentralized system, see: Edward C. Banfield, *Political Influence* (New York: Free Press, 1961), Ch. 8, "The Structure of Influence."
22. *The New York Times*, April 7, 1971, p. 22, col. 1.
23. "Chicago's Daley: How to Run a City," *Newsweek* (April 5, 1971), p. 82.
24. For a biographical account of Mayor Yorty's career, see: John C. Bollens and Grant B. Geyer, *Yorty: Politics of a Constant Candidate* (Pacific Palisades, Calif.: Palisades, 1973).
25. Francis M. Carney, "The Decentralized Politics of Los Angeles," *The Annals*, Vol. 353 (May 1964), p. 116.
26. Jack Langguth, "Yorty Has His Eye on the Big Apple," *The New York Times Magazine* (September 17, 1967), p. 32.
27. *Ibid.*, p. 114.
28. For an account of the 1969 mayoral contest, see: Richard L. Maullin, "Los Angeles Liberalism," *Trans-Action*, Vol. 8, No. 7 (May 1971), pp. 40–51.
29. Levine and Kaufman, "Urban Conflict," p. 14.
30. *Ibid.*, p. 15.
31. Fred Hamilton, *Rizzo: From Cop to Mayor of Philadelphia* (New York: Viking, 1973), and Lenora E. Berson, "The Toughest Cop in America Campaigns for Mayor of Philadelphia," *The New York Times Magazine* (May 16, 1971), pp. 30–31, 52–71.
32. Hamilton, *Rizzo*, pp. 191–204, and *The New York Times*, January 7, 1973, p. 56, col. 3–6.
33. Charles R. Adrian, "The Quality of Urban Leadership," in Henry J. Schmandt and Warner Bloomberg, Jr., *The Quality of Urban Life*, *Urban Affairs Annual Reviews*, Vol. 3 (Beverly Hills, Calif.: Sage Publications, 1969), pp. 388–389.
34. Lockard, *The Politics of State and Local Government*, 2nd ed., p. 392.
35. Pressman, *American Political Science Review*, Vol. 66 (June 1972), pp. 511–524.
36. *Ibid.*, p. 515.
37. *Ibid.*, pp. 518–519.

38. Keith F. Mulrooney, "The American City Manager," *Public Administration Review*, Vol. 31, No. 1 (January/February 1971), p. 8.
39. Karl A. Bosworth, "The Manager is a Politician," *Public Administration Review*, Vol. 18, No. 3 (Summer 1958), p. 218.
40. John C. Bollens and John C. Ries, *The City Manager Profession: Myths and Realities* (Chicago: Public Administration Service, 1969), pp. 18–21.
41. Ronald O. Loveridge, *City Managers in Legislative Politics* (Indianapolis, Ind.: Bobbs-Merrill, 1971); and "The City Manager in Legislative Politics," *Polity*, Vol. 1, No. 2 (Winter 1968), pp. 213–236.
42. Oliver P. Williams and Charles R. Adrian, *Four Cities* (Philadelphia, Pa.: University of Pennsylvania Press, 1963); and Oliver P. Williams, "A Typology for Comparative Local Government," *Midwest Journal of Political Science*, Vol. 5, No. 2 (May 1961), pp. 150–164.
43. Banfield and Wilson, *City Politics*, pp. 177–180.
44. Robert P. Boynton and Deil S. Wright, "Mayor-Manager Relationships in Large Council-Manager Cities: A Reinterpretation," *Public Administration Review*, Vol. 31, No. 1 (January/February 1971), pp. 32–34.
45. *Ibid.*, p. 35.

SUGGESTIONS FOR FURTHER READING

Allen, Ivan, Jr. "Growing Up Liberal in Atlanta," *The New York Times Magazine* (December 27, 1970), pp. 4–5, 32–33.
Discussion of Mayor Allen's political career in Atlanta.

Armstrong, Richard A. "The Re-education of John Lindsay," *The New York Times Magazine* (October 8, 1972), pp. 11, 54–65.
His modest record of achievement did not seem adequate as Mayor Lindsay's political future was uncertain in late 1972.

Banfield, Edward C. *Political Influence*. New York: Free Press, 1961.
Six case studies of civic projects in Chicago which show how the mayor centralizes influence over a decentralized system.

Berson, Lenora E. "The Toughest Cop in America Campaigns for Mayor of Philadelphia," *The New York Times Magazine* (May 16, 1971), pp. 30–31, 52–71.
Indicates the power exercised by Police Commissioner Frank Rizzo before he became mayor of Philadelphia.

Bollens, John C., and Grant B. Geyer. *Yorty: Politics of a Constant Candidate*. Pacific Palisades, Calif.: Palisades, 1973.
Biographical account of the flamboyant mayor of Los Angeles.

Bollens, John C., and John C. Ries. *The City Manager Profession: Myths and Realities*. Chicago: Public Administration Service, 1969.
Brief monograph comparing and contrasting the original structure of council-manager government with modern roles, community environment, and the future of the manager profession.

Boynton, Robert P. and Deil S. Wright. "Mayor-Manager Relationships in Large Cities: A Reinterpretation," *Public Administration Review*, Vol. 31, No. 1 (January/February 1971), pp. 28–36.

Study of leadership interaction patterns find that activist mayors and managers employ a team approach in policy initiation and policy-making.

Dahl, Robert A. *Who Governs?* New Haven: Yale University Press, 1961.
Analysis of community power in New Haven, Connecticut, indicating that Mayor Lee formed an executive-centered coalition in exercising leadership.

George, Alexander L. "Political Leadership and Social Change in American Cities," *Daedalus*, Vol. 97, No. 4 (Fall 1968), pp. 1194–1217.
Identifies political and civic entrepreneurship as key characteristics of program-politician mayors.

Gittell, Marilyn. "Metropolitan Mayors: Dead End," *Public Administration Review*, Vol. 23 (March 1963), pp. 20–25.
A description of how, in the past, most mayors were predestined to political oblivion.

Hamilton, Fred. *Rizzo: From Cop to Mayor of Philadelphia*. New York: Viking Press, 1973.
Biographical account of Philadelphia's politicized police commissioner, focusing upon the primary campaign and general election of 1971.

Lindsay, John V. *The City*. New York: The New American Library, Signet Books, 1969.
Mayor Lindsay discusses his political and policy problems as chief executive of the nation's largest city.

Loveridge, Ronald O. *City Managers in Legislative Politics*. Indianapolis: Bobbs-Merrill, 1971.
Interesting study of diverging policy role perceptions of councilmen and managers in the San Francisco Bay Area region.

Lowe, Jeanne R. *Cities in a Race With Time*. New York: Random House, Vintage Books, 1967.
Big city mayoral leadership in urban renewal and antipoverty programs.

Lowi, Theodore J. "Why Mayors Go Nowhere," *Washington Monthly* (January 1972), pp. 55–61.
Lack of resources hinders effectiveness of New York City mayors.

Maier, Henry W. *Challenge to the Cities*. New York: Random House, 1966.
Milwaukee's Mayor Maier discusses his problems and offers a model of executive decision-making.

Maullin, Richard L. "Los Angeles Liberalism," *Trans-Action*, Vol. 8, No. 7 (May 1971), pp. 40–51.
Analysis of 1969 Los Angeles mayoral contest between Samuel Yorty and Thomas Bradley.

Powledge, Fred. "The Flight From City Hall," *Harper's* (November 1969), pp. 69–86.

Former mayors discuss problems and prospects of managing large cities.

Pressman, Jeffrey L. "Preconditions of Mayoral Leadership," *American Political Science Review*, Vol. 66, No. 2 (June 1972), pp. 511–524.
Analysis of passive leadership style of Oakland's Mayor John Reading.

Rogers, David. *The Management of Big Cities*. Beverly Hills, Calif.: Sage Publications, 1971.
Developing consensus among competing interest groups in New York City, Philadelphia, and Cleveland.

Royko, Mike. *Boss: Richard J. Daley of Chicago*. New York: New American Library Signet Books, 1971.
Muckraking account of Chicago's boss-politician mayor.

Ruchelman, Leonard I., ed. *Big City Mayors*. Bloomington: Indiana University Press, 1969.
Selected essays on political and administrative roles of city chief executives.

Salisbury, Robert H. "Urban Politics: The New Convergence of Power," *Journal of Politics*, Vol. 26 (November 1964), pp. 775–797.
Local decision-making structure is dominated by a governing coalition consisting of the mayor, technical experts, and businessmen.

Serrin, William. "How One Big City Defeated Its Mayor," *The New York Times Magazine* (October 27, 1968), pp. 39, 134–139.
The rise and fall of Detroit's Mayor Jerome P. Cavanagh.

Stave, Bruce M. *The New Deal and the Last Hurrah*. Pittsburgh: University of Pittsburgh Press, 1970.
Analysis of Pittsburgh's Democratic party political machine.

Talbot, Allan R. *The Mayor's Game*. New York: Harper & Row, 1967.
Political and civic leadership of Mayor Richard Lee in New Haven, Connecticut urban renewal and antipoverty programs.

Williams, Oliver P., and Charles R. Adrian. *Four Cities*. Philadelphia: University of Pennsylvania Press, 1963.
Development of a typology to classify communities by functional attributes: economic growth, amenities, caretaker, or arbiter.

Wilson, James Q. "The Mayors vs. the Cities," *The Public Interest*, Vol. 16 (Summer 1969), pp. 25–37.
Identifies a constituency-audience conflict for big city mayors.

6

Black Politics

INTRODUCTION

Municipal and metropolitan reform, with all of its attempts to change the urban political climate and governmental structure, planning, and financial aid, focus primarily on political power as it relates to structure of government and the various forms of mayoral and managerial leadership. At the same time, the previous five chapters emphasized the urban problems of inner-city minorities, particularly blacks. We move next to the political problems and prospects of America's black people. Our goal is to show the relationships between national trends and city politics, particularly the developments of the Civil Rights Movement at the national level and black politics at the local level. Black politics is an important illustration of the roots of urban conflict. We argue that political and policy solutions are necessary to get at the underlying causes of such conflict in order to reduce black-white tensions. This chapter and the subsequent ones focus particular attention on policies that are emerging to deal with these problems.

America's black population is not only the largest racial minority, but it is also the most urbanized. The urban unrest of the 1960s could be explained, in part, as a political conflict between whites and blacks. As blacks migrated from the rural areas and cities of the

South to the industrial cities of the North, Midwest, and West, they affected the character, style, and substance of city politics. By the mid-1960s, the considerable poverty, unemployment, and other social and economic disabilities of blacks led to urban conflicts, riots, and confrontations on a scale never before experienced in the United States.

What are the sources of black political activity in the cities? What are the major strategies and tactics of black politics? What leadership styles are employed by black spokesmen to achieve policy goals? What are the trends of black electoral activity? Until recently, blacks were unable to develop bases of political power which would enable them to participate in decisions affecting their lives. Blacks encountered major obstacles in gaining access to power in the cities. Unlike other ethnic groups, blacks did not benefit from either the material rewards of machine politics or from the "good government" reforms which replaced the bosses. Instead, the black minority was subjected to the political control of the white majority.

More recently, black leaders (and for that matter other minority leaders) have become reform advocates of community control, neighborhood government, and participatory democracy, which harks back to the goals of the early machine politicians (see Chapter 1) who, after all, originally saw themselves as the champions of the downtrodden immigrants.

The protests associated with the Civil Rights Movement beginning in the mid-fifties and the spontaneous rioting in the sixties provided the psychological, political, and organizational bases for politicizing blacks. Specifically, the protest tactics of the Civil Rights Movement led to the passage of the first federal civil rights legislation since Reconstruction. From 1957 to 1965, five major laws were enacted covering access to public accommodations, employment, voting rights, even lynching. Throughout the 1960s, when expectations were running high and evidence of actual progress was meager, the riots served to release the frustrations and pent-up anger of blacks. Indeed, the riots could be viewed as an aggressive reaction to oppressions which replaced the earlier, more common, submissive behavior which involved repression of anger and a loss of self-respect. The riots also dispelled old fears of reprisal and paved the way for the emergence of black leaders after centuries of intimidation and political impotency. The riots also brought white Americans face to face with the contradiction of exclusion and discrimination in a polity dedicated to an egalitarian ethic.

By the close of the 1960s, black attitudes and activism had taken four distinct directions, all of which had historical precedents, but one of which had solid new ground in cities where blacks were approaching majorities or strong pluralities. The four directions were (1) politicalization in cities where blacks had a solid foothold either in numbers or leadership or both; (2) the strengthening of the Civil Rights Movement in increasingly radical actions and in the martyrdom of its most influential leader, Dr. Martin Luther King, Jr.; (3) the rise of insurrectionist and revolutionary activist groups; and (4) the disillusionment and apathy of the deprived masses who bore the brunt of a widening economic gap between blacks and whites. (See Figure 6–1.) This chapter examines each of these aspects of black protest (apathy is a form of silent protest) and their effect on black politics in cities.

A PERSPECTIVE

In the century following the War Between the States, black Americans continued the struggle for the full benefits of legal citizenship accorded them in the Emancipation Proclamation by President Lincoln in 1863 and in the Thirteenth (1865) and Fourteenth (1870) Amendments to the Constitution. They discovered, as have other ethnic groups, that legal citizenship is only the first step toward full citizenship, for citizenship embraces political and social concepts as well as legal ones.[1]

The subsequent rise in the numbers of blacks holding political office at all levels of government throughout the nation is evidence that the voting power of blacks is being translated into effective political power. Across the South 1,144 blacks held elective positions in 1974. In the nation the total had climbed to over 2600—including 86 mayors, 1,149 other elected officials, 657 school board members, and 143 law enforcement officers. The major cities that have elected black mayors since 1967 are: Newark, 1970 (Kenneth Gibson); Gary, Indiana, 1967 (Richard G. Hatcher); Atlanta, 1973 (Maynard Jackson); Los Angeles, 1973 (Thomas Bradley); Cleveland, 1967 to 1971 (Carl Stokes); Detroit, 1973 (Coleman Young); and Washington, D.C., has had a black mayor since 1967 by presidential appointment (Walter Washington). In 1974 blacks controlled the Board of Education, and a black congressman represented the city. There were 209 black lawmakers in thirty-seven state legislatures. Blacks were a majority on the city councils of Brighton, Alabama; Highland Park, Michigan; Maywood, Illinois; Compton, California; and Lawn-

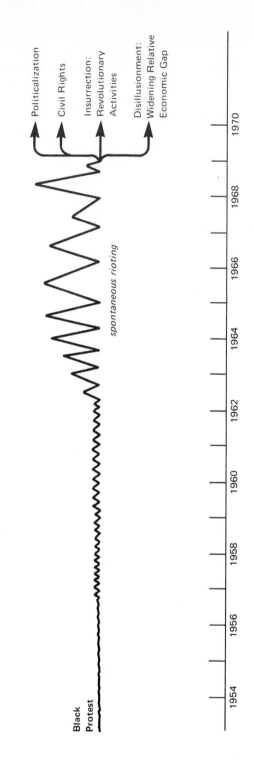

FIGURE 6-1   Black Protest and Politicalization, 1954–1970

Issues:
   Citizen Rights
   Legal-Political-Social
   Assimilation and Integration

Black
Protest

spontaneous rioting

Politicalization

Civil Rights

Insurrection:
Revolutionary
Activities

Disillusionment:
Widening Relative
Economic Gap

1954   1956   1958   1960   1962   1964   1966   1968   1970

side, New Jersey. For the most part, black majority city councils were found in small cities and towns where there was a majority of blacks. There were sixteen black representatives and one senator in the U.S. Congress.

As blacks gain political office, they achieve respect among whites and provide incentive for increased political activity among black citizens. However, social citizenship—the equal and unobstructed access to the channels and institutions of social mobility and welfare —remains the central issue of discrimination and exclusion, and it is this issue to which black protest continues to address its activities. Social barriers, especially in education, effectively hold back the development of leadership, which is the key to political and economic efficacy.

Thus, the problem black Americans still face in achieving full and effective citizenship is pervasive white prejudice; to point out the gradual lowering of discriminatory barriers is not to deny their continuing presence.[2]

While the situation of black Americans is steadily improving, the absolute economic gap between blacks and whites continues to widen. In 1970, blacks were earning more money and were better employed than ever before, but whites were making gains faster. In 1972, 33.7 percent of black families had incomes of $10,000 or more, as compared with 59.2 percent of white families. These figures contrast with those of 1960 when only 13.3 percent of black families had that much income, compared with 35.9 percent of white families. By 1972, the median income of nonwhite families had risen to $7,106, while that of white families had risen to $11,549. Table 6–1 shows other measures of change since 1960 which further illustrate the widening gaps in progress between blacks and whites. These trends average together all ages, levels of education, and regions. The figures outside the South reflect more positive trends where black family income grows more and more equal to that of whites, especially among black males of younger professional families. In the North and West, black males under thirty-five years of age earn 96 percent of the salaries of their white counterparts.[3]

American leadership understands political power and respects it. The problem blacks now confront is no longer so much that of a white heel on the necks of blacks, as it is the blacks' capacity to coalesce a base of political power among themselves and with other minority groups. Why have blacks taken so long in achieving political power when other ethnic groups in the past have succeeded? What explains the disproportionate number of blacks who remain impov-

TABLE 6–1   A Measure of Change Since 1960

	*Non-white	White	Black
Percent of age group who are high school graduates			
25-29 years			
1960	38.6	63.7	
1972		81.5	64.0
Percent of age group who are college graduates			
25-29 years			
1960	5.4	11.8	
1972		19.9	8.3

SOURCE: Bureau of the Census
*All races other than white

	Non-white	White
Professional and Technical workers		
(percent of each work force)		
1960	4.8	12.1
1972	9.5	14.6
Percent of each work force unemployed		
1960	10.2	4.9
1972	10.0	5.0

SOURCE: Bureau of Labor Statistics

	Non-white	White
Percent of families with income of $10,000 or more		
(adjusted for price changes in 1972 constant dollars)		
1960	13.3	35.9
1972	33.7	59.2

SOURCE: Bureau of the Census

	Non-white	White
Life Expectancy at birth (in years)		
1960	63.6	70.6
1972 (prelim.)	65.5	72.1

SOURCE: National Center for Health Statistics

	Non-white	White
Median Income of Families		
(in 1972 constant dollars)		
1960	$4,564	$8,267
1972	$7,106	$11,549

SOURCE: Bureau of the Census

erished, uneducated, and alienated? Why in the past did so many talented black political leaders turn away from the ghetto or exploit it?

The social and political disabilities of the blacks stemmed largely from a historical experience in a uniquely restrictive and brutalizing slavery system, followed by a prolonged period of economic and political subjugation which perpetuated the psychological effects of slavery. That subjugation continues in the present day in forms only less obvious and overt than in the past.

During slavery, self-esteem was gained at the expense of group cohesiveness and ethnic pride. Slaves assigned to household duties had status over field hands, mixed bloods over pure blacks, and so on. There was division between troublesome slaves and "good slaves," and between slaves and freemen. The entire psychological identity of blacks in the slave culture was toward the dominant white. The rivalry in the slave culture was deliberately fostered by the white masters. Slaves adopted the values of their masters because there was no possibility of developing their own, and this fact accounts for the emergence of a black aristocracy of skin color and hair texture, which in turn were symbols of the degree of white ancestry. This orientation persists to the present, and many blacks and most whites still believe in a generalized, if not absolute, inferiority of blacks.

For the middle-class, educated, urban black in the present day who has tried to cast off the negative traits of slavery, the dilemma is one of enforced proximity to abhorrent values and simultaneous exclusion by whites, whose values the aspiring blacks have assimilated. As Ron Karenga, the founder of the black national organization US, once remarked to a group of middle-class blacks: "You want to be white, but the man won't let you be; and you ain't gut-bucket enough to run with the bloods." Thus, the middle-class black is left in limbo between the aspiration of acceptance among whites and rejection of the lower class of the ghetto where he lives.

For decades blacks who achieved middle-class status steered clear of the aspects of white society from which they were barred and drew a wall of social exclusiveness between themselves and lower-class blacks, thus resolving the dilemma in a private world. In the latter years of the 1960s, however, some middle-class blacks found a role in the community control movement and more recently in elective politics.

As background to the discussion about black leadership that emerged out of the upheavals of the past two decades, we draw on

James Q. Wilson's 1960 study, *Negro Politics*, in which he describes four types of community leaders of that earlier period: the prestige leader, the token leader, the organizer, and the "new Negro" leader.[4] We contrast these types of leadership with those which characterize the later and present leadership of the black community.

The *prestige leaders* were successful businessmen or professionals; in their civic activities they avoided controversy; they were cited by other black leaders as having the most extensive contacts with influential white leaders; they were moderate in leadership style and publicly immune from an "Uncle Tom" charge because of noninvolvement. On race issues they displayed a strong sense of racial values but were usually vague on specific means.

The *token leaders* were those who were "selected" (mostly by whites) to represent the black community in civic activities and/or public agencies. They generally lacked the status of the prestige leader, and their contacts with whites were fewer and more focused. They did not represent the militant elements in the community, nor were they spokesmen for groups contending with the agencies on which they served. They were rarely assertive on race issues and seldom took positions on those issues that were in opposition to the agency on which they served. They were generally professional or business people and were hardly ever named as leaders by either the prestige or protest leaders. Their political style was invariably moderate.

The *organizers* were community leaders who maintained organizations whose purpose was the attainment of community goals. They were distinguished by a high degree of commitment to specific ends; they were typically restless, ambitious, eager to improve, and imaginative. Most were men of secondary status, although a few were of high status. They were usually self-employed or otherwise masters of their own time.

The *"new Negro"* was an imaginery composite reflecting wishful thinking in the community. The characteristics of this leader were drawn from exemplary qualities of real leaders like Dr. Martin Luther King, Jr., Adam Clayton Powell, and others. This imagined leader would respond to intangible incentives for civic action, would contribute time and money and energies selflessly, would be immune to corruption, would reject arguments for segregation, and would resist acquiring an exploitative stake in the ghetto. He would be militant, outspoken on racial issues, but would cooperate with other blacks on joint ventures. He would work with whites as an equal partner. The hope for the "new Negro" leader was found principally among militant leaders but was present in every quarter.

The prestige and the token leaders were not leaders in any effective political or civic action sense. They were merely available to white leaders for advice, referrals, or, as with the token leaders, for "window dressing." The organizer, however, was the activist of the late fifties, the predecessor of the militant activist of the sixties. Although the views of militants were cited throughout Wilson's study, they were not among his leadership categories.

Actually, militant voices were heard in the late fifties, but militant groups had not yet emerged on the American scene. The militants of the time were civil rights leaders like Dr. King, whose protest activities, though bold for that period, were boycotts and sit-ins typified by the Montgomery bus boycott of 1955.

THE NONVIOLENT CIVIL DISOBEDIENCE OF MARTIN LUTHER KING

The modern black protest movement began under the leadership of Dr. King as an effort to deal with Southern resistance to the Supreme Court's decision in *Brown* v. *Board of Education* in 1954 and to other earlier decisions bearing upon the desegregation of public facilities. King chose nonviolent civil protest as the main strategy of protest, which included public boycotts, public demonstrations, marches, and sit-ins. It all started on December 31, 1955, when a black woman in Montgomery, Alabama refused to move to the back of a bus in keeping with local custom. A disturbance followed, and King led a black boycott of local buses which lasted until white leadership capitulated.

The emphasis on nonviolence gave the black protest movement in the South the appearance of Christian and nonrevolutionary respectability. As public protest and spontaneous group action, it gave law enforcement agencies a minimum basis for reprisal.

King's group was the Southern Christian Leadership Conference. Other organizations which took part in the protest were the Congress of Racial Equality (CORE) and the Student Non-Violent Coordinating Committee (SNCC). The focus of their protest in the late fifties and early sixties was segregated lunch counters, railroad and bus terminals, washrooms, and drinking fountains. Where direct-action protests were unsuccessful, as in Mississippi and Alabama, CORE and SNCC initiated voter-registration projects. In 1964, SNCC formed the Mississippi Freedom Democratic party, which challenged the seating of the all-white Mississippi Democratic delegation at the National Democratic Convention that year.

These protests, all of which preceded the 1964–69 urban riots, achieved several important goals. They overcame the fears of many blacks of taking action for their own interest and therefore reduced apathy. They made southern whites aware of black grievances and the need for change. They publicized, sometimes dramatically, the lengths to which whites were prepared to go to keep blacks in "their place." In Birmingham in 1963, the police used dogs, firehoses, and cattle prods against the marching protesters; in Philadelphia, Mississippi in 1964 three young white voter registration workers were slain by whites; a march from Selma to Montgomery, Alabama to dramatize a demand for voting rights was forcibly interrupted by local police and state troopers, and two white participants were killed. The Selma march led to the passage of the Voting Rights Act of 1965 which had been pending in Congress. A march on Washington in 1963 attracted 250,000 civil rights sympathizers from all parts of the nation, 20 percent of whom were whites. This event led to the Civil Rights Act of 1964, which provides for equality in economic opportunity, and the federal affirmative action program, which prohibits discrimination in federal contract hiring and employment.

BLACK MILITANCY

Having achieved new federal civil rights legislation, the attention of the black protest movement in the mid-sixties began to turn to the far more difficult problem of conditions in urban ghetto communities, especially those in the North where discrimination was infinitely more subtle than it was in the South. Black immigrants had to settle in the worst sections of cities where rents were high, public services poor, and crime rampant. Whites were leaving, but many remained on the peripheries of their old neighborhoods where they resisted the spread of the blacks. Moreover, white professionals and businessmen controlled the public institutions and businesses of the ghettos. Police either ignored the ghettos or harassed their residents, especially the youth. Under these circumstances, the frustration of blacks rose, and protests against landlords, merchants, social workers, and police began to erupt into community riots. The first of the riots occurred in the summer of 1964 and ushered in a new and spontaneous phase of black protest.

The new militants, who provided the cutting edge of change in the mid-sixties for the political action that followed, emerged in 1963 and 1964 from the "nonviolent" campaigns of SCLC, CORE, SNCC, the Conference of Federated Organizations (COFO), and others. The new militants also were strongly influenced by Malcolm X, the black nationalist who had first been a high official in the Black Muslims, a religious movement headed by Elija Muhammad, but had by 1964 broken away to form the Organization of Afro-American Unity. Unlike the Muslims, Malcolm X was an activist who advocated the integration of political power within black communities as a prior step to integration with the white community. His views influenced the later advocates of community control over institutions in city ghettos. His assassination in February, 1964 cut short his plans for a new separatist organization but made him a martyr of the new black militant leaders and sharpened his influence among them.

The urban riots which began to sweep the country in 1964 refreshed the spirit of these early militants and gave them new impetus. Thus, the advocate of nonviolence, James Foreman, was replaced in SNCC successively by Stokely Carmichael (who later became a leader in the Black Panthers and subsequently an expatriate in Africa) and H. "Rap" Brown, neither of whom would denounce violence as an ultimate instrument of protest. These radical militants provided the models and the scenarios of protest that created scores of followers and imitators across the land.

"Black Power" was the slogan (coined by Stokely Carmichael) which expressed diffuse but substantive goals. John Spiegel once observed that the militant leaders of the sixties shared the following motivations: "A disillusionment with the possibility of obtaining adequate representation for black people in the economic processes of the overall white society; a concern for the weakness of organizations in black communities and a desire to mobilize group consciousness and a feeling of identity for the sake of self-help . . . (and) a desire to create a political program and a style of leadership capable of realizing the aims of self-help and community development."[5]

The radical militants of the sixties also shared the belief that such leadership entailed serious economic and physical risks. Stokely Carmichael and Charles Hamilton warned aspiring militants in *Black Power*: "Jobs will have to be sacrificed, positions of prestige and status given up, favors forfeited."⁶ The radical militants typically refused compromises and were prepared to risk injury and even death against the "oppressor." Resistance to "tokenism," to policies of gradualism, and to white assistance were basic elements of the radical militant position. They tended to simplify issues, to stress the moral principle of their cause, and to base their appeal upon an elaborate set of values. Nevertheless, they differed greatly among themselves in political styles and programs for achieving their aims. Some were hardly visible in the community; others were well known and vocal. There were differences in styles of dress and speech, in the use of symbols of other national or religious cultures, and in the willingness to use violence as defense against the "oppressor." The militants came from backgrounds of varying social and economic classes.

The primary commitment to principle left the militants with a flexible attitude on means. As a result, they expected all sorts of black community organizations to concentrate on stepping up the pace of improvement for blacks. The distinctions between organizations such as the NAACP and the Urban League were unimportant to them. The militants were more interested in "status" gains than "welfare" gains; recognition on grounds of personal merit and integration were much more important than job or other specific improvements in welfare.

In their search for means, the militants favored strategic solutions in public law and policy which had the potential of resolving several problems at a time. Thus, they concentrated on new legislation, key court decisions, or drastic revisions in police policy.

Militants felt justified in the use of civil disobedience as well as political and physical force. During the sixties, however, militant leaders disagreed on the matter of violent force as an instrument for gaining their ends. Many of them used the rhetoric of violence and refused to eschew violence as an ultimate instrument of change, but only a few actually participated in violent action. Some militant groups who at first advocated the use of violent action later denounced this course, although a few moved on the opposite course.

Black nationalists whose origins were working class or lower class paid a great deal of attention to formulating the history and culture of black people, believing that a sense of pride and ethnic identity depended on a knowledge of their historical and cultural roots. They tended to be self-taught, and their insights from reading and contemplation gave their teachings an air of conviction and discovery. Some adopted the role of guru, and their deliberate visibility in the community was accented by exotic dress: a pillbox hat, a bearded chin, a shaved head or "natural" hair style, tunics with an African "tiki" or some other ornamentation hanging from the neck.[7] The style of dress was a rejection of identification with white American culture and emphasized the importance of establishing a separate identity in the African or Arabian tradition.

Most black nationalist militants also believed that blacks should form separate communities either inside or outside the jurisdiction of the United States. Accordingly, they concentrated their efforts in preparing the psychological and social foundations they saw as necessary for the development of black communities. Their recruits were usually black youths who were not under the control of adult or white society and who responded to organization, discipline, and confident and colorful leaders. To facilitate discipline, cadres were sometimes organized in bureaucratic structures complete with titles of rank and hierarchical lines of authority.

Among the radical militant leaders, the black nationalists were the most dedicated to black separation as an end in itself. Since black nationalists did not expect whites to accept separatism, they believed they had to prepare for a violent confrontation. They never discussed plans openly, but they assumed overt attitudes of hostility toward all whites whom they regarded as adversaries.

A second group of militants were young community action workers who held jobs in a variety of public-funded (or foundation-funded) ghetto self-help organizations involved in welfare work, job retraining, legal assistance, school busing, and small business development. These young militants generally were from lower-class ghetto homes. As teen-agers they had participated in street activities, and some of them had acquired a police record. Their lives in the ghetto had brought them into contact with the violence of the street on the one hand and with the achievement-oriented middle-class bureaucracies on the other. The latter both impressed and offended them. Yet they adopted the bureaucratic mechanisms of the white establishment in the cause of black development. They avoided formal political activity because they had little hope of breaking into the citywide political organizations on their own terms. Their main efforts went into mobilizing ghetto residents in community development projects (such as the antipoverty community action program or Model Cities planning) in the interest of forestalling the extreme reactions of apathy or violence. (See Chapter 9.) They were usually well known in their neighborhoods. Although sympathetic to the black nationalists, they were likely to be turned off by the rhetoric, the occasional mysticism, the ideological extremes, and the un-reality of separatist objectives.

A third category of militants were the street leaders, mostly teen-age youths who had acquired organizational and political skill as gang leaders. In some cities, the street gangs were small and in-formal; in others (especially Chicago), they were massive con-federations of smaller gangs which termed themselves "nations." In the sixties, some of the gangs went beyond their delinquent activi-ties into community organization and recreation. As goals shifted in this direction, the gangs retained the leadership of older members who were good at dealing with the larger community. Gang leaders who were marked by the police as criminals could not afford great visibility, even when they were promoting constructive projects. Although their relative invisibility detracted from their significance as militant leaders, the youth gang leaders presided over some of the angriest most violence-prone individuals in the ghetto.

When a riot broke out, it was the teen-agers who were most active in the early stages, and when gang members were involved (as they were almost certain to be), the leaders had to join in the action. After the rioting subsided, the street leaders sometimes confronted local authorities with the complaints of the teen-agers. The authorities usually categorized them (with justification) as criminals, brushing them off or prosecuting them for their participation in the riot, but these actions relieved authorities from confronting their responsibility for conditions which gave rise to the riots and to street gangs.

A fourth category of militants were the insurrectionists and revolu-tionaries whose dramatic style caught the public's attention for a time, but none of these groups ever gained a broad enough base of support in the ghetto communities to sustain them as a political force. Moreover, they were prime targets for police infiltration and harassment and were often plagued by internal power struggles. Nevertheless, the leaders of some of these groups were in their heyday admired by substantial numbers of blacks. For example, a 1970 Harris poll revealed that one out of four black respondents respected the Black Panthers and several of their leaders.

The Black Panthers

Closely related to the goals of black nationalism and ghetto self-determination during the sixties was the issue of self-defense and self-protection which was the prime tenet of the Black Panther party organized by Huey Newton and Bobby Seale in Oakland, California in 1966. This issue had its roots in the slave revolts of the nineteenth century and in the civil rights protests of the 1950s. When Robert Williams, organizer of the Revolutionary Action Movement (RAM), took issue with Martin Luther King's strategy of nonviolent protests, he became the first black leader to express views which were later associated with Black Power. In 1959 Williams was head of a local chapter of the NAACP in North Carolina where he first urged a hard line against segregationists who were "shooting up" black sections of town. He urged blacks to meet violence with violence. When his activities led to charges of kidnapping a white couple, he left the country and lived in China for several years, where he published a revolutionary periodical in which he continued to advocate defense against the brutalization of blacks. His writings had a strong influence on the leaders of the Black Panthers.

Eldridge Cleaver, the author of *Soul on Ice*⁸ and intellectual follower of Malcolm X, initially set out to establish Malcolm's organization of Afro-American Unity in San Francisco in 1969 but after a meeting with Huey Newton, decided instead to join the Black Panther party as minister of information. Cleaver regarded Newton as Malcolm's heir.

A third influence on the formation of the Black Panthers was the writings of Franz Fanon, the Algerian psychiatrist who authored *The Wretched of the Earth.*⁹ Fanon's writings about the oppression of the Algerians under French colonial rule seemed to Newton to parallel the black experience in America. Fanon's analysis of violence turned inward, the symbolic emasculation of the male, and the reversal of male-female relationships all seemed to be reflected in the American black experience. Fanon's teachings that a man cannot be a man until he turns his anger against his oppressor made a deep impression upon Newton, and this philosophy became the essence of the Black Panther program of action against the police.

Thus the Panthers came to view themselves as a revolutionary vanguard protecting their people against police brutality. The Panther leaders instilled in their followers a will to fight and die for their cause. The party platform, which was drafted by Newton and Seale in October, 1966, reflects their revolutionary and protectionist aims:

First, we want freedom, we want power to determine the destiny of our black communities.
Number two: We want full employment for our people.
Number three: We want housing fit for shelter of human beings.
Number four: We want all black men to be exempt from military service.

Number five: We want decent education for our black people in our communities that teaches us the true nature of this decadent, racist society and that teaches black people and our young black brothers and sisters their place in society, for if they don't know their place in society and in the world, they can't relate to anything else.

Number six: We want an end to the robbery by the white racist businessmen of black people in their community.

Number seven: We want an immediate end to police brutality and murder of black people.

Number eight: We want all black men held in city, county, state, and Federal jails to be released because they have not had a fair trial because they've been tried by all-white juries. . . .

Number nine: We want black people when brought to trial to be tried by members of their peer group. . . .

And number ten: . . . We want land, we want bread, we want housing, we want clothing, we want education, we want justice, and we want peace.[10]

The angry rhetoric and bold defensive activities of the Panthers stimulated police harassment and repressive tactics. As a consequence, by 1970 the black revolutionary movement centered mainly in the party, gaining momentum from incidents of mutual provocation. Clashes between the police and the Panthers intensified following the death in 1967 of an Oakland police officer for which Newton was subsequently convicted of manslaughter and sentenced to prison.*

Within the space of nineteen months in 1968 and 1969, at least ten Panthers were killed by police in Chicago, Los Angeles, Oakland, and Seattle. Three more policemen died in gun battles with the Panthers in 1969. Panther headquarters in cities across the country were targets of police raids and harassment during that period.

Meanwhile, Cleaver, who had served a term in prison prior to his affiliation, had his parole revoked after a gunfight with the police in which a young colleague was killed. Instead of returning to prison, Cleaver fled to Algeria where he was an influential figure in the Third World Movement until 1973, when he moved to Paris. Bobby Seale, the cofounder and chairman of the Panthers, was tried with six others in a federal district court in Chicago for conspiring to incite riot and violence in the 1968 Democratic National Convention. In the midst of that famous trial of "the Chicago Seven," Seale was ordered bound and gagged for his repeated attempts to cross-

---

*Mr. Newton was released on August 6, 1970. He was set free after posting $50,000 bail seven days after the Supreme Court had upheld the reversal of his voluntary manslaughter conviction in the 1967 killing of an Oakland policeman.

examine witnesses. In the end, he was convicted to four years in prison for contempt, a sentence which was successfully appealed.

As the party became increasingly radicalized, its leaders adopted an outright anticapitalistic revolutionary position which advocated transformation of the "oppressive capitalistic society into a socialistic society in which each man shall participate in the decisions that affect his life . . ."[11]

In July, 1969, the Panthers attempted to draw together a coalition of other radical minority and white groups to form the National Conference Against Racism. The conference was based on the theme of a united front against capitalism and racism. The conference was an attempt by the Panthers to broaden its base of support against police raids and jailings of Panther leaders. It was also an effort to unite disparate revolutionary groups.

By 1973 the Panther party in Oakland had moved beyond the rhetoric of violence and revolution (none of which had been expressed in its original platform and program except in some paraphrases of the Declaration of Independence) and turned its efforts to supporting Bobby Seale's mayoralty campaign.

Middle-Class Black Activism

Wilson's study of black politics in Chicago and other cities is testimony to the scarcity of middle-class black militant leaders up until 1964. As the riots fueled the black protest movement and provided evidence of police brutality, a dramatic shift occurred among middle-class blacks from traditional noninvolvement or civil rights activism to outspoken militancy. The upsurge of middle-class activism was stimulated by other factors as well: the passage of the Civil Rights Acts of 1964 and 1965; disappointing failures in school desegregation (see Chapter 12); evidence of hardening resistance to change among whites (even liberal whites) in open housing and in the "law and order" response to the riots; the election of hard-line candidates to local and national offices; and indifference to, or outright support of, police brutality in the ghettos.

There was a growing feeling among middle-class blacks that the aim of desegregation was hopeless, and that they had wasted time in futile action. They began to respond with bitter hostility even toward the liberal whites whom they had regarded as their allies. It no longer concerned them that these confrontations stimulated fear and hostility, for they had come to believe that the alliance with whites was a mutually deceptive cover-up of resistance to change.

Most middle-class black leaders were intellectuals and professionals—schoolteachers, lawyers, ministers, doctors, dentists, welfare workers, and writers. Very few well-to-do businessmen (Wilson's prestige leaders) joined them. A few professionals who had previously migrated to the suburbs, however, moved back to the ghetto where they organized and directed community programs which were staffed by the young lower-class community action militants. They exerted pressure on white leaders for changes in discriminatory policies and practices.

By 1970 militancy had become the predominant style of ghetto leadership, and the image of the "new Negro" described by Wilson had taken on a reality. Underneath it all was a craving for aggressive, sure-footed leaders who could stand toe-to-toe with whites and be neither smashed nor forced to back down.

Thus, the emergence of various types of militant leaders described in the foregoing passages represented an experimental phase in the transition from subjugation to self-esteem and independence. During the civil rights period of the fifties and sixties, the "radical" black depended upon the liberal white for support and leadership, but when the alliance seemed to produce little more than token concessions, new black leaders felt impelled to use more aggressive tactics in their assault on discriminatory barriers.

Disillusionment with white allies eventually drove the new leadership to abusive attacks on whites and to the black caucus. However, the tone of the abuse went beyond open defiance. Spiegel explains the intensity of their hostility toward whites as the consequence of ambivalent feelings all blacks harbor toward whites. Living as servants of whites, doing menial work, and being excluded from decision-making, they had learned the dangers of challenging the dominant whites. They had experienced the "legitimate violence" of whites for minor infractions of subordination. The accumulative anger stemming from exploitation and the fear of displaying the anger toward whites was controlled by identification with the whites. To the extent that the identification worked, blacks saw themselves through the eyes of whites as deserving no better treatment and turned their aggressions on themselves. The redirection of hostile energies toward themselves and other blacks made it psychologically possible to regard the whites with admiration and affection.

The degree to which these emotional controls are conscious or repressed varies among blacks. In some blacks the deference toward whites and the ego control it requires has been wholly repressed; in others the deference, shown only in the presence of whites, is conscious. In either case, deference based on identification with the whites has been the salient personality pattern for blacks who were locked into the white system of dominance.

Once the goal of desegregation became popular, the old set of personality mechanisms was no longer appropriate or necessary. The white aggressor was, presumably, disappearing. Therefore, protest in opposition to the injustices was not so dangerous. As anxiety lessened, a redistribution of internal energies was required. It was no longer necessary to love and admire the white man in order to control aggressive impulses which could not be expressed in protest actions. The withdrawal of generalized affection and admiration for whites led to a temporary transfer of the emotional investment to the white liberal who, as it turned out, could not (or would not) give the black activist the required support in his drive for rapid establishment of equality in social arrangements. The disillusionment of blacks with white liberals during the 1960s stimulated anger and a realization of the necessity to do without the dependence on these whites whose weaknesses were exposed.

Thus, the solution of the dilemma was transfer of psychic energy to the self by *internalization of an idealized image of the black person purified of white contamination.* "Under such a solution, the identifications of black people—and thus, the *sense of identity*—would be wholly black."[12]

Meanwhile, control over accumulated internalized aggression may be weakened, which explains the extreme aggression militant blacks express toward each other and toward whites. The intensity of the militant's attack may also be a way of testing his capacity to hurt the white man in order to disturb the latter's indifference or to reject his patronizing attention. Moreover, those who have been victims of powerlessness often enjoy victimizing their oppressors when the opportunity arises.

Black communities are discovering leadership in the militants who have come to terms with themselves as blacks. The effective leaders are those who escaped both the psychological damage of subjugation and the self-destructive identification with the white man, and who value themselves and are governed by standards of their own. In recent times, the freedom and the isolation of the ghetto produced blacks who escaped white domination. The pain of exclusion is no longer so much associated with the status and power of the white as it is with injustice. Once the fact of legal and political citizenship was established in national law, and the rhetoric of equality became standard in campaign liturgy, the problem was no longer that of psychological subjugation but that of "getting what's coming to me."

The abrupt decline of rioting following Martin Luther King's death in 1968 gave way to constructive efforts in many black communities to secure political and economic power. The community control movement, for example, drew its leadership from militant middle-class blacks who in an earlier generation would have taken no part in community affairs. The new generation of leaders who spearheaded the community control movement were impatient, organized in the style of traditional interest groups, and political in the pragmatic sense.

One serious weakness of the black control movement was that many of its emerging leaders had little experience in the political and organizational practices of whites. They confronted and attacked, but they could seldom outmaneuver. Although the established civil rights groups whose programs were always aimed at social and economic mobility had spectacular growth in contributed funds during the same period, the new militants and radicals provided a cutting edge of direct action. As the established civil rights groups consolidated gains, they brought into their organizations some of the leadership that emerged from militant and radical groups.

As Kenneth Clark has observed, the militants and the radicals propelled the more orderly and stable groups toward acceptance of direct-action methods "not only because the older leaders found the ardor of youth contagious but also because . . . they sensed that bolder programs would be necessary if their own roles were not to be undermined."[13]

In effect, the more radical groups took on the role of change agent, while the older groups cautiously exploited the opportunities that were created. It is doubtful that much progress would have occurred in the absence of *either* component. The vigor and enthusiasm of the youthful militants might have been quickly suppressed if the established organizations had not been present to interpret their aims (and frustrations) to the threatened white leadership. By the same token, the older groups needed the thrust of the new to avoid stagnating in the painfully slow progress that had theretofore characterized the Civil Rights Movement.

Of the four major civil rights organizations that dominated the black protest movement a decade ago—the NAACP, SNCC, CORE, and the SCLC—only the NAACP has retained its original identity as blacks redirected their efforts into groups with more narrowly defined purposes: the National Welfare Rights Organizations, the National Association of Community Developers, the National Sharecroppers

Fund, the Movement for Economic Justice, the Urban Coalition, and others. After Martin Luther King's death, SCLC lost financial and organizational stability. CORE became a black nationalist organization without a clearly articulated philosophy. SNCC flirted briefly with militant black nationalism and then faded away.

The sixties was a decade of rapid emergence of new political leadership among black Americans. Relying primarily on Wilson's work *Negro Politics*, we have described the general types of black leadership that were predominant before blacks could establish a substantial political base in their own communities. We followed this discussion with an account of the rise of militant styles of leadership which mainly developed from 1963 onward. As we have noted, the Voting Rights Act of 1965 and the follow-up efforts of both the federal government (acting under authorization of the act) and the Civil Rights Movement played major roles in getting black voters registered, especially in the South. These voter registration efforts encouraged black candidates to run for office at all levels of government. As a result of their successes, black protest activities gradually gave way to black political activities which followed the traditional patterns of American politics.

Thus, Hanes Walton, Jr., a black political scientist writing in 1972, describes several categories of black politicians who reflect the main orientations among contemporary black political leaders: the *integrationists*, who seek cultural assimilation and to gain their ends initiate and support strong civil rights and welfare legislation; the *accommodationists*, who concern themselves with the good of the larger society on the assumption that the good of the whole will benefit that of minorities; the *cultural pluralists*, who cater to black consciousness and press for black control of black communities as well as development of black culture and experience; the *black nationalists;* and the *revolutionaries*.[14]

What is different in the seventies is that these categories have taken on substance and legitimacy as black leaders have gained recognition in the larger society. Moreover, these categories are more likely to represent *styles* of leadership rather than exclusive categories of leaders. Thus, a particular candidate or political leader may seek the support of diverse elements in the community by projecting the image of a moderate in one setting, a militant in another, and perhaps even a black nationalist in still another. Of course, the revolutionary stance is the most difficult one to articulate publicly because of the close and effective surveillance of serious revolutionaries by law enforcement agencies. However, Bobby Seale, a cofounder of the

Black Panthers who once claimed aspiration to revolutionary aims, ran for mayor of Oakland in 1973 and attracted enough support to force a run-off election with a Republican opponent.*

In the end, black politicians have gone the way of all politicians. The successful ones who get elected to office are those who deliver in some measure solutions to the needs of the community they represent. Walton arranges them into four classes which are not mutually exclusive: (1) the *machine politicians,* who provide tangible goods including patronage jobs; (2) *rhetoric politicians,* who respond to certain psychological needs with promises and slogans; (3) *activist politicians,* who combine rhetoric and organization with programs and opportunities that contribute to the economic and social needs of their constituents; and (4) *accommodationists,* who spend their main efforts satisfying white supporters.[15]

Walton's categories do not sound very different from Wilson's because the basic issues in black communities have not greatly changed. Even where blacks have majorities or strong minorities in central cities, they are still no more than a 10 to 12 percent minority in the nation at-large, a fact which means they can hope only to gain control of a dozen or so large cities. Even in those cities, they may be outvoted in the state legislature where power and resources can be controlled by a suburban-rural vote.

In the end, black politicians are always forced to team up with white leaders to realize any substantial goals. Many of the problems their constituencies face are among the most intractable the nation confronts. It is therefore easier for established black politicians, especially those who serve at the national level, to lend their efforts to the less difficult, more interesting, and more prestigious programs which have a chance of success. Local black politicians, for their part, find it easier to deal with the day-to-day issues of routine political management than to be fighting near-hopeless battles for beneficial change.

Yet some black civic and political leaders have chosen that troubled route. Toward the end of the sixties, as the riots died down and it became evident that little progress was being made in improving the schools, the welfare system (in spite of the War on Poverty), or the police, the activists began to press for community control of these services and facilities. The community control movement

---

*In the run-off election of May 15, 1973, Seale received 35 percent of the total votes cast (43,719 votes for Seale and 77,476 votes for incumbent Mayor John Reading). See: *The New York Times* (May 17, 1973), p. 16, col. 1.

(described in Chapters 9 and 12 as it affected poverty and schools) was an important step from civil rights activism and rioting to politicalization.

In the heat of the times, it was also inevitable that a few blacks would turn revolutionary. Some could not reconcile their sense of injustice with the gradualism of the American political process and the extreme reluctance to implement policies and programs at the local level which were formulated at the national level to relieve conditions for blacks. There were also the few who could not contain their frustrations and who either lashed out in acts of destruction (such as attacks on police or bombings) or who turned away in disgust and apathy.

The Community Control Movement

The demand for community control was a move by citizens who were determined to engineer improvements which they regarded as critical to the well-being of their areas.

The objectives of the community control movement (also known as the black control movement) were schools, police, and public services which black leaders insisted could be decentralized and effectively operated within the community. The movement also aimed to place blacks in positions of ownership or management of private business and industrial firms in black communities.

The demands of the movement, coming mainly from the educated black middle class, were demands for local self-government, to do a job that the white community had abandoned or ignored. The struggle for community control was also evidence that moderate black leadership had given up the hope of moving into the larger society at a fast enough pace to insure opportunities for them and their children. As with the militants before them, the leaders of the black control movement sought the goals of self-development and a secure sense of self-esteem which superseded the more traditional, concrete goals of housing, education, and jobs.

The position of the community control movement on schools by 1970 was this: "Let our first goal be quality education, but let us do the job within our own communities with professionals of our choosing." The message to the white community was this: "You have barred those of us who would have joined you in your search for quality education, so let us do the job ourselves." But they soon found that most schools are part of a centralized bureaucracy under white control with diminishing fiscal resources; that they were controlled by intricate networks of entrenched interest groups as well as agencies of city government. (See Chapter 12.)

The assault of the community control movement on the welfare system also met with mixed results, although it produced a vigorous national organization which focused public attention on the inadequacies of local and state welfare systems. It also developed the concept of the rights of welfare recipients with an emphasis on the preservation of dignity as opposed to the debilitating paternalism which has characterized the existing systems. (See Chapter 8.)

In Boston, the demands of the militants associated with the black control movement led to a confrontation with welfare officials in 1967 that precipitated a riot. In the years following the Boston disturbance, reforms in the Massachusetts welfare system were slow, but the organized activities of the welfare mothers contributed to the development of a cadre of politically sophisticated community leaders who subsequently formed the basis of a community control movement in that city. In Massachusetts, the Mothers for Adequate Welfare organization eventually got welfare mothers on the State Welfare Board, and placed mothers in training programs to become social workers.

A demand for control over police in some cities blended into the issue of improved police protection. Black communities have demanded improved police protection to control crime and other forms of social deviancy which are sources of disturbance and insecurity. (See Chapter 7.)

The future of the community control movement is uncertain, for there is no single organization or even a coalition of similar ones. Many of the early leaders have found a place in the traditional civil rights organizations, in government, in the political system, or in the professions. Yet many community organizations that were founded in the period of upheaval following the riots have survived, and the black community is developing its leadership resources at a faster pace than ever. Unlike the white underclass, the natural leaders of the black underclass are not readily siphoned off to the suburbs. Unwelcomed in the suburbs and challenged by outspoken militants, black leaders have begun the tedious work of grappling with long-standing problems, and in doing so they are struggling for influence in local institutions that are vital to the community. Community control may be critical to the long-range interests of blacks in some cities where blacks are permanently in a minority position. But in cities which develop a substantial black population in the range of

35 percent or more, the more profitable course is control of city hall. Table 6–2 lists the central cities of 100,000 or more whose black populations have a majority of blacks or the estimated year when this turning point is likely to occur.

BLACK POLITICAL POWER

The development of effective political leadership in the urban ghettos of America is critical to the long-range goal of black domination of city government where blacks predominate and to increased representation in state and federal legislative and executive offices.

The problem the blacks face is to establish a solid political base in central cities where their greatest strength lies, and from this base to establish coalitions at the state and national levels with whatever groups they find commonalities on particular issues. The black vote in the North and in many large southern cities is concentrated in central cities and is solidly Democratic. This vote has proven to be a crucial determinant in the outcome of close presidential, senatorial, and gubernatorial elections. The degree of difference it makes in cities which have less than a 30 percent black vote is hard to determine because there are often other economic, ethnic, and religious voting groups which sometimes vote as a bloc: the Catholics, the Jews, and labor are examples. Also, the influence of the urban black vote may be diluted by the fact that it is predictable regarding party

TABLE 6–2   Black Population in Central Cities of More than 100,000

City	% of Black Population, 1970 Census	Projected Date of 50% Black Population (Estimated in 1968)*
Washington, D.C.	71%	—
Newark, N.J.	54%	—
Gary, Indiana	53%	—
New Orleans, La.	45%	1971
Richmond, Va.	42%	1971
Baltimore, Md.	46%	1972
Cleveland, Ohio	38%	1975
St. Louis, Mo.	41%	1978
Detroit, Mich.	44%	1979
Philadelphia, Pa.	34%	1981
Oakland, Calif.	35%	1983
Chicago, Ill.	33%	1984

*SOURCE: Report of the National Advisory Commission on Civil Disorders, p. 216.

affiliations. What is *not* certain is the turnout. Many a liberal urban candidate who was certain of the black vote and therefore concentrated a campaign elsewhere and on issues not relevant to the black community lost the election because of a failure to persuade black voters to go to the polls. In fact, it is very hard to convince ghetto residents that the social and economic conditions which trouble their everyday lives can or will be changed by a vote for particular candidates—black or white. As a result, "politics" often seems irrelevant to the low-income black.

As black political leaders develop solid bases in central cities, some of them may concentrate on an agenda of priorities relevant to the problems of their black constituents, articulate this agenda in their campaigns as a test of its meaningfulness to the constituency, and once elected, proceed to seek out whatever coalitions may be put together on an issue-by-issue basis. No other strategy makes sense at the state and national levels. At the city level, coalitions are necessary if the blacks are not in a voting majority, or if a voting majority lacks solidarity of purpose. One effort in this direction is the National Black Political Assembly which was organized at the National Black Political Convention held in Gary, Indiana in March, 1972. The council, led by Imamu Amiri Baraka of Newark (also known as Leroi Jones, the poet-playwright) and by Mayor Richard Hatcher of Gary, was formed as an effort to establish a political agenda on which blacks of all political persuasions could unite. The agenda of the Gary convention called for a minimum of sixty-six black congressional representatives and fifteen senators and for proportionate black employment and control at every level of the federal government. There were also recommendations on economic, human, and rural development; suggestions for black influence on American foreign policy, especially in relation with Africa and the Caribbean; and demands for massive federal support for quality education of every black youth. Representative Charles C. Diggs, Jr., the influential black congressman from Michigan, was chairman of the National Black Assembly and Mayor Hatcher was chairman of the assembly's forty-three-member political council which carries on the work of the assembly between national meetings. The assembly's 427 delegates range from political conservatives to black nationalists and Pan-Africans (Baraka, for example, was head of the Pan-African Congress of African People). A primary objective of the National Political Assembly is to build a bipartisan political base for the 1974 and 1976 elections—with the principal leadership coming from elected black officials rather than from civil rights leaders. Although the leadership of the assembly is comprised mainly of elected officials, the black caucus in Congress declined to participate as a group. The long-range viability of this group remains to be seen.

Old-Fashioned American Politics Elects Black Mayors

Richard G. Hatcher became mayor of Gary, Indiana at the age of thirty-four in 1967. He did so by attracting and holding a black vote which constituted a bare majority of the city population and by beating down the attempts of an entrenched white-dominated Democratic political machine to play games with voting lists. He also was forced to run as an independent in order to get on the ballot. He was no newcomer to Gary politics, however, having served on the city council since 1963. In the mayoralty race Hatcher was up against the most powerful Democratic county machine in Indiana: one that had produced Democratic majorities for a quarter century. The party chairman also was county clerk, secretary of the county election board, and secretary of the board of canvassers.

In the primary, Hatcher opposed the incumbent mayor and won by gaining a solid black vote; the white vote was split between two white candidates. In the general election he continued to emphasize his independence from the Democratic machine, refused to enter into any alliances, and promised an all-out fight on crime and corruption. As a result, the Democratic organization backed the Republican candidate, and tried to enroll phony names on the voter lists in white areas and remove the names of enrolled voters in black areas. The day before the election Hatcher and the U.S. Department of Justice got an order from the federal district court to have over 1,000 fictitious white names stricken from the rolls and 5,000 black names restored to the rolls. Hatcher won the election by 1,389 votes out of 77,271 cast, thus receiving 50.9 percent of the vote. Nearly 80 percent of the eligible voters went to the polls; Hatcher got 95 percent of the black vote and carried all of the city's black precincts. His opponent carried all white precincts, but Hatcher got 4,000 white votes compared to the 1,000 black votes gained by his opponent.

Carl B. Stokes was elected mayor of Cleveland, Ohio in 1967, the first black to be elected in a major city which had not attained a black voting majority. Stokes had been in the Ohio state legislature since 1952, the first black elected to that body. His strategy in both an unsuccessful race in 1965 and in a winning campaign in 1967 was to attract the black vote and a liberal white vote. He adopted the stance of a moderate and avoided racial issues.

In his unsuccessful 1965 race, his strategy was to run in the general election as an independent in order to bypass the Democratic primary and avoid a challenge to the incumbent mayor. He had hoped that the white vote would split between the Democratic and Republican candidates in the general election and that he could pick up enough white votes to win. Stokes lost by less than 2500 votes out of the 236,577 votes cast in the election. He had won only 6000 white votes.

In 1967, Stokes ran in the Democratic primary against two white candidates and won with 52.5 percent of the vote. He spent less time campaigning in black areas, but aided by a Ford Foundation grant to CORE, large numbers of blacks were added to the voter registration lists. In preparation for the general election, Stokes made an effort to build a coalition which would attract a maximum of white support. He got newspaper and union support, the backing of the Democratic party, and the endorsement of the outgoing mayor.

His opponent was Seth Taft, the grandson of former President William Howard Taft and nephew of former Senator Robert Taft. The candidates largely avoided the race issue and stressed their dedication to civil rights. Stokes won the election by holding together the coalition. Although his margin was only 2501 votes, he had increased his white vote from 16,000 in the primary to over 35,000 in the election.

Two years later, Stokes won reelection by a margin of 3,753 votes, 1,252 more than in 1967. The black vote, while solidly for Stokes, was lower than in 1967, but he increased his support in all-white precincts. His opponent (who later succeeded Stokes as mayor) refused to raise the racial issue on "law and order." Both candidates concentrated their campaigns on the white liberal vote.

From Protest to Politics

1975 provides a vantage point from which to assess the outcome of the black protest movement of the 1950s and 1960s. The nonviolent protest activities of the fifties provided the basis for the more aggressive actions of the early sixties. The protest phases of the movement served to reduce the fear of lethal reprisal from agents of the dominant whites and actually produced major concessions in both law and policy at the national as well as the local level—in public attitudes and in the customs and habits of social life. In spite of these changes, and perhaps to a large extent because of them, the intensity of the protest mounted, culminating in spontaneous rioting in hundreds of cities across the land over a five-year period lasting from 1964 to 1968.* But like the protest activities which preceded them, the riots had a further cleansing effect on the discrimination and racism that pervaded an otherwise egalitarian society. The riots revealed to local officials and civic leaders the depth of frustration and anger that minorities felt in consequence of the social and economic conditions in which they were forced to live. These conditions, once revealed, became the focal point of debate about solutions among white politicians and black, the latter thus gaining a basis upon which to claim their greater competence in judging appropriate solutions. Thus, the whole black protest movement, including the riots, provided a great variety of opportunities for the emergence of leadership. It also gave the public, both black and white, a view of different kinds of black leaders in action. As the black protest movement progressed, each of these types of leaders contributed to the needs of a people struggling to find a place of substance and dignity in the larger society. Nevertheless, the leaders who survived to win positions of power were those who were ready to deal with the political realities of the American system. Over the ten-year period dating from the Voting Rights Act of 1965, as we have previously noted, black leaders have won elective office at every level of government, from minor local posts to the U.S. Congress.

The routes to political leadership in America are many and tortuous, but every one is marked by compromise and trade-offs. Thus, in the South, as Professor Dye has shown, the organizational style of black participation was successful in achieving legal justice within the system but failed in bringing about significant changes in the everyday living conditions of the masses of blacks. In the North, Dye observes, black political organizations in cities have concentrated on jobs, favors, and other material rewards, but they also have not been able to bring about much change in the condition of people in the ghettos.[16] The function of protest was to pave the way for political participation, but protest itself was no direct route to power for those who had made the sacrifice. The Stokes, the Hatchers, the Gibsons,

---

*Rapid change in law and policy which is not so rapidly translated into practical improvements in the everyday life of aggrieved people can create severe frustration and anger. This is one explanation of the ghetto riots of the 1960s which in fact followed major advances in national civil rights legislation and major civil rights victories at the local level.

the Bradleys, the Youngs, the Chisholms, the Jordans, and all the others who have made their way to distinguished positions in the political system did so by dint of extraordinary talent and hard work, but they owe much to the cutting-edge militants who preceded them.

NOTES

1. Talcott Parsons, "Full Citizenship for the Negro American? A Socio-logical Problem," in "The Negro American," *Daedalus*, Proceedings of the American Academy of Arts and Sciences, Vol. 94, No. 4 (Fall 1965), pp. 1009–1054.
2. See: "Public Attitudes in the United States on Black-White Relations," Appendix I, in Ralph W. Conant, *The Prospects for Revolution* (New York: Harper's Magazine Press, 1971), pp. 225–236.
3. For a fuller discussion of this latter point, see: Daniel P. Moynihan, "The Schism in Black America," *The Public Interest*, No. 27 (Spring 1972), pp. 3–24.
4. James Q. Wilson, *Negro Politics* (New York: The Free Press, 1960), pp. 255–280.
5. John P. Spiegel, "The Social and Psychological Dynamics of Militant Negro Activism: A Preliminary Report," in *The Dynamics of Dissent: Science and Psychoanalysis*, Proceedings of the American Academy of Psychoanalysis, ed. Jules H. Masserman, Vol. 13 (New York: Grune & Stratton, 1968), p. 138.
6. Stokely Carmichael and Charles V. Hamilton, *Black Power* (New York: Random House, Vintage Books, 1967), p. 15.
7. Spiegel, "The Social and Psychological Dynamics of Militant Negro Activism," in *The Dynamics of Dissent*, ed. Masserman, p. 140.
8. Eldridge Cleaver, *Soul On Ice* (New York: Dell, Delta Books, 1968).
9. Frantz Fanon, *The Wretched of the Earth* (New York: Grove Press, Evergreen Editions, 1963).
10. Gene Marine, *The Black Panthers* (New York: New American Library, Signet Books, 1969), pp. 35–36.
11. Huey P. Newton, "Black Panthers," *Ebony* (August 1969), pp. 106–112.
12. Spiegel, "The Social and Psychological Dynamics of Militant Negro Activism," in *The Dynamics of Dissent*, ed. Masserman, p. 152.
13. Kenneth Clark, "The Civil Rights Movement: Momentum and Organization," in "The Negro American-II," *Daedalus*, Proceedings of the American Academy of Arts and Sciences, (Winter 1966), p. 258.
14. Hanes Walton, Jr., *Black Politics* (Philadelphia: Lippincott, 1972), pp. 202–208.
15. *Ibid.*, pp. 209–224.
16. Thomas R. Dye, *The Politics of Equality* (Indianapolis: Bobbs-Merrill, 1971), p. 157.

SUGGESTIONS FOR FURTHER READING

Aberbach, Joel D., and Jack L. Walker. *Race In The City*. Boston: Little Brown, 1973.

Survey analysis of racial attitudes and policy implications in Detroit, Michigan.

Bailey, Harry A., Jr., ed. *Negro Politics in America.* Columbus, Ohio: Charles E. Merrill, 1967.
Selected readings on comparative black politics.

Barbour, Floyd B., ed. *The Black Power Revolt.* Boston: Porter Sargent, 1968.
Selected readings on black power.

Baron, Harold M. "Black Powerlessness in Chicago," *Trans-Action,* Vol. 6, No. 1 (November 1968), pp. 27–33.
Analysis of systematic exclusion of blacks from the decision-making structure in Chicago.

Bellush, Jewel, and Stephen M. David, eds. *Race and Politics in New York City.* New York: Praeger, 1971.
Five case studies show that blacks encountered difficulty in influencing the local political system.

Blake, J. Herman. "Black Nationalism," *Annals,* Vol. 382 (March 1969), pp. 15–25.

Breitman, George, ed. *Malcolm X Speaks.* New York: Grove Press, Inc., Evergreen Black Cat Editions, 1966.

Breitman, George. *The Last Year of Malcolm X.* New York: Schocken Books, 1968.

Brink, William, and Louis Hanes. *Black and White.* New York: Simon and Schuster, paperback, 1967.

Carmichael, Stokely, and Charles V. Hamilton. *Black Power.* New York: Random House, Vintage Books, 1967.
Development of the causes and reasons for black power. Particularly recommended for discussion on coalition politics.

Cleaver, Eldridge. *Soul On Ice.* New York: Dell Publishing Co., Inc., Delta Books, 1968.

Cook, Fred J. "Mayor Kenneth Gibson says—'Wherever the Central Cities Are Going, Newark Is Going to Get There First'," *The New York Times Magazine,* (July 25, 1971), pp. 7–9, 32–40.
Policy problems encountered by Newark's first black mayor.

Dye, Thomas R. *The Politics of Equality.* Indianapolis: Bobbs-Merrill, 1971.
Survey of politics of race relations.

Dymally, Mervyn M., ed. *The Black Politician.* Belmont, Calif.: Duxbury Press, 1971.
Collection of original essays, articles, and speeches by leading black politicians.

Emer, Virginia B., and John H. Strange, eds. *Blacks and Bureaucracy.* New York: Crowell, 1972.
Articles showing relationships between blacks and governmental agencies.

Fanon, Frantz. *Black Skin, White Masks.* New York: Grove Press, Evergreen Books, 1967.

Foner, Philip S., ed. *The Black Panthers Speak.* Philadelphia: Lippincott, 1970.
Selected articles on the politics and programs advocated by the Panthers.

Grant, Joanne, ed. *Black Protest.* New York: Fawcett Publications, 1968.
Excellent collection of articles showing condition of blacks in America from days of slavery until the Black Power awareness of the 1960s.

Greenberg, Edward S., Neal Milner, and David J. Olson, eds. *Black Politics.* New York: Holt, Rinehart and Winston, 1971.
Selected articles on black politics, the police, conflict, violence, and protest.

Greer, Edward, ed. *Black Liberation Politics.* Boston: Allyn and Bacon, 1971.
Selected articles on black politics, including a case study section on Gary, Indiana.

Grier, William H., and Price M. Cobbs. *Black Rage.* New York: Bantam Books, Inc., 1969.

Hadden, Jeffrey K., Lewis H. Masotti, and Victor Thiessen. "The Making of the Negro Mayors 1967," *Trans Action,* Vol. 5, No. 3 (January–February 1968), pp. 21–30.
Interesting analysis of Mayor Carl Stokes 1967 electoral victory in Cleveland.

Kahn, E. J., Jr. "A Reporter At Large: Who, What, Where, How Much, How Many?" I, II, *The New Yorker Magazine* (October 1973).

King, Martin Luther, Jr. *Where Do We Go From Here: Chaos or Community?* Boston: Beacon Press, 1968.

Keech, William R. *The Impact of Negro Voting.* Chicago: Rand McNally, 1968.
Analysis of black voting impact in Durham, North Carolina, and Tuskegee, Alabama.

Knowles, Louis L., and Kenneth Prewitt. *Institutional Racism in America.* Englewood Cliffs, N.J.: Prentice-Hall, 1969.
The effects of pervasive institutional racism on blacks. Chapter 6 examines racism in political institutions.

Lynch, Hollis R. *The Urban Black Coalition: A Documentary History, 1866–1971.* New York: Crowell, 1973.

————, ed. *The Making of Black America: Essays in Negro Life and History.* Vol. I, The Origins of Black Americans. New York: Atheneum, 1969.

Major, Reginald. *A Panther Is A Black Cat.* New York: William Morrow, 1971.
In-depth study of Black Panther organization in Oakland, California.

Marine, Gene. *The Black Panthers.* New York: The New American Library, Signet Books, 1969.

A history of the origins of the militant Black Panther organization.

Matthews, Donald R., and James W. Prothro. *Negroes and the New Southern Politics.* New York: Harcourt, Brace & World, 1966.
Analysis of increasing black political participation in the South during the 1960s.

Meier, August, and Elliott M. Rudwick. *From Plantation to Ghetto: An Interpretive History of American Negroes.* New York: Hill and Wang, 1966.

————, eds. "The Nation of Newark," *Society*, Vol. 9, No. 10 (September/October 1972), pp. 19–58.
Four articles examine recent political, social, and economic problems of New Jersey's largest city.

Naughton, James M. "Mayor Stokes: The First Hundred Days," *The New York Times Magazine* (February 25, 1968), pp. 26–27, 48–62.
A critical review of initial problems and prospects of Cleveland's first black mayor.

Osofsky, Gilbert. Harlem: *The Making of a Ghetto.* New York: Harper & Row, Torchbooks, 1968.

Parenti, Michael. "Power and Pluralism: A View from the Bottom," *Journal of Politics*, Vol. 32, No. 3 (August 1970), pp. 501–530.
Black powerlessness in relation to white community decision structure is documented for Newark, New Jersey.

Patterson, Ernest. *Black City Politics.* New York: Dodd, Mead, 1974.
In-depth analysis of black politics in St. Louis.

Pettigrew, Thomas F. "When A Black Candidate Runs for Mayor: Race and Voting Behavior," pp. 95–118 in *People and Politics in Urban Society:* Vol. 6, Urban Affairs Annual Reviews, ed. Harlan Hahn. Beverly Hills: Sage Publications, 1972.
Study of five recent mayoral elections suggests that relative deprivation rather than white "backlash" may explain white resistance to black candidates.

Piven, Frances Fox, and Richard A. Cloward. "Dissensus Politics: A Strategy For Winning Economic Rights," *The New Republic*, (April 28, 1968), pp. 20–24.
Argues that a dissensus strategy within the Democratic party will achieve long-term economic gains for urban blacks.

Powledge, Fred. "A New Politics in Atlanta," *The New Yorker Magazine*, Vol. 31 (December 1973).

Rustin, Bayard. " 'Black Power' and Coalition Politics," *Commentary* (September 1966), pp. 35–40.
The major hope for urban blacks is to form new and effective coalitions with sympathetic and influential whites.

Rustin, Bayard. "From Protest to Politics: The Future of the Civil Rights Movement," *Commentary* (February 1965), pp. 25–31.
Emphasizes that black political power and influence will be achieved by establishing coalitions with white leaders.

Scheer, Robert, ed. *Eldridge Cleaver: Post-Prison Writings and Speeches.* London: Jonathan Cape Ltd., 1969.

Silberman, Charles E. *Crisis in Black and White.* New York: Random House, Inc., Vintage Books, 1964.

Stone, Chuck. *Black Political Power in America,* rev. ed. New York: Dell, Delta Books, 1970.
In-depth analysis of black politics through 1969.

U.S. Commission on Civil Rights, *Political Participation.* Washington, D.C.: U.S. Government Printing Office, May 1968.

Walton, Hanes, Jr. *Black Politics.* Philadelphia: Lippincott, 1972.
Comprehensive survey of black politics at the national, state, and local levels.

Weinberg, Kenneth G. *Black Victory.* Chicago: Quadrangle 1968.
Analyzes Carl Stokes' political career which culminated in his election as mayor of Cleveland in 1967.

Wilson, James Q. *Negro Politics.* New York: Free Press, 1960.
An analysis of black political and civic leadership in Chicago.

Zelnick, C. Robert. "Gibson of Newark: Quiet Diplomat on a Racial Battleground," *City,* Vol. 6, No. 1 (January–February 1972), pp. 11–21.
Analysis of Mayor Kenneth Gibson's leadership in Newark, New Jersey.

"HELP!"

Reprinted with permission from *The Herblock Gallery* (Simon and Schuster, 1968).

part two

The Urban Crisis: Problems and Prospects

7

Civil Protest and Law Enforcement

INTRODUCTION

As indicated in Chapter 6, the black protest movement reflected the concerns of disadvantaged inner-city minorities that the established institutions of society (local government, schools, welfare agencies, and the police) were not responsive to their needs. Although the urban riots of the 1960s had their own special momentum, they also served to dramatize the inability of community organizations to serve the poor, the inadequacies in police service, the shortcomings of schools, and the quality of health services and housing (all policy problems which will be discussed in subsequent chapters). Thus, the riots of the 1960s abruptly confronted the nation with the realities of problems which had long been ignored by complacent local, state, and national leaders and contained (after a fashion) by police and welfare agents whose actions sometimes provoked extreme resentment in ghetto communities (as indicated in this chapter and Chapter 8). The policy chapters on public assistance, antipoverty services, community health, housing, and education describe efforts over the past two decades to provide solutions to urban problems that have caused severe tensions in the cities. In a sense, the urban riots of the 1960s and the police response to them provided both an index to progress and a measure of the intensity of resistance to change. As we shall see, progress on solutions to problems para-doxically caused widespread impatience with the speed of imple-mentation; unrest stemming from the impatience caused resistance among established groups. Their fears, in turn, were reflected by frequently repressive police policies in response to active protest and rioting.

Our principal concern in this chapter is the police response to civil protest, particularly to ghetto riots. While the local police in the United States have modified their policies, and to some extent their attitudes, toward extralegal forms of civil protest and even toward rioting, they are inclined to treat any protest activities, except strikes and legal demonstrations, as criminal behavior—which most are in the technical legal sense. Also, police are inclined to apply local law and custom over the national standards of justice when the two are in conflict. We try in this chapter to present the case for tolerance toward dissent and for the value of protest—even when it involves violence. We also attempt to show how the police policy toward protest is shaped by the police officers' training, attitudes, and perceptions of society's expectations of law enforcement. Toward the close of the chapter, we suggest a few general guidelines for police policy that could, by their application, head off the confrontations between police and protesters which so often in the past have escalated peaceful demonstrations into violent ones or turned threat-ening provocations into full-scale riots.

Rioting is a spontaneous form of social protest akin to an outburst of anger in the individual. The psychological origin of riot-producing anger is in acute feelings of *relative* deprivation; one does not have to be deprived (by some objective measure) to *feel* deprived. In its acute stages, relative deprivation is the primary source of internal strife in all societies. Rioting is a very specific form of protest not to be confused with civil disobedience or insurrection, and these latter forms of protest should not be confused with revolution. The distinc-tions that follow are important in the formulation of public policies which govern law enforcement, for it is possible, in the blurring of the distinctions, for officials to treat civil disobedients or rioters as though they were insurrectionists or revolutionaries.

In order of severity, civil disobedience, rioting, and insurrection are the principal forms of protest, short of revolution, through which citizens express their objections to the injustices of misused political or administrative power or to discriminatory private practices. Civil disobedience and insurrection by definition involve defiance of civil authority and a challenge of some public policy, law, or action which the protesters believe runs counter to a constitutional principle or to some basic right of conscience, dignity, or welfare. Whereas civil disobedience does not usually involve violence, insurrection is deliberate violence intended to terrorize adversaries by personal injury or property destruction. Rioting is a spontaneous form of protest against public authority or private inequity; planned or deliberate "rioting" is insurrection.

RIOTS AND CIVIL PROTEST

Rioting and other forms of protest are part of the tradition of democratic action in the United States and other free societies. Though seemingly a contradiction, civil protest in all its forms, both violent and nonviolent, has proven to be an indispensable corrective ingredient in democratic policies. In the United States, civil protest has been as much a functioning institution in the body politic as have representative legislatures, courts of law, administrative offices, lobbying groups, and war. This is because civil protest generally aims at establishing good public policies or modifying bad ones, airing grievances of the powerless, and shaking up or turning out of office leaders who pursue undesirable policies. As such, civil protest is a means of bringing extraordinary pressure to bear on the machinery of government, thus short-circuiting cumbersome or time-consuming procedures of government. A tradition of protest makes it an "option" in political action and an alternative to formal channels which may become blocked or hard to use. The "option" of protest therefore lends an element of resilience to a governmental system which tends toward rigidity. The extent to which a political system lacks tolerance of diverse or opposing views on crucial public issues is the extent to which it is vulnerable to revolutionary action. In a pluralistic community such as the United States where values are in perpetual competition, the possibility for civil protest—even rioting—reduces the pressure for revolution.

In America, protest, even violent protest, has always been regarded as a natural course for citizens to take when they were denied redress to some intolerable grievance. Still, we habitually deceive ourselves about the role and acceptability of violent action in our political life because we have ambivalent feelings toward violence. We believe in law and order and that conflict should be settled peaceably—but not at all costs. The fact is that Americans are simultaneously peace-loving and willing to resort to violent action when other avenues to legitimate goals seem closed or ineffective.

In recent years, violent protest has been an instrument of minority groups to break through oppressive discrimination in housing, education, employment, and political rights, much of which is likely to be judged by history as justified in terms of deeply held egalitarian values. The strife that tore at the fabric of an emerging industrial economy for over a half century is in restrospect interpreted as the constructive conflict which was directly responsible for establishing the bargaining rights of labor. In a generation or two, the urban riots of the sixties will likely be seen as having contributed to the perfection of our system of justice.

In the United States, social movements (of which rioting and rebellion are merely a symptom) with few exceptions have limited their aims to gaining access to the nation's opportunity structure, and movements which have sought to tear down the system have never achieved widespread favor. Thomas Jefferson's speculation on the need for periodic revolution and Abraham Lincoln's homage to the right of revolution meant revolution to reconstruct the original design should it be corrupted by anticonstitutional or antilegal forces.

Political authorities are often centrally involved in generating mass protest because it is their business to intervene in actions that threaten life and property and, of course, because some of the threat is directed at the authorities themselves. In the act of intervention, authorities seek to retain a monopoly on the use of force and violence. Most ghetto disturbances in the United States during the 1960s involved violent confrontations with the local police or the National Guard.

A distinctive phase of civil protest in the United States evolved from the discriminatory basis on which rights and privileges have been distributed to minorities; thus, the riots associated with the black protest movement in cities during the last decade were a direct consequence of ambitious promises and gradual or token delivery. The promises were intended to meet the persistent and aggressive demands of the blacks, and, of course, they squared with our egalitarian ideals. The gradualism was simply a political and social response to the realities of massive resistance. As the gap widened between the expectations created by the promises and the actual fulfillment of those promises, the frustrations of blacks rose, and riotous outbursts mounted.

Black protest, including the riots, by and large appeared justified to white political leaders, especially at the national level. As a result, black leaders (most of whom were never personally involved in a riot) found the white community receptive to the demands they articulated on behalf of blacks. Certainly, white leaders were less punitive in their response to black aggression than ever before in history. The rapid developments in the black protest movement during the sixties (described in Chapter 6) and the displays of aggression which characterized the riots reflected the gradual relaxing of white resistance.

The riots and the constructive response of political leaders, however, also produced intensified white resistance in those segments of the population that were most threatened by the advancement of blacks, *viz.* the lower classes and the working classes for whose homes, schools, and jobs the upward- and outward-moving blacks were competing. This reaction was manifested in the popularity of the "law and order" issue of the late sixties, and the black counter-reactions to some extent polarized the ethnic conflict and increased the incidence of direct clashes between blacks and whites—an aspect of the earlier history of race riots which was largely absent from ghetto rioting in the sixties. Most of these clashes have taken place in the public schools, which are an unusually sensitive point of contact between the races. The increased frustration of young blacks, turned off by public schools and bypassed in the labor market, drove some of them to enlist in insurrectionist or criminal activities. (See Chapter 12.)

THE CAUSES OF RIOTS

An aggrieved population can erupt into violent outbursts on the basis of a preexisting set of hostile beliefs about adversaries in the dominant community. This was the nature of the riots in the ghetto communities of American cities in the 1960s. Tracing this class of riots to World War II, Janowitz has termed them "commodity" riots because they are outbursts against the agents and symbols of the dominant society.[1] The extensive looting of white-owned neighborhood stores gave symbolic meaning to these outbursts. In the earlier period, between World War I and World War II, urban riots were "communal" in character in that they were interracial clashes which took place at the boundaries between white and black neighborhoods, especially at points where the blacks were pushing into white areas. In a still earlier period, from around the turn of the century up to

"Keep A Sharp Lookout For Outside Agitators"

Reprinted with permission from *The Herblock Gallery* (Simon & Schuster, 1968).

World War I, rioting took the form of whites reacting to black aggression and "insubordination" by mob assault which involved shootings and lynchings (Springfield, Ohio, 1906; Atlanta, 1906).

The earlier periods prior to World War II, according to Janowitz, had two predisposing elements. Large numbers of new immigrants, both black and white, were living in segregated urban enclaves under conditions which permitted limited alternatives. Thus, riots were direct clashes between blacks and whites at the edge of neighborhoods where blacks were moving in and trying to expand the "territory" available to them. In the South, violence usually arose from violations of customs and community norms, for example, attempts to counter the doctrine of white supremacy, slurs against whites, lack of deference to whites, and the raping of white women by black men. In the North, violence was more likely to grow out of black "encroachments" on jobs, housing, and transportation as they moved into new areas.

What was common to all three periods of rioting was the weak or vacillating action of the police and other law enforcement agencies, which also had limited capacity for dealing with mass violence and usually had little or no warning as to when an outbreak would occur. Sometimes the police actually aided whites in attacks on blacks, for example, in the East St. Louis riots of 1918, which were later investigated by Congress. In the earlier riots, the police were regarded by blacks as the armed protectors of the white community, rather than as neutral arbiters between whites and blacks. This perception of the police carried into the riots of the 1960s.

In the sixties, many rioters in urban ghettos believed in the malevolence and duplicity of whites and in their basic commitment to the oppression of blacks. An important component of the hostile belief system is that the expected behavior of the adversary is seen as beyond accepted norms. In urban ghettos, people were convinced, for example, that the police would behave toward them with incivility and physical brutality far beyond that displayed toward whites in similar circumstances.

The hostile belief system provides the volatile basis for a precipitating incident leading to a riot. Such an incident is a concrete illustration of a hostile belief. Thus, when a police officer shoots and kills a young black suspected car thief (San Francisco, September 1966) or beats and bloodies a black taxi cab driver (Newark, July 1967) such incidents dramatize and seem to confirm the hostile belief that police do such things to blacks out of hatred for them. An ensuing melee, however violent or destructive, is justified in the minds of rioters who share the hostile belief. Rumors of further brutality during the riot are seized upon to bolster feelings of justification, and any provocations by police are utilized to escalate the rioting.

Hostile beliefs, of course, bear varying relations to "reality." Many whites indeed want to keep blacks "in their place" or to allow them advancement only gradually, but most whites do not consciously want to oppress and harass them.

As stated earlier, an important and perhaps universal cause of rioting is the perception of real or imagined deprivation. The aggrieved see a gap between the conditions in which they find themselves and what they could hope to achieve if given the proper opportunities.

Ghetto residents of cities in the United States use middle-class-white suburban living standards as a comparison, and they feel acutely deprived, not so much of goods and services, but of the access to the job and salaries which would put them within the reach of middle-class standards. The areas of relative deprivation for black Americans are political and social as well as economic. Blacks are not adequately represented in governing councils at the local or national levels, and they are excluded from social opportunities. The riots have not continued, however, partly because the number of blacks holding elective political office since the Voting Rights Act of 1965 has increased from a few hundred to several thousand. Professional job opportunities have broadened substantially, as have educational opportunities, especially in colleges and universities.

Another cause of rioting is the lack of effective channels for bringing about change. Lieberson and Silverman, in their study of riots in U.S. cities between 1910 and 1961,[2] noted that cities in which riots occurred were cities where blacks and other minorities were not likely to get adequate representation in local governing councils, usually because the officials were elected at-large rather than from districts. As a result, these groups felt deprived of a political channel through which to air their grievances.

The "forest fire" effect played a significant role in the crescendo of riots in 1967 and 1968. Ghetto residents were known to feel that things could not be made worse and that riots might achieve concessions from the dominant community. As the disturbances spread, the riots became a threat weapon of militant black leaders whether riots had occurred or not. Although no one could claim to be able to start a riot, the fear that rioters might attack white neighborhoods and white business establishments located in the ghetto was sometimes enough of a threat (though unspoken) to give ghetto leaders a temporary advantage in negotiations on ghetto problems. Actually, any hard-pressed people who hope to improve their situation are riot prone, especially if they see others in similar conditions making gains from rioting. What happens to start a riot may be accidental and spontaneous, but hope for change raises the combustion potential.

RIOTERS AND THE POLICE

One of the characteristics of the conflict between blacks and whites is that communications have been largely blocked by white denial and black intransigence. This condition intensifies the hostile belief systems of each group against the other, and among black citizens it sets the stage for rumors to amplify a potential incident into a riot trigger.

A communications gap between an aggrieved community and the local civil authorities is symptomatic of the distrust and bitterness which intensified between whites and blacks during the 1960s. In many cities, relations between minorities and city hall were damaged beyond repair by hostile outbursts in the aggrieved community and by repressive action from the local authorities.

Once a riot is underway, how far it will go depends on the process of interaction between the governing authorities and the aroused community.[3] The matter of control policy is critical, and its failure is of two sorts: *undercontrol* and *overcontrol.*

The condition of undercontrol exists where the normal forces for social control in the community are ineffective. These forces include law enforcement personnel, the family, and formal and informal community neighborhood leaders. In a situation of undercontrol, dissident groups, noting the weakness or ambivalence of the authorities, seize the opportunity of a spontaneous precipitating incident to express hostility and anger. Inactivity of the law enforcement personnel is a further stimulation for the aggrieved to act out their suppressed feelings, free of the social or legal consequences of unlawful behavior. In the advanced stages of a riot, undercontrol can produce a rapid spread of looting; a sudden reversal of tactics replacing undercontrol with overcontrol can produce brutal acts of suppression as police officers release their own pent-up frustrations. Police officers cannot be ordered to stand by while looting is going on and then be expected to act with restraint when they are turned loose to stop it.

When overcontrol is exerted in the early stages of a riot, it can generate an intense reaction in the aggrieved community. Rioting can worsen under the provocation of extreme repression, or, if the forces of control are sufficient to contain the rioters' action, the anger that was its root cause is not worked out in the catharsis of violent behavior.

The consequences of such repression are hard to predict. Short of sustained and overwhelming force, overcontrol usually leads to increased frustration and repeated conflict. Ghetto residents see the police as violent and strike back with increasing intensity, which may lead to insurrectionist activities.

Several conclusions may be drawn from studies of interactions between rioters and police: (1) the presence of police tends to create an event, provide a focal point, and draw people together for easy rumor transmittal; (2) too few police may encourage uncontrolled deviant behavior; (3) police activity seen as legitimate by riot participants will not escalate the event, but police observed being rude, unfair, or brutal may touch off further rioting; (4) a successful police withdrawal during a riot depends upon the officials contacting recognized community leaders who can organize control mechanisms; and (5) the presence of police who do not exert control encourages the acceptance of deviant behavior as normal.

Furthermore, the sooner appropriate police action is taken and the sooner authorities seek out recognized ghetto leaders and satisfy grievances, the sooner the riot stops. As the audience ceases watching the riot activity, the disturbance simmers down. The greater the degree of normality maintained in the daily routine of the community during the disturbance, the more likely the riot will be to cease.

INSURRECTION

If community grievances go unresolved for long periods, growing despair may impel established, aspiring, or self-appointed leaders to organize acts of rebellion against the civil authorities. Such acts, in that they are premeditated, constitute insurrection; however, terrorism, an especially virulent form of insurrection, is more commonly associated with revolutionary violence than with protest movements.

Although insurrection is deliberate rebellion, the insurrectionist (unlike the revolutionary) is not out to overthrow the system, but *only those in power*. His aim is to force persons in power to abandon discriminatory policies and adopt more acceptable ones—or leave office. The original Black Panther party and the Revolutionary Youth Movement (RYM II) of the Students for a Democratic Society were not true revolutionary groups; the Progressive Labor party (PLP) and the Weatherman factions of the SDS were.[4] Although factions of the Black Panther party steadily moved toward revolutionary aims (as discussed in Chapter 6), the main efforts of the party have been directed toward reforms in the system, especially with respect to police and court practices which put blacks at a disadvantage. RYM II of the SDS also emphasized reforms in its protest activities, its principal targets being the Vietnam War and racism. The Progressive Labor party is a revolutionary group which follows the teachings of the Chinese leader Mao Tse Tung. The principal aim of the PLP is to replace the U.S. system of government with a communist form and to bring about societal reforms which parallel those of Communist China. The Weatherman movement, which advocates the overthrow of the established power structure by armed struggle, is underground.

Like the civil disobedient or the rioter, the insurrectionist wants specific adjustments in the system: increased representation on governmental bodies, a change in political leadership, repeal of an objectionable law, and abandonment of an unjust policy. Insurrection is, in effect, a stage of civil protest that develops out of the same conditions and grievances that inspire acts of civil disobedience or rioting. Although riots do not ordinarily turn into insurrection, the chaos offers insurrectionists a "protective cover" for organized violence to further their goals. Indeed, protesters and rioters are seen by the insurrectionists as representing potential security for the future of organized violent protest and as possible converts to insurrectionist tactics—not so much by the local insurrectionists as by their own disillusionment and frustration.

Insurrectionist activities characteristically involve very few members of an aggrieved community, for it is hard for organizers of insurrection to persuade ordinary citizens to participate in planned violence. Most people, even militants, will not risk physical danger and possible punishment without extreme provocation. Also, the various social controls in the community, quite aside from the law enforcement agencies, inhibit willful acts of premeditated violence and, most of the time, even inhibit civil disobedience. Although law-abiding citizens may get caught up in the contagion of rioting, they are not easily turned toward insurrection.

Persons who can be recruited are those who have previously participated in some form of criminal or borderline criminal activity. Insurrection is more readily organized in a community with a tradition of rioting or insurgency than in a community with a history of peace and stability. A community whose governing authorities are widely recognized as unresponsive or repressive is especially ripe for insurrectionist activities.

As a practical matter, one cannot readily separate the activities associated with spontaneous civil disturbances from those of insurgency. In the early stages of protest stemming from widespread discontent, insurrectionists may await the occurrence of a riot as a cover. As insurrectionists carry out their acts of destruction, they may encourage and assist rioters in similar but unplanned violence, thus fueling the riot and giving it momentum. Revolutionaries may also become involved in their classic role as *provocateurs*.

Contrary to a commonly held belief, there was no documented case of an urban ghetto riot during the 1960s that was set off by either insurrectionist or revolutionary activities. Insurrection that takes place during a riot ordinarily has little effect. Its prime impact may be in the months or years after severe rioting has ceased to be a threat weapon, and when negotiations in the community have subsided short of significant change. At such a point, a well-organized insurrectionist movement could play a crucial role as a renewed threat to recalcitrant authorities. Periodic strikes at police or military headquarters, power stations, and business establishments could continue to dramatize the unresolved grievances.

THE POLICE AND CIVIL PROTEST

The importance of maintaining a nonrepressive policing response to extralegal protest has been stressed as a means of giving the system the capacity to absorb constructive attack from within. The durability of a democratic polity depends upon the degree of resiliency and prudent tolerance in all of its institutions—including the police. While the police cannot stand by when protesters break laws or violate legally constituted policies, they must be trained to differentiate between purely criminal acts and acts of protest stemming from legitimate social, economic, or political grievances.

Civil disobedience, unlike rioting, is the open and intentional violation of a public law, policy, or regulation for the sake of principle or the welfare of the community. But civil disobedience is by definition a nonviolent form of protest. The disobedience may take the form of either doing what is prohibited or failing to do what is required, but disobedience is a premeditated act, understood by the disobedient to be illegal and to carry prescribed penalties. As a form of nonviolent protest, civil disobedience is usually justified by the disobedient under one of the following circumstances:

1. When an oppressed group of citizens is deprived of lawful channels for remedying its grievances
2. When used as a means of refusing to participate in an intolerable evil perpetuated by civil authorities, as for example, a policy of genocide or enslavement

3. When government policies violate the values on which the political system was established
4. When a law or policy is clearly unconstitutional
5. When a change in law or policy is required by social or economic need, and normal procedures are obstructed or in the control of antilegal forces
6. Finally, when the actions of government are so divergent from one's personal values that one would be betraying his conscience in submitting to laws or policies which support those actions as, for example, the Fugitive Slave Law.

An act of civil disobedience under any of these conditions should generally be regarded as obligatory in terms of the highest principles of citizenship and morality. As a practical matter, however, acts of civil disobedience cannot be ignored by civil authorities. On the contrary, aside from the damage such inaction would do to the effectiveness of the protest (which usually *benefits* from the publicity of arrest and punishment), it is the obligation of the government to punish a lawbreaker so long as the violated law is in force. It is a principle of civil disobedience that the individual has the right to refuse to go along with the community, but that the community, not the individual, determines the consequences of such an action. For government to operate otherwise would be to concede the right of individual veto over its every act.

POLICE TRAINING AND ATTITUDES

Police are trained to enforce the laws and customs of the community. They are not encouraged to question the basis or legitimacy of those laws and customs. In this sense, democratic ideals occupy a place secondary to law enforcement in the police profession. In theory, the police officer above all others must accept the law because he is permitted the maximum amount of discretion in its enforcement. Society has granted the policeman the license to violate the law in order to enforce it; he may speed to catch a speeder, kill to subdue a killer, destroy property, invade privacy, and arrest on suspicion. The sense of power a policeman gains from the exercise of these special privileges often imbues him with the notion that he is above the law. Thus policing procedures must be carefully spelled out by civilian authority, and extralegal procedures have to be regulated so that they are not, in fact, unlawful. The policeman must have extralegal procedures for use in crime control, but he must not be put in the position of having to violate the law in order to enforce the law. To prevent this, police procedures usually state the circumstances under which he may lawfully exceed speed limits, lawfully destroy property, or lawfully kill a suspected criminal.

Such procedures, to be effective, must be promulgated in local law by elected authorities. Such policies include appropriate constraints upon those whose duty it is to intervene when a crime is committed.

Control of rioting, insurrection, revolution, and some forms of disobedient protest normally falls within the jurisdiction of the local police. What is required is the development of police policies which reflect an appropriate and judicious balance between the maintenance of order and tolerance of aggressive political activities, some of which involve violence.

Traditionally, local police bureaucracies are among the most conservative and authoritarian institutions in our society. In the words of Joseph D. Lohman, the eminent sociologist and former sheriff of Cook County (Chicago):

> The uniform police, by the nature of their mission to maintain law and order and secure the established institutional arrangements are . . . supportive of the status quo . . . visible and tangible representatives of an intransigent social order . . .[5]

Police conservatism can be traced to the dangers, hostilities, and challenges to authority which are ever-present in the lives of police officers. The danger in police work trains the police officer to be suspicious and supportive of the status quo. Anything out of the ordinary in the daily routine of the beat is a subject for investigation. Moreover, if a policeman did not believe in the system of laws he was responsible for enforcing, he would risk a serious personal conflict, a condition psychologists term "cognitive dissonance."[6]

The recruit who enters the system with conservative attitudes (that is, an inclination to maintain the status quo) has no difficulty in adjusting to the conservative imperative of the police culture. It is the liberal-minded recruit who must somehow rationalize the discrepancies between the objective demands of law enforcement and his own propensity for tolerance of change.

The conservative attitudes of police and their inclination to discourage change alienate groups which press for change. The confrontation, the disorders, and the general disrespect for the law which follow are situations which all but a few local police organizations are neither able to comprehend in political and social terms nor trained to manage as technical police problems. For this reason, public confidence in the police was greatly impaired during the ghetto riots of the 1960s. Some of the most serious consequences as reported by the President's Commission on Law Enforcement and Administration of Justice are summarized as follows:

1. Negative public attitudes are reflected in inadequate manpower supply. Able young men are reluctant to enter an occupation which, lacking the respect of kinfolk and neighbors, has low status among occupational alternatives. Nearly all major police departments are currently operating under their authorized limits of personnel strength, and difficulty in recruitment has become a chronic condition of the public service.
2. Hostility toward the police impairs the morale of the policemen. Correspondingly, the police are disposed to become cynical; low morale is reflected in excessive turnover and early departure for the service.
3. A dissatisfied and disapproving public fails to support the police when issues such as salaries, number of officers, necessary equipment, and building construction and repair are pending before state legislatures, city councils, or executive authorities.
4. An antagonistic public is not likely to cooperate with the police in reporting violations, even as victims. There is a general indisposition, as well as reluctance, to report suspicious persons or incidents, appear as witnesses, or provide information. Considering the relatively small proportion of all crimes known to the police and the even smaller number which are cleared up through investigation, the lack of citizen cooperation compounds the problem and causes it to reach critical proportions.[7]

POLICE-COMMUNITY RELATIONS

In spite of damaged public confidence and antagonistic relations in ghetto communities, local police for a long time resisted public pressure for an effective police-community relations staff. Community relations units that have been set up in local departments are usually given a public relations assignment to interpret police work to the community and to appeal for public support and cooperation. Police-community relations units that have tried to do a serious job of developing sympathetic relations in socially explosive communities are almost universally seen as a threat to the departments in which they exist. This is because such units are a natural receiving point for citizen complaints against the police. If community relations officers press for redress of complaints, they risk alienating the line force; if they do not, they are seen as ineffective by the community.[8]

The community relations unit in the San Francisco police department under Lieutenant Dante Andreotti from 1962 to 1967 is a case in point. Andreotti shunned away from creating a system of informers in the new unit and he had no taste for mere public relations. He set out to learn what was going on in San Francisco's black and Mexican-American communities, what the issues were, and what people thought the problems were. He sought to open up channels to community segments never before considered reachable. Andreotti learned that community relations could not be dedicated to "selling" the police. If the police product were salable, Andreotti once said, "you wouldn't have to have community relations. . . . Explaining the police department is something you can do after you have proved yourself. You can . . . fatmouth to your heart's content, but if people don't see tangible results . . . you have lost them."[9]

Andreotti's operation won support among minority groups in San Francisco because it followed through on complaints and sponsored programs that the ethnic communities valued: coaching black youth for union apprentice exams, raising funds for recreation programs, working with Upward Bound to get minority youngsters into college, and interpreting police records of job applicants to prospective employers. But the community orientation which Andreotti's community relations unit adopted got him into trouble with the rest of the department. Policemen, he said, are hung up on law and order. "Instead of trying to communicate with the Negro, to make him feel that the law is for him too, they are busy espousing the thin-blue-line theory, the idea that they stand between you and chaos."[10] The 1966 riot in the Hunter's Point section of San Francisco undermined high-level support by city hall of Andreotti's program, and the rank-and-file pressures in the department prevailed.

POLITICALIZATION OF THE POLICE

Local police bureaucracies in most cities control the policy framework within which they operate. The extreme dispersal of political power and the typically high turnover of local political leadership weakens the public control over the police and policing policy. Thus, the day-to-day routine of police work adds up to the policing "policy" of the community. By default, the police themselves create the community's standards and guidelines for the maintenance of law and order. Frequently these standards involve a short-circuiting of due process in the interest of preserving order and enforcing acceptable behavior: summary punishment on the street or in the station house, prolonged detainment incommunicado, failure to inform the suspect of his constitutional rights, and obtaining confessions under various forms of physical or psychological duress.

In most American cities, the "police establishment" is a political force in its own right, often capable of mustering formidable support for the issues it favors.[11] For example, in New York City in 1966, the Patrolmen's Benevolent Association succeeded in getting a referendum vote which abolished the Police Review Board that Mayor John Lindsay had created by executive order.[12]

The issue of a civilian-dominated police review board has arisen in the past decade or two in almost every city that has a substantial black, Puerto Rican, or Mexican-American population living in poverty-ridden neighborhoods where crime rates are high. Complaints against the police have come mostly from these neighborhoods, and the issue is whether or not the police can deal effectively and fairly with complaints of harassment and brutality. Proponents of civilian review boards argue that the police review of complaints inevitably favors the accused, while the police counter that an independent review procedure would unduly restrain law enforcement, undermine police morale, and impair efficiency in crime control.

In the past, local police departments have had political significance both as part of the local patronage structure and as a combination sounding board and organizational base for neighborhood political work. Probably the advent of civil service and mobile patrols reduced somewhat the political influence of the police between 1930 and 1960. In the past decade, however, the police unions and professional associations have exerted a significant new political influence on behalf of the police interests.

As police unionism takes hold, the organized political power of the local police will be enhanced; it is a short step from union organization to political activism. The sharp rise in crime rates, the urban riots of the sixties, student unrest, and war demonstrations were the issues that precipitated the latent political activism of the embryonic police unions—issues which also brought into the open the potential activism of the ostensibly nonpolitical local police associations.

THE POLICE CULTURE

Lacking firm and consistent direction from higher political authority, the police rely on their own values and experiences in formulating policy. In the American tradition, the local police in larger cities, especially in the Midwest and the East, are likely to be recruited from one or two ethnic groups, for example, the Irish in Boston and New York, whose leaders hold influential positions in the municipal hierarchy. Typically, the pay is low and the opportunities for advancement are limited in comparison with those in skilled trades or other professional or civil service areas. Educational requirements for the police have been minimal, and although physical standards are commonly stressed at the recruitment stage, they are not rigorously maintained in service.

From the vantage point of the police, social homogeneity within the department is important in maintaining a structure of mutual support against the hostile environment in which the police operate. The recruiting process in most departments reinforces this homogeneity, which means bringing in men who fit an established pattern of social and educational background. In New York City, most police candidates in the two decades following World War II were from the working class, and only about 5 percent had any college training. The typical features of the contemporary police recruit are a working-class background, a high school education or less, average or below average intelligence, a cautious personality, and a physical superiority.[13]

Prevailing values among the police-conforming behavior, group loyalty, morality, and authoritative behavior—are entirely incompatible with the militancy, radicalism, and generally uninhibited behavior associated with rebellious protest and rioting. At the very least, the perception (or misperception) of values attributed to each protagonist by the other is in itself sufficient cause for severe friction in a confrontation. Whatever values are held by individual police officers, the militants engaged in protest or the citizens participating in a riot see all police as willing agents of an oppressive society. On their side, the police see rioters and protesters as a threat to peace and order, as subversives, or worse.[14]

The police as a group share the conservative norms and values which are grossly offended by the attitudes and rhetoric of radical militants and the angry outbursts of aggrieved minorities. The trouble is that the police often fail to make distinctions among the different types of protest, and therefore may try to suppress legitimate protest as though it were insurrection or revolution. Also, police who come from working-class backgrounds are especially sensitive to the aggressiveness of the ambitious lower-class blacks who seem to threaten the meager hard-won resources of whites just above them on the economic ladder. They also resent welfare programs from which poverty-stricken minorities benefit, for these programs at the local level are largely supported by rising property taxes.

The class prejudices and values held by a police recruit when he enters the police system are likely to be reinforced by training and experience throughout his career. His antiblack and antiradical attitudes are supported by older officers as well as by contemporaries. Arthur Niederhoffer, a sociologist and former New York City police officer, asserts that after five years the patrolman on street duty becomes increasingly cynical, authoritarian, and generally hostile to the nonpolice world. The least desirable assignments in the ghetto areas generally fall to the least able patrolmen; the more able ones are promoted to supervisory positions or transferred to specialized administration assignments, training duties, recruitment, and juvenile work.[15]

THE NEW IMMIGRANTS AND CIVIL LIBERTIES

We have passed through the period in our social and political development when extreme decentralization of political power served a useful function in settling and assimilating new ethnic and cultural groups. We no longer admit large numbers of immigrants whose diverse backgrounds require a wide range of local governing options for easy assimilation. The "new immigrants" come from the rural and underdeveloped areas to the cities. It is true enough that these people also require a just, benevolent, and relatively undemanding transition in their new surroundings. In order to create such a milieu in the face of pervasive racial discrimination in local bureaucracies, the moral imperatives of constitutional democracy must be brought into play.

Local police bureaucracies, operating entirely within their own subculture and within the framework of the dominant community they serve, are not likely to deal sympathetically with new ethnic groups whose life styles and values differ significantly from the prevailing ones within the community. Nor are local police likely to adopt peacekeeping policies in dealing with the protest activities of aggrieved minorities which do not have the sanction of local public policy.

At the heart of current social change is the erosion of long-established values rooted in the traditions of locally dominant ethnic groupings which has left local police with tenuous guidelines on which to operate. Moreover, the police have lagged behind the general shift to a national value orientation and are thus caught in the middle of the intense conflict which characterizes the replacement of local values (customs and laws) with national ones based on long-established but dormant constitutional principles of equity and justice.

An example of the shift in values which directly affects police work is the application of Fourteenth Amendment requirements for due process and equal protection of the laws to state and local criminal law. In several cases (*Mapp* v. *Ohio, Miranda* v. *Arizona,* and *Gideon* v. *Wainwright*) the Supreme Court affirmed the application of basic constitutional rights to criminal proceedings in the states.[16] Theretofore, the states had been free to extend or withhold such rights so long as the criminal proceedings were wholly within their jurisdiction. Standards of justice were considered to be divisible within the federal system in deference to the principle of local over national governance.

In recent years the Supreme Court has taken many opportunities to resolve differences between federal and state standards of justice. The next step is to bring police practices into line with the established law of the land. But the difficulties in doing so are enormous because of police dedication to local values and traditional practice. The more the police cling to the old ways, the more alienated they become from the main thrust of social change in the land.

Policy in crime control is fairly clear in most police jurisdictions, however, in spite of these actions by the Supreme Court there continues to be a considerable area of disagreement between police administrators and the federal courts over the substance and application of the due process requirements of the federal Constitution. Various landmark Supreme Court decisions have reaffirmed the principles of constitutional law. When local police ignore them, it is because they feel that an emphasis on due process unduly hampers crime control activities.

POLICE ATTITUDES TOWARD THE COMMUNITY

Policy guidelines for management of protest activities are not so clear, except for the few that have the sanction of law, for example, labor strikes and picketing. As a consequence, during the ghetto riots of the 1960s, the police response to protest was frequently as spontaneous and violent as the actions of the rioters themselves. In many cases, the police provoked or escalated riots. Such situations were documented by official investigations in the Newark riot of 1967 and in the Chicago disturbance of 1968.[17]

Police policy, as well as the range and quality of local police services, is still substantially determined by the expectations of middle- and upper-class citizens in the community (as the police interpret them). The police take their cues from these groups in stressing the maintenance of order and the protection of property as reasons against the expression of individual rights and freedom of protest. In situations of potential or actual social upheaval, the police ordinarily serve as a protective buffer between the "respectable" citizenry and the varieties of disorderly behavior among the disgruntled.

Furthermore, the attitudes police officers have toward various groups in the community determine the type and quality of police service and the treatment that these groups are likely to receive in their contacts with the police. For example, a black or a hippie may be treated quite differently in a given circumstance than a white businessman in the same situation if the officer happens to dislike blacks or hippies. Some police officers lump all blacks together and treat them with suspicion and hostility, and a majority of local police officers oppose rapid integration of minority groups. These attitudes crop up in routine contacts and, even more often, during community disturbances. Even so, the role of racial prejudice in police encounters with citizens is probably exaggerated by critics. A 1966 study of police-citizen encounters in three major U.S. cities found that white suspects may be twice as subject to improper police treatment as are black subjects.[18]

A survey for the President's Commission on Law Enforcement and Administration of Justice (1966) reported that of policemen (both black and white) working in black neighborhoods, 45 percent of the white officers were found to be "extremely anti-Negro," a classification that was used when an officer referred to blacks as subhuman, suggested an extreme solution to the "Negro problem," expressed hatred, or used pejorative nicknames for blacks. In these same black neighborhoods, another 34 percent of white officers were prejudiced, although to a lesser degree than the first, 10 percent were neutral, and only 1 percent were "pro-Negro." This survey also showed that 28 percent of black police officers were prejudiced against their own race.[19]

The survey indicated, however, that class, rather than racial prejudice, may have been the prime motivation for discriminatory actions. The main victims of police harassment and brutality were lower-class men, both white and black. In the study, no middle-class or upper-class offender, white or black, was victimized; also, no white women and only two black women were victims.

Nevertheless, one survey's conclusion was that blacks generally distrust police officers, viewing them as mercenaries of the white society put into the black community to protect the surrounding white communities against possible incursions of blacks. This belief seemed to blacks to be confirmed during the riots of the sixties when police typically were used to seal off black districts when disturbances broke out. It is a fact that whites see the police in a far more favorable light than do blacks, indicating that whites more often see the police as service agents and protectors; whereas blacks, by and large, see them as harassing agents.

A nationwide survey conducted in 1966 by the President's Commission on Law Enforcement and Administration of Justice showed these contrasting attitudes of blacks and whites. Twenty-three percent of all white persons thought that the police were doing an excellent job of enforcing the law, while only 15 percent of blacks agreed. Only 11 percent of whites thought the police were doing a "poor" job, whereas 16 percent of blacks held that view. The report noted roughly the same response to a question on how well the police protect citizens. Sixty-three percent of whites and 30 percent of blacks thought the police were "almost all honest." One percent of whites and 10 percent of blacks thought the police were "almost all corrupt."[20]

Two years later, in the spring of 1968, as the urban ghetto riots in the United States were at their height, the *Report of the National Advisory Commission on Civil Disorders* (the Kerner Commission Report) showed that blacks were far more likely than whites to feel that people in their neighborhood did not receive prompt police service. One out of every four blacks reported that he personally had experienced poor service. The blacks were also twice as likely as the whites to say they knew people who had experienced poor police service. The survey showed that two or three times as many blacks as whites had experienced disrespect or insulting language by the police, knew someone who had had the experience, or believed it happened to people in their neighborhood. The 1968 survey also revealed that three times as many blacks as whites believed that the police in their neighborhood "search people without good reason." About the same proportion reported having had the experience personally.[31]

Black hostility toward the police is not confined to the poor or to those engaged in unlawful activities. Many black businessmen, doctors, lawyers, and police officers share these beliefs. As evidence, black professionals have led the attacks on police abuses. For example, the Guardians, an organization of black police officers in New York City, endorse a proposed civilian review board in opposition to organizations of white officers.

Excessive force is most likely to be used by police officers when their authority is threatened or seems to be. Albert Reiss reported that 48 percent of cases he studied had involved open defiance of police authority or resistance to arrest: "Open defiance of police authority . . . is what the policeman considers *his* authority, not necessarily official authority."[32] In 40 percent of the cases that police officers considered open defiance, no arrest was made. It seems to be a question of "who is in charge."

A police department which condones the use of excessive force and harassment tactics in routine control of crime and deviancy finds it easier to allow (and even encourage) an adaptation of such tactics in the control of civil disobedience, rioting, and other forms of non-sanctioned protest. From the standpoint of the police officer who has acquired the habit of brutality as a method of deviancy control, such tactics seem all the more appropriate in response to mass attacks which seem to threaten not only the police but government itself.

Unfortunately, the police and civilian authorities as well tend to blame violence which grows out of dissent on troublemakers. The police then see themselves as the protectors of the community. The "troublemakers" premise leads to a double standard of law enforcement as it applies to an aggrieved or dissident group. Thus, there is a presupposition by many police (with respect to minorities) of the inevitability of vice or law violation when there are contacts between persons of differing racial extraction. Thereby, police also presuppose the necessity to enforce the social customs and traditions of the community apart from the law, for example, the necessity to invoke special action against minority groups which is not invoked against other citizens, such as stopping them for questioning if they are in the "wrong" place at the "wrong" time.

REGULATING THE POLICE

Blaming troublemakers and the failure to recognize legitimate protest is one set of problems between citizens and the police. The absence of effective channels for airing grievances against the police is another perhaps more serious one. Complaints of police abuse of civil rights fall upon deaf ears, for the police insist on the "right" to investigate such complaints.

The issues of justice and objectivity are submerged in debate over the issue of "policing the police," although this element is crucial to the principle of democratic governance. The absence of any effective machinery for mediating between the police and the ghetto communities they "serve" is a formidable deficiency in the law enforcement systems of the nation in view of the critical social stresses on the current urban scene.

To meet this problem, mediating machinery needs to be developed between aggrieved groups and the official agencies of the community to reduce the potential for violent outbursts when confrontations occur. As Dean Lohman once remarked, it is not the changes in society which affect police morale but the failure of the police to adapt to those changes.[23]

If the protest of the 1950s and 1960s is viewed in these terms, the police appear in the wrong, because they have been so overtly resistant to change. The "villain analysis," of course, almost never corresponds to the objective situation. The police have reacted to protest as they have interpreted their duty to the larger community, and they have responded according to the rules and practices by which they have been trained. Until publication of the Kerner Commission Report in March, 1968, no authoritative source at the national or local level had asserted that police response to protest should be under any set of rules other than the traditional ones. The Kerner Report, however, criticized local police for overreaction to riots. The report also criticized local police for prejudicial behavior toward ghetto residents and other disadvantaged groups and offered guidelines for improving police behavior in minority neighborhoods and for effective response to civil disturbances. However, following the publication of the report, neither President Johnson, who created the commission, nor presidential candidates Hubert Humphrey and

Richard Nixon made any definitive statements in acknowledgement of the commission's findings.

Thus, the police felt unjustly criticized and more determined than ever to use repressive tactics. The seven-day "police riot" at the Chicago Democratic National Convention in 1968 reflected the temper and inclination of police throughout the nation in the period immediately following the crescendo of riots across the nation in the aftermath of Dr. Martin Luther King's assassination. Ugly police reaction to a black mayor's efforts at riot deescalation in Cleveland a few weeks earlier (July 1968) may also have been another consequence of the failure of national leadership to recognize a need for firm direction in the interest of local order and social justice. A responsible and restrained presidential reaction might have laid the groundwork for establishing national guidelines of local police response to protest.

Guidelines for police policy in response to social change should take into account elements of our values which pertain to the administration of justice: respect for individual rights as set forth in the Constitution regardless of social or economic status; respect for the dignity of the individual regardless of personal condition or deviant actions; enforcement of the law within the bounds of sound judgment based on knowledge of the community; and protection of life and property against the destructive intent of deviant persons.

These principles demand a degree of maturity, restraint, and professional efficiency in police organizations which is beyond the capacity and outside the tradition of many departments.

VARIETIES OF POLICE BEHAVIOR

James Q. Wilson has described three varieties of police behavior in a selection of cities across the nation.[24] In every case, he observed, the police are found to adopt a style of behavior which the local administration believes to be the suitable "fit" with community values. The "watchman" style works best in communities which place a higher value on maintenance of order than on strict law enforcement. Common minor violations may be ignored, a certain amount of gambling and vice tolerated, and so on. Police who operate in ghetto communities generally believe that black people want (or "deserve") less law enforcement than middle-class white neighborhoods, and they tend to play the "watchman" role in those neighborhoods, emphasizing law enforcement only when ordered to "crack down" in the event of a serious crime or disturbance. The "watchman" style is also characteristic of police in cities where organized crime (largely vice and gambling) are tolerated and/or protected by the local authorities.

The "legalistic" style prevails in communities whose police administrators regard law enforcement as the principal function of the department. In Wilson's description, "A legalistic department will issue traffic tickets at a high rate, detain and arrest a high proportion of juvenile offenders, act vigorously against illicit enterprises, and make a large number of misdemeanor arrests even when . . . the public order has not been breached. The police will act, on the whole, as if there were a single standard of community conduct."[25] Thus, the "legalistic" department takes no account of the different standards of conduct which normally exist within a heterogeneous community. In effect, what is expected of the middle-class businessman is also expected of the juvenile, the drunk, the unemployed, the newcomer, the tramp, and the dispossessed.

The "service" style of police administration predominates in well-ordered, small communities whose populations are relatively homogeneous, prosperous, and stable. The "service" style gives serious attention to law enforcement and order maintenance, although actual arrests and formal sanctions are less likely to be applied than in the "legalistic" department. In communities where the "service" style prevails, the police see their responsibility as protecting the public order against intruders or unruly local youths.

It seems reasonable to conclude that the "service" style is most compatible with the dominant values of our emerging national community. "Legalistic" police administration can only be appropriate in a community in which the need for citizen discipline is great— where citizens are so accustomed to being strictly regulated that they would become a potential threat to each other should the discipline be relaxed, or where there exists a lethal internal or external threat of such proportions as to require a discipline-oriented citizenry to ward off the danger.

Moreover, since legalisms can always be invoked to block or suppress protest prior to a joining of the substantive issues, "legalistic" law enforcement can be a threat to legitimate protest activities. Local authorities can stop an antiwar demonstration on the grounds that it would preempt normal use of a street or park without ever considering the issue of the war, even though that issue might involve a legitimate challenge to a national policy. Legalism for its own sake inhibits creative change, and overreverence for the law can be as serious an obstacle to change as dictatorial power. Respect for the law, not reverence, is the proper basis of order in the democratic society.

The "watchman" style, on the other hand, encourages and promotes disrespect for the law and for the moral and ethical standards of society on which the law is based. Moreover, the deliberate abrogation by public officials of widely held social standards almost always generates within the community a strong desire for reform. Reform movements against corrupt public leaders sometimes lead to the adoption of rigid, legalistic standards of law enforcement.

The "service" style, characterized by restrained and knowledgeable attention to problems of law enforcement and order maintenance, opens the door to the development of police procedures which take into account both the rights and dignity of citizens who come into contact with the police, and the requirement of order and the protection of life and property. It seems imperative that police service throughout the nation should come within guidelines which characterize the "service" style. Our national standards of justice demand it, and the implementation of these standards are a prerequisite to national maturity.

CONCLUSIONS

The dissent and violence of the past two decades originated in the widespread resistance to the efforts of minorities to gain a place of dignity and achievement in the society. Further trouble grew out of the inability of the national government to avoid a catastrophic involvement in a war in Southeast Asia. Local police were psychologically, tactically, and logistically unprepared for the protest and rioting that ensued. Because they were unprepared, they frequently initiated or contributed to the escalation of the violence that took place, then justified their acts of brutality on the grounds that the law must be enforced. Because so many of the issues which the local police are called upon to confront are of national concern, we cannot afford to leave law enforcement policy entirely to local law enforcement agencies.

Enforcement procedures in response to civil protest—including riots—should be governed by policies of restraint which effectively maintain public order, protect nonparticipating persons and property, and prevent gross disruption of normal community activity. Policies of restraint should specify a style of police response to protest-related incidents, alternative methods of containment, and a variety of arrest and detainment procedures dependent upon circumstances. Such policies should rule out punitive actions and provocative behavior by the police at the scene and should seek to control fear-inducing responses by the police which escalate disturbances and radicalize dissent. The assertion of such guidelines reveals a fundamental dilemma in the policing of a democratic society: the demand for bureaucratic flexibility versus strict law enforcement procedures.[26]

In short, the police in a democratic society must not be cast as agents of exclusion to discriminate against some groups or to inhibit constructive change. Neither should the police play a role in maintaining barriers of economic, political, or social class. To the extent that the police are used in these latter functions, the democratic basis of the society is undermined, and a totalitarian police state is substituted.

We must recognize in this regard that new demands upon local police require new resources. If we are right in the judgment that problems confronting local police are increasingly those of national concern and that local resources are inadequate, then future resources for local police service should be supported by substantial federal programs. Such national programs could provide better standards for administering law enforcement and modernizing local police policies.

NOTES

1. Morris Janowitz, "Patterns of Collective Racial Violence," in *The History of Violence in America: A Report to the National Commission on the Causes and Prevention of Violence*, eds. Hugh D. Graham and Ted R. Gurr (New York: Bantam Books, 1969), pp. 412–444.
2. Stanley Lieberson and Arnold Silverman, "The Precipitants and Underlying Conditions of Race Riots," *American Sociological Review*, Vol. 30, No. 6 (December 1965), pp. 887–898.
3. The stages of a full-scale riot are described in Ralph W. Conant, *The Prospects for Revolution* (New York: Harper's Magazine Press, 1971), pp. 32–35.
4. *Ibid.*, Chapter 8.
5. Joseph D. Lohman, "Comments on the Relations of the Police Force to Society," *West Michigan 1980*, Proceedings of the Grand Rapids Conference sponsored by Television Station WOOD (Grand Rapids, Mich., March 26, 1968), pp. 1–7.
6. See: Arthur Niederhoffer, *Behind the Shield: The Police in Urban Society* (Garden City, N.Y.: Doubleday, Anchor Books, 1967).

7. Report by the President's Commission on Law Enforcement and Administration of Justice, *The Challenge of Crime in a Free Society* (Washington, D.C.: U.S. Government Printing Office, 1967).
8. See: James Q. Wilson, "The Police in the Ghetto," in *The Police and the Community*, A Supplementary Paper of the Committee for Economic Development, ed. Robert F. Steadman (Baltimore: Johns Hopkins University Press, 1972), pp. 51–90.
9. Eleanore Carruth, "Our War with the Police Department," *Fortune* (January 1968), p. 195.
10. *Ibid.*, p. 196.
11. For an analysis of the police as a political force, see: Jerome H. Skolnick, *The Politics of Protest*, A report submitted by the Task Force on Violent Aspects of Protest and Confrontation of the National Commission on the Causes and Prevention of Violence (New York: Ballantine Books, 1969).
12. Jewel Bellush and Stephen M. David, eds., *Race and Politics in New York City* (New York: Praeger, 1971).
13. See: Niederhoffer, *Behind the Shield.*
14. See: Skolnick, *The Politics of Protest.*
15. See: Niederhoffer, *Behind the Shield.*
16. *Gideon* v. *Wainwright*, 372 U.S. 355 (1963). In the Gideon case, the Supreme Court ruled that in all criminal prosecution, whether federal or state, counsel must be provided to any defendant who can not afford to hire a lawyer. Also, see: *Mallory* v. *U.S.*, 354 U.S. 449 (1957); *McNabb* v. *U.S.*, 318 U.S. 332 (1943); *Miranda* v. *Arizona*, 348 U.S. 436 (1966); and *Mapp* v. *Ohio*, 367 U.S. 343 (1961).
17. See: Governor's Select Commission on Civil Disorder State of New Jersey, *Report for Action* (Trenton, N.J., February 1968). Also see *Rights in Conflict*, The Walker Report to the National Commission on the Causes and Prevention of Violence (New York: Bantam Books, 1968). The subject of the report was the confrontation of demonstrators and the police in Chicago at the site of the Democratic National Convention in 1968. See also Ralph W. Conant, *The Prospects for Revolution*, pp. 174–176.
18. Albert J. Reiss, Jr., "Police Brutality—Answers to Key Questions," *Trans-Action* (July-August 1968), pp. 10–19.
19. Albert J. Reiss, Jr., "Studies in Law Enforcement in Major Metropolitan Areas," A Research Report Prepared for the President's Commission on Law Enforcement and Administration of Justice, 1967.
20. President's Commission, *The Challenge of Crime in a Free Society.*
21. *Report of the National Advisory Commission on Civil Disorders* (Washington, D.C.: U.S. Government Printing Office, 1968).
22. Reiss, "Studies in Law Enforcement in Major Metropolitan Areas," p. 8.
23. Lohman, "Comments on the Relations of the Police Force to Society."
24. James Q. Wilson, *Varieties of Police Behavior* (New York: Atheneum, 1968). Also, see: Jesse Rubin, "Police Identity and the Police Role," in *The Police and the Community*, A Supplementary Paper of the Committee for Economic Development, ed. Robert F. Steadman (Baltimore: Johns Hopkins University Press, 1972), pp. 12–50. Also, see: David P. Stang, "The Police and Their Problems," in *Law and Order Reconsidered*, co-directors James S. Campbell, Joseph R. Sahid, and David P. Stang, Vol. 10, National Commission on the Causes and Prevention of Violence Staff Study Series (Washington, D.C.: U.S. Government Printing Office, 1969), pp. 285–308.

25. Wilson, *Varieties of Police Behavior,* p. 172.
26. See: Charles B. Saunders, Jr., *Upgrading the American Police* (Washington, D.C.: Brookings Institution, 1970).

SUGGESTED READINGS

Protests, Riots, and Community Order

Boskin, Joseph, ed. *Urban Racial Violence in the Twentieth Century.* Beverly Hills, Calif.: Glencoe Press, 1969.
Selected essays with commentaries on the history of urban racial conflict.

Conant, Ralph W. *The Prospects For Revolution.* New York: Harper's Magazine Press, 1971. See especially: Chs. 2, 3, and 7.
A study of riots, civil disobedience, and insurrection.

Connery, Robert H., ed. *Urban Riots.* New York: Random House, Vintage Books, 1969.
Original essays on violence and social change.

Conot, Robert. *Rivers of Blood, Years of Darkness.* New York: Bantam Books, 1967.
Vivid first-hand description of the Watts, Los Angeles riot of 1965.

Fanon, Frantz. *The Wretched of the Earth.* New York: Grove Press, Evergreen edition, 1966.
Strategy for guerilla warfare and revolutionary upheaval.

Feagin, Joe R., and Harlan Hahan. *Ghetto Revolts.* New York: Macmillan, 1973.
Analysis of ghetto rioting and law enforcement responses.

Fogelson, Robert M. *Violence As Protest.* Garden City, N.Y.: Doubleday, Anchor Books, 1971.
Examination of black protest and riot participation.

Gilbert, Ben W., and the staff of *The Washington Post. Ten Blocks From the White House.* New York: Praeger, 1968.
Journalistic account of Washington, D.C. riots of 1968.

Governor's Select Commission on Civil Disorders. *Report for Action.* State of New Jersey, February 1968.
Analysis of 1967 New Jersey urban riots with an especially critical attack on the Newark city administration.

Graham, Hugh D., and Ted R. Gurr, eds. *The History of Violence in America.* A Report to the National Commission on the Causes and Prevention of Violence. New York: Bantam Books, 1969.
An exhaustive and significantly revealing series of essays indicating the roots of violence in American society.

Hayden, Tom. *Rebellion in Newark.* New York: Random House, Vintage Books, 1967.
Brief description of 1967 Newark riots.

Hubbard, Howard. "Five Long Hot Summers on How They Grow," *The Public Interest*, No. 12 (Summer 1968), pp. 3–24.
Analysis of Negro protest within a framework of bargaining and negotiation.

Killian, Lewis M. *The Impossible Revolution? Black Power and the American Dream*. New York: Random House, paperback, 1968.
Pessimistic account of black prospects for change.

Masotti, Louis H., and Don R. Bowen, eds. *Riots and Rebellion*. Beverly Hills, Calif. Sage Publications, 1968.
Collection of original essays analyzing civil disorders.

Report of the National Advisory Commission on Civil Disorders, New York: Bantam Books, 1968.
Comprehensive analysis of 1967 city riots together with prescriptions for change. Highly recommended.

Sears, David O., and John B. McConahay. *The Politics of Violence*. Boston: Houghton Mifflin, 1973.
Analysis of 1965 Watts riot.

Willis, Garry. *The Second Civil War*. New York: The New American Library, Signet Books, 1968.
Interviews with police officials preparing for civil disorders.

Wilson, James Q. "The Urban Unease: Community vs. City," *The Public Interest*, No. 12 (Summer 1969), pp. 25–39.
Neighborhood concern for public order.

————. "Why We Are Having A Wave of Violence," *The New York Times Magazine* (May 19, 1968), pp. 23–24, 116–120.
Contends that recent ghetto riots differ from past civil disturbances.

The Police

Advisory Commission on Intergovernmental Relations. *Making the Safe Streets Act Work*. Washington: U.S. Government Printing Office, September 1970.
Analysis of 1968 federal legislation assisting local law enforcement, the first such comprehensive federal law providing grant-in-aid assistance.

Bellush, Jewel, and Stephen M. David, eds. *Race and Politics in New York City*. New York: Praeger, 1971.
Case studies on welfare, police, housing, education, and health.

Campbell, James S., Joseph R. Sahid, and David P. Stang, co-directors. *Law and Order Reconsidered*. Vol. 10, National Commission on the Causes and Prevention of Violence Staff Study Series. Washington: U.S. Government Printing Office, 1969.
Comprehensive report on problems of disorder, police response, and agencies of law enforcement.

The Challenge of Crime in a Free Society. A Report by the President's Commission on Law Enforcement and Administration of Justice, New York: Avon Books, 1968.

Considerably detailed analysis of crime and police problems in American society.

Chavigny, Paul. *Police Power:* New York: Random House, Vintage Books, 1969.
Study of police abuses and civil liberty violations in New York City.

Doig, Jameson W., symposium editor. "The Police in a Democratic Society," *Public Administration Review,* Vol. 28, No. 5 (September-October 1968), pp. 393–430.
Four interesting articles on police problems and prospects.

Masotti, Louis H., and Jerome R. Corsi. *Shoot Out In Cleveland.* A Report to the National Commission on the Causes and Prevention of Violence. New York: Bantam Books, 1969.
Analysis of the events and causes related to the battle between black militants and the police in Cleveland on July 23, 1968.

Niederhoffer, Arthur. *Behind The Shield.* Garden City, N.Y.: Doubleday, Anchor Books, 1969.
Important evaluation of conflicts in police roles and perceptions.

Rubin, Jesse. "Police Identity and Police Role," in *The Police and the Community,* ed. Robert F. Steadman. Baltimore: Johns Hopkins, Committee for Economic Development, 1972.

Saunders, Charles B., Jr. *Upgrading the American Police.* Washington: Brookings Institution, 1970.
Recommendations for improving the quality of the police for better law enforcement.

Skolnick, Jerome H., director. *The Politics of Protest.* A Report to the National Commission on the Causes and Prevention of Violence. New York: Ballantine Books, 1969.
Controversial study of protest strategies and tactics with an especially interesting chapter on the politicalization of the police.

Summers, Marvin R., and Thomas E. Barth, eds. *Law and Order in a Democratic Society.* Columbus, Ohio: Charles E. Merrill, 1970.
Selected essays on criminal justice, urban violence, and political dissent.

Walker, Daniel, director. *Rights In Conflict.* A Special Investigation Report to the National Commission on the Causes and Prevention of Violence, New York: Bantam Books, 1968.
Detailed study of the violent confrontation between demonstrators and police in Chicago during the Democratic National Convention of 1968.

Wilson, James Q. *Varieties of Police Behavior.* New York: Atheneum, 1970.
Study of various police roles and styles.

8

Politics and Policies of Public Welfare

INTRODUCTION

American cities were confronted by a tremendous rise in the welfare rolls during the 1960s. Past policy problems had caused a social disaster of nationwide implications. The failures of public assistance significantly contributed to the urban crisis. No longer did welfare adequately serve the urban poor. Instead of assisting needy mothers and their children, public welfare policy created a class of dependent poor who used the dole as their primary subsistence for food, clothing, and shelter. Ironically, the greatest pressure on the welfare system occurred during a time of general national prosperity. A booming economy created new jobs, reduced unemployment, and raised the incomes of the poor.

Neither the providers nor the recipients were satisfied with the welfare system. Their discontent was a source of considerable political and social conflict. As the federal, state, and local governments became concerned with the financial demands of ever-expanding relief rolls, efforts were made to reduce aid by discouraging dependency and by eliminating so-called welfare chiselers. At the same time, welfare recipients began to organize to demand more benefits and higher payments from welfare agencies. The ghetto riots of 1967 focused attention on the relief problem. The National Advisory

Commission on Civil Disorders observed that "our present system of public assistance contributes materially to the tensions and social disorganization that have led to civil disorders. The failures of the system alienate the taxpayers who support it, the social workers who administer it, and the poor who depend upon it."[1]

Pressures to reform welfare policy focused upon the Aid to Families with Dependent Children (AFDC) program. By the end of the 1960s the federal government had made efforts to ease the eligibility for public assistance, to provide job training and day-care services for recipients able to work, and to eliminate many of the state and local administrative practices and discrepancies in the levels of aid to the poor. However, none of these adjustments reduced the welfare rolls. Policy solutions shifted attention to income transfer proposals. President Nixon's Family Assistance Plan was the most significant policy initiative to overhaul the welfare system. However, for reasons to be explored later in this chapter, the FAP proposal failed. As the national economy entered a period of nagging inflation and rising unemployment during the 1970s, AFDC remained intact, and the deficient welfare system continued to perpetuate the aggrieved conditions of the urban poor.

ORIGINS AND DEVELOPMENTS OF AFDC POLICY

Direct income maintenance for the unemployable poor originated as federal policy in the 1935 Social Security Act. The depression of the 1930s resulted in large-scale unemployment and considerable social unrest. By 1933 about 15 million men, or one-third of the labor force, were out of work.[2] Several New Deal measures provided for *temporary work relief*, that is, government-supported jobs for the unemployed in such programs as the Civilian Conservation Corps, the Public Works Administration, the Civil Works Administration, and the Works Progress Administration. A second set of policies attempted to protect the labor force against future temporary unemployment and to assist workers who would be retiring. These goals were established as part of the Social Security Act, which provided for two kinds of contributory *social insurance* financed by payroll taxes—unemployment insurance and old age insurance.

Additionally, the national economic collapse dramatized the serious hardships for people who, even under normal economic conditions, were unable to work. *Public assistance*, or direct cash support, was originally considered as a temporary measure for needy persons who eventually would be absorbed into the social security system. The Social Security Act established categorical aid programs for the needy poor—the aged, the blind, dependent children, and (by 1950 amendment) the disabled.

In particular, the dependent children program, as with the other welfare categories, was intended to encourage wider state and local participation for a destitute class of people. Aid to needy mothers for their children had been provided by most of the states prior to 1935. These "mother's pensions" to widows, divorcees, and deserted women permitted their children to remain at home. However, due to local options under various state laws, less than half of the nation's counties were providing such assistance.[3] The federal Aid to Dependent Children categorical program was administered under the broad guidelines established by the Social Security Administration as part of optional grants-in-aid arrangements with the states. The SSA established the conditions and formulas for the distribution of funds to the states, and the states controlled eligibility standards and benefit levels for the recipients. Within the states, city and county welfare agencies provided cash support to eligible recipients.

The goals and objectives of the dependent children program were not significantly changed until 1962. By this time, AFDC was the only public assistance program experiencing large caseload increases. Between 1949 and 1960, AFDC recipients had nearly tripled, increasing from 1.2 million to 3.1 million,[4] while aid for the aged and blind had decreased, and aid to the disabled had only moderate increases. Furthermore, the characteristics of AFDC recipients were changing. Such people were becoming concentrated in the cities; large numbers of black mothers and children were on welfare; and many of the recipients were from broken homes. According to Department of Health, Education, and Welfare estimates, between two-thirds and three-fourths of the 50 percent increase from 1948 to 1955 in the number of absent-father families receiving ADC could be explained by an increase in broken homes in the population.[5]

Concerned with the national economic recession and the need to provide work relief to poor families, the Kennedy administration extended AFDC coverage to unemployed parents. This AFDC-UF program was to be implemented by community work and job training programs, including a $5-million authorization for day-care centers to assist working mothers. However, because of the optional nature of AFDC-UF and strict state eligibility requirements, only half of the states had adopted this program by 1969, and less than 100,000 families, or 5 percent of the AFDC recipients, were receiving such benefits.[6]

Secondly, the 1962 public welfare amendments included a *services* approach for the poor. As recommended by social welfare professionals to the Kennedy administration, expanded social services would encourage the rehabilitation and self-sufficiency of welfare recipients. Social workers would offer counseling to strengthen and preserve family stability and economic self-support including legal advice, child care, employment counseling, training, and job placement. The goal was to reduce and prevent dependency. The federal government increased its share from 50 percent to 75 percent in matching funds to the states for such counseling services. The states had to reduce welfare caseloads to no more than sixty cases per worker. However, Gilbert Y. Steiner observes that the social services approach was a program of "services without servants."[7] The states encountered much difficulty in recruiting new staff, and the service components were vaguely defined. Caseworker pay was low in comparison with private agencies, and many caseworkers were not properly trained to offer family counseling.

Even more significantly, the 1962 amendments had no effect in reducing welfare dependency. Between 1962 and 1967, the number of AFDC recipients had increased from 3.7 million to more than 5 million.[8] Concerned by rising caseloads, increased costs, and ineffective work incentives under previous legislation, Congress imposed strict and punitive employment requirements for AFDC recipients in 1967. Led by Chairman Wilbur Mills (Democrat-Arkansas) of the House Ways and Means Committee, Congress established a Work Incentive (WIN) program. WIN, designed particularly for welfare mothers, was a compulsory work-training program for AFDC adults. Penalties, that is, the loss of AFDC payments, were established for recipients who refused to get jobs or accept training. At the same time, recipients were permitted to keep the first thirty dollars per month in earnings plus one-third of additional wages without having them reduced from AFDC payments. (Previously, each dollar earned was reduced from welfare payments.) Furthermore, the federal government imposed a "freeze" on AFDC financial support to the states under which future aid was restricted to the number of AFDC children on the rolls by January, 1968. (In 1969, Congress repealed the AFDC "freeze.")

Thus, by 1967 the goals of public assistance under AFDC were in serious trouble. Despite efforts to provide social services and work incentives, the number of welfare recipients was increasing at an alarming rate. Welfare dependency was not reduced by family counseling, voluntary or compulsory work training and relief, incentives to retain earnings, expanded social services, or the threatened loss of payments. Apparently, the relief problem was caused by other factors. According to Piven and Cloward, public welfare policy responds to cyclical patterns of expansion and contraction in the national economy. In other words, welfare policy is *not* designed to aid the poor but to force them to accept low-paying jobs when such jobs are available:

> Relief arrangements are ancillary to economic arrangements. Their chief function is to regulate labor, and they do that in two general ways. First, when mass unemployment leads to outbreaks of turmoil, relief programs are ordinarily initiated or expanded to absorb and control enough of the unemployed to restore order; then, as turbulence subsides, the relief system contracts, expelling those who are needed to populate the labor market.[9]

THE WELFARE EXPLOSION

By the end of the 1960s public welfare policy had provoked nationwide concern and controversy. Particular concern focused on the black urban poor who were going on welfare in upwardly spiraling rates. The nation's most populous states and cities were unable to stem the tide of AFDC expansion. According to Daniel P. Moynihan, "Welfare dependency became a 'crisis' in the mid-1960s *not* because it was consuming large amounts of money, or involved large numbers of people. . . . Welfare had to be defined as a crisis because of the rate at which the rolls commenced to grow."[10]

What was the nature of the huge rise in welfare dependency? In comparison with the 1950s when the AFDC caseload increased by 110,000 families or 17 percent, 800,000 families (or an increase of 107 percent) were added to the relief rolls during the 1960s.[11] Most of these AFDC gains took place after 1964 when the welfare rolls increased by 71 percent.[12] At the beginning of the decade about 3 million people were assisted by AFDC, but by 1969 more than 6.7 million people were on the relief rolls. The recipients included 5 million children, 1.4 million mothers, and 300,000 fathers. Accompanying these gains was a threefold increase in welfare payments, which grew from about $1 billion in 1960 to nearly $3.5 billion in 1969. (See Table 8–1.) At the present rates of growth, it is estimated that

AFDC caseloads will increase by 50 to 60 percent and that costs will double by 1975.[13]

TABLE 8-1   Recipients and Amounts of Money Payments Under The Aid to Families With Dependent Children Program 1950-1969

Year	Number of AFDC Recipients (Millions)	Payments (Millions)
1950	2,233	$ 547
1955	2,192	$ 612
1960	3,073	$ 994
1965	4,396	$1,644
1966	4,666	$1,850
1967	5,309	$2,250
1968	6,086	$2,824
1969	6,725	$3,425

SOURCE: U.S. Department of Health, Education, and Welfare.

The welfare explosion affected the nation's largest states and cities most severely. During the 1960s, about 60 percent of the national increase in AFDC occurred in the five states of New York, California, Illinois, Pennsylvania, and Ohio. New York and California together accounted for 44 percent of this upward spiral in welfare dependency, while New York City alone had about 10 percent or one million of the nation's AFDC recipients.[14] The five largest counties—New York, Philadelphia, Cook County (Chicago), Wayne County (Detroit), and Los Angeles—experienced the greatest increases (217 percent) in comparison with the remaining 116 urban centers which had a 135 percent increase.[15] All urban areas contributed 70 percent of the national increases in AFDC, but the five largest counties together accounted for 34 percent of these gains. Regionally, northern urban centers (175 percent) had larger increases than southern ones (121 percent). Nationally, the proportionate share of AFDC cases increased more rapidly in the North (39 percent) and the West (26 percent) than in the South (18 percent) and the North Central (17 percent) regions.[16]

What accounted for the welfare explosion? Clearly, the problem of increasing AFDC dependency was *not* related to improved national economic trends. During the 1960s, the welfare rolls increased as poverty and unemployment were *reduced.* Poverty level incomes, as defined by the Social Security Administration (based upon minimum essential food purchases for a nonfarm family of four) rose from $3,000 to $4,000 between 1959 and 1969. During this time, the number of Americans whose income fell below these minimum levels *declined* from nearly forty million to about twenty-five million. Also, unemployment rates *decreased.* Between 1959 and 1969, the gross national product grew from $484 billion to $932 billion, thirteen million new jobs were created, total employment increased from sixty-five million to seventy-eight million, and the unemployment rate dropped from 5.5 percent to 3.5 percent.[17] But, as Figure 8–1 indicates, the AFDC roles were, during this period, *increasing* by more than 50 percent, and AFDC money payments were more than tripling in cost.

These findings should not be considered unusual. In fact, Gilbert Y. Steiner criticized the apparent "paradox" of rising dependency and increasing employment as early as the 1950s:

> To term rising welfare costs during a period of full employment a paradox assumes some direct relationship between job availability and the dependency status of public assistance clients . . . Public assistance costs have risen sharply despite social insurance and despite full employment because the groups benefited by public assistance are either outside the insurance system, are underinsured under present public policies, or are largely unemployable.[18]

EXPLAINING THE WELFARE EXPLOSION

If welfare dependency dramatically increased even during a time of national prosperity, what explains the AFDC explosion? At least four other factors have been suggested. First, the pool of eligible recipients increased because of deteriorating family conditions among the black urban poor. Second, poor blacks migrated from the South to the North where welfare was easier to obtain. Third, the courts and local welfare agencies relaxed eligibility requirements and eliminated demeaning administrative procedures. Finally, welfare recipients organized and brought pressure on welfare agencies to gain higher benefits and to inundate the welfare rolls.

Broken Families and More Potential Recipients

Was the welfare explosion due to increased family deterioration among the black urban poor which created a larger pool of eligible recipients? Daniel P. Moynihan is the chief advocate of the "broken family" explanation for rising welfare dependency. In his 1965 report for the U.S. Labor Department, *The Negro Family,* Moynihan observed that "the steady expansion of [AFDC] can be taken as a measure of the steady disintegration of the Negro family structure over the past generation in the United States."[19] The Negro family was experiencing a "tangle of pathology" because one-quarter of urban black marriages are dissolved, one-fourth of black births are illegitimate, and almost 25 percent of black families are headed by women.[20]

Clearly, welfare dependency is related to special problems encountered by poor black families, although it is less obvious that such instability was a primary cause for the huge AFDC gains during the 1960s. According to statistical evidence by the Committee for Economic Development,[21] the overall *declines* in the poverty population between 1959 and 1968 were accompanied by *increases* in the proportions of children and female-headed families among the poor. Children under eighteen constituted the largest group of poor persons (10.7 million or 42 percent of all the poor between 1959 and 1968). Dependent children in fatherless homes faced severe hardships. In 1968, there were 7 million poor people living in families headed by mothers, including 4.4 million children. In such households, 62 percent of nonwhites were poor compared with 36 percent of whites. More significantly, the number of nonwhite poor in female-headed families increased by 24 percent (700,000), while the number of poor whites in such families decreased by 16 percent.

Were the increases in the numbers of potential welfare recipients from broken families directly related to increases in AFDC rolls? The evidence is far from conclusive. One estimate is that even if all the new female-headed families between 1959 and 1966 had received AFDC, only about 10 percent of the AFDC increase would have been accounted for.[22] Also, even though AFDC rose during the 1960s, there was no significant change in the illegitimacy *rate*.[23] Neither does the "broken family" thesis explain the tremendous increases in AFDC after 1964. Thus, while many welfare recipients are black, many poor urban black families are headed by women, and such families have a greater tendency to seek public assistance, the huge gains in the welfare rolls cannot be fully explained by the sociological and economic problems of such black families.

Migration Trends and Higher Benefit Levels

A second possible explanation for AFDC increases is that poor black families migrated from the South, where restrictions on eligibility and low benefit levels discouraged dependency, to the North, where AFDC rules were less restrictive and payment levels were higher. The urbanization of the black population was accompanied by the urbanization of the AFDC population, but these two trends did not necessarily explain the welfare explosion during the 1960s. Blacks had been leaving the South since the 1940s. Between 1940 and 1966, almost four million blacks migrated to the cities.[24] From 1961 to 1967, the proportion of AFDC families living in metropolitan areas increased from 58 percent to 71 percent.[25] However, about three-fourths of the black migration had occurred *before* 1960, that is, prior to the huge AFDC increases.[26] By the end of the decade, black migration to the cities had decreased, and yet the welfare rolls were higher than ever.

It is also doubtful that potential black AFDC mothers migrated to northern industrial states and cities because of higher benefit levels. As shown in Table 8–2, the correlation between state population ranking, average monthly family AFDC benefits, and residency patterns of AFDC recipients is rather inconclusive. Of the eight most populous northern states, Pennsylvania and Massachusetts had a higher proportion of AFDC mothers who were permanent residents, while Ohio and Michigan had nearly equal proportions of in-state and out-of-state AFDC mothers. Among the states having very high proportions of migrant AFDC mothers, including California, New York, Illinois, and New Jersey, nearly as many welfare recipients came to these states during the 1950s as the 1960s, and a majority had migrated between 1940 and 1959. Furthermore, there is no direct correlation between black migration and urban areas having higher benefit levels. While not shown in Table 8–2, other studies suggest that more migrating poor whites than poor blacks were attracted to such states and cities.[27] Steiner concludes that even if "variations in AFDC payments [had] been responsible for [southern black] migration, it was too late in 1969 to discourage it by narrowing those variations. But we are in no position to say that the variations were responsible in the first place."[28]

Welfare Litigation and Court Decisions

Successful legal challenges to restrictive and demeaning welfare administration provide a third possible explanation for AFDC increases during the 1960s. The argument is that lawyers working in the neighborhood legal services program, established in 1964 as part

TABLE 8-2   AFDC Recipients, Welfare Payments, and Migration Patterns in Most Populous States, 1967 and 1971

States By 1970 Population Rank	Total Number of AFDC Recipients 1971	Average Monthly AFDC Family Payment 1971	Proportion of AFDC Mothers Never Lived Outside State 1967	AFDC Mother Has Lived Outside State— Year of Last Move Into State				
				Total	1965–67	1960–64	1950–59	1940–49
California	1,625,000	$184.40	31%	68%	8%	14%	23%	13%
New York	1,277,000	289.25	33%	65%	9%	13%	20%	7%
Pennsylvania	607,000	237.80	63%	35%	4%	6%	8%	3%
Texas	373,000	118.10	75%	24%	3%	5%	7%	3%
Illinois	576,000	238.85	33%	65%	5%	11%	27%	4%
Ohio	383,000	165.05	46%	52%	5%	8%	17%	10%
Michigan	417,000	226.25	43%	56%	6%	8%	16%	10%
New Jersey	450,000	255.35	38%	60%	6%	15%	20%	7%
Florida	279,000	90.25	47%	50%	5%	9%	17%	7%
Massachusetts	270,000	242.60	64%	36%	6%	10%	11%	3%

SOURCES: Bureau of the Census, U.S. Department of Health, Education, and Welfare (April 1971), and HEW Materials Submitted to Committee on Ways and Means (*Social Security and Welfare Proposals*, Committee on Ways and Means, House of Representatives, 91st Congress, 1st Session, Part 2, pp. 511–512).

of community action agencies of the War on Poverty, promoted litigation for welfare recipients. Such lawyers made AFDC clients more aware of their legal rights and benefits and assisted many poor blacks in getting on welfare by helping them to untangle the delays and bureaucratic red tape of local welfare agencies.

Various federal court decisions eliminated such practices as welfare residency requirements, "man in the house," "substitute parent," and "employable mother" rules. Also, the antipoverty lawyers successfully established procedural guarantees for recipients at welfare hearings and challenged the rights of caseworkers to enter homes of recipients without search warrants. All of these court decisions had the effect of adding many thousands of people to the welfare rolls.

Welfare residency requirements were struck down by the United States Supreme Court in 1969. In his opinion for the 6–3 majority, Justice William J. Brennan ruled that Connecticut, Pennsylvania, and the District of Columbia had violated the freedom to travel by the newly arrived poor and that the states cannot use a waiting period for AFDC for "the purpose of inhibiting migration by needy persons into the state."[29] The decision had the effect of invalidating forty-two similar state laws which restricted potential recipients from moving to obtain immediate welfare benefits. Subsequently, the Department of Health, Education, and Welfare required the states to tell people who had been denied welfare because of residency laws that they were now eligible. HEW officials estimated that 100,000 to 200,000 more recipients would be added to welfare because state residency requirements were dropped.[30]

In 1968, federal courts invalidated Georgia's "employable mother" rule and Alabama's "substitute father" provision. The Georgia case involved the right of welfare officials to deny AFDC benefits to mothers designated as "employable" even if they could not find jobs. The challengers convinced the three-judge federal district court that the state rule was used primarily to keep black mothers off the rolls and was therefore a violation of the Equal Protection clause of the Fourteenth Amendment.[31]

The Alabama "substitute father" or "man in the house" provision denied AFDC benefits to families where the mother was consorting with a man, whom the state claimed was the legally responsible "parent" for any children in the home. Chief Justice Earl Warren, in a unanimous Supreme Court decision, ruled that Alabama had incorrectly defined parental support under the Social Security Act. "Destitute children who are legally fatherless cannot be denied federally funded assistance on the transparent fiction that they have a substitute father."[32] This decision invalidated eighteen other similar state laws under which approximately 500,000 children were denied benefits because of violations of such "substitute father" rules.[33]

Lawyers for the poor also challenged arbitrary terminations of welfare benefits which denied AFDC recipients the rights of fair procedures in appealing such decisions. In a 1970 decision by the Supreme Court, welfare recipients were afforded constitutional rights to trial-like hearings with trial-like constitutional safeguards before officials could terminate benefits.[34]

Less successful was a legal attack on caseworkers entering welfare clients' homes to determine eligibility and benefits. In 1969 a three-judge federal district court in New York decided that such daytime home visits could not be conducted unless the caseworker obtained a search warrant. Otherwise, the AFDC mother would be subjected to illegal search and seizure in violation of the Fourth Amendment. However, the U.S. Supreme Court overruled this decision in 1971.

Grass-roots Political Pressure by the Organized Poor

If the welfare explosion could not be fully explained either by increasing deterioration of black urban families or as the direct result of southern black migration to northern industrial states—trends which were clearly evident before the 1960s—then it is more likely that the huge AFDC gains were attributable to the poor already living in large cities. As previously indicated, all federal efforts to reduce dependency were accompanied by upwardly climbing welfare rolls. Despite restrictions to contract AFDC, the poor were motivated to obtain public relief because of greater knowledge and encouragement to go on the rolls.

How did potential AFDC recipients overcome the enormous federal, state, and local bureaucratic resistance to expand the welfare rolls? Leaving aside various psychological, sociological, and economic analyses of the poor, the welfare crisis can be directly linked with the ghetto protest, riots, and demonstrations which resulted in the politicalization of the poor. The federal government responded to ghetto disruption by providing new services and programs. Secondly, the National Welfare Rights Organization assisted potential recipients by directly pressuring local relief agencies.

What was the nature of federal responses to urban protest and public welfare? According to Frances Fox Piven and Richard A. Cloward, the various civil rights demonstrations and ghetto riots of the 1960s were precipitated by a "dissensus politics" strategy. Such a strategy required "issues and actions which will drive groups apart . . ." and was developed by black leaders of "a cadre, acting on behalf of a minority within a coalition, [which] engages in actions which are designed to dislodge (or threaten to dislodge) not only that minority, but more important, *other significant constituent groups in that same alliance.*"[35] Black protest leaders threatened the national Democratic party coalition. Presidents Kennedy and Johnson wanted to ease urban disorder, which threatened other groups in the party, and to maintain black voting support.

In 1966, Piven and Cloward applied the "dissensus politics" strategy to the welfare system. They argued that the poor should create a welfare crisis by organizing a massive drive to inundate the AFDC rolls. By doing so, massive bureaucratic disruptions and unbearable financial burdens would result for local and state governments. Such disruptions, they argued, would cause severe strains within the Democratic party, thereby forcing the federal government to ease the welfare crisis by eliminating AFDC and instituting a guaranteed annual income for the poor.[36]

Ghetto protests did coincide with expanding welfare rolls. City welfare agencies began to ease restrictions and to permit more eligible applicants to obtain relief, probably because it was easier to grant welfare than to provide other concessions. Subsequently, the federal antipoverty program became the major governmental response to reduce ghetto disorders by offering a services policy to urban blacks. As discussed in more detail in Chapter 9, the 1964 Economic Opportunity Act provided for "maximum feasible participation of the poor" in implementing and coordinating neighborhood services. The antipoverty programs provided resources to black community leaders in counseling the poor to obtain more relief and assistance from local welfare agencies.

The National Welfare Rights Organization resulted from ghetto organizing activities promoted under antipoverty programs. Organized in 1966 by Dr. George A. Wiley to coordinate various grassroots welfare rights associations, the NWRO by 1970 had about 100,000 dues-paying members representing 350 local groups.[37] Even though NWRO is one of the largest national associations of the poor, the membership comprises only about 1 or 2 percent of all adult

AFDC recipients. The impact of NWRO is more important than its membership size. Its activities and pressures on local welfare agencies to expand AFDC have generally increased the awareness of potential and existing welfare recipients. According to Steiner, the NWRO performs three critically important functions for AFDC mothers which cannot be provided by other social agencies:[38]

1. It provides mutual reinforcement for welfare mothers in their fights against policies and procedures of welfare agencies.
2. It provides for participation in organizational activities and policy decisions which directly affect welfare recipients.
3. It provides an organizational tie and identity which the poor ordinarily do not have.

The NWRO has not, for the most part, employed Piven and Cloward's welfare saturation strategy but has focused primarily on expanding its membership base and achieving increased benefits for AFDC recipients. Protest strategies were used, for example, to demand authorized special welfare grants for clothing, household equipment, and furniture in New York City. In 1968, welfare mothers besieged local agencies with protests and demonstrations to obtain $100 million of these benefits. According to Michael Rogin, "the welfare system seemed on the verge of collapse as clients went off happily waving checks for up to $1,000 without a full investigation . . . before the city and state huddled with HEW and changed the system to exclude these grants."[39]

The welfare rights movement employed a variety of organizational, counseling, publicity, and direct confrontation tactics, all of which affected increased awareness of public assistance among the black urban poor. Consequently, many more potential welfare recipients applied for and received AFDC. Welfare aid was not considered shameful or disgraceful for the deserving poor, but a right for those people who had no other means of subsistence. Between 1960 and 1968 the volume of both applications and acceptances for AFDC dramatically increased. Applications rose by 85 percent and acceptance rates increased from 55 percent in 1960 to 70 percent in 1968.[40] Thus, the welfare explosion of the 1960s involved many complex developments, and one of the most important reasons was the emergent political awareness and protest activities of the poor in the cities.

PROBLEMS OF THE WELFARE SYSTEM

By the end of the 1960s it was clear that the welfare system had totally failed in assisting the nation's dependent poor. Drastic policy reform was necessary to overcome several basic defects of the AFDC program.

First, the welfare program resulted in inhumane, demeaning, and degrading conditions for the poor. AFDC did not eradicate or alleviate poverty. Rather, public relief contributed to family deterioration, destroyed the incentive to work, prevented economic and social mobility, encouraged fraud and invasion of privacy, and caused shame and disgrace among the poor. AFDC encouraged unemployed fathers to desert their families so that mothers and children could obtain relief. Why? Fatherless families could receive more income from welfare than from low-paying jobs. In contrast to Moynihan's "broken families" thesis of welfare expansion, other evidence suggests that welfare is a major cause of family breakups. Studies of welfare mothers in New York City found that nearly 60 percent were separated or divorced *after* they went on relief.[41] Despite the AFDC-UF provisions of 1967 and other state programs of income relief for unemployed parents, the welfare system destroyed work incentives. Most earnings were directly deducted from welfare checks, and recipients could not get jobs with sufficient income to reduce their need for welfare assistance. Without either work incentives or job opportunities, the poor were locked into central city ghettos. They lacked mobility to seek employment in the suburbs where most of the economic growth existed. Since AFDC was their major source of subsistence, many welfare recipients claimed the maximum number of permissible benefits. Caseworkers had to conduct home investigations of relief clients to make sure that their eligibility and entitlements were authorized. Fraud, suspicion, cheating, and lying frequently resulted. Invasion of privacy was particularly degrading. Finally, even with the burgeoning welfare rights movement, the poor often considered welfare a stigma which destroyed their self-confidence and self-esteem.

The desperate plight and destitute status of AFDC recipients was convincingly demonstrated in a 1967 survey by the U.S. Department of Health, Education, and Welfare:[42]

11.2% had no private use of a kitchen.

24.0% had no hot and cold running water.

22.5% had no private use of a flush toilet.

22.4% had no private use of a bathroom with shower or tub.

30.1% had not enough beds for all family members.

24.8% had not enough furniture so that everyone could sit down while eating.

45.8% had no milk for the children sometime in the past six months because of lack of money.

17.4% had children who stayed home from school sometime in the past six months due to lack of shoes or clothes.

Secondly, the welfare system was inadequate and inequitable for the poor. Even with rising relief rolls, most of the poor were not included in any public assistance program. The ten million people receiving public welfare comprised only about 40 percent of the poverty population.[43] The remaining 60 percent included many of the working poor whose incomes disqualified them from relief even though they could not earn enough to exceed established poverty levels.

Thirdly, the poor were victims of both intrastate and interstate variations in program coverage, eligibility restrictions, benefit levels, and local administrative discretion. From its inception in 1935, public assistance had remained an optional categorical grant-in-aid program between the federal government and the states. The federal government established conditions for matching funds, but the states were not compelled to participate in all of the cash or service programs. By the end of the 1960s, more than twenty states did not accept all available federal welfare funds because of their refusal or inability to appropriate required matching amounts. Within the states, poverty budgets determined necessary subsistence levels for people on welfare. However, rarely did AFDC payments approach established state poverty budgets. For example, in 1967 only twenty-one states paid 100 percent of AFDC basic minimums, while the remaining states offered between 3 percent and 20 percent of such cost standards.[44] Additionally, there were considerable variations in *average* AFDC payments to recipients. In April, 1971, the national average monthly AFDC payment for a family of four was $185.40. Payments ranged from a low of $53.50 in Mississippi to a high of $289.25 in New York.[45] These variations far exceeded differences in budgeted cost standards and cost-of-living differentials between the states.[46]

Finally, the variations in state payment levels and eligibility requirements resulted in unequal financial burdens on state and local governments. In effect, the states offering higher AFDC payments received less federal support than the lower-paying states. As noted earlier, total national AFDC payments had nearly tripled during the 1960s. The federal government supported about 50 percent of these total costs. But the range of federal reimbursements was 78.7 percent for Mississippi and 76.7 for South Carolina to only 40.4 percent in New Jersey and 46.3 percent in New York.[47] There was also considerable variation in local burdens of total welfare costs. Local contributions were less than 1 percent in twenty-five states, but ranged up to about 25 percent in the highest-paying AFDC states. Thus, in New York, New Jersey, and California, local governments had to support between 24.4 percent to 18.5 percent of all AFDC costs.[48] Since most of the welfare increases were in the large central city ghettos, the major cities were paying higher proportions of welfare costs and neglecting other important budgetary priorities. For example, New York City, with the nation's highest AFDC caseload, had to budget more than $700 million of city funds for its $2.1 billion welfare expenditures in 1971–1972.[49] This was the most costly city program, exceeding local funds for public education.

INCOME TRANSFER PROPOSALS

In overcoming the serious deficiencies of the welfare system, several economists and study commissions have proposed various income transfer proposals. These recommendations incorporate an "income strategy" for the poor. They attempt to raise the standard of living for the poor by providing them with direct cash support from the federal government. According to Daniel P. Moynihan, the income strategy differs substantially from the "services strategy" which the federal government had been promoting from the 1930s. He observed that established antipoverty and other social welfare measures involved "a good deal of money . . . being expended. It could *not* be shown that it was going to the poor. It *was* going, in large degree, to purchase services, which could *not* be shown to benefit the poor." Consequently, the services strategy, in Moynihan's view, had the actual *effect* of reallocating "resources *up* the social scale . . ." while the income strategy sought "income redistribution down the social scale."[50]

For purposes of comparison and contrast, two negative income tax and two guaranteed income proposals have been selected for a brief analysis. These include Milton Friedman's negative income tax, James Tobin's credit income tax, the universal income supplement program of the President's Commission on Income Maintenance, and the cash assistance grant proposed by the National Urban Coalition. As shown in Table 8–3, the major criteria for evaluating these four plans are:

1. *Adequacy:* Does the plan provide a basic guarantee or minimum income level that provides sufficient subsidies for the poor?

2. *Work Incentives and Tax Equity:* Does the program encourage able-bodied recipients to work? Do the people who receive subsidies without working receive the same incomes as people who are employed? What is the tax rate on additional earned income for people receiving income supplements? What is the "breakeven point," or the level at which recipients no longer receive subsidies but not yet begin to pay taxes?

3. *Costs to Government:* Is the program a reasonable expenditure compared with current federal welfare costs? Does the program reduce state and local costs?

Analysis of the Four Plans

Milton Friedman, an economist at the University of Chicago and chief economic adviser to Senator Barry Goldwater during the 1964 presidential campaign, first proposed the negative income tax in his 1962 book, *Capitalism and Freedom.*[51] Friedman suggests that the solution to poverty and welfare dependency is found in restructuring the federal income tax, from which direct subsidies (or "negative taxes") would be paid to the poor. He reasoned that taxpayers are assessed on their net incomes after subtracting exemptions for family dependents and a minimum standard deduction for essential yearly expenses. However, individuals who earn poverty incomes which fall below these amounts pay no taxes. Friedman proposed that the federal government should compensate nontaxpayers on the basis of half the difference (50 percent) between the sum of their personal exemptions, standard deductions, and initial incomes.

As shown in Table 8–3, Friedman's proposal is applied to a family income of $3,000 per year. Each nontaxpaying family would have the right to a negative tax at the rate of 50 percent of the difference between earnings and allowable exemptions and deductions.

TABLE 8–3 Comparisons and Contrasts of Four Income Transfer Plans (For a Family of Four)

Proposal	Zero-Income Allowance	Tax Rate on Additional Earned Income	Breakeven Point	Additional Federal Cost (Estimated by year)
Negative Income Tax (Milton Friedman)	$1,500	50%	$3,000	$7 to $9 billion (1964)
Credit Income Tax (James Tobin)	$3,000	50%	$9,000	$14 billion (1966)
Universal Income Supplements (President's Commission on Income Maintenance)	$2,400	50%	$4,800	$7 billion (1971)
Cash Assistance Grants (National Urban Coalition)	$4,708	50%	$9,416	$28 billion (1976)

The 50 percent tax rate on additional earnings provides work incentives for recipients. Friedman's plan provides a $1,500 income floor for poverty families. When incomes exceed $3,000 (the breakeven point), subsidies would cease and "positive tax" payments would begin.

The estimated additional federal cost of Friedman's plan in 1964 would have been approximately $7 billion to $9 billion. However, Friedman wanted to replace most other governmental social welfare programs with the negative income tax, including social security (old age insurance), Medicare, all categorical assistance welfare programs, public health, public housing, farm price supports, and the minimum wage. Thus, Friedman envisaged no additional net increase in federal costs for the negative income tax. James Tobin estimates that the proposal would have reduced the nation's poverty gap by about only 50 percent in 1966, or by about $5.5 billion, because the breakeven point of $3,000 did not include all nontaxpayers at established poverty income levels.[52]

A second form of income tax supplements for the poor has been proposed by James Tobin, a Yale economist and former member of the Council of Economic Advisers.[53] Instead of simple tax equity for the poor, Tobin suggests a credit income tax which would integrate public assistance with a minimum income and radical tax reform. The plan would eliminate all exclusions, deductions, and exemptions from the federal income tax. Instead, a credit income tax would entitle each person $750 per year from the federal government and would require individuals to pay back one-third of their incomes, excluding the initial $750. The plan would assist both the poor and the nonpoor. As shown in Table 8–3, a family of four would be guaranteed a $3,000 minimum income, or four times $750 per year. No taxes would be paid until family incomes exceeded $9,000 per year. According to Tobin, in 1966 the plan would have redistributed about $14 billion to the poor, in addition to existing public assistance, and about $29 billion in benefits to nonpoor families, for a net cost of $43 billion.

The President's Commission on Income Maintenance, a twenty-one-member group appointed by President Johnson in 1968 and chaired by Ben W. Heineman, a Chicago corporation executive, issued its report *Poverty Amid Plenty* in November, 1969. The commission recommended a guaranteed annual income floor of $2,400 for a family of four, which would extend coverage to thirty-six million persons. The minimum income was based upon benefit levels of $750 per adult and $450 for children. A 50 percent tax was imposed on additional earnings between $2,400 and the breakeven point of $4,800.

The commission proposed that the guaranteed income would replace all existing welfare programs, including aid to the aged, blind, disabled, and dependent children. Federal costs would increase by $7 billion in 1971, but state costs would be reduced by $1 billion, thus resulting in a $6 billion net cost for all levels of government. Of the $6 billion redistributed to ten million welfare families, $5 billion would be given to the estimated eight million poor families receiving welfare and the remaining $1 billion to families above poverty income levels. This would have eliminated half of the nation's poverty income deficits in 1971. The commission took a pragmatic view in trying to eliminate poverty and welfare dependency. The $2,400 minimum income represented a level chosen not "because we believe it to be adequate, but because it is a level which can be implemented promptly."[54] The commission justified an income floor below existing poverty levels by indicating that a poverty level floor would cost $27 billion per year for twenty-three million households instead of $6 billion for ten million households. However, the commission recommended that payment levels be raised as rapidly as possible.

Finally, the commission's central policy goal was to provide cash support to the poor rather than to establish work incentives. The commission argued: "It is time to design public policy to deal with two basic facts of American poverty: the poor lack money, and most of them cannot increase their incomes themselves. These conditions can be remedied only when the Government provides some minimum income to all in need."[55] Nevertheless, the commission did recommend, as noted above, a 50 percent tax rate on additional earnings below the $4,800 breakeven level to ensure that those who worked earned more than those who did not, thereby eliminating the incentive under the present welfare system not to work.

The National Urban Coalition's proposed cash assistance grant (CAG) plan represents the most ambitious long-range projection to eliminate poverty and welfare dependency. As recommended in *Counterbudget*,[56] the coalition offered a five-year plan (1971 to 1976) for changing national priorities. Beginning with a $2,400 income guarantee for a family of four in 1972, the CAG would be scaled upward to $4,708 by 1976 to reflect the nation's rising standard of living. With cash subsidies geared to poverty threshold incomes, the coalition expected that by 1980 poverty would be eliminated for all families with children and for all other households with family heads under age sixty-five. The plan called for a 50 percent tax rate on additional earnings up to the breakeven point of $9,416. The tax rate would also reflect the diminished take-home value of additional earned dollars for such costs as housing and day-care payments; federal, state, and local income taxes; and the social security payroll tax. Finally, CAG would replace existing categorical assistance programs and would be completely administered by the federal government. Estimated program costs for 1976 were $28 billion.

In analyzing the four income transfer proposals, several policy problems are evident. The criteria selected for the minimum guarantee level, the breakeven point, and the tax rate on additional earnings are all interrelated. A viable income transfer policy requires a necessary balance between (1) income equity for the poor, (2) work incentives that increase the income of the poor and gradually reduce the need for subsidies, and (3) extent of coverage for the near-poor and the nonpoor.

Different social purposes are served by different policy choices made between these three factors. If the basic purpose is to raise the incomes of the poorest groups in the population, regardless of work incentives, the most important considerations should be a high income floor and a high tax rate on additional earnings. Secondly, if the policy-maker wants to raise the standard of living of all people with lower incomes, he should focus upon the breakeven point and the tax rate. Thirdly, if the major concern is work incentives, the policy choice would be concerned with a low tax rate on earnings below breakeven level.

Obviously, these policy choices are not compatible. For example, in raising the incomes of the poor, a high income floor and a low tax rate might be the "ideal" social policy. However, this choice would greatly extend program coverage to many of the nation's near-poor and nonpoor and thereby greatly increase the total costs to government. Could the federal government afford a $25 billion to $50 billion annual expenditure for income maintenance? Also, a low tax rate might be desirable for work incentives to raise the incomes of the very poor and gradually to reduce their need for subsidies. Presently, welfare policy imposes a very high tax rate on additional earnings. But as a high tax rate would discourage work for the very poor, a low tax rate would threaten the working near-poor who would oppose subsidies unless they were included in the plan. The policy-maker would have to decide whether to increase program coverage by raising the breakeven point and increasing total government costs.

In summary, there are four basic questions about income transfer proposals that policymakers must resolve: (1) *Equity*—Should the basic income floor be established at the same level as the poverty threshold or below it? (2) *Work Incentives*—How can income guarantees to the poor be reconciled with work requirements? (3) *Coverage*—How many of the near-poor and nonpoor will be included? and (4) *Costs*—Considering the income floor, the tax rate, and the breakeven point, what will be the total expenditures for government?

OVERHAULING WELFARE: PRESIDENT NIXON'S FAMILY ASSISTANCE PLAN

In 1969 President Nixon initiated the first comprehensive policy reform of the welfare system since the 1930s. In his special welfare message to Congress, President Nixon noted that public assistance had failed recipients, taxpayers, and American society. In proposing a Family Assistance Plan (FAP), the president emphasized six major goals: (1) assurance of an income foundation for all parents who cannot adequately support themselves and their children; (2) a new approach to end the unfairness of the welfare system; (3) creation of stronger work incentives; (4) support for work training and child care programs; (5) reduction of welfare redtape and achieving administrative cost savings; and (6) substantial initial federal investment which will yield future returns to the nation.

These ambitious goals were encompassed in a relatively modest income transfer proposal to replace the AFDC program. As originally recommended, FAP provided a $1,600 income floor for a family of four, based upon $500 per year for the first two family members and $300 for each additional member. Recipients could retain $60 per month or $720 per year in additional earnings, above which a 50 percent tax rate was imposed. The breakeven point was $3,920. Also, provisions were included to alleviate state welfare costs. The federal government would pay 30 percent of state supplemental payments for AFDC, where welfare assistance was above the $1,600 minimum. At the same time, these states (42 of them and the District of Columbia) could reduce their payments by two dollars for each three dollars the family earned. Additionally, food stamps for the poor, which provided about $864 a year, would be continued. The net federal costs of FAP in 1972 would have been $3.8 billion, including about $600 million in fiscal relief to the states. Total cash assistance for families with children would increase from $6.8 billion to $7.8 billion, and welfare costs for adult assistance, administration, day care, Medicaid, and food stamps from $10 billion to $12.4 billion.[57] Also, $600 million was proposed for child-care centers and work training programs.

Compared with the four income transfer plans discussed in the previous section (see Table 8–3), FAP had the following characteristics:

Zero-Income Allowance	Tax Rate on Additional Earned Income	Breakeven Point	Net Federal Costs in 1972
$1,600 (plus food stamps)	50% (1st $720 excluded)	$3,920	$3.8 billion

FAP was quite significant as a policy reform for the seriously deficient AFDC program, but as Theodore Marmor and Martin Rein (and others) indicate, the proposal contained several inconsistencies and apparent contradictions.[58] FAP had the same dilemmas as other income transfer plans in attempting to reconcile the problems of equity, work incentives, program coverage, and federal costs. The Nixon proposal selected a *low* income floor (45 percent below the poverty income threshold), *low* initial federal costs (which had the effect of providing more fiscal relief to the southern states than the highly urbanized industrial northern states), *restricted* program coverage to families with children (although some of the working poor would have been included), and *strong* work incentives and requirements (since only $720 in additional earnings could be retained, after which a 50 percent tax rate was applied). Marmor and Rein observe that "the desire to increase work incentives, to reduce the fiscal burden of the states, to discourage migration and to compel people to work as a condition of eligibility appeared as the central themes."[59]

Considering these policy choices, FAP was *not* a comprehensive scheme to eliminate poverty and welfare dependency. The income floor was too low to alleviate poverty conditions in the cities. Welfare dependency was not considered the result of a complex web of social, racial, and economic conditions for the urban poor. Rather, the Nixon plan attempted to encourage work by AFDC adults. Despite all statistical evidence indicating the reluctance of states to adopt the AFDC-UF provisions for unemployed parents, and the ineffectiveness of the WIN program, FAP sought to deal directly with work requirements rather than with the alleviation of poverty. The Nixon administration did not consider poverty as the cause of welfare, but work as the solution for welfare dependency. "Workfare" was stressed by President Nixon in his nationwide television address of August 8, 1969:

> This national floor under incomes for working or dependent families is not a "guaranteed" income . . . During the Presidential campaign last year, I opposed such a plan. I oppose it now and I will continue to oppose it. A guaranteed income establishes a right without any responsibilities: family assistance recognizes a need and establishes a responsibility. It provides help to those in need, and in turn requires that those who receive help work to the extent of their capabilities. There is no reason why one person should be taxed so that another should live idly." [60]

Secondly, FAP would have aided the southern states more than the rest of the nation. As noted earlier, AFDC resulted in unequal regional fiscal burdens, particularly since the federal government provided less reimbursement to the higher-paying states than to the lower-paying states. With a $1,600 income floor, FAP would have erased welfare responsibility in eight states, all of which offered AFDC minimums below the federal plan. Conversely, the other forty-two states were required to maintain their higher supplemental payments, although FAP provided for a 30 percent federal takeover of these costs. But not all states would share equally in this fiscal relief. For example, New York State with 10 percent of the nation's population and 15 percent of the total welfare recipients would have received only 6 percent of federal assistance under FAP.[61] Mayor John V. Lindsay estimated that New York City, with the nation's highest urban AFDC caseload, would receive only an estimated $20 million under FAP, although its 1971–1972 welfare budget was $2.1 billion.[62] Senator Abraham Ribicoff (Democrat-Connecticut) observed that FAP "sounds great for Mississippi, but what does it do for Hartford?"[63]

Daniel P. Moynihan, who strongly promoted FAP while serving as President Nixon's urban affairs adviser, indicated that 60 percent of the nation's poorest families—those earning less than half of poverty income levels—lived in the South, which had 40 percent of all the poor but only one-third of the national population. Also, between 1966 and 1968, four of the ten states with the highest percentage AFDC increases were southern—Texas, Georgia, Louisiana, and

Alabama.[61] But federal income redistribution for the South could not, at the same time, alleviate welfare cost burdens in the North, which had the highest AFDC caseloads, provided the highest supplemental relief payments, imposed the greatest share of welfare burdens on city governments, and gave more relief to longer-term residents than to recent arrivals (see Table 8–2). If FAP was intended to discourage migration to the northern cities, it was a program providing too little assistance too late. If FAP was intended to provide fiscal relief in the federal system, the program inflicted greater cost burdens on the more generous states while providing greater rewards to the most restrictive and miserly states.

Legislative Deadlock

Congress considered President Nixon's welfare reforms from 1970 to 1972. Two distinct patterns of legislative responses emerged: the House of Representatives approved FAP, with certain modifications, in 1970 and 1971, but the Senate never took affirmative action. FAP was more acceptable to the House than the Senate because the House Ways and Means Committee developed a workable consensus on welfare reform, while the Senate Finance Committee was torn by liberal and conservative dissension over public assistance.

Early reluctance by Chairman Wilbur Mills (Democrat-Arkansas) was soon converted to his substantially strong support for FAP. By March 5, 1970, Mills, working together with the ranking minority member, John W. Byrnes (Republican-Wisconsin) promoted support for an eventual 21–3 vote for FAP on the Ways and Means Committee. Consensus and near voting unanimity were the guiding principles. The proposal went to the floor under a "closed rule" which prohibited any amendments. Considering his high prestige and many years of legislative accomplishment, Mills' committee support for FAP ensured House approval. On April 16, 1970, FAP was endorsed by a 243–155 vote. During the debates, Mills noted the work incentive features which required recipients to register for work or to accept training or jobs as they became available. This emphasis echoed Mills' prior support for compulsory work for training for AFDC mothers in the 1967 Social Security amendments.

Acceptance of FAP by the House did not ensure similar success in the Senate Finance Committee. Marmor and Rein indicate that the "lightly glued welfare-reform package came apart . . ." as "liberals flayed the bill as inadequate and inhumane . . ." while the conservatives "devastated FAP's pretension to consistent welfare reform."[65] The Senate Finance Committee was dominated by small-state, southern, and rural conservatives. In particular, Chairman Russell Long (Democrat-Louisiana) and John J. Williams (Republican-Delaware) led the conservative assault on FAP. During 1970, Williams, soon to retire from the Senate, undertook a crusade to defeat welfare reform. He demanded to know how work incentives would be effective when the tax rate on additional earnings reduced FAP payments by more than two-thirds, considering the recipients' costs for food stamps, housing subsidies, Medicaid, and federal, state, and local taxes. Williams envisioned no work incentives as marginal tax rates exceeded 100 percent. But, as previously indicated, the only way to encourage stronger work incentives was to raise the income floor and to lower the tax rate, both of which would greatly increase program coverage and governmental costs—policy alternatives that were obviously unacceptable both to congressional conservatives and the Nixon administration. By the summer of 1970, the Senate Finance Committee had stifled FAP with its endless probing questions to HEW Secretary Robert Finch and his successor, Elliot Richardson. By October 8, the Finance Committee formally rejected FAP by a 14–1 vote and, instead, endorsed a series of regional welfare reform experiments in a few states and cities (by a 13–3 vote on November 20).

The legislative stalemate persisted throughout 1971 and 1972. Chairman Mills and the Ways and Means Committee again secured House approval of a revised welfare proposal by a 288–132 vote on June 22, 1971. This time the bill raised the income floor from $1,600 to $2,400 and included stronger work incentives. Food stamps were excluded, but states could supplement payments up to the $2,400 minimum. The breakeven point was increased from $3,920 to $4,320. The tax rate on additional earnings rose from 50 percent to 66⅔ percent, but excluded the first $720 in earnings, permitted deductions for day-care expenses, and eliminated social security and income taxes for recipients obtaining jobs. Employable adult recipients were made eligible for the Department of Labor's Opportunities for Families (OFF) program, while mothers with children would be in the Family Assistance Program of HEW (Marmor and Rein note the splintering of administrative responsibilities resulted in the humorous acronym, FAP-OFF[66]). Additionally, recipients would pay a new tax for Medicaid equivalent to a deductible of one-third of earnings above $720 plus state supplemental assistance.[67]

However, the Senate was not in a mood to accept this modified version of FAP, nor even to develop a consensus of its own. Instead, Senator Herman Talmadge (Democrat-Georgia) proposed restrictive work requirement provisions for AFDC adults, which Congress quickly approved in the closing days of the 1971 session. The Talmadge amendment required all AFDC recipients, except mothers with children under six years of age, the ill, and the elderly, to register with the Department of Labor for work or training under penalty of losing benefits. These provisions were reminiscent of the punitive 1967 Social Security amendments, but only 5 percent or about 160,000 unemployed men and 40 percent of welfare mothers were affected.[68] When he signed the bill on December 28, President Nixon strongly supported these "workfare" provisions of his welfare reform: "We are a nation that pays tribute to the working man and rightly scorns the freeloader who voluntarily opts to be a ward of the state."[69]

Meanwhile, Senator Abraham Ribicoff (Democrat-Connecticut) tried to develop a compromise welfare reform proposal that would satisfy liberals, moderates, and conservatives. First, he broadened the original FAP plan by establishing an income floor of $3,000; a break-even point of $3,940 (the poverty level); a comprehensive coverage for families with children, childless couples, and single persons; a federal takeover of 30 percent of state supplemental payments; and the complete federal administration of all welfare assistance by 1976. Secondly, Ribicoff organized a coalition of twenty-three senators and interest groups for his plan, including fifteen governors, the AFL-CIO, the United Auto Workers, the League of Women Voters, Common Cause, the National League of Cities/U.S. Conference of Mayors, the National Association of Counties, and the American Jewish Committee.[70]

Using his welfare reform proposal as a bargaining chip, Senator Ribicoff conducted extensive negotiations with HEW Secretary Richardson and Labor Secretary James Hodgson to work out an acceptable compromise between the 1971 House-endorsed version of FAP and the liberal alternative. They agreed on a $2,600 income floor, a 60 percent tax rate on additional earnings, benefits geared to cost of living increases, payment of the minimum wage to recipients required to work, and additional coverage of several million of the working poor.

However, the Ribicoff-administration compromise was doomed to failure. As the 1972 presidential campaign began, President Nixon turned his attention to such foreign policy matters as the Vietnam War and visits to Peking and Moscow. Also, Senator George McGovern, the leading Democratic presidential candidate, proposed his ill-fated and extravagant "demogrant" proposal, guaranteeing $1,000 to every person, which Senator Hubert Humphrey (Democrat-Minnesota) vigorously criticized during the California primary campaign. President Nixon refused to endorse the Ribicoff compromise because FAP seemed to be a more viable legislative possibility than McGovern's radical demogrant plan.

Furthermore, Chairman Russell Long of the Senate Finance Committee sponsored a "forced work" welfare plan which gained support among committee conservatives. Long's proposal sought to eliminate "welfare chiselers" from the relief rolls. Except for AFDC mothers with children under six years of age who would receive a $2,400 minimum income, all other welfare recipients would be required to work at jobs paying at least $1.20 per hour or $48 per week (or below the minimum wage). For recipients unable to find work, a Federal Employment Corporation would be established to create such low-paying jobs which would provide an annual income of $2,400. Recipients refusing to work would be denied all adult cash benefits.

With no hopes of reconciling FAP, Ribicoff's version, or Long's "workfare" scheme, the Senate buried welfare reform in 1972. On October 3, Senator Long moved to table Ribicoff's proposal, and the Senate agreed by a 52–34 vote. The next day, Senator Adlai E. Stevenson III (Democrat-Illinois) offered a compromise between the financial provisions of FAP and the Ribicoff plan's more extensive coverage, but this was also tabled by a 51–35 vote. The Senate then agreed to a series of limited regional tests of the plans it had just disapproved. However, the House-Senate conference committee deleted this provision. Instead, the 1972 Social Security amendments shifted the blind, aged, and disabled categorical assistance programs to federal cash support under the Social Security Administration. The AFDC program remained untouched, except for the work registration requirements adopted in the 1971 Talmadge amendment.

Why did welfare reform suffer such a resounding defeat? Consensus was impossible when the ideological defenders of the guaranteed income and "workfare" could not accommodate their opposing viewpoints. First, the Nixon administration seemed most willing to adjust FAP with the views of congressional moderate conservatives but not with the extremely hostile conservative opposition to income support for the poor. In effect, the "workfare" issue split the conservative ranks in Congress, especially in the Senate. At the same time, the moderate liberals in Congress could not reconcile their hopes for a higher income guarantee with militant groups (such as the NWRO) who demanded much greater federal support without

272 / The Urban Crisis: Problems and Prospects

any work requirements. The liberals also were unable to achieve presidential endorsement of the Ribicoff-administration compromise because of Senator McGovern's untimely demogrant plan. Without strong presidential leadership, welfare reform proposals were mired in bitter ideological entanglement. Welfare reform became a forum for the mutual antagonism of conflicting interests. President Nixon, who neither cultivated nor had the support of the urban constituencies most affected by his policy changes, diverted his attention to other issues at the very time when he might have reconciled the guaranteed income-workfare policy dispute. Instead, President Nixon politicized "workfare" and made it an election campaign issue. In the end, political antagonism rather than policy compromise ensured the perpetuation of AFDC, even though none of the groups involved were satisfied with the welfare mess.

NOTES

1. *Report of the National Advisory Commission on Civil Disorders* (Washington, D.C.: U.S. Government Printing Office, 1968), p. 252.
2. Frances Fox Piven and Richard A. Cloward, *Regulating the Poor: The Functions of Public Welfare* (New York: Pantheon Books, 1971), p. 49.
3. Daniel P. Moynihan, *The Politics of a Guaranteed Income* (New York: Random House, 1973), p. 43.
4. American Enterprise Institute for Policy Research, *Legislative Analysis: Welfare Reform Proposals* (Washington, D.C., 1971), p. 5.
5. *The Negro Family*, in *The Moynihan Report and the Politics of Controversy*, eds. Lee Rainwater and William L. Yancey (Cambridge, Mass.: M.I.T. Press, 1967), p. 58.
6. Report of the President's Commission on Income Maintenance Programs, *Poverty Amid Plenty: The American Paradox* (Washington, D.C.: U.S. Government Printing Office, 1970), p. 47.
7. Gilbert Y. Steiner, *The State Of Welfare* (Washington, D.C.: Brookings Institution, 1971), pp. 35–38. Also, see: Gilbert Y. Steiner, *Social Insecurity: The Politics of Welfare* (Chicago: Rand McNally, 1966), pp. 34–47.
8. American Enterprise Institute, *Welfare Reform Proposals*, p. 5.
9. Piven and Cloward, *Regulating the Poor*, p. 3.
10. Moynihan, *The Politics of a Guaranteed Income*, p. 25.
11. Piven and Cloward, *Regulating the Poor*, p. 183.
12. *Ibid.*, p. 187.
13. President Nixon's Message to Congress on Welfare Reform, August 11, 1969, in Committee on Ways and Means, U.S. House of Representatives, 91st Congress, 1st Session, *The President's Proposals for Welfare Reform and Social Security Amendments* (Washington, D.C.: U.S. Government Printing Office, 1969), p. 94.
14. Edward C. Banfield, "Welfare: A Crisis Without 'Solutions'," *The Public Interest*, No. 16 (Summer 1969), p. 90, and John V. Lindsay, *The City* (New York: The New American Library, Signet Books, 1970), p. 143.

15. Piven and Cloward, *Regulating the Poor*, p. 185.
16. *Ibid.*
17. Committee for Economic Development, *Improving the Public Welfare System* (New York, 1970), pp. 22–23.
18. Steiner, *Social Insecurity*, pp. 27–28.
19. *The Negro Family*, p. 60.
20. *Ibid.*, pp. 52–58.
21. CED, *Improving the Public Welfare System*, pp. 28–29.
22. Piven and Cloward, *Regulating the Poor*, p. 195.
23. William Ryan, *Blaming the Victim* (New York: Random House, Vintage Books, 1971), p. 104.
24. *Report of the National Advisory Commission on Civil Disorders*, pp. 116–118.
25. Steiner, *The State of Welfare*, p. 42.
26. *Report of the National Advisory Commission on Civil Disorders*, pp. 116–118.
27. Steiner, *The State of Welfare*, p. 87.
28. *Ibid.*, p. 88.
29. *The New York Times*, April 22, 1969, p. 1, col. 6.
30. *Ibid.*, June 3, 1969, p. 28, col. 4.
31. Piven and Cloward, *Regulating the Poor*, p. 308.
32. *The New York Times*, June 18, 1968, p. 33, col. 5–8.
33. *Ibid.*
34. Piven and Cloward, *Regulating the Poor*, p. 310.
35. Frances Fox Piven and Richard A. Cloward, "Dissensus Politics: A Strategy for Winning Economic Rights," *The New Republic* (April 28, 1968), pp. 20–24.
36. Frances Fox Piven and Richard A. Cloward, "The Weight of the Poor: A Strategy to End Poverty," *The Nation* (May 2, 1966), pp. 510–517.
37. Piven and Cloward, *Regulating the Poor*, p. 322.
38. Steiner, *The State of Welfare*, p. 285.
39. Michael Rogin, "Now It's Welfare Lib," *The New York Times Magazine* (September 27, 1970), p. 83.
40. Piven and Cloward, *Regulating the Poor*, pp. 331–334.
41. Banfield, *The Public Interest*, No. 16 (Summer 1969), p. 95.
42. *Poverty Amid Plenty*, p. 120.
43. Joseph A. Kershaw, *Government Against Poverty* (Chicago: Markham, 1970), p. 104.
44. U.S. Department of Health, Education, and Welfare, *Welfare Policy and Its Consequences for the Recipient Population: A Study of the AFDC Program* (Washington, D.C.: U.S. Government Printing Office, 1969), p. 9.
45. U.S. Department of Health, Education, and Welfare, *Aid to Families with Dependent Children*, data for April 1971.
46. *Poverty Amid Plenty*, p. 117.
47. *The New York Times*, January 10, 1971, p. 40, col. 3–8.
48. *Ibid.*
49. *Ibid.*
50. Moynihan, *The Politics of a Guaranteed Income*, p. 55.
51. Milton Friedman, *Capitalism and Freedom* (Chicago: University of Chicago Press, 1962), pp. 191–195.
52. James Tobin, "Raising the Incomes of the Poor," in *Agenda for the Nation*, ed. Kermit Gordon (Washington, D.C.: Brookings Institution, 1968), p. 111.

53. *Ibid.*, pp. 105–108.
54. *Poverty Amid Plenty*, p. 58.
55. *Ibid.*, p. 57.
56. The National Urban Coalition, *Counterbudget* (New York: Praeger, 1971), pp. 50–58.
57. Henry J. Aaron, *Why Is Welfare So Hard To Reform?* (Washington, D.C.: Brookings Institution, 1973), p. 21.
58. Theodore R. Marmor and Martin Rein, "Reforming 'The Welfare Mess': The Fate of the Family Assistance Plan, 1969–72," in *Policy and Politics In America*, ed. Allan P. Sindler (Boston: Little, Brown, 1973), pp. 17–18.
59. *Ibid.*, p. 17.
60. *The New York Times*, August 9, 1969, p. 10, col. 3.
61. *Ibid.*, September 3, 1969, p. 1, col. 1.
62. *Ibid.*, August 10, 1969, p. 1, col. 1.
63. *Ibid.*, August 9, 1969, p. 11, col. 7.
64. Moynihan, *The Politics of a Guaranteed Income*, pp. 41, 85.
65. Marmor and Rein, in *Policy and Politics In America*, ed. Sindler, p. 19.
66. *Ibid.*, p. 20.
67. Aaron, *Why Is Welfare So Hard To Reform?*, pp. 22–23.
68. *The New York Times*, December 19, 1971, Sec. 4, p. 4, col. 3.
69. *Ibid.*, December 29, 1971, p. 1, col. 2.
70. Senator Abraham Ribicoff, "He Left at Half Time: Book Review of Daniel P. Moynihan's *The Politics of a Guaranteed Income*," *The New Republic* (February 17, 1973), p. 25.

SUGGESTIONS FOR FURTHER READING

Aaron, Henry J. *Why Is Welfare So Hard to Reform?* Washington, D.C.: Brookings Institution, 1973.
Analysis of major welfare programs indicating the problems of providing adequate incentives for the poor.

American Enterprise Institute for Policy Research. *Legislative Analysis: Welfare Reform Proposals.* Washington, D.C.: 1971.
Analysis of categorical aid programs and major issues related to legislative proposals for welfare reform.

Banfield, Edward C. "Welfare: A Crisis Without 'Solutions'," *The Public Interest*, Vol. 16 (Summer 1969), pp. 89–101.
A description of how welfare dependency increases even with reform proposals.

Committee for Economic Development. *Improving the Public Welfare System.* New York: 1970.
Analysis of trends in poverty, unemployment, inadequacies of the present welfare system, and proposals for change.

Elman, Richard M. *The Poorhouse State.* New York: Dell, Delta Books, 1966.
Devastating indictment of welfare system from interviews with New York City recipients.

Glazer, Nathan. "Beyond Income Maintenance—A Note on Welfare

in New York City," *The Public Interest,* Vol. 16 (Summer 1969), pp. 102–120.
An examination of how even with massive welfare reforms, the nation's largest city would still have to support a considerably large poverty-stricken population.

Gordon, David M. "Income and Welfare in New York City," *The Public Interest,* Vol. 16 (Summer 1969), pp. 64–88.
A discussion of statistical analyses which indicate the persistence of poverty and welfare dependency in the nation's largest city.

Levitan, Sar A., Martin Rein, and David Marwick. *Work and Welfare Go Together.* Baltimore: Johns Hopkins University Press, 1972.
Evaluation of AFDC program and options for welfare policy that include work incentives.

Marmor, Theodore R., ed. *Poverty Policy.* Chicago: Aldine-Atherton, 1971.
Collection of leading welfare reform proposals.

Marmor, Theodore R., and Martin Rein. "Reforming 'The Welfare Mess': The Fate of the Family Assistance Plan, 1969–72," in *Policy and Politics in America,* ed. Allan P. Sindler. Boston: Little, Brown, 1973. pp. 3–28.
Comprehensive case study of the defeat of the Nixon Family Assistance Plan in Congress.

Moynihan, Daniel P. *The Politics of a Guaranteed Income.* New York: Random House, 1973.
Leading proponent of Family Assistance Plan analyzes the legislative struggle and blames Congress for refusing to accept the Nixon administration's welfare reform proposal.

Piven, Frances Fox, and Richard A. Cloward. *Regulating the Poor: The Functions of Public Welfare.* New York: Pantheon, 1971.
Devastating criticism of the welfare system which, the authors contend, maintains the poor in dependency rather than alleviating their deprivation.

Poverty Amid Plenty: The American Paradox. The Report of the President's Commission on Income Maintenance Programs. Washington, D.C.: U.S. Government Printing Office, 1969.
Commission appointed by President Johnson recommended a guaranteed income supplement for the poor.

Rainwater, Lee, and William L. Yancey, eds. *The Moynihan Report and the Politics of Controversy.* Cambridge, Mass.: M.I.T. Press, 1967.
Collection of articles relating to the controversial report by Daniel P. Moynihan on the black family and welfare dependency.

Steiner, Gilbert Y. *The State of Welfare.* Washington, D.C.: Brookings Institution, 1971.
Comprehensive analysis of federal welfare aid programs.

Vadakin, James C. "A Critique of the Guaranteed Annual Income," *The Public Interest,* Vol. 11 (Spring 1968), pp. 53–66.
An evaluation of five alternative policy proposals together with an argument for family allowances to replace the welfare system.

9

Community Participation
in the War on Poverty

INTRODUCTION

On August 20, 1964, President Lyndon Johnson signed into law the Economic Opportunity Act which launched the War on Poverty. The massively ambitious program was aimed, rhetorically at least, at nothing less than eliminating poverty in America. The program was to be administered by an Office of Economic Opportunity (OEO) directly under the president. Community action agencies* (CAAs) were to be established at the local level to initiate special programs targeted on education, job training, job opportunities, and others whose common theme was opening opportunities to the poor.

The CAPs were to be an improvement over the traditional welfare institutions that had fallen short or failed in the task of relieving the problems of the poor. The CAPs were authorized to bypass the established agencies when necessary in order to carry out their mission. Finally, they were to foster the "maximum feasible participation" of residents and groups in the areas they served. Some would

---

*They were commonly known as the CAP agencies; CAP is short for the community action program within OEO, which sponsored them. We use CAA and CAP interchangeably in the text.

serve on governing and advisory boards, others on planning task forces. Still others could be employed to work on programs, the advantage being that their personal experience with the problems of the community would make them more effective than professionals in administering solutions. The CAPs were to be run by competent professionals who also understood the community and could communicate with the poor. In the experience of the program, as we shall see, the actual participation of the poor was minimal and in many localities almost meaningless. In the end, the CAPs took on the behavioral characteristics of the traditional agencies that preceded them, and the masses of the poor have hardly benefited at all. The program did, however, contribute greatly to the development of new professional and political leadership which may someday be in a position to help develop truly effective national antipoverty programs.

The well-meaning designers of the program, however, saw the OEO community action program as a chance to develop local organizations that would in time become powerful enough to make their own demands upon local and national resources. In some measure, this much was accomplished through a constituency of new professionals and leaders who now have their advocates in the federal bureaucracy and in Congress.

The emphasis in the antipoverty programs of providing opportunities presumed that most poverty was caused by blocked opportunities. This concept had gained currency in the early 1960s from the work of Richard Cloward and Lloyd Ohlin in their study *Delinquency and Opportunity* (1960), which suggested that youth crime in poverty areas stemmed mainly from a malfunctioning social system. The Cloward-Ohlin thesis was that the ghetto youth had absorbed the values of a materialistic society and in committing crimes of acquisition were gaining socially approved objectives by unlawful means. If given the same opportunities for an education and jobs as law-abiding people, the delinquents presumably would not "need" to commit crimes. The solution suggested by the Cloward-Ohlin thesis was to provide the opportunities in education, training, health, and welfare to youth born into poverty equivalent to those of youth born into affluence. In focusing upon a strategy of opening opportunities to the deprived, the antipoverty program failed to take into account poverty which stems from other causes. For example, many poor people are poor because of a cognitive disability which prevents them from holding a job. Many others hold personal or cultural values which render opportunities for "betterment" meaningless.[1]

PRECEDENTS FOR COMMUNITY AND
CITIZEN PARTICIPATION

The Economic Opportunity Act not only provided for involvement of ghetto residents in the antipoverty program, but it also required the federal government to take the initiative in organizing community action agencies to insure their participation. This meant that the federal government was to be responsible for organizing poor people to speak up on their own behalf. On the continuum of protest, it is an easy step from vocalization to aggressive action. (See Chapter 7.)

Why did the federal government take so bold a step? For one thing, no one in Washington foresaw that the local CAAs would become the threat to the local establishment that some of them did. Also, the precedents in local community action programs against poverty which had been sponsored by the Ford Foundation had not yielded any clues as to the potential volatility of the CAPs. These precedents were so promising in their early results that they seemed to give substance to "The New Frontier" slogan of the youthful Kennedy administration whence the program originated. In the early months of his administration, President Kennedy told his Council of Economic Advisers: "Now look, I want to go beyond the things that have already been accomplished. Give me facts and figures on the things we still have to do. For example, what about poverty in the United States?"

The facts revealed an unemployment rate that had gone from 3.5 percent in 1953, to 3.8 percent in 1956, to 5.5 percent in 1959. The situation was much worse for blacks and Hispanics* who had migrated into the industrial cities of America during and after World War II. In 1940 black unemployment was 20 percent higher than that of whites; by 1953 it was 71 percent higher, and it had reached 112 percent in 1963. It was during this period (1950–1960) that 1.4 million blacks left the South for the urban industrial centers of the North and West.

It should be noted that President Kennedy's antipoverty program embodied a dual strategy of jobs and services. In 1963, a few weeks before his assassination, he was preparing a 1964 legislative program which included an $11 billion tax cut to revive the economy and expand employment. The other part of his program focused upon

---

*The generic "Hispanics" is used throughout the text to identify Spanish-speaking Americans whether they originate in Puerto Rico, other parts of the Caribbean, Mexico, or South or Central America.

manpower, training, and education for the jobless who needed new skills for a changing job market. Other services such as health care and legal and job counseling would remove other barriers to the job market.

The stage had already been set for a national initiative by the Ford Foundation's "grey areas" program and by New York City's Mobilization for Youth. The President added a third in his Committee on Juvenile Delinquency and Youth Crime (PCJD) which was headed by Attorney General Robert Kennedy. The antipoverty program had other major precedents: the Civil Rights Movement, Saul Alinsky's Industrial Areas Foundation, and advocacy planning.

All of these community and citizen action programs (except PCJD) were outside of the federal government, and there was little in them that provided an adequate forecast of the effects a massive government-sponsored attack on poverty that involved poverty-stricken citizens. In all previous experience, citizen participation in federal programs had brought local people into advisory councils which were controlled by federal agencies or by local agencies acting for the federal government.

The federal Housing Acts of 1949 and 1954 (see Chapter 11) required that urban redevelopment be carried out with the advice of local citizens, and that public hearings be held prior to implementation of redevelopment programs. The Housing Act of 1954 specifically required citizen participation in city and regional planning, but none of these programs gave over any control to local citizens.

Although citizen participation in government is a fundamental concept in the American system as evidenced in the Mayflower Compact, the Declaration of Independence, the Revolution, the New England town meeting, Jeffersonian theory, and Jacksonian practice —the concept had never specifically included the landless or the ne'er-do-wells.

The Ford Foundation's "grey areas" program. In the late fifties the Ford Foundation initiated community action programs aimed at inducing a concentration of public and private resources for improving life in poverty sections of Boston, New Haven, Philadelphia, and Oakland. The purpose was to involve residents of these areas in finding ways to make the improvements and at the same time to open opportunities for them in jobs and education. Anticipating the federal antipoverty program by several years, the vehicle was an independent community action agency which at both board and staff levels was a coalition of citywide established institutions and inner-city community representatives. The Ford program assumed, as did the later federal antipoverty efforts, that most of the established institutions were too limited in their resources and too conservative in their approach to deal effectively with conditions of the hard-core poor. As the demonstrations matured, officials of the Foundation found a ready audience among White House and PCJD staff members who were looking for ideas for a federal antipoverty program. In due course, some of the Ford Foundation staff joined the antipoverty planners in Washington and eventually all of the "grey area" projects were absorbed into the federal program as prototypes of the CAPs.

Alinsky's Industrial Areas Foundation. Long before anyone else had thought about involving the poor in local decision-making, Saul Alinsky had recognized that no substantial social effort would be made on behalf of excluded minorities—or the underclasses—unless they undertook the effort themselves. For many years before the riots of the 1960s, Alinsky had been putting to work his theories on the politics of confrontation in his Industrial Areas Foundation and in his Chicago Woodland Organization. Alinsky's thesis was that the "powerless" had to generate power as a necessary condition in achieving a position of power and that power was gained through effective organization and aggressive action. Alinsky's work in urban ghettos provided a few working models for the instruction of the community action program leaders (both local and national) in the poverty program. Inspired by Alinsky's example and encouraged by Martin Luther King's tactics of provocation, many of the early CAP leaders challenged the local power centers and actually took control of some local programs and gained a large voice in others.

The Civil Rights Movement, Point Four, and the Peace Corps. The overseas community development programs initiated by President Harry S. Truman in his "Point Four" program of technical aid to underdeveloped nations featured locally initiated plans and self-help. Witnessing the success of community development under this program in the early 1950s, the American Civil Rights Movement began similar efforts in poverty communities of the United States. The approach was one of helping "backward" people develop new techniques and facilities to improve their living standards.

These experiences served as models for the Peace Corps which was the first major program in the Kennedy administration. Peace Corps volunteers helped communities in underdeveloped countries build hospitals, schools, recreational centers, and sewer and water systems. They also helped apply elementary agricultural and food-processing techniques to increase food supplies, as well as techniques and instruction to improve health standards. Volunteers in Service to America (VISTA), also a Kennedy program, applied the Peace Corps experience at home, thus reinforcing the work begun by the Civil Rights Movement. The notion of community self-help, more than any other, translated into the concept of "maximum feasible participation," a phrase which meant participation in both planning and implementation by the residents themselves. In the Kennedy version, upgrading people was as important as upgrading physical facilities, thus, the emphasis on job opportunities, education, and health and welfare services.

Mobilization for Youth and PCDJ. While the Ford Foundation's "grey area" program came up with the specific models for community action agencies for the antipoverty program, the Mobilization for Youth program (MFY) in New York City provided a field test of the Cloward-Ohlin theory of delinquency and opportunity. MFY's objective was reform and reorganization of community institutions aimed at opening channels of opportunity to deprived youth. MFY leaders believed that the indigenous poor knew more about their problems than the social welfare experts, except that in both the MFY program and in the Ford Foundation's "grey areas" projects, community action was a means of obtaining access and acceptance in poverty communities by the social planners who designed and controlled the programs. These programs, including the federal antipoverty program, were never meant to be controlled by community residents. The last thing the planners intended or anticipated was the creation of community action groups that would provide a political base for emerging new leaders in ghetto communities. But this is what happened, and the community action program ran into trouble in city hall, Congress, and the White House when it appeared that new and independent forces were being fostered in the local CAPs.

The President's Committee on Juvenile Delinquency and Youth Crime (PCJD) was set up in May, 1961, to begin planning a series of federal projects to demonstrate and evaluate methods of dealing with juvenile crime. The PCJD staff included Lloyd Ohlin, Richard Boone of the Ford Foundation, and Sanford Kravitz, who later became chief of research and program development in the community action program of the Office of Economic Opportuntiy. The group shared the belief that an intellectual understanding of the problems

of poverty and delinquency combined with "political clout" and resources would provide the solid basis for a "war on delinquency."

The PCJD in awarding planning grants stressed community planning, analysis and action, and, (as with the Ford Foundation "grey
areas" program) participation of public agencies and local political
leaders. Thus, PCJD wanted the involvement of the poor but would
have been horrified at the idea of fostering social upheaval or disrupting local political power. Indeed, the PCJD sought the active
involvement of established local political leaders in implementing
programs.

In September, 1961, Congress enacted the Juvenile Delinquency
and Youth Offenses Control Act which provided $10 million a year
for three years for projects which could demonstrate "effective ways
of using total resources to combat juvenile delinquency in local
communities."

The local projects sponsored by the PCJD and the Juvenile Delinquency and Youth Offenses Control Act were operated by community
action agencies in the general pattern of Mobilization for Youth.
Their emphasis on planning, on coordination of local services, and
on measurement and evaluation of results attracted the support of
the Bureau of the Budget, Congress, and the Council of Economic
Advisors. This was important political groundwork for the antipoverty
legislation which followed.

PARTICIPATION AND PLANNING

The brief span of the Kennedy administration (1057 days) was a
period in which the liberal intellectuals were in ascendancy, inspired
and supported by the Civil Rights Movement, the social experimentation of the Ford Foundation, and other movements. In the spirit of
the times, involving the poor in programs of improvement seemed
natural. The tidal wave of social upheaval which crested after 1965
in the ghetto riots and war protest (as discussed in Chapter 7) was
not foreseen by the antipoverty planners.

By November 1963, the young president was dead, and a nation
in mourning was ready to pay tribute to his memory. Thus, when
President Lyndon Johnson called for the War on Poverty in his first
State of the Union message, the nation recognized the idealism they
associated with the Kennedys.

Drafting the Antipoverty Program

Lyndon Johnson saw the antipoverty program in much the same light as Kennedy had: it could attract to the party a new group of urban voters (1964 was a presidential election year); it was a plausible-sounding vehicle for working on solutions to black unemployment problems; if the program was big enough, it could employ poor people. It might also take some of the pressure off state and local government in the area of urban problems.

A presidential task force on the War Against Poverty was set up in January, 1964, to draft a legislative program. The group was headed by R. Sargent Shriver, President Kennedy's brother-in-law, who had organized the Peace Corps. Much of the debate in the task force centered on the concept of community action and participation: To what extent and for what purposes would residents of "target areas" be involved? To what extent should programs and projects be initiated from the local level? From the federal level? To what extent should the federal program rely upon local leadership? Should the program be used to challenge local institutions or should it be permitted to bypass them? Daniel P. Moynihan, a member of the task force, summarized some of the debate which took place in the early stages of the drafting: "[We] touched on the problem of local leadership in the South, especially, and noted that CAPs could be used to by-pass the local 'power structure' with the use of federal funds. Richard Boone insisted that the community action programs could be 'manned' by the poor themselves. . . . Mayor Arthur Naftalin [warned] not to expect too much from community leadership and . . . that existing bureaucracies must be made to work . . ."[2] instead of creating new ones.

Shriver's skepticism about the workability of community action switched discussions to substantive programs in jobs, education, work study, child health, and others. The president himself had made clear the political necessity of avoiding alienation of local power structures. As Moynihan reports, "Community action remained as an *item* in the antipoverty program . . . but it was no longer the program itself."[3] In particular, the program as settled upon by the task force in February, 1964, was action-oriented and national in scope; nevertheless, community participation became a major feature of the actual bill. Members of the task force insisted that action for federal recourse be included if the poor—and especially the poor Southern black—were excluded from planning and program implementation at the local level. This concern, more than any others, explained why the community action title of the bill provided for maximum feasible participation of the residents. The drafters thought that a requirement for participation would ensure that persons who were intended to benefit from the program would actually benefit. Nevertheless, drafters of the legislation on the White House task force assumed that the programs would be dominated by local power structures. Hence, the community action model in the draft legislation included local political leadership.

To summarize the intent of the presidential drafting group, the local CAP agencies were supposed to be *consensus* structures which would bring together the relevant actors in the political structure, the social agencies and civic organizations, and the residents of the poverty areas to be served—objects, incidentally, that were included in the Ford Foundation programs.

When the "consensus structures" turned out to be generators of conflict and brought some embarrassing protests from several powerful big-city Democratic mayors, there were only a few recorded hints from the designers of the program that anyone foresaw those results. Kravitz later confessed that the task force was aware of "a gnawing question about the capacity of a structure based on 'consensus' to work effectively for broad social change," but, "none of us, in our euphoria over the opportunity to mount the program at a national level, were really prepared to raise openly that question."[4]

Yarmolinsky recalls that the drafting group regarded maximum feasible participation "simply as a process of encouraging the residents of poverty areas to take part in the work of community action programs and to perform a number of jobs that might otherwise be performed by professional social workers."[5] According to Yarmolinsky, there was no "visible concern at the time that the program might (later) be accused of financing revolt and insurrection in the ghetto."[6] The only reference made to it during the congressional hearings on the bill was by Attorney General Robert F. Kennedy when he said: "This bill calls for maximum participation of residents. This means involvement of the poor in planning and implementing programs; giving them a real voice in their institutions."[7] As it turned out, the process of getting the CAP agencies established sometimes involved dramatic, headline-making conflict, but most communities eventually accepted the program.

The matter of "comprehensive community planning" was an issue. In a meeting on May 7 between Shriver and the House Committee on Education and Labor, Title II (the community action program of the bill) was altered to eliminate the requirements for a comprehensive community plan as a basis for action. As Moynihan observed: "Congress . . . wanted action without too much forethought, preparation, planning, negotiating, agreeing, staging. This is what it got."[8]

While the task force appeared not to anticipate that participation might become a disrupting force at the local level, there was a great deal of attention paid to the related but quite different concept of community action and coordination of diverse federal programs aimed at helping the poor. Bureau of the Budget (BOB) members of the task force proposed that ten demonstration areas be selected with a development corporation to be formed in each. "In these areas, federal funds would be provided for a wide range of programs, with the corporation to plan the programs, expend the funds, and provide the coordinating mechanism."[9] BOB argued that a development corporation, as a highly visible new element in the local social service structure, could be given responsibility for selecting among new programs being offered by different government agencies.

Provision for this coordination (but not the ten pilot projects) was made in the 1964 act as follows: "Federal agencies which are engaged in administering programs related to the purposes of this Act, . . . shall . . . cooperate with the Director in carrying out his duties and responsibilities under the Act, . . ." That it never worked at the local level was partly because of resistance from the federal departments. For its part, OEO concentrated on organizing the CAP agencies and on creating the other major programs for which it had direct responsibility. Efforts to coordinate the poverty programs of other federal departments never did gain a high priority in OEO.

The Effects of Resident Participation

[In practice, when coordination was emphasized at the local level, resident participation was neglected. Where resident participation was strong, coordination was not particularly successful.[10] This situation illustrates a point made by Peter Marris that two local organizations are probably needed for disadvantaged minorities: one in city hall which does the planning and coordination and another through which the citizens can make their will felt.[11]]

In the end, the task force endorsed the notion of a single local organization to coordinate public and private antipoverty efforts, but it did not say how the organization should be created, who should create it, or whom it should represent. Moreover, there was no indication that the poor would be encouraged to utilize the program for self-assertion, and planning—which had been so critical an element in the Ford "grey areas" projects, Mobilization for Youth, and PCJD programs—was not emphasized. Action and results were all-important; the time was short before Congress would want results to justify continued support. Thus, it was clear even before the bill became law that OEO would be far less concerned about the "institutional and intellectual organization of reform than about the influence of community action on the distribution of power."[12] The programs of OEO were to address actual needs, not merely add to the understanding of poverty problems; they were to relieve poverty wherever it prevailed, not merely "show how it might be relieved."[13]

President Johnson's antipoverty program thus abandoned his predecessor's inclination to lay stress on planning and experimentation. As early as 1963, though, the projects of Kennedy's PCJD had come under increasing pressure to show what they could do. The dilemma was apparent and OEO opted for what it regarded as the lesser of two evils: it preferred the risk of faulty action programs to no programs.

Once the Economic Opportunity Act was signed into law, the Ford Foundation gave terminal grants to Boston, New Haven, and Oakland, all of which subsequently were funded by OEO. At the same time, twelve of the sixteen projects originally funded by PCJD were transferred to OEO. The others in Washington, Boston, and New Haven and Mobilization for Youth in New York remained under their original auspices to complete their evaluation as demonstrations.

In spite of the fact that Congress and the administration played down community action in the legislation, Title II in the first year received $340 million of the $500 million in "new" funds for the poverty program. In fiscal year 1966, the second year of the program, the amount was nearly doubled.

Meanwhile, events bearing upon the direction and character of the antipoverty program were accelerating. A few scattered but severe riots had occurred in the summer of 1964. As the dimensions and potential of the antipoverty program became known to ghetto leaders and as the effect of the riots on white political leaders became obvious to them, their demands for a controlling role in local program planning mounted. (Because some OEO officials chose to take seriously the mandate to seek maximum participation of local communities, they welcomed the aggressive interest of ghetto leaders.) Many local leaders also saw the antipoverty program as a convenient vehicle for making concessions to spokesmen for the ghettos, once the threat of rioting had sunk in.)

But neither Congress nor the administration (except for some advocates of the poor in OEO) expected or wanted the poor to make *significant* policy decisions. As a practical matter, too, the anti-poverty program was conceived in Washington and then "sold" to hundreds of communities throughout the nation. Federal guidelines, though imprecise, set policy and organizational patterns which local communities were expected to follow. The "prepackaging" effectively preempted the local creativity which the program seemed to be aimed at fostering. There was really no alternative; although the anti-poverty program tried to give the poor an opportunity to articulate what they thought they needed, Congress ultimately had to decide what kinds of programs would be available. As it turned out, local communities could seldom agree upon a locally initiated agenda of needs; too many contending interests were involved.

Participation Becomes a Threat

The planners of the antipoverty program knew that they were breaking new ground with the community action program, and they were aware that a mandate for significant participation of local groups in poverty areas was a radical departure from previous federal policy. But, according to the firsthand testimony of some of the key program planners, neither they, nor the president, nor Congress foresaw that forces were being set in motion among the poor which really could operate—even control—the CAPs and through them bypass established local institutions. Least of all did the president or Congress foresee that the new agencies would generate sufficient potency to *threaten* the local establishment. *Participation* of the poor was the intent of federal policy-makers, but *initiative* was not.

IMPLEMENTING THE COMMUNITY ACTION PROGRAMS

The new director of the OEO Community Action Program, a labor organizer by profession, had a different concept of the function of the local organizations. He was Jack Conway, a former assistant to Walter Ruether of the United Auto Workers. Conway's objective was to create a vehicle of leadership development, participation, and a political base through which poor people could improve their opportunities with normal political methods. The White House task force planners had wanted participation of the poor but not exactly as Conway visualized it. On behalf of the president, they wanted a grateful poor who would constitute a revitalized political base in inner cities. They also wanted to retain the support of the local political regulars, and so it was not in their interest to create politically independent community organizations that would be antagonistic to the regulars. Conway, however, was not the president's man; he was (in his own image) the "people's man," and the "people" responded. The ghettos to which he offered the antipoverty action program were already aroused by the Civil Rights Movement and by the early riots.

Conway's structure for the community action programs was neither innovative nor radical. Like its Ford predecessors, the organization of the OEO community agency was viewed as a three-legged stool which sought the involvement of the established agencies, the leadership groups, and the representatives of the poor. The process of involving the poor in the local CAAs, however, was no *pro forma* exercise. According to OEO guidelines, participation had to be meaningful and effective, with neighborhood elections to CAP boards, forums for discussion of proposed plans, and promotional materials to advertise new programs. The major CAP programs were the Job Corps for school dropouts, a Neighborhood Youth Corps for high schoolers, and a work-study program for college youths. Jobless fathers of dependent children were offered special training.

Also, residents could protest actions of city hall or the CAP or propose changes in the community action program at any stage. Moreover, the tripartite boards of the community action agencies provided an opportunity for poor people, public officials, and civic leaders to cooperate in a common effort.

Ostensibly, the responsibility for organizing and carrying out the various antipoverty programs lay with the local committee. In OEO literature, communities were told to identify their own problems and priorities and to mobilize their available resources accordingly. The emphasis on local initiative presumably meant that there would be no specific federal blueprints or formulas, and federal standards were to be minimal, as required by the act. Also, OEO planners felt that encouraging communities to think through their own problems was essential to the process of mobilizing local resources.[14]

Thus, confusion over federal control versus local initiative plagued the program from its very beginnings. Moreover, it was never made clear by OEO, Congress, or anyone in the administration whether the local CAPs were to be primarily coordinators of federal programs and operators of OEO programs or organizers of and advocates for the poor. OEO itself was accountable to Congress and the administration for program achievement, and it was committed to the people the program served. In its accountability to Congress and the administration, it had to develop specific programs and to carry them out, even if these programs ran counter to objectives hammered out by the local CAPs. If it insisted upon programs developed in Washington, OEO ran the risk of seeming to manipulate people at the local level. If, on the other hand, OEO really did give the local CAPs free rein in program development as it tried to claim, it ran the risk of supporting local programs which it might have difficulty explaining to Congress. Under the leadership of Shriver and Conway, OEO took the extremely bold course of delegating goal-setting and program development to the local community action agencies.

In this course, according to some critics, the Conway group went far beyond the intent or expectations of the president and Congress.[15] But the Economic Opportunity Act contained no specific guidelines and no explicit statements of intent, and so Conway and Shriver had the legal freedom to adopt this course. In setting up the CAPs with maximum delegated responsibilities and control, they set in motion in the urban ghettos powerful forces that were already seething with the frustrations of rising expectations and inadequate implementation of rights.

The poverty program got off to a fast start: it made over 900 grants to CAPs in a thousand counties within the space of fourteen months. As we have observed, probably the most significant long-run effect of the program was the opportunity it provided for new leadership in the ghettos at a time when the populations of blacks in a dozen or so major cities were approaching majorities. In the period from 1964 to 1966, about one-third of local CAP field representatives were blacks, Puerto Ricans, or Mexican-Americans. Staff workers were major beneficiaries of the program as they gained extensive experience in executive, technical, and professional positions in the CAPs. The poverty program in effect took on the function of the old political party system which, as discussed in Chapter 1, afforded opportunities when other avenues of mobility were limited or blocked.

One lasting contribution of OEO was the Head Start Program, which has become standard in most urban school systems. This program gives ghetto children an enriched educational experience in their preschool years. Another lasting contribution, the Neighborhood Legal Services program, is so widely used that it is now taken for granted. These legal services have had a significant impact in expanding welfare roles. (See Chapter 8.) Both programs have been imitated by volunteer groups in churches (preschool programs), law schools (legal services for the poor), and other local institutions.

(For all its positive results in nurturing new political leadership and in launching some valuable local programs, the community action program fell far short of the expectations of its creators. Few residents ever took part in the program in the organizational sense, although many benefited from its services. This was partly because many of the programs were initiated by established (white) local leaders who knew how to go about applying for a government grant but had no idea of how to involve the people the program was supposed to benefit. When asked by OEO staff whether representatives of the poor had participated in preparing plans for the local program, the usual answer was, "Well, not very much, but about as much as feasible. We needed to move fast."[16] When representatives of the poor failed to object, OEO officials called this omission to the attention of local sponsors.)

The first of the poverty representatives to demand participation were the civil rights groups—the local Urban League, the NAACP, and the American G.I. Forum (of the Mexican-American community). Next came the new militants, mostly young black leaders who took up the slogan "Black Power." The role of the militants was to organize opposition to an "establishment committee" which originated a poverty proposal. OEO officials would then urge the applicant committee to meet with the opposition to "work things out." After negotiations, sometimes taking months, the applicant committee usually offered the leaders of the protesting group seats on the governing board and one or more of the top staff jobs. If the leaders accepted, they ran the risk of being dubbed "sellouts" by associates who were not included. At this stage a new protest committee would appear, adopting a more militant stance than the previous one. In most communities this process usually resulted in something approaching an uneasy consensus.

OEO administrators, for their part, adopted an experimental attitude toward the consensus process. As John Wofford, deputy director of the OEO Community Action Program, recalls: "Sometimes the chief problem was to persuade the local health and welfare council to cooperate with the mayor; sometimes it was to reach an accommodation between the mayor on the one side and the county supervisors on the other; sometimes it was to persuade the school system to cooperate, or to get heads of public city agencies such as welfare to agree to participate in innovative programs."[17]

An important issue in the process of local consensus-building often came down to the number of poverty representatives (ultimately the percentage) which constituted reasonable participation. As a matter of policy, federal administrators were careful in the early stages not to specify a fixed percentage for local governing boards.

As a consequence, there were great variations among communities. A congressional requirement written into the Economic Opportunity Act of 1967 (the Quie Amendment) settled on one-third, a standard which was derived in part from Conway's "three-legged stool" notion of involving local public officials, the old-line social service agencies, and the poor. Wofford notes that OEO guidelines never required that representatives of the poor themselves be poor. The 1965 guidelines read in part: "In determining whether the requirement for *representation* has been met, it is not the incomes of the representatives that (are of) concern; it is the degree to which they represent the persons to be served by the community action program."[18]

Even so, nowhere among the nine-hundred-odd CAPs was there to be found a *community* effort that involved enough people to have any discernible effect upon the quality of life in the community. The CAP governing boards were elected by neighborhood vote, but the turnout was never over 5 percent, except in a few smaller cities. Commonly the turnout was 1 percent or less.

It was apparent by 1965 that consensus politics was not going to work in any community action program where militant politics was on the rise. It is also clear that the CAPs were not *the* source of the militancy as some observers have claimed. The CAPs were merely one vehicle for a movement which had its impetus in the frustrations and hopes that had been building among blacks at least since the case of *Brown* v. *Board of Education*, the Montgomery bus boycott, and the Civil Rights Acts of the period. The riots of the 1960s were not the source either, but rather the expression of a mood which was overready for the riots and the militant leadership that followed. In Wofford's words: "the pulling and hauling, the alliances and counter-alliances developed in the course of creating a local community action structure . . . served to familiarize one set of leaders with another in a period when 'more extreme elements' were entering local politics."[19] Seen in this light, it is not surprising that in the riots of 1967 and 1968, local community action workers, far from fomenting trouble, were among the most active peacemakers. The time was one of conflict, not of consensus.)

The greater tragedy of the community action program (brought on by inadequate federal funding and a gradual withdrawal of presidential support) was the retreat (after 1966) of the local CAPs into organizational maintenance tactics; concern for survival crowded out innovation.

As the local programs developed, some abuses came to light: internal battles over agency control diverted attention from programs; funds were sometimes misused; trusted associates were brought in by those who gained the controlling positions. All of this was in the fashion of a new political organization in the making. From the standpoint of many ambitious minority leaders whose opportunities for political advancement had been blocked, the antipoverty program was an opportunity for a share in local power. Were the poor benefited? One might observe that the poor who were ready to be benefited got a great deal out of the program both in political opportunity and in services that were not previously available.

(With all of these problems, the community action programs never were able to become the coordinating agencies that the Bureau of the Budget had hoped they might. Far from being in a position of coordination, many of them had to battle against the very agencies they were supposed to coordinate. As a result, the need for coordination not only went untended, but it was further complicated by the addition of the CAP agency.) A lesson of the community action program was the discouraging fact that the "enemy" included established local institutions that were supposed to be allies in the battle against poverty.*

Many of the activities and policies of OEO itself tended to restrict, if not discourage, citizen participation (for example, in the emphasis on national priorities and programs). Naturally, the extent to which program development originated in Washington rather than in the communities was the extent to which local participation was relatively less important. Congressional criticism of the program forced OEO to increase its own involvement in program decisions, and this involvement adversely affected local participation. The limited funding of the program in relation to the original intent and design also forced OEO to make decisions about local programs which greatly

---

*This phenomenon crops up in all areas of planning which affect autonomous agencies. The natural enemies of health planning, discussed in Chapter 10, are health professionals who run autonomous institutions.

limited the effective role of local citizens. The pressure on local groups to produce program proposals in the face of unfamiliar federal procedures was also discouraging to citizens. Constant changes in OEO regulations which defined who constituted the "poor" or who was to be counted among the "residents of the area involved" caused disruptive changes in the membership of local CAA boards. In some cases participation was limited by professional standards established for staff members, especially among senior professional positions. These standards sometimes restricted the opportunities for the poor and minorities. Also, OEO failed to produce enough technical assistance and financial support for participation, and what technical assistance was available in the early stages was cut drastically after 1967.

[An unfortunate aspect of the local programs was the tendency to bring blacks into conflict with each other for control of well-funded programs and high-paying jobs. The rivalry caused many citizens to avoid participation altogether. Saul Alinsky, mindful of the hard-won position of the local programs he had helped organize years before, once referred scornfully to the "vast network of sergeants drawing general's pay" in the poverty program. He also noted the speed with which consulting firms sprang up to assist indigenous groups prepare OEO applications.]

Another unfortunate aspect of the program was that community initiative seldom translated into priorities, and many communities set no priorities at all. Gregory Farrell, who had directed a community action agency, observed that the task of priority-setting was made impossible by OEO's demands on the CAPs to press simultaneously for effective programs and for organization for advocacy activities. Since federal funds for community organization were inadequate, local CAP staff members often found themselves playing dual and incompatible roles. They had to play both roles because OEO insisted upon stressing community organization to achieve maximum feasible participation of affected residents. The dilemma caused near-paralysis in many CAP programs. Farrell's agency avoided the dilemma by opting for a strong program thrust.[20]

Community participation also failed to achieve its full potential because of the "promise-delivery gap." Robert A. Aleshire observes that "Planning is basically expansionist in nature since it implies that problems once identified can be solved and solutions once developed can be implemented. If resources for implementation are not available, the frustration of all those involved rises . . . creating a major risk of social unrest."[21]

By 1967 the Johnson administration had been thrown off balance by the twin blows of a war that had got out of hand and by urban riots that seemed to threaten the peace in cities. A presidential commission* traced the cause of the riots to the racist policies and discrimination which pervaded American life. The commission recommended programs in jobs, education, and housing to close the gap of "relative deprivation." From the standpoint of the president, those were precisely the goals of the War on Poverty which (he now believed) were being subverted to radical objectives. He had been told that extremists on the CAP staffs were undercutting his Democratic supporters in city halls and were using the CAPs to build political bases which would serve as vehicles of revolution. Members of Congress, particularly those who had never supported the program, were spreading similar tales from their home districts.

The CAPs that came under heaviest attack during this period were generally the more aggressive CAPs which had no ties to local government. Many of the CAPs in city halls were disappointing from the standpoint of providing services which were valued by the local poor. Others, hampered by inexperience and the limited talent of their staffs, made undistinguished records and were generally ignored by the leadership of the larger community.

In Chicago, Mayor Daley held his ground with the local CAP agency by insisting upon making the decisions about the content of the program and the allocations to be made from it. At the same time he saw to it that the poor were employed by it. Daley's CAP did the coordinating job, and the role of the poor in policy-making was kept to a minimum.²² Reformers who were looking for institutional change saw Daley's example as subversive.

The principal source of opposition to the community action programs, as we have noted, came from the big city mayors. John F. Shelley, Democratic mayor of San Francisco, accused OEO of undermining the integrity of local government by sponsoring "militant politically active groups." In June, 1965, Mayor Shelley and Mayor Samuel Yorty of Los Angeles (also a Democrat) sponsored a resolution at the U.S. Conference of Mayors which attacked Shriver for "fostering class struggle." The policy of insisting upon maximum participation of the poor failed, they said, "to recognize the legal and moral responsibilities of local officials who are accountable to the

*National Advisory Commission on Civil Disorders, commonly known as the Kerner Commission after its chairman, Governor Otto Kerner of Illinois. The commission's report was published by Bantam Books in 1968. For a further discussion see Chapter 7.

taxpayers for . . . local funds."[23] Although the resolution was shelved, the message got through. (It is worth noting that Mayor Shelley later gave way to pressures from blacks who demanded a majority on San Francisco's Economic Opportunity Council as the price for their support of a $4 million OEO grant to the city.)

The pressure on OEO was intensified by a resolution adopted by the Executive Committee of the U.S. Conference of Mayors which urged OEO recognition of city hall–endorsed local agencies as the "proper" channels for community action projects. In a meeting with Vice-President Humphrey (who was the White House liaison to the cities), the mayors reiterated their objection to CAPs which were independent of city hall. The pressures from the mayors typified a growing resentment of the CAPs among established local leaders. The president's reaction took the form of gradual retreat, silence, and a reluctance to press Congress for the passage of new antipoverty legislation. The president's attitude prompted officials of the Bureau of the Budget in 1966 to issue "instructions" to CAP officials to interpret "maximum feasible participation" as using the poor primarily to work in local programs rather than in planning them. Shriver at first turned the "instructions" aside, insisting that there would be "no retreat from . . . earlier policies and no slackening in [the] efforts to press for vigorous and creative compliance. . . ."[24] Before long, however, Shriver backed off in the light of political realities.

\From 1966 on, Congress limited funds for the antipoverty program while simultaneously restraining the freedom of action of its administration. In 1966, Congress allocated only about 20 percent of the OEO appropriation ($332 million of $1.563 billion) for unspecified CAP activities; most community action funds were earmarked for Head Start and for several new programs (initiated by Congress) for drug rehabilitation, emergency family loans, and special employment for the hard-core poor.)

By 1967, the main emphasis of the CAP agencies was on services funded by OEO rather than on community action. However, in the few communities where the poor gained a majority on the governing board of the CAPs, the emphasis was on social and political action.[25] In most communities, resident participation was achieved in traditional ways: by membership on CAA governing boards; by employment of residents in staff positions, especially at the subprofessional level; by neighborhood boards and area councils; by program advisory committees, parent groups for Head Start, and school programs; by independent citizen organizations; by neighborhood meetings; and by newsletters.

In 1968, the House repeatedly tried to cut the OEO budget by $3–4 million from $2.1 billion, and the president repeatedly limited the amount of funds allocated to OEO because of the pressing demands of the Vietnam War. Meantime, some congressional Democrats representing urban constituencies felt themselves increasingly threatened by the political ambitions of some of the CAP executives. Some of these congressmen attacked the CAP agencies, claiming they were creating "explosive situations" in their districts, and used the riots as examples of what could happen. The real threat, however, was an emerging new leadership in black communities that was gaining practical political experience at federal expense. From the standpoint of officeholders, the antipoverty program was training political rivals.

In March of 1967, President Johnson requested several amendments to the act, four of which placed limits on the community action program. One was directed at requiring the local CAPs to improve their planning, auditing, and personnel systems. A second was aimed at giving local public officials and other interested groups a greater voice in the policies of the CAPs. A third was aimed at strengthening the role of the states, especially in rural aspects of the antipoverty program. A fourth was an attempt to encourage more participation by private enterprise. In other proposed changes, the administration would have barred partisan political activities of CAP staffs, ruled out the use of federal funds for illegal picketing or demonstrations, screened out "troublemakers" from the Job Corps, and required annual audits.

Congressional conservatives were also on the attack. Many of them wanted the poverty program ended, except for Head Start and other "popular" programs. The riots fueled the opposition: several of the worst, including Detroit and Newark, occurred in the summer of 1967. But poverty workers, if they had a role at all, helped to minimize community involvement and to negotiate changes in local policies—especially police policies—designed to alleviate further violence. Poverty workers understood the frustrations that were behind the outbursts and, as in Newark, had participated in nonviolent demonstrations against the police prior to the riot.[20]

As opposition in Congress grew and the Johnson administration was reconsidering its political and practical values, the local CAPs were building constituencies that had already begun to counteract the opposition. The uneasiness in city halls during the period of ghetto rioting (and the uncertainty of its occurrence) caused the mayors to seek communication with ghetto spokesmen. The old "token" leaders could not be trusted to have influence with the riot-prone youths. City hall could not deal directly with the rioters, but it could deal with the poverty workers who could talk with the youngsters. Thus, many of the mayors who had at first expressed hostility to CAP leaders learned to value them.

With all the concern in Congress over the community action program, the only significant change in the 1967 legislation was the Green Amendment which provided local governments with the option of bringing the community action programs under the control of city hall or county government. (Only a few did—48 by 1968.) Moreover, the program was accorded a two-year extension, and its appropriation was substantially increased.

After 1967, some northern Democrats whose power base was in the cities and some southern Democrats who were determined to hold the line against any black incursions into politics in their districts joined forces to curb the threat they saw in the CAPs. A few Republicans took a stand against this *ad hoc* coalition of northern and southern Democrats, criticizing the lack of clear guidelines on participation that could be applied in every community action program in the country. Shriver responded that the great variety of local situations required "flexibility" in federal standards and opposed any specific statutory requirement of representation.

Thanks to support in both parties, the community action program survived to make a substantial contribution to the achievement of political inclusion of minority groups who had previously been excluded from public policy decision-making. David M. Austin concluded from his study of community action programs in twenty cities that community mobilization and conflict in target areas and experience on CAP boards had strengthened leadership resources among blacks. He observed that many of the political gains appeared to have continued, although a few basic issues in education, housing, employment, urban development, and police practices had not been resolved to the satisfaction of black citizens. Also, he observed, in the contest between newly empowered groups of citizens and entrenched political and civic leaders, resident participation had had a significant impact in one-third of the CAPs he had studied.[27]

The progress in political participation and development of leadership appeared substantial, but the impact upon established institutions was much less, at least in the short run. Austin's study revealed that resident participation had failed to institutionalize "a broadly decentralized process of citizens' participation in organizational decision making." The OEO community action program fostered structural and operational participation similar to that of the traditional nongovernmental social welfare service agencies—the very pattern the OEO community action program had set out to break. Thus, although by 1968 the program had survived the controversy, it had achieved stability at the expense of concessions that threatened the most innovative elements of the program. In the end, most of the CAP agencies were under the control of precisely those local institutions which had previously failed to break the poverty cycle.

But in Wofford's view, community action had laid the groundwork for a constructive role in conflict resolution (between the haves and the have-nots) after a long process during which communities worked out basic structural and political problems in creating new directions of social policy at the local level. In Wofford's view, the "new directions" took the form of breaking down patterns of racial exclusion and opening channels of opportunity to the poor as well as to minorities.

Although the OEO continued to stress resident participation, it never did achieve much success either at the federal or local level in coordinating antipoverty programs of other departments of the federal government or agencies in the local community.

THE MODEL CITIES PROGRAM

The coordination role was in 1966 turned over to the Model Cities Program, established that year by the Demonstration Cities and Metropolitan Development Act.* In addition to providing federal funds for a variety of projects and activities, the act required the participating cities to have "administrative machinery . . . for carrying out the program on a consolidated and coordinated basis."** The act also required "widespread citizen participation" but placed the local programs (of which there were 150) under the control of city government. The Model Cities Program in its attempt to de-emphasize participation of the poor was intended as a counter to OEO in the latter's role as the advocate of the poor. Indeed, the Model Cities Program was in part a response to pressures in Congress to provide local government with an antipoverty program which urban officials

---

*The Model Cities Program is also discussed in Chapter 11 from the standpoint of its impact on housing problems and policy.

**Section 103(a), Demonstration Cities and Metropolitan Development Act of 1966, P.L. 89–754.

could control. The resident commissions of the program were elected in neighborhoods affected by the program, but few participating cities gave over any substantial decision-making power to them. The main tasks were local coordination of federally sponsored social service programs, institutional change where it was deemed necessary, and evaluation of results.

Unlike the antipoverty program, Model Cities was to go through a one-year planning period after which a comprehensive plan and action program would be produced over a five-year period. The plan was to identify the basic problems of the neighborhood and the strategies, programs, and projects through which the community proposed to meet the problems. The planning goals were to form the basis of an evaluation.

Even though the Model Cities program called for widespread participation, residents were seldom involved in the designation of the target neighborhoods or in working out the organizational and programmatic framework of the funding applications. The excuse (reminiscent of the antipoverty program) was the time pressures placed on the local agencies (CDAs). The "process" of citizen participation often started after the program was designed, funded, and prepared for operation.

In both the Model Cities and antipoverty programs, federal deadlines frequently squeezed out effective participation. According to Aleshire, "Neighborhood boards and representatives were told, honestly, that unless a decision was made by a certain time and the program package submitted, the program (would) die."[28] With assurances that amendments could be made at a later time and a sense that the community had no presumptive right to the funds, the citizens usually acceded.

The influence of the resident commissions in most cases depended upon the degree to which city officials were sympathetic to the concept of community participation in the social planning process. Between citizen participation and coordination, the latter was more important in Model Cities because of the connection with the mayor. By the time the Model Cities Program had got underway in the participating cities, the OEO community action programs operating in the same cities had pretty much settled into a service function.

EVALUATING CITIZEN PARTICIPATION

Participation of the poor in the antipoverty programs has contributed to their competence and cooperation in institution development. As the CAPs assumed a program role, however, their capacity as advocates of the poor diminished. In some localities the staff jobs were preempted by charismatic community leaders who often turned agency goals toward the status quo, preserving their jobs at the cost of substantive response to community problems. The "poverty hustler" was the worst of a breed of CAP staffers who did great harm to the community action program and provided grist for the conservative opposition. Yet both the Model Cities and the CAPs employed more blacks and low-income persons than had any previous federal programs, especially in management positions and on decision-making bodies.

The discord and agitation which the community action program fostered was seen by the established local interests as subversive or worse. But from the standpoint of the poor, the social order had to be disturbed if oppression and exploitation were to be eliminated. Yet, in the end there was no subversion, and the changes that were brought about were almost wholly within established institutions.

The poor, who are relatively powerless, need the opportunity to decide what type of local organization best serves their needs. What is important is that such decisions be based upon the perspective of the neighborhood resident, not that of "distant bureaucracies," suggesting that community action agencies should serve as catalysts in behalf of federal agencies for assisting neighborhoods to find an effective method of organization. Yet, as Aleshire has observed, "The history of the last decade has been that citizen participation (in federally sponsored) programs has usually meant participation within the context of guidelines and values imposed by federal administrators and the Congress as a reflection of the mores of 'the country'."[29] Still, the active promotion of citizen participation through the antipoverty program has had a crucial symbolic meaning to excluded minorities. For a time in the mid-sixties, if an aspiring or incumbent officeholder was against such participation, he or she was seen as antiblack, anti-Chicano, or whatever. The participation policy has thus had the effect of bringing these groups closer to full citizenship, and this process has not been slowed. Furthermore, the impact of the participation policy has spread to local institutions of all kinds which have gradually, although sometimes reluctantly, opened up their staffs and governing boards to minorities.

The policy of participation of minorities as employees of institutions both public and private has been continued and expanded in the "affirmative action" policy of the federal government under the authority of the Civil Rights Act of 1964.

Unresolved Issues

The question of "appropriate" participation never was resolved within the antipoverty program or by the theorists, critics, and political "experts." The purists insist that citizen participation can mean no less than direct representation on the decision-making bodies that control the programs and funds of antipoverty agencies, that the community action agencies should be controlled by the citizens who are to be helped by the programs, and that local government should regard the CAPs as an opportunity to bring the alienated residue of society into the political mainstream.

The militant purists insist upon nothing less than total control both of program and community. The moderates are satisfied with citizen representation on antipoverty agencies which are controlled by city hall but want separate organizations which are organized by the poor and serve as advocates of the interests of the poor. The moderates also favor including the poor as employees of the antipoverty agencies on the grounds that the employment both relieves the economic problems of the poor and provides opportunities for training and experience.

The issue of who should participate has not been resolved. The Economic Opportunity Act of 1964 said that affected residents should be represented, but it left open the questions of whether the representatives of the poor had to be poor, and if most of the residents were black, whether the representatives had to be black.

The Nixon administration from the outset evidenced a lack of interest in citizen participation in the antipoverty program by not encouraging participation prior to funding, by denying funds for organizational activities, by transferring OEO programs to other agencies, by giving emphasis to research and planning as opposed to action, and by reducing funds in general. In the Model Cities Program, the Nixon administration tried to limit the powers of the neighborhood commissions. In May, 1969, a Model Cities memo banned exclusive initiation of projects by citizens groups and required all Model City agencies to assure HUD that "the city's ability to take responsibility for developing the plan" would not be impeded. Thus, the nation would have to await a more sympathetic administration before new initiatives were taken to reduce poverty. Experience indicates that action in this area must be initiated by the federal government where resources are sufficient to give a powerful nationwide thrust to solutions and where coherent programs can be developed that will benefit the entire nation.

A new approach must attempt to strengthen social service programs and play down the focus on the poor (an aspect of present antipoverty programs which stigmatizes beneficiaries). A new national program to eliminate poverty must include some form of guaranteed income. Lacking this element, a substantial portion of the poor will remain in poverty and form the basis of a permanent underclass. (See Chapter 9.)

Citizen participation in various forms is crucial to the attainment of these objectives in the context of American politics. For American political history shows that no group gets its share of social, economic, and political opportunities unless it acts from a position of social, economic, or political strength. If a goal of the nation is the abolition of economic poverty, poverty groups must be encouraged to organize for effective political action on their own behalf. The national government has a responsibility to provide the moral leadership and policies which further this end. A vigorous beginning was made in the community action program of the War on Poverty. Other programs and policies at the national and local levels which follow upon its precedents must be shaped into a coherent social policy which will end poverty and lay the basis for achieving a good life for every citizen.

NOTES

1. Edward C. Banfield argues that poverty can be attributed to "present-orientedness" and that this condition stems from three causes: psychological incapacity to take the future into account or to control one's impulses; circumstances that make any concern for the future impossible or unprofitable; or a preference for the life-style of poverty. See especially: *The Unheavenly City* (Boston: Little, Brown, 1970), pp. 216 ff.
2. Daniel P. Moynihan, *Maximum Feasible Misunderstanding* (New York: The Free Press, 1969), p. 83.
3. *Ibid.*, p. 84.
4. James L. Sundquist, ed., *On Fighting Poverty* (New York: Basic Books, 1969), p. 60.
5. *Ibid.*, p. 49.
6. *Ibid.*
7. U.S. Congress, House, Committee on Education and Labor, Subcommittee on the War on Poverty Program, *Hearings on Economic Opportunity Act of 1964,* 88th Congress, 2nd Session: Part I, March 17–20, April 7–14 (Washington, D.C.: U.S. Government Printing Office, 1964), p. 305.
   See also Lilian Rubin's authoritative discussion of the differences between apparent intentions of the planners and policy-makers and

the subsequent reality as to what was meant by the phrase, "maximum feasible participation" in "Maximum Feasible Participation: The Origins, Implications, and Present Status," *Poverty and Human Resources Abstracts,* Vol. 2 (November-December 1967), pp. 5–18. Also, see Rubin's article, "Maximum Feasible Participation: The Origins, Implications, and Present Status," *The Annals,* Vol. 385 (September 1969), pp. 14–29.

8. Moynihan, *Maximum Feasible Misunderstanding,* p. 93.
9. Sundquist, ed., *On Fighting Poverty,* p. 22.
10. Howard W. Hallman, "Federally Financed Citizen Participation," *Public Administration Review,* Vol. 32 (September 1972/Special Issue), p. 425.
11. Peter Marris, "The Strategies of Reform," a paper presented at a conference on community development held in San Juan, Puerto Rico, December 1964, 11 pp. mimeo.
12. Peter Marris and Martin Rein, *Dilemmas of Social Reform* (New York: Atherton Press, 1969), p. 210.
13. *Ibid.,* p. 211.
14. Sundquist, ed., *On Fighting Poverty,* p. 76.
15. Moynihan, *Maximum Feasible Misunderstanding,* p. 95.
16. Sundquist, ed., *On Fighting Poverty,* p. 80.
17. *Ibid.,* p. 81.
18. *Ibid.,* p. 83.
19. *Ibid.,* p. 100.
20. *Ibid.,* p. 156.
21. Robert A. Aleshire, "Power to the People: An Assessment of the Community Action and Model Cities Experience," *Public Administration Review,* Vol. 32 (September 1972/Special Issue), p. 433.
22. See J. David Greenstone and Paul E. Peterson, "Reformers, Machines, and the War on Poverty," in *City Politics and Public Policy,* ed. James Q. Wilson (New York: John Wiley & Sons, 1968), pp. 267–292.
23. Quoted in Sundquist, ed., *On Fighting Poverty,* p. 168.
24. Quoted in *Ibid.,* p. 98.
25. Hallman, "Federally Financed Citizen Participation," *Public Administration Review,* Vol. 32 (September 1972/Special Issue), p. 425.
26. For a summary of the role of community leaders in the riots and in aftermath "negotiations," see Ralph W. Conant, *The Prospects for Revolution* (New York: Harper's Magazine Press, 1971), p. 47.
27. David M. Austin, "Resident Participation: Political Mobilization or Organizational Co-optation?" *Public Administration Review,* Vol. 32 (September 1972/Special Issue), p. 420.
28. Aleshire, "Power to the People," *Public Administration Review,* Vol. 32 (September 1972/Special Issue), p. 432.
29. *Ibid.,* p. 428.

SUGGESTIONS FOR FURTHER READING

Advisory Commission on Intergovernmental Relations. *Intergovernmental Relations in the Poverty Program.* Washington, D.C.: U.S. Government Printing Office, 1966.

This report examines the background of the Economic Opportunity Act of 1964 and describes its development by the administration and Congress.

Alinsky, Saul D. *Reveille for Radicals*. New York: Random House, Vintage Books, 1969.
New edition of community organizer's strategies for local action against social disabilities.

Altshuler, Alan. *Community Control*. New York: Pegasus, 1970.
A penetrating analysis of the demand among black leaders for participation in and control of institutions which are in black communities.

Bachrach, Peter, and Morton S. Baratz. *Power and Poverty*. New York: Oxford University Press, 1970.
Analytical study of community power and its application to the War on Poverty in Baltimore.

Beer, Samuel H., and Richard E. Barringer, eds. *The State and the Poor*. Cambridge, Mass.: Winthrop Publishers, 1970.
Twelve essays on the role of the states in alleviating poverty with special emphasis on Massachusetts.

Blaustein, Arthur I., and Roger R. Woock, eds. *Man Against Poverty: World War III*. New York: Random House, Vintage Books, 1968.
Problems and prospects of American and international poverty conditions.

Bloomberg, Warner, Jr., and Henry J. Schmandt, eds. *Urban Poverty*. Beverly Hills, Calif.: Sage Publications, 1968.
Twelve essays on poverty and the governmental response.

Cahn, Edgar S., and Barry A. Passett. *Citizen Participation: Effecting Community Change*. New York: Praeger, 1971.
A casebook of studies on citizen participation in a wide variety of settings and sponsorship.

Caplovitz, David. *The Poor Pay More*. New York: Free Press, 1967.
Exploitative consumer practices against ghetto low-income residents.

Clark, Kenneth, and Jeannette Hopkins. *A Relevant War Against Poverty*. New York: Harper & Row, 1968.
Analysis of community action programs of the War on Poverty.

Donovan, John C. *The Politics of Poverty*. New York: Pegasus, 1967.
Evaluation of executive and legislative history leading to the passage of the 1964 Economic Opportunity Act.

Ferman, Louis A., Joyce L. Kornbluh, and Alan Haber, eds. *Poverty in America*, rev. ed. Ann Arbor: University of Michigan Press, 1968.
Extensive collection of important essays and articles defining poverty and suggesting programs for change.

Gladwin, Thomas. *Poverty U.S.A.* Boston: Little, Brown, 1967.
Very perceptive arguments analyzing the political and social deprivations of America's poor. Highly recommended.

Halloran, Daniel F. "Progress Against Poverty: The Governmental Approach," *Public Administration Review*, Vol. 28, No. 3 (May-June 1968), pp. 205–213.
Examination of the federal government's role in alleviating poverty.

Harrington, Michael. *The Other America: Poverty in the United States*. Baltimore: Penguin Books, 1964.
Classic study of poverty, deprivation, and hopelessness among low-income groups in America.

Hutcheson, John D., Jr., and Frank X. Steggert. *Organized Citizen Participation in Urban Areas*. Atlanta, Ga.: Emory University Center for Research in Social Change, ca. 1970.
A review of the process and impact of organized citizen participation in urban areas. Includes an excellent bibliography on the subject.

Irelan, Lola M., ed. *Low-Income Life Styles*. U.S. Department of Health, Education, and Welfare, Welfare Administration, Division of Research. Washington, D.C.: Government Printing Office, 1968.

Kershaw, Joseph A. *Government Against Poverty*. Chicago: Markham, 1970.
Analysis of 1964 EOA and OEO with conclusion that antipoverty programs have been stymied by inadequate federal support.

Kramer, Ralph M. *Participation of the Poor*. Englewood Cliffs, N.J.: Prentice-Hall, 1969.
Comparative case studies of CAP programs in four California communities.

Levitan, Sar A. *The Great Society's Poor Law*. Baltimore: John Hopkins Press, 1969.
Comprehensive examination of various programs of the War on Poverty.

Marris, Peter, and Martin Rein. *Dilemmas of Social Reform*, 2nd ed. Chicago: Aldine, 1973.
Origins and analysis of community action programs to combat poverty.

Miller, S. M., and Martin Rein. "Participation, Poverty, and Administration," *Public Administration Review*, Vol. 29, No. 1 (January-February 1969), pp. 15–25.
Review of "maximum feasible participation" provisions of the 1964 EOA.

Moynihan, Daniel P. *Maximum Feasible Misunderstanding*. New York: Free Press, 1969.
Scathing attack on the CAP programs of the War on Poverty.

————, ed. *On Understanding Poverty: Perspectives from the Social Sciences*. New York: Basic Books, 1968, 1969.
A collection of essays from a seminar on American domestic problems sponsored by the American Academy of Arts and Sciences.

————. "What Is Community Action?" *The Public Interest*, No. 5 (Fall 1966), pp. 3–8.

Public Administration Review. Special Issue: Curriculum Essays on Citizens, Politics, and Administration in Urban Neighborhoods. Vol. 32. Washington, D.C.: American Society for Public Administration, October 1972.

Silberman, Charles E. "Up From Apathy—The Woodlawn Experiment," *Commentary*, Vol. 5, No. 37 (May 1964), pp. 51–58.

Spiegel, Hans B. C., ed. *Citizen Participation in Urban Development.* Washington, D.C.: Center for Community Affairs, NTL Institute for Applied Behavioral Science, 1968.
Selected readings on issues in community development; see especially Section 3 on the antipoverty program and Section 4 on Alinsky.

Walinsky, Adam. Review of Moynihan's *Maximum Feasible Misunderstanding, The New York Times Book Review* (February 2, 1969), pp. 1–2, 28.

Waxman, Chaim I., ed. *Poverty: Power & Politics.* New York: Grosset and Dunlap, Universal Library, 1968.

10

Politics and Policies of Community Health Planning

INTRODUCTION

The American people enjoy better health than ever. Average life expectancy is seventy-one years, among the highest in the world. Infant mortality rates are on a downward trend. Most communicable diseases have been brought under control through extensive application of advanced epidemiological techniques, and some of these techniques are being applied to the big killers of the present day. Developments in medical science promise eventual prevention and cure of these and other lethal afflications. Hepatitis, measles, scarlet fever, strep throat, venereal disease, and tuberculosis are still troublesome but receding problems. Cancer may be curable within a decade. Injuries and deaths from accidents still occur in appalling volume, but the *rate* has fallen in many categories, especially in auto fatalities. Nutritional problems elude effective solutions, but technical knowledge is making strides in this field. Substantial advances are being made in birth-control technology as well as in the public education and acceptance of it.

As a consequence, Americans of all classes expect to live a fairly long and healthy life and are willing to pay the cost. Annual personal expenditures of all health services (public and private) reached $30 billion in the 1960s and will probably rise to over $100 billion in 1975,* a considerably faster rate than increases in population and personal income.

The trend in the expansion of the health industry seems likely to continue far beyond 1975. A comprehensive federal health insurance program extending benefits similar to Medicare to the entire population, almost certain of adoption within a few years, can be expected to provide a powerful new impetus to the expansion. So will a further steady rise in personal income, as well as the eventual adoption by the federal government of some form of guaranteed income to reduce poverty.

The rising expectations and expanding demand have created severe organizational and manpower problems in the health industry and explain the rising costs. This situation calls for radical changes in the methods of distributing health and medical services. The first steps include: the identification of critical gaps and wasteful duplications, the creation of links among related components of the health system, and solutions to manpower problems. The foundation for these changes can best be established in a comprehensive planning process which relates the components of the existing health system to each other and to the needs of individuals and committees.

The purpose of this chapter is to explore efforts that have been made over the past two or three decades at federal, state, and local levels to develop comprehensive health planning. Most recent efforts have their origins in the provisions of the Public Health Service Act of 1966 (P.L. 89–749, sections 314[a] and 314[b] which created the federal Partnership for Health Program. Sections 314(a) and (b) provided for the establishment of comprehensive health planning agencies at the state level (the "a" agencies) and at the local or regional level (the "b" agencies). These agencies were supported by federal matching funds.**

Before 1966, health planning took a variety of forms. The Hill-Burton Hospital Construction Act of 1946, whose primary purpose was to provide federal funds for hospital construction, required a state plan and encouraged the establishment of local or regional hospital planning councils. A large number of local United Fund organizations sponsored community health planning whose programs were usually broader in scope and substance than those of the hospital councils. A few city and county governments attempted to coordinate

---

*Expressed in absolute dollars adjusted for inflation.

**Throughout the chapter we use the terms "local CHPs," "local CHP agencies," and "'b' agencies" interchangeably. The terms "'a' agencies" and "state CHPs" or "state CHP agencies" are also used interchangeably.

public health and welfare facilities within their jurisdictions.[1] In a few other places, civic leaders have tried to encourage the communitywide coordination of health and medical facilities. This chapter describes some of these earlier efforts, as well as the more recent planning activities sponsored by the Partnership for Health Program.

THE NATURE AND FUNCTION OF COMPREHENSIVE HEALTH PLANNING

Comprehensive health planning in the broadest sense is the effort to accumulate and make rational use of private and public resources (talent, money, goals, and services) to meet all important health problems, including those of the poor. Ideal comprehensive health planning would leave no important gaps in services to individuals, in environmental health control, or in availability of services, and it would eliminate unnecessary or costly duplications.

Comprehensive health planning for acute, long-term, and chronic illness implies the availability of a continuum of care from preventive measures through various stages of institutional care to follow-up care at home (or in a nursing facility). Comprehensive planning for environmental health control implies a complete range of coordinated activities by the agencies responsible for controlling environmental threats to health. The geographical range of administrative and technical controls insures against gaps or duplications between or among jurisdictions.

Comprehensive health planning would identify optional market areas for major health services according to the capacity and availability of facilities as well as the quality of services required to meet needs. A difficult task? Only to the extent that health planners lack the training, experience, or will to do the job. For example, techniques of optimal market identification are taught in graduate schools of business, and there is no reason why health planners should not learn and apply these techniques.

Comprehensive health planning must proceed from a basis of detailed information and analysis of all significant health problems in the community of jurisdiction. Once the facts are established and placed in a perspective of community values, courses of action can be laid out to correct gaps and duplications and improve substandard services and facilities. Comprehensive health planning must periodically reevaluate goals and standards of services in the light of new or refined technical knowledge and changing values. Planners have a continuing responsibility to maintain fresh analyses of health problems, services, and facilities. Planners have a further responsibility to assist policy-makers in sorting out priorities, in establishing long-range goals, and in identifying the interim steps toward the goals. Planning also includes a political analysis to determine the character, strength, and staying power of groups in the community that support and oppose the planning objectives of the policy-makers. A political analysis keeps the planner alert to potential shifts, splits, and coalitions among community and professional groups on specific health issues.

The essential ingredients of comprehensive health planning include: (1) knowledgeable, determined leadership especially skilled at resolving conflicts among contending interests; (2) legal authority and enforceable sanctions; (3) a reliable source of money in proportion to established goals; (4) the capacity to combine public and private resources of the community with those of other levels of government; and (5) the capacity for a skilled analysis of community health problems (i.e., a highly trained research staff).

Leadership. Basic to successful community health planning are committed, intelligent leaders who are familiar with health problems in the community, who know how to work out solutions, and who can gain acceptance for and implement solutions. Generally, the leadership works best when it has a base in a health planning organization.

The Achilles heel of leadership is the problem of succession. Throughout history this has been the most difficult problem of political organization. No foolproof solution has ever been invented, although durable organizations have devised some form of institutionalized leadership in which the office exists independently of the incumbent and the successor is chosen by procedures which are carefully described in the laws of the organization. The difficulty is not so much in the legal structure and legal procedures of institutionalized leadership, as in the guarantee of superior leadership succeeding superior leadership. To capture and hold in legal and institutional forms the elusive qualities that elevate some persons to roles of leadership is to capture the force of the wind in a bottle. Nevertheless, great institutions stand the best chance of attracting outstanding leaders, and the elements of a great institution lie in the quality and flexibility of its structure and of those who people it, in the breadth and social value of its mission, and in the extent of its authority and its resources.

A Reliable Source of Funds. It is obvious that a community health planning program cannot move towards implementation without a reliable source of revenue that is in proportion to projected plans. Government agencies are usually in a stronger position in this regard than private voluntary ones. By the mid-1960s new federal grants were stiffening the support of reluctant state and local governments. Private and voluntary agencies which in the past had relied almost entirely on voluntary contributions have in recent years been forced to develop a capacity to attract public resources as a matter of survival.

Legal Authority and Enforceable Sanctions. Planning is a political process in which policy-makers choose among alternative goals and alternative courses of action. Legal authority or other enforceable sanctions are the *sine qua non* of effective implementation of the choices. In the absence of legal authority and sanctions of enforcement, the courses of action that policy-makers select may be blocked, neutralized, or cancelled at the whim of opposing forces.

Research Capacity. Sound comprehensive planning is founded on factual knowledge of community problems. Indeed, planning can survive outside the context of political decision-making wholly as a service in fact-gathering and education. In all community health planning efforts, an indispensable element of goal achievement is careful research into the problems for which solutions were sought. The findings of research are by no means always the persuasive element in implementing planning decisions. Often the choices of policy-makers are based primarily on political considerations, but a factual basis can add substance to a political decision.

THE ORIGINS OF COMMUNITY HEALTH PLANNING

The concept of comprehensive community health planning goes back to the 1920s in the work of the Committee on the Costs of Medical Care. This group, set up and financed in 1927 by eight leading foundations, issued twenty-eight reports in five years—the most thorough survey of medical economics up to that time. In 1932, the committee published a summary report which called for group practice for physicians and health insurance for patients. In 1935 President Roosevelt established the Interdepartmental Committee to Coordinate Health and Welfare Services, and three years later the committee sponsored a National Health Conference and issued a National Health Program. This program went to Congress as the Wagner Health Bill (Senate Bill 1620, 76th Congress). This bill, if it had passed, would have become the first national health act. It incorporated maternal and child health services, hospital construction, disability insurance, and state-operated medical care programs to be aided by federal grants. These early initiatives of the president and Congress came to nothing, and although they had little immediate influence either on national policy or on public opinion, they gave impetus to a precedent-setting program in the state of Maryland of medical care for the poor and indigent elderly.[2]

The 1946 Hill-Burton Act was the first federal health program which had a significant impact on local communities. Under the auspices of this program, many local communities got adequate hospital facilities for the first time. However, the only planning done under the program was by individual hospitals who had to meet minimum federal standards. In some communities where more than one hospital wanted Hill-Burton funds, institutions had to coordinate the planning of similar facilities. Almost without exception such conflicts were settled short of any communitywide health planning research.

In the quarter century following the passage of the Hill-Burton Act, efforts at planning and coordination among hospitals in communities were generally minimal or absent in spite of the requirement of a state plan. This was because antiplanning hospital and medical interests controlled the program from the federal level on down. Serious studies of hospital needs were undertaken only when local institutions were competing for funds, or at the state level only when the state allocation was insufficient to meet the demands within the state. The few studies that were done concentrated on hospital needs from the standpoint of hospital administrators and physicians, not from that of the community. Moreover, there was no substantial effort within the Hill-Burton program to require hospitals to provide for indigent patients, to give priority to public hospitals which served the poor and medically indigent, or to provide facilities and services for the chronically ill. The steady increase in federal categorized grant-in-aid health programs since Hill-Burton testify to a growing public demand for expanded health and medical services, especially for the indigent. However, health planning was even less a requirement of these programs before 1966 than it was in the Hill-Burton program.

The next major federal health programs after Hill-Burton were

Medicaid (for welfare patients) and Medicare (for the elderly of all classes) both of which were enacted in 1965. Neither program had any direct impact on health planning, although because of the magnitude of the demand these programs created for hospitals and other health facilities, the *indirect* pressures for planning were enormous. The Partnership for Health Program was adopted in 1966 in response to this need.

A Partnership for Health. The Partnership for Health Program provided for the establishment of regional comprehensive health planning agencies (the "b" agencies) throughout the nation. The "b" agencies were guided by the state health planning agencies also established under the program (the "a" agencies). The purpose of the "b" agencies was to develop effective relationships with all of the principal health and medical institutions, agencies, and programs in their areas (most CHPs cover a metropolitan area or several counties). The new planning agencies were to develop a comprehensive approach to health planning which was to take into consideration the full spectrum of local health services and facilities, including environmental health matters and services to the poor and indigent. A regional health plan was to set goals and priorities and the means of achieving them. The "b" agencies were required by law to have at least 51 percent consumer representation on their policy boards.

In the period from 1966 through 1973, 195 local CHPs were organized across the nation. The uneven success among the "b" agencies in the early years can be attributed largely to the strong antiplanning and anticollective tradition in the medical and health professions.[3] Indeed, the American Medical Association until recently has frowned upon group practice in which the one-to-one physician-patient relationship might be disturbed. Medical centers and clinics are very largely a development of the last twenty-five years, and "community medicine" was until the 1960s generally regarded in the profession as off-beat or radical. Health maintenance organizations (HMOs) are still regarded with suspicion and hostility by many physicians and hospital administrators. The predominant view of health planning among physicians and most health professionals (other than health planners) is that planning might lead to "socialized medicine" (in which the government maintains hospitals and health clinics and reimburses physicians for most medical services). Planning is also regarded by hospital administrators as a threat to the independence of their institutions.

Health planning on a comprehensive basis has also been held back by the limited and sometimes negative role that local and state health departments have played in attending to their responsibilities in their jurisdictions for environmental and epidemiological health problems. Typically, the resources and authority granted to them are inadequate in relation to the problems for which they are held responsible. Moreover, these agencies are usually controlled by organized medicine which insists that they play a minimal role in providing health services. The reasoning is that any intrusion of government into the domain of medicine constitutes a threat to private practice and must not be tolerated. As a consequence, very few state or local public health departments engage in broad research into local health problems, much less in health planning.

Developing Health Planning. Prior to the Partnership for Health legislation, a few spontaneous efforts in comprehensive health planning were developed at the community level in several American cities. These efforts usually were in response to some specific local problem or situation that seemed to require a special planning effort or a special study of local health conditions. In most cases, a leader or coalition emerged who recognized the need and was willing to do something about it.

The politics of health planning are generally so complex and time-consuming for those who become intimately involved that the leaders of health planning efforts, including the professional staff, sometime lose sight of the goals of health planning. In many of the recently established "b" agencies, for example, substantive goals have often been obscured in the struggle among contending interests. In other cases, the haste to qualify for federal funds has not infrequently resulted in the conjuring up of community "objectives" out of suppositions and guesswork, thus discrediting health planning before any genuine research and planning is started.

In spite of the coolness to planning among health professionals, much of the impetus for comprehensive health planning in the past decade or so has come largely from health professionals who have recognized a need for reorganizing health care systems. Such attempts at reorganization have usually proposed centralization of some services and facilities and decentralization of others. One task of health planners is to sort out the aspects of services that require centralized facilities from those which are beneficial in decentralized forms. The scale of organization that favors big hospitals, big research laboratories, and regional health departments is determined by the need to make optimum use of professional manpower, high cost equipment, as well as by the economics of the market area for which the services are organized. The trend toward decentralized services stems from the demand for ready accessibility to emergency care facilities, and for the need for easily available health maintenance and diagnostic services in community or neighborhood facilities.

The growing complexity and specialization in the health and medical professions in response to specific and pressing demands is another impetus for health planning. Resistance to planning has come mainly from individuals and institutions who are relatively self-sufficient in the scope of services they offer, who operate successful health institutions, or who derive professional satisfaction and economic gain as individual practitioners. The supporters of planning tend to be civic leaders and/or professional planners who have a communitywide or "systems" view of health services and facilities. Their motives are various: the professional planners have a stake in devising and implementing some scheme of planning, although it is seldom as inclusive as the definition offered earlier in the chapter. Doing a professionally creditable job is, of course, a principal motivation. Civic leaders who get involved in health planning usually have had some experience as members of a hospital board, as health or medical practitioners, as lawyers or insurance executives with clients in the health profession, or in government service. Health planning activities reward these civic leaders by bringing them into contact with a variety of health professionals and institutions, thus keeping them abreast of health problems in the community and informed of developments in government policies and programs in health. Health planning is also an exceptionally interesting political arena. The issues can be extremely sensitive; the stakes are high, and the conflict can be both subtle and fierce.

The shift from *laissez-faire* activities to a planned system inevitably results in gains to some interests and losses to others. In the beginning stages of planning, the political battles are mainly fought over *anticipated* gains and losses. Hospitals feel obligated to offer a certain range of services and to protect their staff physicians from loss of patients to colleagues attached to better-equipped hospitals. Should a planning authority with the power to do so decide to award, let us say, a cobalt therapy unit to hospital A and deny the equipment to hospital B, the latter is likely to resist the action because of an anticipated loss in advantage or prestige. At the stage when the establishment of such a planning agency is being considered, both hospitals are likely to oppose the move, anticipating that its decisions, although unknown in advance, might at some future time be harmful to their interests. The most skillful planners take care to include the relevant health interests throughout the planning process, and in doing so try to win over or neutralize antiplanning interests.

Local health planning in the period just prior to the advent of the federal Partnership for Health Programs was characterized by local initiative based upon community needs for orderly cooperation among health institutions and programs in the interest of economy and improved services. Even in communities where vigorous health planning efforts were initiated, success was mixed with frustration and failure. Sooner or later, most of them were captured or co-opted by the health and medical interests, whose idea of planning generally is an "equitable" division of available resources among competing agencies. Case studies of health planning in Rochester, New York and Lincoln, Nebraska illustrate these points. The problems faced by community leaders in initiating planning invariably carried over into later efforts under the Partnership for Health Program in the same localities.

In Rochester, hospital interests had submitted "need" estimates to a local hospital campaign fund which were double what local business and industrial interests thought could be raised. In Lincoln, a hospital council was set up by interests representing major business donors to hospital campaigns when it became apparent that the local funds might not be used as economically and effectively as the civic campaign leader believed they should. In both cases, planning came out of a desire by local givers to get the most out of their local resources.

Case Study: Hospital Mergers in Rochester, New York[1]

The Rochester health planning effort began in the early 1960s, under the experienced leadership of former Secretary of HEW Marion Folsom, a retired officer of the Eastman-Kodak Corporation which has its home offices in Rochester. His knowledge of health problems, his national and local stature, his intellectual agility, persistence, and political acumen, and his desire to make Rochester an example in community health planning enabled him to engineer precedent-setting decisions on health matters in that city. In the process, he organized a regional health planning council which in 1968 became a "b" agency under the Partnership for Health Program. The precedents set in Rochester also helped to shape new laws and policies in health planning at the state level.

In 1961, shortly after Folsom returned to Rochester at the close of the Eisenhower administration, he was appointed chairman of a hospital fund allocations committee which was to be responsible for dividing $14 million of privately raised local and federal funds among six local hospitals. Among the proposed uses of the funds was a claim by the hospital administrators that 500 new beds were needed in the area. In such a situation, the hospitals commonly have the last word in determining what new facilities are needed, and the task of an allocations committee is to act as a referee in dividing the campaign funds.

Folsom, however, arranged for an independent study of bed needs in the community and for the development of a communitywide hospital plan. The bed study and the hospital plan served as the basis for allocating the campaign funds among the six hospitals. To oversee the research and planning, Folsom initiated the Patient Care Planning Council (PCPC) which was representative of all community and health interests in Rochester.

The bed study revealed that Rochester in 1961 already had a comfortable leeway in general hospital bed capacity, provided that other suitable facilities could be made available for patients who required facilities other than those in a general hospital, e.g., long-term care facilities. The Hospital Review and Planning Division of the State Department of Health provided an estimate of the total needs of Rochester hospitals at $16.4 million and suggested that plant and equipment modernization should take priority over new general hospital beds. On the basis of the reports of the Patient Care Planning Council and those of the state, the Rochester Hospital Fund Campaign raised $15.4 million. The Hospital Fund used PCPC's recommendations as guidelines in the allocations, but before negotiations were completed, PCPC "conceded" 140 new beds, and hospital interests agreed to add 144 extended and intermediate care beds.

In the next four years, PCPC under Folsom's chairmanship brought about the merger of Rochester Municipal Hospital with the University Medical Center and Strong Memorial Hospital, and the affiliation between the county infirmary and the University of Rochester Medical Center to provide improved medical care for infirmary patients. PCPC also was responsible for a mental health study which resulted in the abandonment of plans to build a small independent psychiatric hospital and for the inclusion in the plans of a local general hospital of out-patient and in-patient psychiatric units.

Furthermore, PCPC established its own successor organization, the Health Council of Monroe County, which combined the community health planning work of the Rochester Council of Social Agencies and PCPC. The council was delegated authority from the Rochester Regional Hospital Council to review requests for construction and equipment as to "public need."

The hospital merger illustrates Folsom's skill in working out an agreement in which all parties stood to gain so that the normal psychological and bureaucratic resistance of the leaders and functionaries of the affected institutions was minimized. Folsom's plan was to turn over to the University of Rochester, the Rochester Municipal Hospital plant. The university would get twenty-one acres of land adjacent to its medical center for future expansion. The medical center and the municipal hospital were in adjoining buildings, and for several decades the medical center had provided contract medical services to the municipal hospital. The city wanted to get rid of the hospital because many of its patients could not pay full costs. In the case of indigents, the county had for many years refused to pay the full cost of their care. As a result, the municipal hospital had run an annual deficit of half a million dollars which the city wanted to recover. Other advantages in the arrangement were that the facilities could be more closely integrated with the medical center; the university would get a large teaching hospital plant at practically no investment. The university medical center staff had for years been using the hospital for research and teaching.

The big obstacle was the deficit, and so PCPC arranged for a reimbursement schedule that would approximate actual costs. The new rates also applied to indigents who used other hospitals in the community, so that all hospitals benefited from the arrangement. Thus, the merger resulted in a considerable saving to the city, a shift of indigent hospital costs to the county where by law they belonged, an improvement in medical services to municipal hospital patients, and an opportunity for the medical center to expand its plant on newly acquired land.

The proposed affiliation between the university medical center and the county infirmary was a more difficult problem because the principal beneficiaries were to be the infirmary patients rather than either of the two institutions. The county infirmary had always been under the supervision of the County Welfare Department and a medical director. The professional salaries were low; facilities were crowded; the equipment was old or outmoded, and there was a chronic shortage of supplies. The infirmary was previously a custodial facility with limited rehabilitation services. A few years earlier, the institution's accreditation had been withdrawn by the Joint Commission on the Accreditation of Hospitals. Many of the staff physicians were foreign trained and had difficulty qualifying for state medical licenses.

The gap between medical service standards in the medical center and in the infirmary was both the main obstacle in negotiations and the key argument for the proposed affiliation. Medical center officials feared that the infirmary would make excessive and uncompensated demands on its resources and drag down the university's standards of medical practice. From the standpoint of the university, the infirmary presented a problem of restaffing and retooling to bring standards to an acceptable level. From the standpoint of the county welfare director, the demands of the medical center exaggerated the conditions in the infirmary. In the proposed affiliation agreement, the county would give up control of patient care and admissions but would continue to support the facility. The agreement, promulgated after four years of study and discussions, was made possible by sound fact-finding and persistent, careful negotiations for which Folsom was largely responsible.

The Health Council of Monroe County, established in 1966 to replace PCPC, was created by Folsom to continue health planning in the region. The council combined the functions of PCPC, the health division of the Council of Social Agencies, and the mental health council. All the municipal health interest groups in the region were included on the board of directors. The planning review authority that the Health Council got from the Regional Hospital Council was the crucial first step in converting the group from one whose planning "authority" had depended on the leadership of one individual to one whose planning function rested upon a legal mandate.

Case Study: Lincoln, Nebraska[3]

In Lincoln, Nebraska in the early 1960s, the situation was different. A local hospital council was organized in 1962 by business leaders who arranged for its control by lay leaders rather than health professionals. Hospitals and physicians were represented, but in a minority.

In scores of American communities prior to 1966, health planning was vested in hospital councils set up to coordinate the allocation of monies from local campaigns and federal hospital construction funds. As noted earlier in the chapter, most of the hospital councils originally were organized in response to the Hill-Burton requirements of state planning for hospital development. However, most of the hospital councils were never more than trade associations. They collected data and did some limited research on hospital needs, but they hardly ever initiated broad community-oriented health studies. A few attempted to work out a division of labor on certain high-cost, low-demand services that typically run a loss.

The council's initial efforts were to coordinate planning among three local hospitals, Bryan, Lincoln General, and St. Elizabeth's. A consultant's study recommended a plan of hospital development on the basis of which the council hammered out a $12.6 million program of modernization and replacement affecting the three hospitals. At the time, Bryan Hospital had 258 beds in a new and remodeled plant and was aiming for 375 by 1970. Lincoln General had 163 beds in an old plant. St. Elizabeth's had 264 beds in an obsolete plant. Thus, Lincoln already had 685 beds at the time of the study. The council plan recommended a total of 750 beds in the city by 1970: 216 for Lincoln General, 282 for St. Elizabeth, and only 254 for Bryan. Lincoln General's 216 beds would be in a new plant connected with a county public clinic and long-term care facility; St. Elizabeth's would be moved to a new facility in a section of the city where no hospital was located; Bryan was to halt expansion plans. Lincoln General and St. Elizabeth's accepted the plan, but Bryan rejected it, claiming that the occupancy rate at its new hospital already exceeded the 82 percent level at which a hospital would normally plan expansion.

After intensive negotiations, Bryan got the council to approve an additional 50 acute-care beds by 1970 and received priority for Hill-Burton extended-care funds. Bryan was also approved for 50 long-term care beds to occupy an uncompleted floor in Bryan's new plant. The council plan included equipment specifications for the long-term care unit. Bryan rejected these recommendations and in doing so retained the option of converting the space to acute care. The council thought that Bryan could not change a Hill-Burton allocation in the plan, but it was wrong, for in 1972 the extended-care beds were converted to a more profitable acute-care facility.

To balance Bryan's 50 additional beds, the council persuaded St. Elizabeth's to accept 224 beds, 58 less than the plan recommended and 40 less than the hospital had in its existing plant. In return, St. Elizabeth's was promised 70 percent of the proceeds from the hospital campaign. Lincoln General came out with 220 beds (4 more than the plan) and a Hill-Burton priority over St. Elizabeth's.

Who Got What. Bryan got 25 percent of the campaign (which

raised $2 million); approval to complete two "shell" floors; 50 additional acute and 50 chronic beds; and, as noted above, remained in a position to convert the 50 chronic beds to acute ones. Lincoln General got a new building and 57 extra beds, approval of three additional floors for eventual chronic care use and approval to retain its old building for future chronic care use, council support of a $3.6 million bond issue, and priority for Hill-Burton funds. St. Elizabeth's got a new location, a new building, 70 percent of the campaign funds, and second priority for Hill-Burton funds, including priority over Bryan's next expansion. The consultant's report had revealed that some of St. Elizabeth's buildings were not fire resistant by state standards, a fact which weakened that institution's bargaining position. What saved the hospital was its long service in the community and a strong Catholic constituency (Lincoln is about 20 percent Catholic).

The headway the Lincoln Hospital and Health Council made in inducing cooperation among the community's three hospitals between 1962 and 1966 rested upon determined lay leadership which formed a majority of the council, a competent study with realistic recommendations, sizable resources from a council-sponsored local campaign, and availability of federal funds. However, none of these factors had the permanency which could provide the basis for sustained community health planning. The lay leadership on the original council eventually faded away. The council itself had no regulatory or review powers, and the leverage of locally raised funds was lost once they were dispersed, as was that of federal funds.

In 1966 the council received a grant under the Partnership for Health Program and expanded its jurisdiction to seventeen counties as the Southeast Nebraska Health Planning Council (SENHPC). While the council had maintained a substantial majority of lay members on its board, SENHPC by federal law needed only 51 percent "consumer" representation. The irony was that the 51 percent consumer rule in the Partnership for Health Programs, which was meant to guarantee a consumer majority on local health planning agencies, virtually negated in Lincoln an established consumer dominance. The new "b" agency, which was dominated by health interests, almost at once adopted a policy of "voluntary participation" in health planning meaning that health institutions and agencies, including hospitals, could cooperate if they wanted to but that there was to be no more of the "coercive tactics" of the former council. SENHPC went so far as to oppose the state-sponsored certificate-of-need legislation that would have given the agency some review authority over proposed new health facilities. During the transition from the council to SENHPC, there was a great deal of talk about "getting away from a conflict orientation" which "pitted consumer against provider." The council, it was claimed, pressured the providers unreasonably: "the public was used to beat the providers over the head."

As the original council leadership faded and SENHPC took over, the hospitals in Lincoln went their own ways. Lincoln General opened 80 new acute-care beds in August, 1972, after having "closed" 80 obsolete ones. The new beds were supposed to replace the old ones, but the latter were almost immediately renovated so that Lincoln General had 306 beds by October, 1972. This number far exceeded the 216 recommended by the original council plan. Also, Lincoln General added the radio-isotope equipment which in a 1967 agreement had been assigned to St. Elizabeth's for sharing among the three institutions. Bryan by 1972 had 346 beds which exceeded the earlier agreement by 92 beds. Also, Bryan discontinued all extended-care beds "due to inadequate reimbursement and difficulties in record keeping."

While all of this hospital expansion was going on, SENHPC was organizing, setting goals, and steering clear of controversial issues. Its main goal was "to raise the level of health of all citizens of the region to that desired by its citizens through cooperative voluntary planning efforts." Specific goals included: broadly based consumer and provider participation in determining community health goals (a goal to set goals) and in "developing procedures to encourage current and proposed health programs and services to be in accord with community health goals." The plan in fact failed to specify any community goals. The activities of the agency included data collection, health policy establishment, consultation with area providers, and evaluation of programs. The general principles of SENHPC included stipulations that hospitals should "relate to each other," share services and avoid duplications, and base their services on community need.

In actuality, SENHPC got very little effective goal-setting done and implemented almost none of the few programs it attempted to set up. There was no sign (in 1972) of a comprehensive health planning program, except in the rhetoric of various goal statements. SENHPC's stand against certificate-of-need legislation and its insistence upon the principle of volunteerism in participation seemed evidence that SENHPC was playing the role of the dummy corporation whose actual purpose was to go through the motions of planning, thus preventing any effective planning from taking place. Professional health interests in Lincoln had had their fill of the lay-dominated Hospital and Health Council, and they wanted no more. As a result, Lincoln by 1972 was over-bedded in acute-care units and short of facilities for long-term and indigent care.

EVALUATING THE EFFECTIVENESS OF COMMUNITY HEALTH PLANNING

In most communities, health and medical services are not organized in such a way that the ordinary consumer (of any class) knows what services are available. Nor is there any easy way for a person to enter the health care "system" and be sure he will be properly examined and diagnosed. The lay citizen depends almost entirely upon his personal physician for preliminary diagnosis of medical problems. The location and transfer of health and medical records is haphazard. There is no systematic or centralized record-keeping as there is in the military services. Facilities for periodic physical checkups are nonexistent or specialized. Health planners in effect are dealing with a nonsystem largely organized for the convenience and profit of health and medical professionals; whereas the goal of community health planning as implied in the federal Partnership for Health Program is the creation of a health system designed to serve the consumer. A consumer majority on local health planning agencies presumes to give the consumer a sufficient voice in the planning of facilities and services to counter the self-serving interests of professionals in the planning process, but the experience of the Partnership for Health Program has been to the contrary.

Consumer Participation. There are several problems with consumer participation in health planning. One is that consumers often find themselves at a disadvantage in discussions with the physicians and administrators about health and medical services. The consumer members of a CHP agency may have a "feel" for the needs of the community they represent but may not know enough about the specifics of those needs to translate them effectively to the health planners. They may also hesitate to counter the views of the professionals when these views differ from their own.

Another problem regarding consumer representation is that some consumers are closely allied with the health professionals. Hospital board members and insurance executives are examples. Some business people are philosophically sympathetic to the private entrepreneurial ethic of the medical profession and share the antipathy to public planning.

Also, consumers, especially those who represent poverty or minority segments of the community, are often unable to participate regularly in the policy and planning meetings of agency boards. Sporadic attendance limits their effectiveness and places them at a further disadvantage in board deliberations. In most cases, consumer participation in the CHP agencies has been consistently and significantly lower than professional participation.

Thus, although the health and medical profession at first feared domination of the CHPs by lay interests because of the 51 percent rule, in most cases the effect of the requirement has been the opposite. Ordinarily, the "b" agency boards have no more lay membership than the law calls for, and its ineffectiveness in representing consumer interests is low compared with that of the professional interests. In some places like Lincoln, and perhaps even Rochester, health planning may be worse off in the Partnership for Health Program where preemptions of policy positions in the new CHP agencies leave little incentive for lay leadership of the calibre and public orientation of a Folsom.

Service to the Poor. A second major issue in the Partnership for Health Programs is the matter of service to the poor and otherwise disadvantaged. Most of the CHPs give a high priority in planning to this problem, at least in rhetoric. This is partly because federal guidelines require it and partly because service to poverty groups is a major health problem in most communities. The main problem is that the poor cannot pay the cost of an adequate level of service whether they are on welfare or not, except for the elderly who qualify for Medicare. Even Medicare has the built-in disadvantages of an initial "deductible" fee, a twenty percent share in costs paid by the patient, and time limits of coverage. These drawbacks are a severe burden to the poverty stricken.

In spite of the sometimes ambitious-sounding objectives of CHPs to develop plans for delivering health and Medicare services to the poor, much time and energy is actually spent in organizational goals such as broad community participation in fund-raising to meet federal-matching requirements and in heading off hospital expansions. For example, in Birmingham, Alabama two years of intensive activity by the "b" agency's Committee on Health Services for the Poor failed to introduce any significant change in the health service delivery system to improve care for the poor. Three major obstacles accounted for this failure: power struggles over consumer participation in policy-making, interagency conflict, and uncertainties of federal funding.[6]

Another problem of comprehensive health planning is that there are no firm criteria for the division of services between the public and the private sector, though there does seem to be general agreement that basic health services should somehow be made available to all citizens regardless of their means. The question is: how should responsibility for services be allocated to avoid gaps or duplications while at the same time striking a reasonable balance between public obligation and private capability.

Health Planning in Councils of Government. Another issue in comprehensive health planning is its relationship to general regional planning and to the planning activities of local municipalities (see chapter 4). The problem of these relationships stems from the fact that separate federal departments are responsible for general regional planning (the Department of Housing and Urban Development) and the comprehensive health planning (the Department of Health, Education, and Welfare). In spite of efforts by the Office of Management and Budget to secure coordination at the federal level, in most states the CHPs are autonomous and not subject to review by the HUD-sponsored regional planning agencies or the councils of government. In many instances, the two agencies battle each other for planning authority on matters of mutual interest (as for example, regional sanitation facilities). In a few states, however, regional councils of governments are the official sponsors of comprehensive health planning. Texas and Maryland are examples.

In these states, conflicts in health planning shift from the issue of cooperation to the issue of who *controls* health planning. The boards of autonomous CHP agencies have the final say on health planning within their jurisdictions, but those which are under the jurisdiction of COGs must have their decisions approved by their COG boards which can override or modify them. Since the COG boards are by federal law dominated by local elected officials, the question arises as to the intent of the Partnership for Health Program to have health planning policy dominated by consumer interests.

Placing health planning within the COG structures has the following advantages: (1) superior representativeness of the public interest; (2) a broad mandate for comprehensive planning in social, economic, and environmental development; (3) a lesser commitment to existing patterns of health-care delivery; (4) greater opportunities for consumers and public officials to influence health matters; (5) closer relations with local governmental units, and (6) reliable financial backing to provide the local share of support.

Moreover, the few CHPs that are located in COGs are more likely to see health planning issues in the context of other social, economic, and environmental problems. Regional planning agencies such as the one in Baltimore generally facilitate such coordination and provide a data base that is broadly valuable to health planners. Where CHPs have a regulating function, their locus in a COG has the advantage of accountability to an official public agency which possesses a broad planning mandate.

A disadvantage of COG sponsorship of health planning is that the public officials who make up the COG boards are inclined to shy away from issues which involve political risk. As representatives of their localities, they do not readily support regional interests at the expense of local prerogatives. Even when local officials do not have a vested interest in establishing patterns of health care, they tend to favor approaches to decision-making that minimize political conflict. It has not been demonstrated that consumers have any more leverage on public policy in a COG structure than in an autonomous agency. In Maryland, consumer members of the Baltimore regional CHP found themselves in an advisory role; several who were interviewed indicated that their influence on health planning policy was minimal.

Planning Review. The review and regulatory functions of the CHPs remains one of the critical issues in local and regional health planning. The heart of the issue is whether and to what degree those agencies should have the authority to approve the plans of public and private health groups to develop health facilities and services with public resources. There is, of course, no contest about the right of private groups to use private resources to develop such services and facilities, except where they voluntarily submit to CHP's authority. The question of legal authority to review and approve plans utilizing public resources has been partially resolved in several states which have adopted certificate-of-need laws. Some of these states require that plans for new or expanded facilities and services be submitted to a CHP for review and comment or approval before the state certifies the need for the proposal facility or service. The certification-of-need procedure varies, but in most of the states where it exists, it tends to strengthen CHP's authority.

Is Community Health Planning Necessary?

The answer is straightforward but complex. The sheer pressure of population expansion and congregation in cities makes it increasingly difficult to provide adequately for health services on an economical and equitable basis. Their availability requires decisions about the magnitude and location of facilities, the assembly and organizations of professional and managerial talent, and priorities in relation to resources. All such decisions must be based upon a knowledge of health problems and upon the demands and preferences of the community. An accurate assessment of these factors is the essence of planning.

Also, the recent advances in medical and health services and technologies mentioned earlier in this chapter have created both a demand for these services and an expectation of further successes. The successes attract resources for additional research on problems. The rising expectations and accompanying demands put pressure on costs. As costs rise, a demand is created for a greater level of efficiency and economy. A function of planning is to match the demand for services to the scale of the facilities which are created to meet those demands. A related function of planning is to arrange for optimal efficiency in the distribution of services.

Moreover, the equalitarian ethic of our society impels us to regard health care as a basic right to which every citizen is entitled. These equalitarian attitudes (however ambivalent they appear to be at times) have led to the establishment of public programs which aim at establishing access to services regardless of capacity to pay the full costs. Of course, the more people who have access to services with limited facilities and personnel, the greater the pressure on costs. This situation requires planned phasing of new health insurance programs in conjunction with planned expansion of scarce professional manpower resources through expanded training programs. It also calls for new professional specialties such as physician assistants and a further gradation of nursing services.

In sum, the need for planning arises when ad hoc management fails in its capacity to deal effectively with all relevant components of the health care system. Recent moves to establish health planning is a response to the need to improve the distribution of health services in the total demand market. The demand market is increasingly difficult to serve by traditional patterns of health and medical services based upon the one-to-one physician-patient relationship and the entrepreneurial hospital. Also, cities are hard to get around in, suburbs are remote, and the proliferation of hospitals and other health institutions and agencies make it difficult for people to know where to go when they have a health or medical problem.

THE FUTURE OF COMMUNITY HEALTH PLANNING

The key to the survival and success of comprehensive community health planning is in the quality and staying power of the federal government's programs and policies in health planning. Should the present federal programs lose momentum, comprehensive health planning at the state and local levels could be set back for many years.

The continuing vitality of the programs depend upon the vigorous development of planning by all three partners: the federal government which sets the pace and standards of planning, state health planning which has the responsibility for overseeing the local CHPs, and the local CHPs which have the critical role of developing regional health planning. If the latter are weak or fall victim to contrary interests, there is no alternative local mechanism (in most places) capable of performing comprehensive planning functions. Should the federal government withdraw its support, many of the CHPs would wither or be taken over by the professional groups which blocked earlier efforts in local health planning.

Experience shows that even in communities where health planning has resulted in impressive studies, few concrete goals are ever implemented. Planning goals are seldom well defined. Indeed, efforts at establishing well-defined goals often make organizational and planning progress difficult. This is because there are many conflicting interests involved in the health industry, and most of them operate from well-situated bases in the community. A major function of comprehensive planning, therefore, is the management of conflict among competing groups.

Also, health issues tend to get a low priority in local communities except during periods of crisis. This is partly because civic leaders believe that health problems are being met by existing services and partly because they want to avoid the costs involved in solving the problems. Moreover, a great majority of Americans are poorly informed about health matters, and as a result they appear apathetic. Civic leaders who are not actually involved in health agencies are ordinarily hard-put to discuss knowledgeably any local health problems. Civic leaders who *are* involved in health agencies may not take seriously the fact that large segments of the population do not have ready access to health services. The ignorance and apathy of citizens and civic leaders about local health conditions has usually left the responsibility for planning and action to the professionals, many of whom are more concerned with protecting their own jurisdictions than in cooperating with fellow agencies to improve the health system.

The most active foes of comprehensive health planning are the hospitals and physicians. They, along with the health insurance interests, are also among the most active participants in the CHPs. This is the main reason why the Partnership for Health Program requires that consumers be a majority on the policy boards of the CHPs.

The rare cases of the professional and civic leaders who have been effective in health planning were able to do so through imaginative leadership, skillful maneuvering among contending groups, tough decision-making (with leverage), organizational talent, personal prestige, aid from government, and improvisation in peculiar local situations. But comprehensive health planning on a scale calculated to meet the needs of *all* citizens also requires the financial and legal security of a governmental base. The CHP agencies enjoy this crucial advantage.

Comprehensive health planning is most likely to attain its proper goals where the focus of planning is a single institution or in a set of similar ones (e.g., hospitals). Hospital administrators find planning among hospitals easier to manage than planning between hospitals and other health organizations. This is because similar institutions (and professionals) share similar problems as well as common aspirations. In fact, there is much to be said for hospitals assuming the lead role in the coordination of health and medical services in the community. Yet, many health educators, planners, and hospital administrators point out that hospitals are unwilling to take on this broader and more challenging responsibility.

The main point against hospitals in this role is they may be too deeply committed to the treatment of acute illness to be capable of shifting to an emphasis on preventive medicine and ambulatory care—the concept of health maintenance. Specialists in health maintenance believe that a whole new set of institutions may be required to give the maintenance concept an important place in the health care systems of the future. They may be right; transforming hospitals into comprehensive health maintenance organizations would indeed require a radical reorientation from traditional concerns to a broad concern for all health conditions in the community.

Some hospitals have taken a self-interested initiative in creating community medical centers in which acute and emergency services are combined with health maintenance services. Although community medical centers are well-established in some localities, very few offer a complete range of health and medical services. Reorganizing more hospitals into medical centers and expanding the range of hospital functions would preclude the need to organize new kinds of institutions.

Comprehensive health planning should concentrate on the development of a coherent health care system at the community level, whether or not the system involves the specific reorganization of existing institutions. Planning that does not lead to the institutionalization of functions, responsibilities, and relationships is endless ad hocism which serves only the short range interests of established, disconnected components of the health industry. In such circumstances, the public—all segments of it—pays a high cost for badly organized, seriously deficient services. Medicare revealed how unprepared the health industry was to absorb a bonanza of federal dollars into its overworked and overused services.

The puny scale of federal aid in the early years of the Partnership for Health Program guaranteed its puny offspring. With few exceptions, funds for staffing have been so skimpy that CHPs were hard-put to perform the demanding role spelled out for them in the Partnership for Health Program. Lacking an adequate and continuing source of funds from *outside* a community or region, the CHPs have had to do their money-grubbing in the community where support is limited largely to the natural enemies of health planning. Some CHPs have been able to raise funds from private sources other than those in the health industry but hardly ever on a sufficient scale or sustained basis to give them the independence and clout they need to do an effective job of health planning. Money buys research, but it takes *independent* money to buy objective research.

The federal government cannot be serious about establishing effective comprehensive health planning if funds are too meager to support serious health planning. They have been so far. The reason heard from federal officials seemed valid enough: that the initial funds were for start-up organizing. That was acceptable, provided that follow-up funds were at a sufficient scale to develop the start-ups into effective planning agencies. But so far they have not. Indeed, the Partnership for Health Program has been threatened with a phase-out or a modification of purposes which seems to reveal a turnabout in federal policy, a lack of confidence in the value or feasibility of local planning, and perhaps a philosophical affinity to the health and medical interests that oppose planning.

Professor William Curran of the Harvard School of Public Health has asked whether the CHPs are ready to take on the task of community decision-making, whether they are prepared to be technically trained and equipped to conduct equitable reviews and hearings and to make decisions in individual cases on firm legal foundations. Most of them are not but should be, otherwise they will not be worth the slim funds on which they were started.

At the present stage in the development of comprehensive health planning, the CHPs are still experimental. The basic techniques of health planning are not yet well established. For example, no one knows for sure what an optimal health market area is or how to go about delineating one. This is the case partly because health services are so diverse. Thus, communities that take the lead in planning have had to begin by experimenting with organizational devices that in some cases attempt to cover whole urban areas, while others have begun on a more modest geographical basis.

Judging from the uncertain development of the federal Partnership for Health Program, the future of comprehensive health planning seems precarious. The CHPs seem to have been valued in recent years primarily as local sounding-boards for federal health program and planning policies. Thus, for the time being, the CHPs are not likely to be encouraged in aggressive or authoritative planning and are certainly not likely to be encouraged to design new health systems.

NOTES

1. San Mateo, California is a prime example. See "The Political Administrator—San Mateo," a case study in Ralph W. Conant, *The Politics of Community Health* (Washington, D.C.: Public Affairs Press, 1968).
2. See "Three Decades of Experience—Maryland," a case study in Conant, *The Politics of Community Health.*
3. This statement, a main theme of the chapter, is documented in a series of case studies of "b" agencies which are included in a manuscript under preparation on the politics of comprehensive health planning by Ralph W. Conant and Jonathan West at the Institute for Urban Studies, University of Houston, Houston, Texas.
4. *Ibid.,* "A Recipe for Civic Leadership—Rochester, New York."
5. *Ibid.,* "Who Got What in Lincoln."
6. The case material cited in this chapter, including updated portions of the Lincoln and Rochester studies, is drawn from a manuscript under

preparation on the politics of comprehensive health planning by Ralph W. Conant and Jonathan West at the Institute for Urban Studies, University of Houston, Houston, Texas.

SUGGESTIONS FOR FURTHER READING

Alford, Robert R. "The Political Economy of Health Care: Dynamics Without Change," *Politics and Society* (Winter 1972), pp. 127–164. Argues that the crisis of health care has arisen due to the conflicts between the professional monopolists—seeking to protect their control over research, teaching, and care—and the corporate rationalizers—seeking to extend their control over the organization of services.

Altshuler, Alan A. *The City Planning Process.* Ithaca: Cornell University Press, 1965.
A general criticism of certain aspects of city planning theory based on four planning cases in Minneapolis and St. Paul and other sources. Includes a chapter on hospital site selection controversy.

Anderson, D. M., and M. Kerr. "Citizen Influence in Health Service Programs," *American Journal of Public Health*, 61:1518–1523, 1971.
A study of citizen participation in community health groups focusing on group interaction, group members' perceptions on division of labor, and the group's formal documents.

Ardell, Donald B. "CHP, Regional Councils and the Public Interest: A Case for New Leadership," *Inquiry*, Vol. 8, No. 4, pp. 27–35.
Advocates greater use of multifunctional regional councils as the organizational base for areawide health planning activities.

Ardell, Donald B. "Public Regional Councils and Comprehensive Health Planning: A Partnership?" *Journal of the American Institute of Planners* (November 1972), pp. 393–404.
Makes a case for merging health planning with comprehensive metropolitan planning under the leadership of public regional councils.

Banfield, Edward C. *Political Influence.* Glencoe, Ill.: Free Press, 1961.
Case studies illustrating the numerous ways in which political influence can be exerted. One chapter focuses on a hospital planning decision.

Blum, Henrick L., et al. *Notes on Comprehensive Planning for Health.* San Francisco: American Public Health Association, 1968.
Chapters 5, 14, 15, and 16 deal either directly or indirectly with the political ingredients of health planning.

Breslow, Lester. "Political Jurisdictions, Voluntarism, and Health Planning," *American Journal of Public Health* Vol. 58, No. 7 (July 1968), pp. 1147–1153.

Discusses the roles governmental and voluntary agencies should take in health planning.

Brieland, D. "Community Advisory Boards and Maximum Feasible Participation," *American Journal of Public Health.* 61:292–296, 1971.
Reviews the uses for community advisory boards and guidelines for setting them up.

Burke, E. M. "City in Participation: Strategies," *Journal of the American Institute of Planners,* 34:287–294 (September 1968).
Analyzes strategies available to planners to deal with conflicts which arise between participatory democracy and professional expertise.

Burns, Eveline M. *Health Services for Tomorrow: Trends and Issues.* New York: Dunellen, 1973.
A selection from the writings of an eminent critic of health services tracing the development of health systems over several decades.

Cater, Douglas and Philip Lee, eds. *Politics of Health.* New York: Medcoin Press, 1972.
An edited book growing out of a series of lectures and seminars on the politics of health conducted at the University of California in San Francisco. It covers national health politics, community health politics, and international health activities.

Cohen, Harris S. "Regulating Health Care Facilities: The Certificate-of-Need Process Reexamined," *Inquiry,* Vol. 10 (September 1973), pp. 3–9.
Discusses the political aspects underlying the certificate-of-need process.

Conant, Ralph W. *The Politics of Community Health.* Washington, D.C.: Public Affairs Press, 1968.
Five case studies of successful health planning prior to the passage of the Partnership for Health Act.

Curran, William J. *National Survey and Analysis of Certification-of-Need Laws: Health Planning and Regulation in State Legislatures.* American Hospital Association, 1972.
Reviews the health care facilities certification-of-need laws now on the books in twenty states.

Elling, R. H. "The Shifting Power Structure in Health." *Milbank Memorial Fund Quarterly,* Vol. 46; Suppl.: 119–143, Part 2 (January 1968).
Considers social power in general; power changes internal to the health establishment; and the changing role of government, lay community leaders, and the consumer public in health.

Hochbaum, G. M. "Consumer Participation in Health Planning: Toward Conceptual Clarification," *American Journal of Public Health,* 59:1698–1705, 1969.
Considers the problems and potential of consumer participation with examples of the conflicts apt to arise between consumers and health professionals.

Hyman, Herbert H., ed. *The Politics of Health Care.* New York: Praeger, 1973.
Nine case studies of innovative planning in New York City.

Jonas, Steven. "A Theoretical Approach to the Question of 'Community Control' of Health Services Facilities," *American Journal of Public Health*, 61:916–921, 1971.
Considers the implications of the community control movement on the provision of health care and on the role of the professional.

Kaufman, H. "The Political Ingredient of Public Health Services: A Neglected Area of Research," *Milbank Memorial Fund Quarterly*, 44:13–34, No. 4, Part 2 (October 1966).
An extensive review of political science and public health literature through 1965 identifying the political dimensions of public health.

Morris, Robert and Robert H. Binstock. *Feasible Planning for Social Change.* New York: Columbia University Press, 1966.
Discusses ways the planner can assess the feasibility of his goals and the strategies for influencing or overcoming the resistance of target organizations.

Mott, B. J. F. *Anatomy of a Coordinating Council.* Pittsburgh: University of Pittsburgh Press, 1968.
Reviews the evolution of an effective state-level council stressing the reasons for its successes and failures.

Reinke, William A., ed. *Health Planning: Qualitative Aspects and Quantitative Techniques*, Baltimore, Md.: Johns Hopkins University School of Hygiene and Public Health, 1972.
An edited volume which covers the planning process; information gathering for a health planning data base; methods for analyzing and synthesizing information; and the special features of mental health, environmental health, and population planning. Chapter 6 deals with the politics of health planning.

Roseman, Cyril. "Problems and Prospects for Comprehensive Health Planning," *American Journal of Public Health* (January 1972), pp. 16–19.
Identifies immediate past and future problems confronting those involved in comprehensive health planning and assesses prospects for survival of CHP and its likely role in innovation.

Strauss, Marvin D., and Idode Groot. "A Bookshelf on Community Planning for Health," *American Journal of Public Health*, Vol. 61, No. 4, pp. 656–679.
Introductory essay and bibliography on community health planning.

Swanson, Bert. "The Politics of Health," in *Handbook of Medical Sociology.* Englewood Cliffs, N.J.: Prentice Hall, 1972, pp. 435–455.
Develops a paradigm on the politics of health which identifies seven factors shaping the health system, including system output, levels of stress, system inputs, power structures, political ideologies, political focuses, and system change processes.

"The Politics of Health Planning: A Symposium." *American Journal of Public Health.* 59:795–813, 1969.

Four papers stressing the interaction of politics and planning, the political element in health planning, and the effective use of political influence in the planning process.

11

Housing Problems
and Policies

INTRODUCTION

America's urban problems are most visibly evident in the sprawling slums of central city ghettos. Here, one can observe the decay and neglect of many years—poverty, crime, filth, teen-age gangs, drug addiction, overcrowding, and other forms of social malaise. It seems incredible that our powerful, affluent, post-industrial society tolerates such miserable living conditions. In an age which has witnessed manned spaceflight to the moon, developed instant communications throughout the world, and produced highly sophisticated computer technology, the existence of ghetto slums is incompatible with America's image of its own many remarkable achievements. Perhaps the affluent white majority wishes to deny the existence of these slum areas, taking action only when impoverished minorities begin to move toward the suburbs. The run-down city slums and ghettos with their rubble, boarded-up windows, disassembled buildings, abandoned structures, garbage piles, and broken glass symbolize a nation at war with itself. A few years ago, when a group of big-city mayors visited the Brooklyn neighborhood of Bedford-Stuyvesant, one of them remarked that its appearance was worse than the bomb-devastated city of Dresden, Germany after World War II.

Various government programs have focused upon the housing

problems of the poor, but none of them have been very successful. Over the last forty years, such programs have destroyed more low-income housing than they have constructed in the central cities. On balance, as this chapter will show, government housing policies have been biased against the poor and in favor of the middle-class and business interests. Minority groups have not generally benefited from housing programs specifically designed to meet their needs. Curiously, public housing and other low-income subsidy efforts have been condemned as socialistic or as threats to community stability and property values, while federal urban renewal assistance for downtown commercial redevelopment and luxury high-rise apartment buildings, as well as FHA mortgage insurance for suburban housing

"These Weren't Damaged In The Riots — They Went To Pieces Years Before"

Reprinted with permission from *The Herblock Gallery* (Simon & Schuster, 1968).

and federal income tax deductions for mortgage interest and property taxes are accepted as rightful subsidies for the middle-class and business interests. Until government housing policies can overcome public attitudes which blame the poor for creating the slums they are forced to occupy and can adequately fund low-income housing programs which are enacted with avowedly humanitarian objectives, it seems unlikely that the most serious problems of the nation's slums and ghettos will be alleviated.

HOUSING CONDITIONS

Estimating, analyzing, and evaluating America's housing conditions are not simple tasks. Clearly, slums and ghettos exist, central cities contain vast numbers of run-down dwellings, and the poor and minority groups occupy the worst housing. However, accurate and reliable national statistical data indicating these trends has not been developed by government agencies. Neither the federal government, the states, nor localities have refined their research methods to compare over time changes and improvements in housing quality. Thus, the discussion below requires at least two preliminary cautions. First, the 1960 Census Bureau categories of *sound, deteriorating,* and *dilapidated* housing relate only to exterior physical structural conditions and interior plumbing facilities. These classifications, according to the National Commission on Urban Problems, amounted to only a crude measure of housing quality, or that of "a nearly weathertight box with pipes in it."[1] Omitted from the census definitions were such interior conditions as room size, ventilation, light, and the regularity of heat and hot water. Also, the relationship of housing to community services and environmental influences was not considered. The census definitions excluded such criteria as adequate sewage and sanitation services, street lights, road maintenance, fire and police service, decay of surrounding buildings, noise levels, and noxious or foul odors from industrial plants. Second, neither the two preceding censuses nor the succeeding 1970 census used the same standard-substandard definitions of the 1960 census. The 1970 housing census avoided solutions to the earlier problems of classification and comparison by shifting to data collection of household conditions such as the number of rooms, the year of construction, heating, air conditioning, washing machines, and other home appliances, rent and property taxes, available automobiles, etc. Thus, it is extremely difficult to compare housing conditions and housing quality over time. Only special studies provide some comparative insights, and these will be referred to in Table 11–1.

In considering the limitations of adequately defining satisfactory and unsatisfactory housing conditions, the 1960 census provided the following summary portrait of America's housing inventory.

TABLE 11–1   America's Housing Inventory 1960 Census

Classification of Housing Conditions	*Number of Units (in Millions)*	*Percent of Total*
Sound	47.3	81.1
Deteriorating	8.1	13.9
Dilapidated	2.9	5.0
Totals	58.3	100.0
Standard		
A) Sound, with all plumbing facilities	43.1	
B) Deteriorating, with all plumbing facilities	4.6	
Subtotal	47.7	81.8
Substandard		
A) Sound, with inadequate plumbing facilities	4.2	
B) Deteriorating, with inadequate plumbing facilities	3.5	
C) Dilapidated	2.9	
Subtotal	10.6	18.2

SOURCE: Frank Kristof, *Urban Housing Needs Through the 1980s: An Analysis and Projection.* Prepared for the Consideration of the National Commission on Urban Problems, *Research Report* No. 10 (Washington, D.C.: U.S. Government Printing Office, 1968), p. 89.

Based upon the housing inventory findings shown above, the National Commission on Urban Problems observed that the nation's minimum housing needs in 1968 required the removal or replacement of about eleven million housing units (or about three units out of every twenty), including the seven million structures without adequate plumbing facilities and the four million overcrowded standard units.[2] More particularly, the commission found especially serious housing problems in a special study of poverty areas in 101 metropolitan areas, problems indicating the concentration of deficient housing and the sense of outrage by poverty area residents. Although such poverty neighborhoods of central cities contained one-third of the housing units on less than one-quarter of the land, such areas had:

> Four out of five of all housing units occupied by nonwhites;
>
> Three out of four of the substandard units;
>
> Nine out of ten of the substandard units occupied by nonwhites;
>
> Over half of the overcrowded units;
>
> Five out of six of the overcrowded units occupied by nonwhites;
>
> Four out of ten of all housing structures built before 1940, or those which were almost a third of a century old or older; and
>
> Five out of six of all the structures built before 1940 which were lived in by nonwhites.[3]

In analyzing the 1967 ghetto riots, the National Commission on Civil Disorders found a close relationship between urban disorder and dissatisfaction with slum housing. In the riot cities, 47 percent of the housing occupied by nonwhites was substandard, 24 percent of the units were overcrowded, a high proportion of the residential structures were poorly maintained and seriously violated city housing codes, and blacks paid a higher proportion of their incomes for rents than did whites.[4] The commission observed that "[t]he result has been widespread discontent with housing conditions and costs. In nearly every disorder city surveyed, grievances related to housing were important factors in the structure of Negro discontent."[5]

AN OVERVIEW OF HOUSING POLICY OBJECTIVES

While government policy-makers have long been aware of the nation's slum problems, the various programs enacted have not really provided sufficient and adequate housing for the poor and entrapped minority groups. Low-income housing programs are limited by (1) a consistent public bias which favors detached, single-family, owner-occupied homes and opposes apartments and other renter-occupied multi-family housing; (2) a "social cost" approach to the slums which seeks to eliminate only the external effects of decayed housing; and (3) only very limited support for a social welfare approach which would dramatically improve housing opportunities for the poor by improving economic, social, and community conditions and by adequately funding existing governmental housing programs.

Nathan Glazer indicates that America's preference for single-family, detached housing with a bit of land around it is "perhaps the most distinctive constraint on American housing policies."[6] The cost of such housing is beyond the economic means of most of the poor unless government provides them with direct subsidies. Furthermore, as shown below, most of the newer single-family housing is located in the suburbs where the greatest opposition to low-income housing exists. The 1970 housing census showed that 69 percent (including the 3 percent of mobile homes and trailers) of the nation's forty-seven million dwelling units were single-family residences and that about 60 percent of such homes were owner-occupied. Another 3 percent were one-family attached, 13 percent were structures containing two to four units, and 15 percent were multi-family structures of more than five units. Table 11–2 shows that more than two-thirds of the single-family housing was located in the suburbs and that the greatest proportion (more than 60 percent) of the rented housing was in the central cities.

TABLE 11-2   Housing Type and Location, 1970 Census

		Occupancy		Location	
				Percent	
	Percent	*Percent*	*Percent*	*Central*	*Percent*
Housing Units in Structure	*of Total*	*Owner*	*Renter*	*Cities*	*Suburbs*
Single-Family, Detached	66	86	33	45	73
Mobile Homes or Trailers	3	4.4	1	1	3
Single-Family, Attached	3	3	3	6	2
Multi-Family, 2 to 4 units	13	5.4	26	21	10
Multi-Family, 5 or more units	15	1.2	37	28	12
Totals	100	100	100	100	100

SOURCE: U.S. Department of Commerce, Bureau of the Census, "1970 Census of Housing: Supplementary Report Detailed Housing Characteristics for the United States, Regions, Divisions, and States." Series HC (S1)-6. (Washington, D.C.: U.S. Government Printing Office, June 1972).

The problems connected with social cost and social welfare housing policy approaches are provided by Lawrence M. Friedman. Following the Civil War, millions of European immigrants came to American cities seeking economic opportunities and improved living conditions. However, many immigrants were crowded into ethnic ghettos where their housing was less than adequate. Reformers such as Jacob Riis decried the filth, disease, crime, and overcrowding of immigrant housing. They called for slum clearance, health and safety measures which would not only benefit the poor but the middle and upper classes as well. In other words, slum housing resulted in social costs such as public health hazards, contagious disease, epidemics, and fires. New York was the first state to use its general police power to regulate health, safety, and welfare in tenement housing. In the tenement house laws of 1867, 1879, and 1901, New York State provided for minimum standards of construction, maintenance, ventilation, light, and sanitation. Such laws were adopted by eleven other states by World War I, but all of them dealt only with external housing conditions. The "social cost" approach did not consider the community environment of slum housing; neither did such regulations include any direct government housing assistance for the poor unless the middle-class and business interests also benefited. Friedman observes the shortcomings of the social cost orientation in housing policy:

> . . . A man who emphasizes the price society pays for the results of slum housing is apt to look for measures which, for the fewest dollars, eliminate the evil as it touches him. . . . The law has emphasized fire prevention, sanitation, minimum standards of building and maintenance, and outright demolition of the slums. These are the ways of protecting society from contamination arising out of the slums. The pathology of this branch of the social-cost approach is its tendency to disregard the problems of the people who live in the slums.[7]

In contrast to the social cost considerations, the social welfare approach to housing policy considers the slum problem "as a problem of the suffering people who live there, whether or not the slums hurt society at large."[8] Consequently, government housing policies for the poor should raise their incomes by direct subsidies, construct low-income housing, improve neighborhood conditions and facilities, and provide residents with better economic and social opportunities. Aside from a few limited state and local housing efforts, most of the federally oriented low-income housing programs specifically designed for the urban poor followed earlier New Deal and urban renewal projects. The objectives of the antipoverty programs of 1964 were succeeded by housing efforts such as rent supplements, model cities, and the various components of the 1968 Housing Act. However, the poor were never an effective political force in lobbying for these programs, and the lofty objectives of these various social welfare approaches to housing were never adequately funded.

NEW DEAL RESPONSES: FHA AND PUBLIC HOUSING

The national economic collapse of the 1930s severely affected housing in American cities. Before the depression years, housing policy was traditionally a concern of private enterprise and state and local governments. With few exceptions, the financing of nearly all residential construction, repair, and maintenance was provided by private lenders who charged homeowners high interest rates, required large down payments, and demanded short loan repayment terms of usually seven to ten years. Cities and states had adopted building codes, zoning laws, and other health and safety measures under their general police and regulatory authority, but, by and large, they were not directly involved in either home construction or the financing of residential property. This localization and decentralization of housing policy encountered drastic problems during the 1930s. High unemployment rates threatened homeowners who could not maintain their mortgage payments. In 1932 about 273,000 homeowners lost their properties from mortgage defaults and foreclosures.[9] Housing construction came to a virtual stand-still, and banks could not extend mortgage credit to borrowers. Between 1928 and 1933, residential construction fell 95 percent, declining from an annual average of 900,000 units during the 1920s to an annual rate of only 90,000 units in 1934.[10]

New Deal housing relief measures included financial aid for banks, mortgage insurance for home lenders, temporary work relief for the unemployed, and government subsidies for public housing. Homeownership and social cost emphases were the foundations of these policies. The federal government wanted to restore previous levels of housing construction by putting people to work and by expanding the sources of mortgage credit. Two early measures included the creation of the Federal Home Loan Banks (1932) to provide home finance capital to savings and loan banks, and the establishment of the Home Owners' Loan Corporation (HOLC) in 1933 to refinance homeowners' mortgages facing foreclosure. By 1936, the HOLC had loaned about $3 billion to refinance the mortgages of over a million homeowners.[11]

The most significant New Deal housing policy innovation affecting financial credit for homeownership was established in the 1934 Housing Act which created the Federal Housing Administration. FHA programs were intended to expand mortgage credit by reducing the risks of mortgage lenders and to induce them to make credit available on more liberal terms. FHA guaranteed lenders that mortgage loans to borrowers would be repaid even if borrowers defaulted on such loans. Federal mortgage insurance to banks was backed by charging borrowers a premium against the risk of default.

FHA policies encouraged homeownership opportunities for young families and substantially contributed to suburban growth, development, and expansion after World War II. In effect, FHA mortgages enabled young middle-class families to leave the central cities and to buy homes in the suburbs. FHA mortgage insurance eased previously stringent home loan requirements by enabling banks to charge lower interest rates, to require lower down payments, and to provide for gradual amortization of mortgage principal—all of which resulted in lower monthly payments for borrowers. As long as families had some savings and could show a bank they were a good credit risk, the mortgage would be approved, conditioned only by where the new home was located. Since 1935, FHA mortgages have resulted in the construction of more than seven million new homes and apartments, or about one-fifth of all privately financed nonfarm units.[12] The vast number of FHA-insured mortgages were in the suburbs, contributing to the tremendous expansion and housing construction in metropolitan areas.

In contrast, the FHA and private lenders, with their fiscally conservative mortgage policies, refused to invest in older city neighborhoods, particularly in the slums and areas with high concentrations of blacks and other impoverished minority groups. FHA supported racially restrictive covenants, or refusals by white homeowners to sell to blacks and other minorities, until the U.S. Supreme Court prohibited such practices in 1948. Also, until the 1968 Housing Act, FHA policies discriminated against the poor and deteriorating city areas because FHA would not extend loans to "economically unsound" groups. Furthermore, FHA and private lenders had an unwritten understanding not to provide mortgages in slums, declining neighborhoods, and other city areas having unfavorable economic conditions. Mortgage lenders were not interested in reversing the tide of central city decay. In 1965, for example, only 11 percent of FHA-insured mortgages were held by the poor and the lower-middle class, while 83 percent of FHA mortgage purchasers were in the middle-income and upper-middle-income groups.[13] Section 102 of the 1968 Housing Act eliminated the "economically unsound" restrictions to low-income groups by authorizing FHA to give mortgage preferences to families forced to leave public housing whose incomes had risen above local maximums and to those groups eligible for public housing who were displaced from urban renewal areas.[14] Also, FHA was permitted to insure mortgages for repair, construction, or purchase of homes in older, declining urban areas "which could not meet all the normal eligibility requirements because of the nature of their areas,"[15] and particularly to support the housing needs of low-income and moderate-income families.

Public housing was another significant federal policy innovation of the New Deal era. The program developed from earlier federal work relief projects. In 1933 Secretary of the Interior Harold Ickes, designated by President Roosevelt as chief of the Public Works Administration, established a Housing Division to provide construction jobs by direct federal authority, to make loans, and to buy or build housing projects. Between 1933 and 1937, PWA demolished 10,000 substandard structures and constructed 21,639 units in forty-nine low-income housing projects.[16] However, these accomplishments were small in relation to national housing needs, and PWA, with its direct federal powers, encountered local opposition and legal challenges to acquiring and demolishing slums for public housing. More importantly, PWA efforts set the stage as the forerunner of the 1937 Housing Act.

The public housing program of 1937 recognized the homeownership, social cost, and social welfare approaches to housing policy. Government subsidized, owned, and managed housing was not originally designed to encourage or to support the abject, dependent poor but was primarily to aid the deserving poor, that is, underpaid workers or members of the submerged middle class who were "innocent victims of economic reverses, who needed a break to tide them over the lean years."[17] Housing assistance for the temporarily needy "depression poor" was considered necessary because they could not afford private housing and because private enterprise could not "build an adequate supply of decent, safe, and sanitary dwellings for their use."[18] The government provided subsidized housing as temporary assistance until such families could assume their own responsibilities. In this sense, the 1937 Housing Act had the same limited social welfare objectives as the AFDC program of the 1935 Social Security Act, as discussed in Chapter 8. Moreover, the general welfare was served by assisting local government "to alleviate present and recurring unemployment."[19] Social cost goals were promoted by clearing unsightly slums which had "unsafe and unsanitary housing conditions . . . that are injurious to the health, safety, and morals of the citizens of the Nation."[20]

In implementing these policy goals, the 1937 Housing Act established the U.S. Housing Authority (which later became the Public Housing Administration and then the Housing Assistance Administration in the Department of Housing and Urban Development) with the authority to provide loans and grants to local housing agencies for the development and construction of public housing. Unlike earlier PWA efforts, the federal government no longer had direct responsibility for determining low-income housing needs. Instead, a national-local partnership was created in which the federal government provided 90 percent of project development costs as conditional grants-in-aid, and localities determined participation in the program, decided how many units they required, and assumed ownership and management of public housing projects. Federal subsidies resulted in controlled rents for public housing residents since localities needed to pay only for current operating expenses which were supported by tenants' rents, while interest costs and amortization of principal were met by the federal annual contribution contracts.[21]

The 1937 law also required that slum clearance and public housing be pursued together. The principle of "equivalent elimination" meant that public housing projects would be located in areas where other substandard housing was demolished, condemned, or rehabilitated. Thus, public housing was not intended to compete with private enterprise, to disperse the poor from central city slums, to seek project sites where land was cheapest, or to encourage metropolitan planning for publicly subsidized housing. Instead, such projects would simply replace unsightly and decaying dwellings in slum neighborhoods. The result was to concentrate the poor by not encouraging them to resettle outside of the slums. Moreover, public housing did not substantially increase housing opportunities for the poor since the policy was to replace existing slums rather than to expand the total supply of low-income dwellings.

Public housing construction was not vigorously pursued by the federal government and the nation's cities. From 1939 to 1948, about 170,000 units were built. The 1949 Housing Act authorized construction of an additional 810,000 public housing units (or a total of about one million units) by 1955, but this goal was not reached until 1970 when 870,000 units were completed.[22] Among other problems, public housing encountered serious construction delays. To shorten the estimated three- to four-year time span required for planning, executing, and building public housing, HUD introduced the "turnkey" method in 1967, under which 30,000 new units were begun in 1969 by private developers who constructed public housing on their own land and, upon completion, turned the projects over to the local housing authorities.[23] Additionally, only 3,000 localities or 15 percent of all potentially eligible communities were participating in the program by the end of the 1960s.[24] Most public housing was concentrated in the largest cities although many smaller communities were involved in the program.

As public housing became increasingly identified with welfare dependency and minority groups, the original social welfare goals of the 1937 Housing Act were considerably modified. In effect, policymakers were unwilling to provide sufficient subsidized housing for the "undeserving poor." The depression of the 1930s was followed by the postwar prosperity of the 1950s, resulting in large-scale private housing development in the suburbs. Many of the formerly submerged white middle class were now able to afford their own housing due to rising incomes and favorable mortgage policies provided by FHA and the Veterans' Administration.

In contrast, the poor and increasingly large numbers of blacks, who had migrated to the nation's largest cities during the 1940s and 1950s, were victimized by inadequate housing conditions. Public housing was the only available alternative for these forgotten Americans. By the 1970s, about 60 percent of the approximately three million families in public housing were from minority groups, including 50 percent black families.[25] They suffered severe socioeconomic problems—broken families, unemployed parents, dependent children, and low incomes. In 1967, approximately 60 percent of nonwhite public housing tenants were poor, as compared with 35 percent of poor nonwhites in the total population.[26]

Even these figures do not adequately dramatize the high correlation between poverty and public housing. Minimum income requirements for rents excluded the hard-pressed poor. The approximately $2,800 average annual incomes of all public housing tenants in 1966 do not accurately reflect the dire housing straits of those without any financial support.[27] Only some form of rent supplements could assist the abjectly poor. Furthermore, maximum income limits threatened public housing families with improving economic circumstances. The threat of eviction discouraged financial self-improvement when rising income was not accompanied by expanded housing choices. For those families who did leave voluntarily, their loss deprived public housing of tenant leadership because "they tended to be the more energetic, ambitious, and 'responsible' tenants . . . who were active in providing structure and organization in the public housing communities."[28] The National Commission on Urban Problems recommended that tenants be permitted to retain three-fourths or four-fifths of any additional income provided that they agree to pay about one-quarter or one-fifth of excess income as additional public housing rent.[29]

Public housing was also severely criticized for its institutional, confining, and drab appearance which frequently resembled massive, high-rise, prison fortresses. Suburbanites and middle-class city dwellers deplored such huge housing projects, but, at the same time, they did not welcome public housing in their own neighborhoods. Consequently, city governments sought economy of scale in high-cost inner-city sites by constructing as many units as possible on available land. Such massive buildings contributed to the social disintegration of the poor. One example is found in the St. Louis Pruitt-Igoe public housing complex, consisting of forty-three structures on fifty-seven acres of central-city land, which was nearly totally ravaged by 1970. Built at a cost of $36 million in 1955–1956, the project encountered social, architectural, and financial disaster. In 1970, twenty-six of the eleven-story apartment buildings were vacant because the nearly 12,000 tenants could no longer tolerate a whole series of daily problems, as reported by John Herbers in *The New York Times:*

> Robbers, burglars, narcotics pushers and street gangs roamed at will through the buildings. Anarchy prevailed. Windows were broken faster than they could be replaced. . . . The steam pipes were not covered and children were seriously burned. People fell out of windows or walked into elevator shafts to their deaths. Drainage was not proper and water would back up on the grounds. . . . Last winter, with windows out, pipes froze and broke on some of the top floors, sending streams of water through the buildings and forming glaciers on the stairs . . . [Consequently,] the poorest of the poor would rather live in a dilapidated hut than endure Pruitt-Igoe's concentrated misery . . .[30]

Suggested solutions for improving both the quality and quantity of public housing are considerably restrained by the lack of commitment by policy-makers to provide decent, adequate, and safe shelter for the poor. The 1968 Housing Act, which will be discussed later, did contain several provisions to alleviate many of the existing deficiencies in public housing. However, the homeownership and social cost biases in housing policy continue to stand in direct opposition to social welfare goals, which should benefit the poor and minority groups who live in public housing. The National Commission on Urban Problems summarized these long-standing objections to public housing: (1) a dislike of public activity in such an intimate family matter as housing, (2) the fear of undue government expenditures,

(3) the desire to keep the poor physically at a distance, and (4) deep racial prejudices on the part of some whites.[31]

Until recently, the political powerlessness of public housing residents has prevented them from bringing about any meaningful policy changes in their own behalf. In his study of the rent strike movement in New York City during 1963–1965, Michael Lipsky concluded that "relatively powerless groups" cannot effect public policy because they "lack the minimum resources necessary to initiate or sustain protest activities which would bring their demands before a wider public. . . . [Such groups lacking political resources are] the groups in which constituents are poor, relatively unorganized and unschooled in organizational techniques, lacking in status and the refinements which accompany income, education, and social position . . ."[32]

By the 1970s, public housing tenants began to organize and to seek changes in severely restrictive local housing authority management practices. This occurred at a time when many city housing authorities were encountering serious financial difficulties which resulted in further deterioration, decay, vandalism, lack of security, and inadequate maintenance in public housing projects. In a twenty-three-city survey conducted by the Urban Institute, only four—Philadelphia, Oakland, Milwaukee, and Atlanta—had rental incomes which exceeded operating costs, which, by 1970, were rising more than 8 percent a year while tenants' incomes were increasing only by 3 percent annually.[33] The National Tenants Organization, formed in 1968 as a clearinghouse to service some 144 local groups in seventy-two cities,[34] began to pressure the Department of Housing and Urban Development to overcome such public housing problems as "eviction for 'social' reasons without a hearing, entry of the authorities without notice of permission of the tenant, adding fines for breakage even if the tenant was not responsible, and lack of a voice in the management of public housing."[35] In 1971, HUD responded with a model lease policy for the nation's 1,900 local public housing authorities. The model leave was designed to protect tenants' rights to procedural due process in both complaints and threats of eviction.

URBAN RENEWAL

The federal urban renewal program was the major housing policy for American cities from 1949 until enactment of subsequent federally subsidized low-income programs, including rent supplements, the

Model Cities program of 1966, and the 1968 Housing Act. Unlike the limited scope of the 1937 Housing Act, which combined slum clearance with public housing for the poor, urban renewal became a major effort to transform the physical deterioration of central cities. Construction of low-income housing was only part of the program's overall objectives. After World War II, the cities faced a serious housing shortage, substantial slum blight and decay, and declining land values coupled with a shrinking tax base and diminishing tax revenues. The cities were neglected as private enterprise, including real estate firms, lenders, and builders, was attracted to investment opportunities in the suburbs. Federal mortgage policies encouraged suburban home-ownership opportunities for the white middle class, and business followed this outward metropolitan expansion by constructing new shopping centers and industries.

Federal urban redevelopment and renewal policies were intended to reverse the tide of central city housing and financial malaise by combining private entrepreneurial, social cost, and social welfare objectives. These policy goals were incorporated in the preamble of the 1949 Housing Act:

> The Congress hereby declares that the *general welfare and security of the Nation* and the health and living standards of its people require *housing production and related community development* sufficient to remedy the *serious housing shortage*, the elimination of sub-standard and other inadequate housing through the *clearance of slums and blighted areas*, and the realization as soon as feasible of the goal of *a decent home and suitable living environment for every American family*, thus contributing to the development and redevelopment of communities and to the advancement of the growth, wealth, and security of the Nation (emphases added).[36]

The "slum clearance and community development and redevelopment" provisions found in Title I of the 1949 Housing Act had three major purposes: *First*, to speed up the clearance of slums and badly blighted residential areas; *second*, to facilitate the provision of decent, adequate, low-income housing by assisting in financing the acquisition and preparation of appropriate sites; and *third*, to give private enterprise the "maximum opportunity" in redeveloping these areas.[37]

City governments and private redevelopers could begin major rebuilding programs in slum areas with federal subsidies which supported most of the costs for slum clearance. Acting alone, private enterprise could not afford to acquire, condemn, demolish, and rebuild blighted areas. City governments had the power of eminent domain to obtain slum properties, but they clearly lacked the financial resources to prepare such areas for private construction.

Title I authorized a five-year federal expenditure of $500 million to cover the "write-down" costs of preparing renewal sites for private redevelopers, that is, a subsidy of two-thirds of the difference between the costs of assembling and clearing the slums and the price paid by the redevelopers for the cleared land. Renewal sites could then be sold to private redevelopers at substantially less than the actual market value. Thus, urban renewal provided a considerable incentive for large-scale private investment in the cities. The partnership between city governments and private redevelopers, supported by federal conditional grants-in-aid, would, as described by Charles Abrams, yield the following results:

> . . . Given such federal impetus and municipal cooperation, new buildings would supplant the slums, new revenues at least five times more than the old sites yielded would pour into the slack city treasuries, slums would disappear, the cities would begin to convalesce, and the general welfare would be served all around.[38]

Between 1949 and 1954, urban renewal did not achieve many significant results. Only 60 of 211 cities had reached even the initial land acquisition stage, and only $74 million of the available $500 million federal grants had been allocated to the cities by the Urban Renewal Administration.[39] The 1954 Housing Act expanded the scope of urban renewal by moving beyond slum clearance to housing rehabilitation and conservation in "gray areas" not requiring land acquisition and demolition by local renewal agencies. Private residential development and relocation assistance were encouraged by special FHA mortgage insurance programs in Sections 220 and 221 which provided aid for new and rehabilitated housing in renewal projects and for people displaced from renewal sites requiring moderate and low-income housing.

Additionally, the 1954 Housing Act required local renewal agencies to develop "workable programs," or overall community development plans, in qualifying for $500 million in available rehabilitation, conservation, and construction grants for new housing in urban renewal projects. Workable program components included adequate health and safety codes, analyses and identification of blighted neighborhoods, administrative organization to coordinate and carry out renewal projects, evidence of local financial resources, housing relocation sources for people displaced by renewal, and assurance of community knowledge of and participation in renewal programs.[40]

Despite all of the moderate and low-income housing provisions of federal urban renewal legislation, the program became primarily an instrument for commercial investment in rebuilding central business areas and for constructing luxury, high-rise apartments. Many profitable and prestigious city rebuilding projects contributed to tremendous construction activity and considerably enhanced the reputations for accomplishment by the program-politician mayors during the 1950s and 1960s (see Chapter 5). City centers were transformed by new department stores, shopping malls, high-rise office and apartment structures, expensive town houses, parking garages, government facilities, medical centers, sports and convention complexes, etc. By 1964 the scope of urban renewal activity included:

> Boston . . . has laid waste to 60 slum acres in the center of town and is erecting there a $200 million Government center; Washington has turned a 560-acre jungle south of the Capitol into a paradise of gracious living; New York City has so much private building that the streets are all but impassable. . . . Chicago has 27 redevelopment projects and four conservation projects that in five years will have transformed 514 city blocks, . . . Los Angeles . . . has 17 projects on 917 acres under way. St. Louis has miles of riverfront teeming with bulldozers and unfinished dreams. San Francisco is ripping and riveting at the rate of $1,000 a minute; Cleveland is trying to turn itself completely around to re-embrace the waters of Lake Erie. . . .
>
> In central Philadelphia . . . workmen were finishing two towering modern office buildings . . . a $120 million complex of transit and bus terminals, hotels, shops, restaurants, offices, underground concourses, sunken gardens and pedestrian malls called Penn Center . . .[41]

Slum clearance and redevelopment projects provided many cities with a necessary face-lifting and stimulated considerable economic recovery by a construction boom which attracted many commercial investors, businessmen, and apartment dwellers to downtown areas. For example, between 1966 and 1968, 65 percent of federally approved urban renewal projects were in or near central business districts.[42] But much of this rebuilding came at the expense of the poor, the blacks, and other ethnic minorities whose homes and apartments were destroyed by the urban renewal bulldozer. By 1968 urban renewal projects had demolished about 400,000 housing units (a majority of which were occupied by moderate and low-income groups) and had replaced only about one-tenth of them with 41,580 new low and moderate-income units.[43] Less than one-tenth of the total new units were planned for public housing while 62.3 percent were for middle and upper-income housing.[44]

Urban renewal resulted in tremendous displacement of the poor and became commonly known among blacks as "Negro removal." Slum sites considered desirable for luxury high-rise apartments and town houses resulted in subsidizing the rich at the expense of the poor. For example, in his study of the predominantly Italian West End section of Boston, Herbert J. Gans criticized the typical urban renewal process which demolished a "slum," as defined by the values of upper-middle-class housing experts:

> In summary, the West End was a low-rent district—both physically and socially—rather than a slum. Total clearance might have been justified if the end result had been better living conditions for the West Enders. . . . But none of this would have been possible under the urban renewal policies of the 1950's, which required the relocation of site residents and rebuilding for a new set of occupants by private enterprise.[45]

Urban renewal could not substantially assist the poor, the blacks, and other minorities as long as such housing was not profitable for private redevelopers. The crucial problem was that the private entrepreneurial and social cost approaches to urban renewal were pursued at the expense of social welfare goals. According to Lawrence Friedman, "The root of the problem lies in the nonwelfare orientation of redevelopment and renewal. Cities, for example, are passionately eager to tear down skid row. But skid row is a social, not an architectural phenomenon. The skid-row bums do not vanish from the earth when their bars and their flophouses vanish."[46] Urban renewal failed to help the poor whose homes were destroyed. The program did not provide moderate and low-income groups with either sufficient on-site housing or relocated living facilities and thereby denied them "a decent home and suitable living environment" as originally stated in the 1949 Housing Act.

Subsequent federal legislation attempted to ease the serious plight of people victimized by the urban renewal bulldozers. In 1965, Title I was amended to provide not only $200 per family for moving expenses and direct property losses, but also relocation "adjustment" payments up to $500 per family for rentals while seeking alternative housing. The 1964 Housing Act also established a $50 million revolving loan fund for residential rehabilitation by property owners and long-term tenants in renewal areas.[47] A 1965 amendment required that residential renewal had to afford "a substantial number" of housing units for low and moderate-income families and had to "result in marked progress in serving the poor and disadvantaged people living in slum and blighted areas."[48] Finally, the 1968 Housing Act required that future renewal projects be for predominantly residential uses and that at least 20 percent of new housing must be for low-income families. Rehabilitation grants were increased to $3,000 for low-income homeowners, the rehabilitation revolving fund was increased to $150 million, $15 million was allocated as preventive action against blight to alleviate harmful neighborhood conditions before renewal was necessary, and relocation and rehousing payments were increased.[49] Between 1967 and 1969, as many new low and moderate-income units were constructed on renewal sites as had been completed from 1950 to 1966.[50] However, even these substantial changes in the urban renewal program encountered federal cutbacks as the Nixon administration, seeking to control inflation by reduced government spending, budgeted only $1 billion for 1971 even though Congress had authorized $1.7 billion.[51] As urban renewal goals moved toward assisting the poor, the concern for providing adequate federal aid diminished.

Urban renewal could never become a program benefitting the poor, blacks, and other minorities unless there was a genuine change in policy emphasis. In 1965 Herbert Gans, in commenting upon the failure of urban renewal, suggested a useful series of recommendations which might resolve the program's deficiencies. Note, however, that Gans' suggestions require a substantial change in attitudes among groups who support the private entrepreneurial and social cost emphases in renewal policy:

> The solution, then, is not to repeal urban renewal, but to transform it from a program of slum clearance and rehabilitation into a program of urban rehousing. This means, first, building low and moderate-cost housing on vacant land in cities, suburbs, and new towns beyond the suburbs, and also helping slum-dwellers to move into existing housing outside the slums; and then *after* a portion of the urban low-income population has left the slums, clearing and rehabilitating them through urban renewal . . .[52]

MODEL CITIES

By the 1960s, federal housing programs were compartmentalized, disjointed, uncoordinated, and operating under different assumptions with conflicting objectives. Due to bureaucratic delays and congressional cutbacks, public housing had not achieved the authorized 810,000 new units under the 1949 Housing Act. Urban renewal, while successful in rebuilding many central business areas, was destroying ten times as many moderate and low-income housing units as it was providing.

The Model Cities program greatly differed from past federal policies to the cities because it included the goals of a national urban policy rather than separate and specialized program objectives. As enacted by Congress in 1966 upon the initiative of President Johnson, Title I of the Demonstration Cities and Metropolitan Development Act was a major policy innovation to improve the quality of urban life by welding together public housing, urban renewal, and other federally subsidized low-income housing programs with other social welfare and antipoverty programs:

> The persistence of widespread urban slums and blight, the concentration of persons of low income in older urban areas, and the unmet needs for additional housing and community facilities and services arising from the rapid expansion of our urban population have resulted in a marked deterioration in the quality of the environment and the lives of large numbers of our people while the Nation as a whole prospers.[53]

Model Cities not only recognized the homeownership, social cost, and social welfare approaches of the past, but the program also sought to encourage new and comprehensive city plans which would coordinate existing, but disjointed, federal programs in rebuilding entire slum neighborhoods. With a three-year $1.2 billion congressional authorization (reduced from President Johnson's original six-year request of $2.3 billion), the Department of Housing and Urban Development would select sixty to seventy cities of various sizes to develop demonstration plans. HUD would provide 80 percent of the planning costs for local needs and financial requirements in developing demonstration plans. Thereafter, HUD would offer "block grants," or combined federal categorical assistance instead of separate grants-in-aid, to cover 80 percent of all federally assisted project activity containing such "new and imaginative proposals to rebuild or revitalize large slum and blighted areas" as:

1. Expanding housing, job, and income opportunities
2. Reducing dependence on welfare payments
3. Improving educational facilities and programs
4. Combating disease and ill health
5. Reducing crime and delinquency
6. Enhancing recreational and cultural opportunities
7. Establishing better access between homes and jobs
8. Improving living conditions for the people who live in such areas.[54]

The original purposes of the demonstration grants, as developed by the Johnson administration, were to assist localities of all population sizes in a concerted attack on slums, poverty, and other related social and economic problems. In developing comprehensive plans, local officials would work together with neighborhood residents in the target areas. When results proved effective in model neighborhoods, the program could be enlarged as a total attack on the urban crisis. The full range of urban problems was evident in Model Cities applications to HUD. For example, in Rochester, New York the model neighborhood area had "the worst slum housing. . . . Approximately 39 percent of the 12,200 dwellings in the area are substandard. . . . [the area had] a staggering range of interconnected problems which have been growing for decades and which, if no attempts are made at correction, can only continue to grow worse."[55] Suggested solutions included Atlanta's first-year action plan in eleven functional areas with such proposals as "A new Nonprofit Housing Corporation . . . to develop, direct and/or assist others in the development of Housing for Model Neighborhood Residents . . . [E]stablishment of an intra-neighborhood bus service . . . [Organizing] a Neighborhood Development Corporation [to] assemble a $2 million pool . . . to make loans to existing and new businesses."[56]

Despite the lofty objectives of Model Cities, the program soon encountered financial limitations and charges of political favoritism. The greater needs of large cities clashed with those of medium-sized and smaller localities. Congressional limits on first-stage planning grants severely undercut program objectives. By May 1967, 193 cities had applied for the available $11 million in planning funds, but requests from the 12 largest cities totaled nearly $8 million, including about $4 million requested from Chicago, Los Angeles, Philadelphia, and Detroit.[57] In allocating planning funds to the 63 selected cities in November 1967, HUD had to limit the awards and to exclude some of the major cities from the program. Also, critics charged the Johnson administration with political maneuvering and favoritism. For example, only 9 of the 63 cities were in Republican congressional districts. Several grants went to smaller communities represented by key Democratic congressional committee chairmen, while Los Angeles and Cleveland did not receive planning funds.[58]

Further problems ensued as the Nixon administration changed the scope of the Model Cities program without a corresponding increase in federal financial support. In 1969, President Nixon reorganized Model Cities by giving local officials authority to expand the program to all city poverty areas, even though many of the first-stage planning grants had not yet been completed. Instead of using the demonstration programs to upgrade selected blighted areas, Model Cities now became part of a decentralization plan to limit federal participation in urban programs. According to John Herbers, the Nixon administration abandoned "the primary goal of Model Cities—to build gleaming examples of urban renaissance—and appl[ied] a secondary goal—reform of administrative techniques—for administering all new and existing social and housing programs in almost all urban poverty areas."[59] The federal government continued to provide block grants to the cities, but with much less supervision and control than under the original 1966 law. In effect, Model Cities would replace the antipoverty program and thereby fit in with President Nixon's view of reduced federal involvement in city affairs.

Additionally, the Nixon administration sought to achieve these goals with less federal funding. Instead of the $1 billion projected for Model Cities in the 1968 Housing Act, the Nixon administration requested only $675 million, and Congress appropriated only $575 million for 1969–1970. Reduced federal funding for Model Cities continued throughout 1971–1973 so that the 150 participating cities (87 of which had been added to the program in 1968) had less support to achieve their planning goals. Consequently, by 1973 many Model Cities programs were no longer viable and the program had become "just another poor man's pork barrel—empty."[60]

FEDERAL HOUSING SUBSIDIES

In alleviating the deficiencies of public housing and the displacement of moderate and low-income families from urban renewal projects, the federal government moved toward strengthening social welfare objectives and private entrepreneurial incentives in housing policy during the 1960s. However, the three major housing subsidy programs—assistance for moderate-income groups (the Section 221 (d) (3) program), rent supplements, and homeownership for low-income groups (the Section 235 program of the 1968 Housing Act)—encountered the same difficulties as previous federal efforts. These problems, as elaborated below, included very slow implementation of original program objectives, a serious bias against the very poor, inadequate federal funding, fears of racial integration, and considerable corruption resulting in large-scale housing abandonment in central city poverty areas.

Section 221 (d) (3) BMIR Subsidies

The 1961 Housing Act included a program to assist families displaced from urban renewal projects whose incomes were too high to qualify for public housing but too low to afford private housing. The Section 221 (d) (3) program was essentially a federal subsidy to provide "below market interest rates" (BMIR) for private developers including nonprofit associations, limited-dividend corporations, and cooperatives, who were encouraged to build moderate-income rental housing. The federal government offered such developers forty-year FHA-insured mortgages at maximum 3 percent interest rates to cover 100 percent of development, construction, and long-term financing costs. In return, sponsors had to limit rents for occupants which amounted to about 25 percent below existing levels under conventional mortgage loans at unsubsidized market interest rates.

The BMIR program was not intended to assist the abjectly poor nor did it aid many of the near-poor families who could not find adequate housing outside of urban renewal sites. In various policy statements, congressional priorities included displaced families (the 1961 law), the elderly and handicapped (1964), tenants occupying housing destroyed or damaged by natural disaster, and other "low and moderate-income persons" not to exceed 10 percent of the occupied BMIR apartment units (1966). Furthermore, localities tended to establish family income ceilings far above nationally established poverty and near-poverty levels. In a survey of fifty large cities conducted by the National Commission on Urban Problems, BMIR family income eligibility ceilings exceeded the 1968 family income median of $8,000 in twenty-two cities, while only ten cities had ceilings in the $6,000 to $7,000 range.[61]

Additionally, the BMIR program had only very limited results in providing adequate amounts of subsidized moderate-income housing. The original program goal was 40,000 units per year, but by 1970 only 175,000 units had been started and 140,000 units completed.[62] In fact, it took five years to complete BMIR's first-year construction objectives. BMIR never seriously competed with the unsubsidized private housing industry. By 1967, BMIR units represented only 1 percent of the total volume of private housing construction and even with increased participation after 1967, the 221 (d) (3) program resulted in less than 3 percent of the total private housing starts.[63]

BMIR never gained momentum because nonprofit sponsors frequently lacked expertise and "seed money" for professional guidance in planning, initiating, and carrying out housing proposals. FHA procedures were so complex and time-consuming that private developers were frustrated. For example, the FHA manual for BMIR included 283 pages of required steps for applicants and FHA processing time required 376 working days between approved applications and actual construction.[61] Finally, since the program was a local option, developers could not participate unless local housing authorities included BMIR in the urban renewal "workable programs" as required under the 1954 Housing Act. Suburbs seeking to exclude racial minorities and other "problem families" could simply refuse to adopt workable programs.

Rent Supplements

In 1965, BMIR was incorporated into a new rent supplement program, although HUD had originally proposed that such subsidies would be a partial substitute for public housing and would replace BMIR by providing benefits for moderate-income groups through added incentives for private developers to build more subsidized housing. Congress rejected HUD's version of rent supplements by restricting the program to low-income groups eligible for public housing and by continuing the existing BMIR program. In effect, rent supplements shifted low-rent housing responsibilities from local housing authorities to private developers. BMIR sponsors—nonprofit associations, limited-dividend corporations, and cooperatives—and profit-motivated developers could now accept low-income groups in rental housing. Under the program, the federal government paid direct subsidies to landlords covering the difference between 25 percent of an eligible tenant's income and the computed fair-market rent for such housing. Not all tenants would qualify for rent supplements, and those with rising incomes would pay a higher proportion of such gains in added rents. Thus, rent supplements served as a kind of inverse income transfer (similar to some of the welfare reform proposals discussed in Chapter 8) because those families with lower incomes received higher subsidies and paid lower rents, while other groups with higher incomes received less in subsidies and paid more rent.

The Johnson administration hoped that rent supplements would encourage racial and economic integration. Most tenants would pay full rents, and only landlords would know which families were subsidized by rent supplements. Poverty or near-poverty status would not automatically disqualify families from obtaining adequate housing.

No stigma would be attached to such families, and they could be dispersed throughout the cities and metropolitan areas. Presumably, mixed tenancies would be more acceptable to community living standards than public housing, which contained only the poverty-stricken.

However, Congress responded to local objections and middle-class fears of the specter of widely dispersed governmental housing subsidies. Rent supplements were restricted to no more than 70 percent of fair market rents, thereby placing a greater economic burden on the lowest-income tenants. Dollar limits on construction costs and low maximums on fair market rentals were additional obstacles faced by developers. Furthermore, Congress was less than enthusiastic in funding the program. Of the $150 million authorized by 1968, only $42 million was appropriated, with nothing at all appropriated in 1967.[65] Local obstruction was permitted by requiring either specific local approval or inclusion of rent supplements in urban renewal workable programs. Nonprofit sponsors were frequently "repelled by what they regarded as cold, bureaucratic, and at times actually hostile treatment at the hands of FHA."[66] The National Commission on Urban Problems indicated that while top FHA officials were sympathetic to rent supplement developers,

> . . . the rank and file officials in district and local offices were, in many cases, highly unsympathetic. They were accustomed to dealing with the conservative real estate and financial community. They did not feel at home in having business dealings with churches and philanthropists whom they tended to regard as soft and impractical. Neither did they welcome the poor as their constituents. This was a social class whom they had never served and who seemed alien to their interests and associations.[67]

Consequently, it was not surprising that between 1965 and 1970 only 55,000 apartment units in rent supplement projects had been started and only 33,000 completed.[68] The formidable resistance to rent supplement housing found in local objections, insufficient federal funding, congressional restrictions, and FHA hostility easily undermined the program's original racial, economic, social welfare, and private entrepreneurial objectives.

Section 236   Rental Housing

The 1968 Housing Act contained a rental housing provision that was designed to replace both BMIR and rent supplements. The Section 236 program provided 1 percent FHA mortgage financing to nonprofit housing sponsors which would result in lower rents than under BMIR's 3 percent mortgage financing. Rent subsidies were similar to the 1965 provisions, that is, the federal government paid landlords the difference between 25 percent of an eligible tenant's income and fair market rentals. With maximum rent subsidies established at $50 to $60 per month, Section 236 would provide benefits primarily to families in the $4,000 to $6,500 range. The very poor would not qualify for 236 assistance, and in high-construction-cost cities, even moderate-income families might be excluded from such projects. Finally, Section 236 was not tied to local urban renewal workable program requirements. The early results of Section 236 apartment construction were not promising. Congress authorized construction of 700,000 units over a three-year period, and the Johnson administration had hoped to rehabilitate or begin construction of 90,000 units by 1970, but actual production was only two-thirds of this goal. Nonprofit sponsors were hindered by low levels of congressional appropriations and skyrocketing mortgage interest rates, which by the 1970s had significantly narrowed the pool of available home financing funds, particularly for government subsidized housing projects.[69]

Section 235 Homeownership Program

By 1968, thirty years of federal housing assistance had produced construction of only 800,000 rental subsidized units, which was far below the national needs for moderate and low-income groups. Formidable opposition by real estate groups, homebuilders, cost-conscious congressmen, and middle-class homeowners successfully halted any efforts to increase the production of federally subsidized housing programs. However, the 1968 Housing Act, which President Johnson proclaimed as the "Magna Carta to liberate our cities,"[70] pledged a ten-year national goal of six million new and rehabilitated housing units, including both rental and homeownership assistance for moderate and low-income families, thus reaffirming the 1949 goal of "a decent home and suitable living environment for every American family."

Homeownership subsidies represented a sharp departure from past federal housing policies which had provided direct housing for the poor (public housing), assistance to private developers and nonprofit corporations (urban renewal and BMIR), rent supplements, aid for housing rehabilitation, and FHA-insured mortgages. Presumably, homeownership assistance would not threaten the private entrepreneurial and middle-class value system which opposed governmental aid to the "undeserving poor." Homeownership was an acceptable goal for every American family because it fit in with the majority view of social and economic goods and contributed to community and neighborhood stability. Subsidized homeownership would assist families with initiative and the desire to own private property. In these various respects, the homeownership program compared favorably with the temporary public works programs of the 1930s and FHA mortgage insurance for suburban middle-class homeowners.

The Section 235 program provided homeownership opportunities to moderate and low-income families by subsidizing mortgage loan interest rates as low as 1 percent, by extending mortgage terms for as long as 40 years, and by requiring downpayments as low as $400. Eligible families would pay at least 20 percent of their incomes toward monthly mortgage payments. In making up the difference between full market interest rates (more than 8 percent in 1970) and the 1 percent mortgage subsidies, FHA would reimburse lending institutions with insured mortgage loans. With mortgage interest subsidies providing about $40 to $70 a month, the program would benefit families in the $3,000 to $7,000 income range. Such families could purchase homes for a maximum of $15,000, although mortgages up to $17,500 were permitted in high-cost areas and mortgages of up to $20,000 were allowed for large families in high-cost areas.[71] Finally, Section 235 developers were not limited by profit ceilings, and the program did not require local urban renewal workable program approval.

By the end of 1970, the Section 235 program had provided nearly 118,000 new and rehabilitated homes to about 130,000 moderate and low-income families at federal governmental costs of $140 million.[72] Homeownership was particularly attractive to the Nixon administration's housing policies because it fit in with the overall de-emphasis of federal assistance for public housing, urban renewal, model cities, and antipoverty programs, while encouraging decentralized urban objectives through greater attention to the private sector and individual initiative. However, the 235 program also resulted in serious deficiencies including spurious real estate speculation, poor housing construction, scandalous FHA appraisals, rapid property deterioration, mortgage defaults, large-scale housing abandonment, and federal takeovers of vast numbers of inner-city homes at huge losses. Such despairing and depressing conditions contributed to the further victimization of the near-poor, blacks, white ethnics, and other minorities. Consequently, federal policy directly contributed to worsening the housing conditions for those families with the greatest housing needs.

In January, 1971, the House Banking and Currency Committee uncovered the Section 235 scandals by revealing that (1) So-called "suede shoe" (or shady "fast buck" real estate swindlers) would buy inner-city homes at very cheap prices, perform a cosmetic or superficial rehabilitation at minimal costs, and then sell such homes to unsuspecting purchasers at profits of several thousands of dollars; (2) Many new and rehabilitated 235 homes had "faulty plumbing, leaky basements, leaky roofs, cracked plaster, faulty wiring, rotten wood, loose stair treads, paper-thin walls, inoperative furnaces and appliances, inadequate insulation, and the like"; (3) Such homes were of such poor quality that they could not survive the life of the FHA-subsidized mortgages; (4) FHA appraisers worked together with the shoddy real estate operators by evaluating 235 homes far above true market values and thereby substantially adding to the speculator's profits. For example, in Detroit, speculators would purchase shabby homes at $3,000 to $4,000, spend about $1,500 for superficial repairs, and then have FHA appraisers value such homes at $12,000 so that the FHA would insure the mortgage at that figure. Thus, the speculators easily doubled their initial investments at the expense of the homebuyer, who received an inferior structure; (5) Section 235 homeowners found they could not afford major, costly repairs, would stop making mortgage payments, and eventually would default on their mortgages. Then, FHA repossessed such properties at huge losses after they had been abandoned, gutted, and vandalized.[73]

The disastrous financial scandals resulting from federal housing subsidies under the 1968 Housing Act led to a 1973 freeze on all new commitments for Section 235 and Section 236 mortgage assistance. The Nixon administration sought to find new solutions for alleviating the existing and projected mortgage losses resulting from defaults on an estimated 240,000 housing units. Such prospects were compounded by the current and expected $8 billion annual federal expenditures for six million new and rehabilitated moderate and low-income housing units which would cost $200 billion by 1978. Clearly, the private homeownership policy objective of federal housing subsidies had failed to serve the inner-city poor, just as public housing, BMIR, and rent supplements did not adequately achieve their intended social welfare goals.

CONCLUDING NOTE

With all of the various, complex, and well-intended federal policies for housing assistance to the cities, none seemed to be working very well by the 1970s. The federal government, including both the executive and legislative branches, was unable to generate the necessary assistance for those urban groups with the greatest housing needs. The summary table below indicates that slightly more than 1.5 million federally sponsored low and moderate-income housing units were completed by 1970 with another 1.8 million under construction. As indicated earlier, the nation's *minimum* housing needs in 1968 alone required removal or replacement of 11 million substandard units. Even the projected 6 million new and rehabilitated subsidized units by 1978 called for in the 1968 Housing Act would not meet the nation's low and moderate-income housing needs of 1968. Thus, the federal housing policy toward the cities would seem to require a drastic reappraisal to meet the nation's minimum housing requirements. Either massive housing assistance to the poor by direct federal intervention or a substantial federally supported income redistribution policy may serve to overcome past policy failures. Otherwise, housing assistance for the poor will continue to be plagued by lofty goals without sufficient financial support.

TABLE 11–3   Production Under Federal Low and Moderate-Income Housing Programs As of July 31, 1970

Program	Completions	Starts
Public housing	867,000	973,000
Rent supplements	33,000	55,000
221(d) (3) BMIR	140,000	175,000
235 Homeownership	68,000	110,000
236 Rental Apartment Subsidies	9,000	64,000
Other HUD low and moderate-income programs	56,000	67,000
Farmers Home Administration low and moderate-income programs	330,000	350,000
Totals	1,503,000	1,794,000

SOURCES: Department of Housing and Urban Development and Department of Agriculture, Farmers Home Administration.

NOTES

1. *Building the American City*, Report of the National Commission on Urban Problems to the Congress and to the President of the United States, 91st Congress, 1st Session (Washington, D.C.: U.S. Government Printing Office, 1968), p. 68.
2. *Ibid.*, pp. 73–74.
3. *Ibid.*, pp. 77–78.
4. *Report of the National Advisory Commission on Civil Disorders* (Washington, D.C.: U.S. Government Printing Office, 1968), p. 259.
5. *Ibid.*
6. Nathan Glazer, "Housing Problems and Housing Policies," *The Public Interest*, No. 7 (Spring 1967), p. 29.
7. Lawrence M. Friedman, *Government and Slum Housing: A Century of Frustration* (Chicago: Rand McNally, 1968), p. 12.
8. *Ibid.*, p. 10.
9. Jewel Bellush and Murray Hausknecht, eds., *Urban Renewal: People, Politics, and Planning* (Garden City, N.Y.: Doubleday, Anchor Books, 1967), p. 4.
10. *Building the American City*, p. 94.
11. Bellush and Hausknecht, *Urban Renewal*, p. 5.
12. Joseph P. Fried, *Housing Crisis U.S.A.* (Baltimore: Penguin Books, 1972), p. 68.
13. *Building the American City*, p. 100.
14. *Ibid.*, p. 102.
15. *Ibid.*
16. Friedman, *Government and Slum Housing*, p. 103.
17. *Ibid.*, p. 109.
18. *Building the American City*, p. 108.
19. Friedman, *Government and Slum Housing*, p. 106.
20. *Ibid.*
21. *Ibid.*, pp. 108–109.
22. Fried, *Housing Crisis U.S.A.*, p. 72.
23. *Building the American City*, p. 120.
24. Fried, *Housing Crisis U.S.A.*, p. 72.
25. *Building the American City*, p. 114.
26. *Ibid.*, p. 115.
27. *Ibid.*
28. Leonard Freedman, *Public Housing: The Politics of Poverty* (New York: Holt, Rinehart and Winston, 1969), p. 108.
29. *Building the American City*, p. 117.
30. *The New York Times*, November 2, 1970, p. 1, col. 2–4; p. 36, col. 1.
31. *Building the American City*, p. 129.
32. Michael Lipsky, *Protest in City Politics: Rent Strikes, Housing and the Power of the Poor* (Chicago: Rand McNally, 1970), pp. 202–203.
33. *The New York Times*, June 25, 1970, p. 25, col. 1–6.
34. *Ibid.*, October 29, 1970, p. 47, col. 3–6.
35. *Ibid.*, February 24, 1971, p. 1, col. 7; p. 29, col. 1.
36. "Housing a Nation" (Washington, D.C.: *Congressional Quarterly*, 1966). p. 28.

37. *Building the American City*, p. 152.
38. Charles Abrams, *The City is the Frontier* (New York: Harper and Row, 1965), p. 77.
39. *Ibid.*, p. 86.
40. Robert C. Weaver, *The Urban Complex: Human Values in Urban Life* (Garden City, N.Y.: Doubleday, 1964), p. 83.
41. *Time* (November 6, 1964), pp. 60, 69.
42. *Building the American City*, p. 162.
43. *Ibid.*, p. 163.
44. *Ibid.*
45. Herbert J. Gans, *The Urban Villagers: Group and Class in the Life of Italian Americans* (New York: Free Press, 1962), pp. 316–317.
46. Friedman, *Government and Slum Housing*, p. 159.
47. *Housing a Nation*, p. 52.
48. Fried, *Housing Crisis U.S.A.*, p. 92.
49. *Building the American City*, p. 177.
50. Fried, *Housing Crisis U.S.A.*, p. 92.
51. *The New York Times*, March 1, 1970, p. 1, col. 4.
52. Herbert J. Gans, "The Failure of Urban Renewal," in *Urban Renewal: The Record and the Controversy*, ed. James Q. Wilson (Cambridge, Mass.: M.I.T. Press, 1966), p. 545.
53. *Demonstration Cities and Metropolitan Development Act of 1966*, Title I, Section 101, Public Law 89–754, 89th Congress, November 3, 1966.
54. *Ibid.*
55. *The Christian Science Monitor*, August 8, 1967, p. 16.
56. *The Model Cities Program*, Department of Housing and Urban Development (Washington, D.C.: U.S. Government Printing Office, 1969), p. 29.
57. *The Christian Science Monitor*, July 8, 1967, p. 5.
58. *The New York Times*, November 17, 1967, p. 1, col. 8; p. 36, col. 6–8.
59. *Ibid.*, May 11, 1969, Section 4, p. 2, col. 1–6.
60. Fried, *Housing Crisis U.S.A.*, p. 104.
61. *Building the American City*, p. 146.
62. Fried, *Housing Crisis U.S.A.*, p. 97.
63. *Building the American City*, p. 147.
64. *Ibid.*, p. 148.
65. Fried, *Housing Crisis U.S.A.*, p. 100.
66. *Building the American City*, p. 150.
67. *Ibid.*
68. Fried, *Housing Crisis U.S.A.*, p. 99.
69. *Sources:* Fried, *Housing Crisis U.S.A.*, pp. 110–111; and *A Decent Home*, The Report of the President's Committee on Urban Housing (Washington, D.C.: U.S. Government Printing Office, 1969), pp. 65–66.
70. *Building the American City*, p. 173.
71. *Sources: A Decent Home*, p. 66; and Fried, *Housing Crisis U.S.A.*, pp. 107–109.
72. *The New York Times*, January 15, 1971, p. 1, col. 6–7; p. 12, col. 6–8; and *Ibid.*, January 3, 1972, p. 1, col. 3–4; p. 20, col. 1–5.
73. The source for these exposés is the excellent reporting of John Herbers in *The New York Times*, January 6, 1971, p. 1, col. 8; p. 41, col. 1–2; December 4, 1971, p. 1, col. 4–5; p. 21 col. 4–6; and January 3, 1972, p. 1, col. 4–5; p. 44, col. 1–6.

SUGGESTIONS FOR FURTHER READING

Abrams, Charles. *The City Is the Frontier*. New York: Harper and Row, Colophon Books, 1967.
An important study of governmental roles in housing policies, with particular emphasis on the pros and cons of urban renewal.

A Decent Home. The Report of the President's Committee on Urban Housing. Washington, D.C.: U.S. Government Printing Office, 1968.
Appointed by President Johnson in 1967, the committee, headed by Edgar F. Kaiser, offered a detailed analysis of the role of private enterprise in providing adequate housing for the poor.

Anderson, Matrin. *The Federal Bulldozer*. New York: McGraw-Hill, 1967.
A highly critical and controversial attack on federal urban renewal programs.

Bellush, Jewel, and Murray Hausknecht, eds. *Urban Renewal: People, Politics and Planning*. Garden City, N.Y.: Doubleday, Anchor Books, 1967.
Collection of articles surveying public housing and urban renewal policies.

Building the American City. Report of the National Commission on Urban Problems. 91st Congress, 1st Session, House Document 91–34. Washington, D.C.: U.S. Government Printing Office, 1968.
Comprehensive survey of federal housing policies, building codes, housing codes, zoning, and urban government by the commission appointed by President Johnson. Excellent source materials for housing developments to 1968.

Clark, Kenneth B. *Dark Ghetto*. New York: Harper and Row, Torchbooks, 1967.
A highly recommended and important analysis of social and psychological aspects of black slum life.

Freedman, Leonard. *Public Housing*. New York: Holt, Rinehart and Winston, 1969.
An analysis of legislative process and interest-group struggle over public housing together with an evaluation of public attitudes over race, poverty, and public ownership.

Fried, Joseph P. *Housing Crisis U.S.A.* Baltimore: Penguin Books, 1971.
Excellent overview of recent housing policies indicating that effective solutions are lost in an abyss of confusing legislation.

Friedman, Lawrence M. *Government and Slum Housing*. Chicago: Rand McNally, 1968.
Using "social cost" and "social welfare" goals in providing housing to the poor, the author indicates the inadequacies of federal public housing and urban renewal policies.

Gans, Herbert J. "The Failure of Urban Renewal: A Critique and

Some Proposals," *Commentary* (April 1965), pp. 29–37.
In attacking federal urban renewal programs, Gans suggests that suburban integration and slum improvement should precede demolition of housing for the poor.

Gans, Herbert J. *The Urban Villagers*. New York: Free Press, 1962.
An excellent insight into the life of an Italian community in Boston and its demise resulting from an urban renewal project.

Glazer, Nathan. "Housing Problems and Policies," *The Public Interest*, No. 7, (Spring 1967), pp. 21–51.
Author observes that most housing policies have benefited the middle and upper classes while neglecting the poor.

Goldwin, Robert A., ed. *A Nation of Cities*. Chicago: Rand McNally, 1966.
A collection of essays analyzing the assumptions of President Johnson's Model Cities proposal.

Greer, Scott. *Urban Renewal and American Cities*. Indianapolis: Bobbs-Merrill, 1965.
Study of federal-local implementation of urban renewal policy.

Hunter, David R. *The Slums*. New York: Free Press, 1968.
A comprehensive examination of slums and government programs to combat urban poverty.

Lipsky, Michael. *Protest In City Politics: Rent Strikes, Housing and the Power of the Poor*. Chicago: Rand McNally, 1970.
Study of the rent strike movement and political resources of the poor in New York City.

Lowe, Jeanne R. *Cities In a Race With Time*. New York: Random House, Vintage Books, 1967.
Implementation of housing policies in a variety of cities.

Sternlieb, George. *The Tenement Landlord*. New Brunswick, N.J.: Urban Studies Center, Rutgers—The State University, 1966.
A study of problems, maintenance, and eradication of slum housing.

Weaver, Robert C. *Dilemmas of Urban America*. New York: Atheneum, 1965.
A discussion of housing and race problems.

Weaver, Robert C. *The Urban Complex*. Garden City, N.Y.: Doubleday, 1964.
An evaluation of urban renewal by the first federal cabinet secretary of Housing and Urban Development.

Wilson, James Q. *Urban Renewal: The Record and the Controversy*. Cambridge, Mass.: M.I.T. Press, 1966.
Comprehensive collection of articles concerning the federal urban renewal program.

Wolman, Harold. *Politics of Federal Housing*. New York: Dodd, Mead, 1971.
An analysis of federal housing through a policy and decision-making framework.

12

Political Problems
of Urban Education

INTRODUCTION

This chapter focuses on the two problems which have plagued the public school systems of American cities ever since they were defined as problems by the courts of the land. One is the matter of segregation by race, which was ruled unconstitutional by the U.S. Supreme Court in *Brown* v. *Board of Education of Topeka*[1] in 1954. The other is the matter of fiscal disparities among school districts due to the universal reliance on the local property tax which, because property values vary among districts, gives some a considerable advantage over others in their capacity to support public education. While the Supreme Court has refused to do so, several state courts have condemned this system of school support as a violation of (state) constitutional provisions that guarantee equality of educational opportunities.

The chapter traces the development of *de facto* segregation to patterns of residential and suburban development in metropolitan areas both before and after the case of *Brown* v. *Board of Education,* showing how efforts to enforce this decision actually hastened the segregation process in cities. We show that resorting to busing in desegregation programs provoked so strong a reaction among both white and black voters that the president of the United States felt

369

compelled to take a political and policy stand in opposition to busing. The failure to achieve stable integration in city schools and the steady deterioration of conditions in schools serving black communities led to demands for community control of these schools. Such demands revealed the stakes the white-dominated education profession had in the ghetto schools (which they protected through their unions) and the unresponsiveness of the white-dominated school system bureaucracy to the special problems of minority communities. We show how experiments in community control were repressed or defeated and in several large cities converted into proposals for decentralization. Some of the decentralization plans made provision for community decision-making, but without exception the community decisions were subject to the approval or ratification of a central administration and policy board.

Following the discussion of community control and decentralization, we summarize a few ideas about how urban school systems might be restructured so as to address the issues of social and racial mix, the quality of educational programs, the equality of educational opportunities, the fiscal disparities among districts, and the shared decision-making between the city or metropolitan level and the community-neighborhood level.

Finally, we discuss the problem of fiscal disparities among school districts and summarize the court and legislative actions that have been and are being taken in different states to reduce such inequities.

PRESENT PROBLEMS OF AMERICAN PUBLIC SCHOOLS

A serious problem of urban education is the deterioration of the quality of the instructional programs of inner-city schools. As upwardly mobile families have moved to the suburbs, the better teachers and administrators have followed. What is left behind are the less-qualified staff and the less-motivated pupils from lower-class families whose interest in education is undermined by a sense of hopelessness, low self-esteem, and a resulting inability to visualize the values of education. These attitudes breed delinquent behavior both in and out of school, and they are reinforced by the frequent examples of deviant behavior of adults with whom they are in daily contact. Upwardly mobile whites, even those of modest means, have usually been able to move out of the worst neighborhoods, but the blacks have had to stay behind because of housing discrimination and hostility in white areas. The outward movement of whites, even poor whites, has left most city school districts with a nearly insoluble problem of compliance with court orders commanding integration. Thus, many inner-city schools have become more segregated over the past two decades than they were before 1954.

A 1967 study of the U.S. Civil Rights Commission[2] found that the majority of students still attended segregated schools, that school segregation was most severe in metropolitan areas (where 70 percent of the nation's population resides), that 75 percent of black students (1.2 million of 1.6 million) in seventy-five cities attended schools where the student populations were more than 90 percent black, whereas 88 percent of the white students (2 of 2.4 million) went to schools that were more than 90 percent white. The report found that racial isolation was sanctioned by government at all levels; perpetuated by the effects of past segregation; reinforced by demographic, fiscal, and educational changes in urban areas; and compounded by the policies and practices of urban school systems. None of this has changed very much, as we shall see.

THE COLEMAN REPORT

While the U.S. Civil Rights Commission was tracking the expansion of segregation in public schools, Congress, under Section 402 of the 1964 Civil Rights Act, authorized the U.S. Office of Education to do a study of the effects of *de facto* segregation on the achievement levels of black students. In 1967 Professor James Coleman of the John Hopkins University and his associates published *Equality of Educational Opportunity*, a massive report which confirmed the findings of the Civil Rights Commission on the lack of progress in school integration. In addition, the Coleman study found that black pupils were likely to be taught by black teachers. Before 1967, 65 percent of all teachers were white. The study found that on the average, the minority pupil (excluding Orientals) scored significantly lower on achievement tests than white pupils. The deficiency in achievement was found to be progressively greater for minority students as they moved to higher grade levels. At grade one, the score of the black child was on the average 1 year behind the average white child; at grade twelve, the black student was 3.3 years behind the white.

The study revealed, however, that the expenditures for teachers, facilities, and curriculum were similar for predominantly black schools and affluent white schools. The main difference was that black teachers did not do as well as white teachers on tests of academic ability. On a national basis, black students had less access to physics, chemistry, and language laboratories than white students. They also had fewer books per pupil in the libraries and fewer texts in the classroom.

The expected relationship between inferior schools and low student achievement was not proven by the study. Scores in achievement tests were not related to the kind of school attended. Black and white students of similar family background did not show higher achievement in schools where expenditures were higher as compared with students of similar background in schools where expenditures were lower. The critical factor in achievement were the *attitudes toward learning of the other children in the school*. Thus, a predominance of highly motivated students in any school had a positive influence on the less motivated students. In contemporary American culture, black students, by and large, come from impoverished backgrounds and tend to lack the incentive to learn. If such children attend schools where most others also lack motivation, the general achievement level is likely to be below any national average. Because the majority of white students in predominantly white schools are from families whose parents have gained substantial advantages from their educational background, the students are motivated by the knowledge that education is essential to "success." Thus, a major finding of the Coleman Report was *that peer group influence on educational achievement is more related to attitudes developed outside the school than in school.*

In summary, variations in the facilities and curricula of schools had a negligible effect on student achievement, but the quality of teachers showed a somewhat stronger relationship to student achievement and was more important to minority students than to white students. If a minority pupil from a home lacking in educational support were put into a school where most students came from strong educational backgrounds, his or her achievement was likely to increase. In an analysis of the Coleman Report, Christopher Jencks and a group of colleagues at Harvard concluded that while students probably do influence peer achievement, the effect may be relatively small and thus not worth the political and economic cost of integration.[3]

Coleman himself has favored a policy of school integration but emphasizes that neither piecemeal integration of schools nor upgrading of ghetto schools by compensatory programs can substantially improve the achievement of students. As long as blacks are excluded from opportunity by the dominant society and are labeled as inferior, black children will feel inferior, and those feelings are likely to be the principal obstacle to educational achievement. Putting them in schools with white children will be an aid to their achievement only if: (1) they are at least as bright to begin with, (2) they are *treated* as though they are by their peers and by their teachers, and (3) if they do not experience substantial discrimination. Thus, integration carried out without regard for the psychological condition of the individual child and without regard for the social attitudes of both the students and teachers in the schools risks serious damage to certain children. Moreover, integration programs which take a few children out of ghetto neighborhoods in the morning and return them in the afternoon, effectively preclude the social ties through which children learn to live in a pluralistic society. Forced and temporary school associations may make racists out of children (both black and white) who hear their parents verbalize their doubts and fears as the integration issue boils through the community. The mutual insecurities felt by black children and white children toward each other in a newly integrated school never get worked out in the neighborhood play experiences in which youngsters "get inside" the personalities of one another.

Kenneth Clark, the distinguished black psychologist, has pointed out, however, that segregation in schools has never had any other more important purpose than "to remind blacks and whites that blacks had an inferior status in society." His solution is to "remove every vestige" of the old system, which means "maximum integration" in school systems everywhere, pushing out beyond district and municipal boundaries into white suburbs where necessary. Clark rejects the arguments of black "separatists" who, in his view, want to avoid being confronted by the challenges of a nonsegregated society and those of the social scientists who "argue through one route or another that desegregation of schools is not going to be very helpful." The challengers, he maintains, attack desegregation without providing evidence "that separate schools can be any less damaging now than in the past."[4]

BUSING TO ACHIEVE RACIAL BALANCE

The response of the nation to school integration programs up to 1969 was grudging acceptance in the face of increasing pressure by the courts to produce workable plans. In most parts of the South—where black population in many cities is scattered and segregation had been maintained by law in dual school systems—progress in integration

"Man, We Were Lucky—We Rode On Those Things Before Anyone Realized How Terrible They Are."

Reprinted with permission from Herblock's *State of the Union* (Simon & Schuster).

was accomplished by direct court orders. In other parts of the country, no easy solution could be applied because of segregated residential patterns.

Busing in many cities seemed the only solution, yet the logistical problems in some of the larger cities proved so awkward as to provide a ready-made excuse to delay such efforts. Moreover, busing children away from their neighborhoods proved to be as abhorrent to black parents as to white. In 1970 national polls reflected a near-majority among blacks opposed to busing plans and an overwhelming majority opposition among whites. A 1973 Gallup survey reported that a majority of Americans still favored public school integration, but only 5 percent—9 percent of blacks and 4 percent of whites—favored busing over other alternatives. Twenty-seven percent favored changes in school boundaries to permit more children from different economic and racial backgrounds to attend the same schools. Twenty-two percent felt that more low-income housing placed in middle-income neighborhoods would be the best course to achieve school integration. Of the blacks in the survey, 32 percent favored this method. Nineteen percent of whites and 9 percent of blacks opposed public school integration. The survey revealed that most of the opposition to busing apparently was based less on racism than on such concerns as its effect on local school taxes, sending children into strange (and perhaps hostile) neighborhoods, and the infringement on personal liberties. Only 27 percent of white parents in the North and 36 percent in the South indicated objection to having their children in schools where less than half of the pupils were black. But 63 percent in the North and 69 percent in the South objected to schools that had a majority of black students. In 1970 only 51 percent of parents in the North had felt this way. Thus, while the views of southern white parents have changed very little since 1970, the attitudes of northern parents have become more like those of southern parents.

Because of the strength of these attitudes at that time, many states passed or gave serious consideration to legislation that would bar state agencies from requiring busing as a local solution to integration. Few politicians could afford to support busing.

From 1968 onward, busing was the focal point of the school integration issue and it reached a peak of intensity in public reaction in 1971 and 1972. The issue was precipitated by the 1968 U.S. Supreme Court ruling in the *Green* v. *New Kent County* case,[5] that quick and substantial desegregation was imperative even if the remedy involved busing of students to schools in other neighborhoods. In the *Green* case, the court said that there should be massive mixing and that the racial make-up of each school should reflect that of the system. The Johnson administration promptly incorporated the substance of the *Green* decision in HEW guidelines designed to assist school systems in complying with court-ordered desegregation plans or in initiating their own. As a sanction, the HEW Office of Civil Rights could recommend a cut-off of federal funds to a noncomplying school district.

During the first year of his administration, President Nixon directed the attorney general and the secretary of HEW to develop revised guidelines; these reaffirmed the old ones except for school districts with *bona fide* educational and legal problems. The Nixon administration promptly applied this exception to thirty-one school districts in Mississippi which had resisted earlier pressures to integrate dual school systems. The president then sent Justice Department attorneys into the Court of Appeals to argue against desegregation in the Mississippi cases. In October of that year, however, the Supreme Court headed by Chief Justice Burger, who had been appointed by Mr. Nixon, declared that "the standard of allowing all deliberate speed for desegregation" (set by *Brown* v. *Board of Education* 15 years earlier) was "no longer constitutionally permissible." The Court went on to assert that "the obligation for every school is to terminate dual systems at once and to operate now and hereafter only unitary schools."[6]

Meanwhile, the U.S. Civil Rights Commission issued a statement on September 12, 1969, in which it charged that the administration's actions on school desegregation constituted "a major retreat in the struggle to achieve meaningful desegregation." The statement also accused the Nixon administration of issuing inaccurate and misleading information.

Meantime, a federal district court in North Carolina ordered a desegregation plan for Charlotte which involved massive busing of blacks to white schools. While that order was not received by the Supreme Court until April, 1971, the appeals process did not delay immediate implementation. The racial conflict which the court action set off in Charlotte seemed to bode ill for the future of involuntary busing plans. The Nixon administration commenced intensive work on plans to prevent any further forced busing. On March 24, 1970, the president announced his opposition to involuntary busing and his support for maintaining the neighborhood school. At the same time, he proposed to seek $1.5 billion from Congress to aid school districts in the implementation of desegregation plans.

Once again the Civil Rights Commission, whose chairman, Father Theodore Hesburgh, had been appointed by Mr. Nixon, criticized the statement as inadequate and overcautious. The commission pointed out that much segregation throughout the nation was traceable to the actions of government at all levels.[7] Several northern states had required school segregation by law or condoned it by policy until the 1940s and 1950s, while several others had been guilty of deliberate segregation by the placement of schools and boundary lines. Where school segregation resulted from residential patterns, government at all levels was directly or indirectly responsible. The report cited racial zoning ordinances, restrictive real state covenants, segregation expressly required in federal housing prorgams, and indirect influence on segregation patterns in federal highway and urban renewal programs. The situation the nation faced in school segregation was, therefore, "not accidental or purely *de facto*."[8]

Following upon his antibusing statement, the president directed the Office of Civil Rights in HEW to work with southern school districts in organizing citizen committees to insure that school openings in the fall would be peaceful. That year the proportion of blacks attending previously all-white schools rose from 18.4 to 38.1 percent.

The following April (1971), as the Nixon policies seemed to have allayed the fears of southern school officials, the Supreme Court authorized a lower court to use busing as a tool to end segregation.[9] In a March meeting with the attorney general and secretary of HEW, the president had ordered these officials "to be cooperative rather than coercive but to get the job done."[10] But when the HEW Office of Civil Rights came up with a desegregation plan for Austin, Texas which required extensive busing over strong local objections, Nixon announced (August 3, 1971) that the Austin court did not have to accept the HEW plan and that his administration henceforth would hold busing "to the minimum required by the law."

The next spring (March 1972), Mr. Nixon proposed a flat ban on busing for one year and a requirement that judges consider other ways of integrating schools before ordering busing. He urged Congress to outlaw involuntary busing as a means of achieving racial balance in schools. He also rcommended the inclusion of $2.5 billion in special aid to ghetto schools.

On March 29, the Civil Rights Commission declared that if enacted, the president's program "would work a major governmental retreat." And in May the commission issued the pamphlet, "Your Child and Busing," in which it stated flatly that "In rejecting busing in the racially segregated situation in which most Americans live today, we also reject integration."

Following the president's lead, Congress passed a bill on June 8, 1972, which delayed implementation of court desegregation orders on busing or transfer of students until all appeals were exhausted or until January 1, 1974. The bill also said that federal funds could be used for busing only if requested by the community, but that these funds could not be granted if the busing would risk the health, safety, or education of the children involved or would force attendance at inferior schools. Most federal judges ignored the new law. Justice Lewis Powell, a Nixon appointee, wrote a decision for the Supreme

Court in which he brushed aside the antibusing provision as not applicable to a case in Augusta, Georgia because the objective of busing there was to end segregation (long since declared unconstitutional), not to overcome "racial imbalance" which was the language of the legislation.

In April, 1973, the U.S. Court of Appeals in Washington, D.C. denied an administration request to halt court-ordered desegregation in cities of seventeen states. The Nixon administration had argued for the development of voluntary desegregation plans and against court-imposed busing in those districts.

Meanwhile, in Richmond, Virginia a plan approved by the federal district judge would have created one school system which included the city (70 percent black) and two adjacent counties which were 90 percent white. The plan involved busing about 78,000 of 100,000 pupils in the metropolitan area, but only 12,000 more than were already riding buses. A U.S. Circuit Court of Appeal had ruled that the district judge had exceeded his authority in requiring local governments to restructure themselves to achieve racial balance in their schools. The Appeals Court stayed implementation. When the case reached the Supreme Court, the Nixon administration joined the defendants in seeking disapproval of the Richmond plan. The Court divided 4–4 on the case with Justice Powell not participating, a result that left standing the ruling of the circuit court against the Richmond plan.[11]

In June, 1973 the Supreme Court ruled for the first time on a desegregation case involving a northern city. Denver, Colorado school authorities were charged with having created and maintained segregated schools. The defendants argued that whatever segregation that existed was due to residential patterns which the school system had nothing to do with developing. The High Court held 7–1 that the burden was on the Denver school board to prove that it had not deliberately segregated students by race in drawing school boundaries and in other actions. It further declared that if the authorities had pursued a policy of intentional segregation in a substantial part of the district, then the entire district must be included in a desegregation process. In addition, the Court made clear that it would apply equally rigorous desegregation standards to areas where racial separation was produced by social patterns as it had to areas where segregation was produced by law. Effective desegregation in Denver required a redrawing of school boundaries and a large-scale busing program.[12]

One of the toughest unresolved desegregation issues is white flight to independent suburban districts and to private schools. The Richmond city-county merger plan had attempted to provide a solution. A similar plan was proposed in Detroit, where a federal district judge ordered the merger of the city and the surrounding suburbs. The plan was approved in a 6–3 ruling by the Sixth Circuit Court of Appeals.

Since the tie vote in the Richmond case set no precedent on the issue of metropolitanwide application of court-ordered school integration plans, a decision upholding the Sixth Circuit Court in the Detroit case would open the way for remedies against the white exodus from the central cities, an opportunity that many city school districts would welcome. (A federal district court in Virginia in August, 1973, ordered private schools in the South to begin immediately accepting black pupils. This order, if upheld, could head off the other kind of white flight.) In July, 1974, however, the U.S. Supreme Court reversed the Sixth Circuit Court ruling that it could not approve an interdistrict remedy unless both the suburban and urban school districts were racially segregated because of constitutional violations. In a narrow 5–4 decision, the Court held that the lower courts had not presented any evidence that the suburban school districts were guilty of illegal segregation and so they could not be included against their will in a metropolitanwide integration plan.[13]

Current problems of desegregation are primarily *de facto* segregation which is the pattern in every urbanized area in the nation which means people segregating themselves by socioeconomic status. The Denver case laid to rest the spurious distinction between *de facto* and *de jure* segregation within school systems and mandated a systemwide desegregation process where deliberate governmental actions were responsible for school segregation. Since then, the Supreme Court has decided that a similar principle can be applied to metropolitan areas containing independent school districts only if all districts involved in an integration plan have violated the Constitution in deliberately maintaining segregated schools.

COMMUNITY CONTROL AND DECENTRALIZATION

Long before President Nixon reintroduced a neosegregationist policy in his position against busing, impatient black leaders were urging community control of institutions in ghetto areas with public schools as a prime target. In their book, *Black Power*, Stokely Carmichael and Charles V. Hamilton argued that:

Black parents should seek as their goal the actual control of the public schools in their community; hiring and firing of teachers, selection of teaching materials, demonstration of standards, etc. . . . The principal and as many of the teachers as possible should be black [so that] [T]he children will be able to see their kind in positions of leadership and authority . . . The fact is in this day and time, it is crucial that race be taken into account in determining policy of this sort. Some people will . . . view this as reverse segregation or as 'racism.' It is not. It is emphasizing race in a positive way; not to subordinate or rule over others but to overcome the effects of centuries in which race has been used to the detriment of the black man.[14]

Between 1967 and 1970, many black leaders, both militant and moderate, and many white liberals were advocating a shift in emphasis from integration to quality education in neighborhood schools. The white liberals were disillusioned by failures to make significant headway in integration. Black parents and community leaders were disgusted and impatient with the duplicity and delay of whites and with the poor condition of their schools. Many were ready to give up on integration and improve the schools in their communities if they could get the resources and the authority. Demands for community control usually entail a corollary demand for the decentralization of public bureaucracies.

Community control is, as Carmichael and Hamilton suggest, a pattern of organization in which the local community through its elected representatives has control over programs, services, and decisions which affect the residents of the neighborhood and its institutions. Effective community control requires a substantial delegation of authority by a higher governing body and in most cases also requires some form of districting to delineate the boundaries of the community. Community control of schools, in the rare cases where it has occurred, has involved the transfer of the decision-making authority to locally elected school boards in areas of personnel selection, curriculum design, and budget allocations.

Decentralized school systems typically retain in the central board all decision-making authority on personnel, budget, and curriculum, while the powers of local boards may range from advisory functions to delegated authority with final approval by the central board. Community control advocates often settle for forms of decentralization that permit local participation in educational decision-making.

Although the concept of community control described in terms of local self-government is as old as the nation itself, such demands by militant ghetto leaders have been viewed by whites as new and threatening. When ghetto leaders in Ocean Hill–Brownsville, Detroit,

Washington, D.C., and other areas called for locally controlled (and even separate) school districts, they were actually demanding what whites already had in their suburban communities. But the demand of blacks for community control often constitutes a very substantial threat to the stakes whites have in their ownership of private property and their positions in the public institutions of the ghettos. For example, whites hold the most important positions in the public school, police, and welfare bureaucracies and control new jobs that open up in those agencies. The opposition of whites to community control is largely a defense of those stakes.

As black leaders slashed away at the ties which bound their community institutions to the larger white-dominated system, they discovered (sometimes to their amazement) the extent of the stakes whites have in black areas. They also discovered how painful it was for whites to give up those stakes and how difficult it was for a relatively powerless minority to gain anything approaching full control of white-owned or sponsored institutions in their communities.

Seen from the perspective of local power politics, community control of schools and the inseparable issue of decentralization have also been areas of struggle for new bases of power for aspiring community leaders. As many analysts have pointed out, the issue of quality education for children has not always been the central issue in these struggles. Thus, the power struggle of aspiring community leaders was matched in most cases by the incentives of upwardly mobile parents who saw the schools as a means for economic improvement and social advancement. Many supporters of community control were also concerned with practical matters such as overcrowding, discipline, and hostility between teachers and students and between students of different racial and social backgrounds. Thus, the ghetto parents who have been among the leaders in efforts to gain local control of schools have been motivated by values very similar to those of the earlier upwardly mobile white ethnic groups as well as to those of their white middle-class contemporaries who have moved to the suburbs.

In the big city school systems, the conflict between whites and blacks (and other minorities) has been over the issue of how the schools can simultaneously serve the needs of minority and disadvantaged groups and those of the middle and upper-class whites. Where minorities have appeared to gain influence in the school system, whites have feared that the schools were no longer serving their children and that the values and life styles of an "underclass" would become predominant. It is this fear more than anything else that has impelled whites to leave the cities or to place their children in private schools. White fears have been compounded as minorities (especially blacks) employed tactics of aggressive protest to challenge educational bureaucracies.

In recent years dissatisfied blacks and Hispanic-Americans in some cities have taken to challenging predominantly white teaching staffs who are unionized. The union teachers depend upon union leadership to protect their job rights and to improve their wages and working conditions. The teachers' unions in turn depend upon the central school administration· to carry out bargaining procedures which generally yield predictable results. The relationships between the teachers' unions and the central administration puts the unions at odds with demands for community control, especially on issues which touch upon teacher transfers and job security. Teachers' unions sometimes support decentralization but not community control of school administration.

The intensity and persistence of the community control issue appears to be related to the size of the minority population in cities. In general, the smaller the percentage of blacks in a city, the greater the demand for community control. One explanation is that an important objective of community control is to have minority teachers and principals in predominantly minority schools. Thus, where minority students and teachers are already a majority, this demand tends to dissipate. In cities where this particular demand has been met, the pressure for community control tends to recede. When demands for community control were at their strongest, however, the conflicts were hard-fought and often bitter. Witness, for example, the turmoil that resulted from the attempt of community leaders to gain control of their schools in the Ocean Hill–Brownsville district of New York City, and in Detroit.

Ocean Hill–Brownsville

This three-year long dispute was mainly between the governing board of the Ocean Hill–Brownsville experimental school district in New York City and the United Federation of Teachers. The New York City school system is the largest in the nation with more than 900 schools and 1.1 million students, with black and Puerto Rican students outnumbering whites two to one. The exodus of whites included movement to the suburbs as well as a substantial shift to private schools within the city. By 1967 when the dispute broke out, whites had controlled the public schools long after the black and Hispanic students were in a majority.

The Ocean Hill–Brownsville case illustrates how the teachers' union responded to the issue of community control in New York and how the union promoted instead a decentralization plan that was more favorable to union interests. Seniority rights and rating systems which bore up promotions and assignments to particular schools were central issues.

From the standpoint of minority leaders, when minority enroll- ment in schools reaches a majority, black leaders have a basis for challenging white control. The community control issue arose in New York City when community leaders in a section of Harlem (later to be included in the Ocean Hill–Brownsville district) objected to the location of a new school because it would be comprised entirely of black students. Demands that white students be bused to the school were fruitless, and as the debate progressed, someone suggested the idea of demanding community control of the school as a way of in- suring a quality program. It was agreed that if this objective could be achieved, integration demands would be dropped. In response, the Board of Education created several experimental community districts of which Ocean Hill–Brownsville was one. The decision-making authority of the new districts was left vague, but a community advisory board created by the central school administration was to be consulted on matters such as the selection of administrative personnel.

The Ocean Hill–Brownsville district contained eight schools with 9,000 students enrolled in them. It was an impoverished area whose population was 70 percent black and 25 percent Puerto Rican; 56 per- cent of the residents had lived in the area less than ten years; 68 percent had not completed school; more than half earned less than $5,000 per year.

Following upon a long-standing interest in promoting community participation in local institutions (see Chapter 9), the Ford Foun- dation awarded a planning grant to a group of parents representing the schools in the area. The funds were used for the development of a governing board of parents, teachers and principals elected by their respective groups. This governing board and an administrator was to make all decisions on personnel, curriculum, and fiscal allocations in the district.

The United Federation of Teachers of New York City (UFT) recog- nized that the governing board's scope of authority over personnel decisions could force the union to deal directly with the district in contract bargaining and that a citywide precedent could deprive the UFT of citywide bargaining power. Also, the union feared that the community governing board might try to replace white teachers with blacks and Puerto Ricans, older teachers with younger ones, or conservative teachers with radicals. In the face of such threats, the UFT regarded Ocean Hill–Brownsville as a critical battleground.

The new governing board speedily selected a black administrator as well as several black principals. These appointments were made over the objections of union teachers on the governing board.

The rift between the UFT and the board widened following a citywide teachers strike when the UFT barred union teachers from serving on the district board. Subsequently the UFT joined the Council of Supervisory Associations (an organization of school administrators) in challenging the local board's appointments of five principals.

Meanwhile, Mayor Lindsay had persuaded the state legislature to increase educational aid to New York City, provided that the city could work out a decentralization plan for the schools. Subsequently, a decentralization planning committee, appointed by the mayor, proposed decentralized, nearly autonomous districts to be run by a board of local residents. Ocean Hill–Brownsville was to be regarded as a demonstration of the effects of community control on the quality of education in the schools. When the Ford Foundation planning funds were used up by Ocean Hill–Brownsville, the Foundation declined to provide additional funds unless either the Board of Education or the legislature gave the board official recognition. No such recognition was granted and so the governing board was still operating under the vague authority previously delegated to it by the Board of Education. Under these circumstances, it was left in a seriously weakened position *vis-a-vis* the UFT. Friction between the governing board and union teachers led to the summary dismissal (in May, 1968) of thirteen teachers and six administrators. The UFT protested that the nineteen had been dismissed without due process. Meanwhile, a local court ruled that the five principals hired by the board the previous summer had been illegally appointed. A further blow to the authority of the governing board occurred when the central administration ordered the nineteen dismissed staff members to return to their schools. The UFT also insisted that formal charges be brought against the nineteen and backed the demand with a strike against the district schools. When the Board of Education agreed to the UFT demand, the governing board retaliated by dismissing 350 teachers who participated in the strike.

In the midst of the dispute, the state legislature passed a decentralization bill which authorized the Board of Education to develop a decentralization plan; permitted Mayor Lindsay to appoint four additional members to the board; gave the legislature the option to review the board's plan; declared Ocean Hill–Brownsville and two other demonstration districts to be local school districts; and gave the Board of Education the power to delegate to the districts any powers and duties required to operate them.

In September, a two-day strike got all of the dismissed teachers reinstated, but the Ocean Hill governing board, which had not been a party to the settlement, refused to assign them to classrooms. The UFT promptly called a second strike which resulted in the removal of the governing board by the state education commissioner and the jailing of UFT officials.

The second strike ended when the Board of Education lifted the suspension of the Ocean Hill board and once more ordered the ousted teachers returned to the district schools with arrangements for observers to report on any harassment of returning teachers. But the trouble continued and after a third UFT strike lasting five weeks, the State Board of Regents set up a trusteeship for the district and a State Supervisory Commission for the city school system. The governing board remained under suspension until March, 1969, and the ousted teachers returned to classroom assignments in the district.

The School Decentralization Act of 1969. The UFT's victory over the Ocean Hill–Brownsville governing board effectively killed aspirations of community control of the schools. The focus then shifted back to the unfinished business of decentralization. When the Board of Education failed to agree on a plan which the legislature could accept, the UFT stepped in and negotiated a decentralization bill with the Republican leadership of the city. This bill became the Decentralization Act of 1969.

The new legislation permitted the city school system to be divided into districts with locally elected boards empowered to appoint a superintendent and other supervisory personnel from central eligibility lists. The boards controlled promotions, but involuntary transfers had to be heard for cause. Tenure and other rights of professional and administrative staff were protected. The central board retained authority in negotiating union contracts and in preparing the budget. Districts whose students ranked in the bottom 45 percent on citywide reading tests could hire any teacher who passed the National Teacher Examination with an average score or better, thus giving districts the leeway to employ teachers of their own ethnic background.

Although the community control concept lost out to administrative decentralization, the Decentralization Act permitted the central administration to delegate to the local boards sufficient powers for a considerable degree of local control. What the legislation tried to hedge against was a take-over by local groups who might use the districts for self-serving bases of power or corruption.

The Detroit Case

A battle over community control and decentralization in Detroit in the late 1960s offers the contrasting case of a major school system in a city in which blacks were rapidly approaching a voting majority. The conflicts in Detroit schools over integration and decentralization, however, paralleled those of New York.

But, by the mid-sixties the threat of integration had caused many whites to leave the city. Moreover, voters had repeatedly rejected tax increases for school improvement, and the worse the schools got, the deeper public dissatisfaction became, especially among middle-class blacks.

Beginning in 1948, a Labor-Democratic party coalition had dominated Michigan politics with its base in Detroit; by 1960 the coalition included Detroit's black leadership. This coalition controlled the Detroit school system. Due to the influence of Detroit blacks in the coalition, the percentage of black teachers and administrators (42 and 38 percent respectively) was higher than that of any city, which explains why there was less trouble with the teachers' union and the supervisors' association in decentralization and community control issues than in New York. It also explains why the Detroit blacks were more willing than New York blacks to settle for decentralization over community control.

A peculiarity of the Detroit situation was that the commitment to integration came more from the liberal wing of the Board of Education than from black groups. Although most blacks (except the separatists) were committed to the *principle* of integration, they did not favor desegregation schemes that involved extensive busing among school districts. Most Detroiters, both black and white, wanted at least the option of having their children in their own neighborhood schools. A long history of racial conflict in Detroit, including the bloody 1967 riot, was behind much of the fear of massive racial mixing in the schools. Also, neighborhood homogeneity along racial and ethnic lines was very important to Detroiters.

Community Control. In 1968 a black Detroit legislator, whose constituency was a poverty-stricken ghetto area, introduced a bill that would have divided the city school system into sixteen independent school districts, each with its own tax base. The goal of the bill was to put blacks in control of black schools and whites in control of white schools. The bill was defeated by opposition from the Detroit civic and school establishment and by most black groups.

Within a year, however, black leaders in Detroit organized Citizens for Community Control. The Ocean Hill–Brownsville struggle was a source of inspiration; conferences on community control listened to the leaders of the embattled New York district. A proposal for locally elected community boards and regional high school boards emerged from these discussions but was never given serious consideration by the Detroit Board of Education, although it helped arouse public interest in decentralization.

Decentralization. Shortly thereafter, an influential black state senator from Detroit* successfully sponsored a bill in the legislature (Act 244) which authorized the creation of seven to eleven regions with elected boards and a delegate from each to serve on a central board. The regions could make their own budgets within central board allocations; determine curricula, testing, and use of educational facilities; hire regional superintendents from central board lists; and control school employees, subject to a review by the central board. Collective bargaining was left with the central board; rights of transfer, tenure, seniority, and other teacher benefits were protected.

The Detroit Board of Education. Meanwhile, the Board of Education was considering several decentralization plans, some of which would meet federal integration standards and some which would not. The plans which attracted wide public support in both the black and white communities were those which proposed racially and ethnically homogeneous districts. The NAACP urged that consideration be given to areas with a prevailing sense of community. A black separatist leader whose views were widely respected among Detroit blacks wanted decentralization to guarantee black control of black schools. Whites favored maintaining the community identity of the neighborhood schools: integration was acceptable so long as their children

*Senator Coleman Young, who was later elected as Detroit's first black mayor in 1973.

were not bused and not too many blacks were transferred to their schools. Thus, Act 244 was not to be a vehicle for integration. In spite of the propensity to community schools, a majority of the seven-member Board of Education stuck to the federal integration guidelines and adopted a decentralization plan which increased both integration and busing.

A white group called the Citizens Committee for Better Education (CCBE) was formed to fight implementation of the board plan. The Detroit Federation of Labor reluctantly supported the board plan because of a commitment to integration. The black establishment, in spite of strong inclinations toward community control, supported the board's plan, although the separatists did not. In June, 1970, the blue-collar white neighborhoods rallied around a successful CCBE campaign to recall the four members of the Board of Education who had voted for the integration plan.

Shortly thereafter, the legislature voted almost unanimously to replace Act 244 with new legislation (Act 48) which mandated eight regions in place of the seven which the Board of Education had created under Act 244. District lines were drawn by a special Governor's Boundary Commission which, in accordance with the act, would "enable students to attend a school of preference" and in the event of overcrowding to give priority to students living nearest the school. In effect, the legislation repealed the board's plan. The Boundary Commission, composed of two whites (a city councilman and a professor of law) and a black clergyman, *agreed that integration was not to be the goal.* The commission's plan kept existing school districts nearly intact and avoided changes in the school feeder patterns. That fall, Detroit voters chose regional boards of education and at-large candidates for the central board that gave a substantial edge to the antibusing and anti-integration forces.

The Federal Courts Move on Integration.   Shortly after the elections, the federal courts intervened in response to black establishment groups who were disappointed by their failure to gain a stronger position in the new regions. Prior to the school elections that fall (1970), the U.S. Sixth Circuit Court of Appeals had ruled that the legislature could not negate an integration effort of a local school board and turned the case back to the federal district court in Detroit for hearings on a new integration plan. The Detroit Board of Education, which at that time (prior to the elections) had four gubernatorial appointees to replace the members who also had been recalled, offered a "magnet school" plan which was conditionally accepted by the court. After an unsatisfactory trial in the fall of 1971, federal District Court Judge Stephen J. Roth ordered a plan which involved busing between the city schools (which were then 66 percent black) and fifty-two suburban districts (which were 3 percent black). It was this plan which was struck down by the U.S. Supreme Court in July, 1974 after having received approval of the U.S. Sixth Circuit Court of Appeals. In denying the existence of grounds for involving the sub- urban communities in the integration plan, the Court nevertheless argeed that the Detroit system itself was unconstitutionally segre- gated, and so the case was sent back to the federal district court for consideration on a Detroit plan for desegregating the urban system. It remains to be seen how a new plan for integrating Detroit's schools will affect the decentralized pattern of regional districts.

ALTERNATIVES TO COMMUNITY CONTROL

A Metropolitan School District

In the view of some educational planners, a metropolitan school dis- trict such as Judge Roth suggested in Detroit could be an appropriate step in upgrading ghetto schools and providing a realistic basis for integration. A pioneering model was the Boston-area Metropolitan Council for Educational Opportunities (METCO), a voluntary pro- gram formed by five Boston suburbs in 1966–1967 to bus 240 chil- dren from inner-city ghetto neighborhoods to their schools. METCO was entirely financed by a $239 million grant from the U.S. Office of Education and the Carnegie Corporation; therefore, it cost the sub- urbs practically nothing. The black children were selected by the receiving school system for their academic potential on the basis of scholastic records supplied by the Boston School Department.

The METCO program, initiated by suburban and black leaders, had mixed results. It took some of the best students out of the already troubled ghetto schools and confronted them with adjustments to an affluent suburban culture from which some of them they could not fully benefit. There is no reliable evidence, however, of the program's effect on the students. Operation Exodus, another voluntary Boston program organized by black parents, was shown by Professor James G. Teele to have had positive effects on the reading scores of par- ticipating elementary students. Teele suggested that voluntary attend- ance and parental interest were the main factors in motivating the children in academic improvement.

Peter Schrag, the author of *Village School Downtown*,[15] taking the METCO program as a model, has also urged the metropolitanization of city and suburban school districts. He has suggested a single metropolitan school district based upon a single property tax. A metropolitan school board would be elected from districts in the region, would serve long terms, and would appoint a general superintendent to be responsible for central administration. It could create regional high schools that could serve several thousand students with optimally staffed academic and training programs. It could also operate specialized schools to meet the needs of the exceptional and the handicapped.

Schrag's plan would divide the metropolitan system into "neighborhood subdistricts" of 50,000 people (about 10,000 school-age children), each to elect its own school committee, and in consultation with the central administration, each would have the authority over local curriculum and educational policy. Each district would receive a standard per-pupil allocation of funds for instructional facilities and materials. Districts would receive a cash bonus for pupils who chose to enroll from other districts: a plan intended to give substance to an open enrollment policy and add an element of competition among districts.*

The Community School Concept

For as long as anyone can remember, public schools in America have been more or less centers of community activities outside the regular school program. In any case, the notion that the schools ought to function as community centers is at least as old as the days when the country schoolhouse served as a local meeting place. John Dewey was a strong advocate of community-centered schools organized to provide

---

*This aspect of Schrag's plan mimics the voucher system which has been tried in a few school districts since the Office of Education adopted it for experimental purposes. The most publicized voucher experiment has been in Alum Rock Union School District in San José, California where in 1973, 4,000 pupils in 6 out of 24 districts' schools were freely choosing where to enroll in participating schools. An interesting account of the Alum Rock experiment appeared in the June 4, 1973, *Wall Street Journal*. It is noteworthy that the Alum Rock community is predominantly Mexican-American and that school officials were primarily interested in the OE program as a means of decentralizing educational decision-making to the level of the parents. By contrast, New Rochelle backed out of a commitment to vouchers apparently out of concern for the "stability" of the schools. Moreover, many parents objected to the busing feature of the proposed program. New Rochelle has a substantial black population.

educational opportunities for adults as well as children. In most cities, high schools have a long tradition of the "night school" for people who wanted to learn English, art, mathematics, or a vocational skill. Countless immigrants have qualified for citizenship in such programs.

In Flint, Michigan, with the sustained assistance of the Mott Foundation, all public schools operate as community centers. Ever since the decade of the 1930s when the foundation first began to support "community outreach" programs, the schools have added recreational programs, health and social services, youth meetings, senior-citizen affairs, cultural events and even job counseling and placement. Their success is reflected in the strong public support of the schools: voters approved (as of 1973) twelve consecutive tax issues over a twenty-year period. In Flint, schools contributed to a sense of community, and so the issue of community control hardly arises.

The Educational Park as Community School

One solution which has not been fully enough explored by any large school system is the educational park designed at a scale to reflect the racial and social mix in the city and, at the same time, to incorporate educational, recreational, health, library and other facilities. A city of one million, for example, would require twelve to fifteen such campuses to accommodate in each a cross-section of the city's population. The campuses could occupy unused city spaces, each large enough to avoid crowding of students. Some of the campuses could be located over freeways and would therefore occupy space that could readily be separated into areas for different kinds of use. For example, the facilities of a high school and a two-year college might be placed at one end, thus enhancing the functional relationships between the two. Elementary areas and especially kindergarten and pre-school areas could be remote from the upper grades and the adult segments of the campus and could be designed on a scale suitable for young children.

The campuses could have a range of community facilities, programs, and services that would bring them within easy access to every resident. These might include a health clinic (complete with diagnostic service and preventive care), a library and information center (or series of such centers to serve different kinds of information and research needs), and recreational facilities which would be designed physically and programmatically to serve the entire community seven days a week.

The campuses would be located to take maximum advantage of the transportation networks and facilities ranging from mass transportation and freeways to bicycle trails and pedestrian walkways. A linear campus design of up to a mile in length could permit easy access by foot, bicycle, or motorbikes. Automobile, bus, and rail access could not only provide entry at several points into each campus, but would provide linkages among the different campuses. Such linkages would make it both feasible and desirable for each campus to have one or more major facilities and/or programs that could not be provided in all of them.

The educational park concept is utilized in a few places. But with all the agonizing conflict over desegregation, rising educational costs, and the search for community, no one has seriously proposed the abandonment of the neighborhood school to be replaced by an educational park that is in scale with the great metropolis of the present day. There is a need for the preservation of community through institutions which offer high quality education at all levels, a need for ready access to vital community facilities, and a need for contact among the various and diverse elements of the society. The retreat into neighborhood institutions which were in scale with a less complex and demanding world, the retreat into the socially comfortable isolation of an earlier day, and the attempt to create socially homogeneous cocoons for children in small-scale suburban schools are not appropriate answers to the demands of a sophisticated modern society.

A restructured educational system must be thought of as both physically and socially integrating. The public education system of the future must be open to the entire society, not only to children of "school age." The world of the future demands that education (and for that matter training) be a continuing process. Our city school systems should provide such opportunities on a basis that fully meets the educational needs of our society. A student attending school in an educational park of the scale and diversity suggested here would be exposed to opportunities reflecting the real world of creativity and work. Imagine the child of the upwardly mobile middle-class suburban family whose inclination is to be an automobile mechanic (an interesting and well-paid occupation) but whose parents would prefer for him or her to go into an occupation of greater prestige and earning power. In the educational park the opportunity would exist for the child to follow his or her own inclinations because an automobile mechanics course would be readily available. The ghetto child of high talent in the setting of the educational park would be exposed to every kind of educational opportunity and would be encouraged to choose any career or any area of concentration without artificial restraints. The same opportunities would be available to every member of the community without respect to age, race, economic condition, sex, or religion.

Social mix in the educational system is important to the maintenance of the democratic ethic in a society which encourages the rise of a natural aristocracy. Social mix in an educational system which is dedicated to the maintenance of high standards is a long step toward assuring equality of educational opportunities which in turn assures that talented children born into poverty have their chance and that the less talented find satisfying and productive places in the system. Public schools designed to assure social mix in an educational setting in which quality is the chief goal would reaffirm our dedication to democratic ideals, to equality of educational opportunity, and thus to the appropriateness of merit as the just basis of one's career and position in society.

As we have suggested in discussing alternatives to community control, the trend in the public school systems is to remake the schools into community institutions emphasizing quality educational opportunities. To achieve this goal, it will be necessary to expand school districts to encompass metropolitan areas so that a cross-section of the area population attends each school complex. Thus, the campuses will be large enough to be appropriate locations for community services, and fiscal disparities will disappear within the single metropolitan district.

A major problem to which the metropolitanwide reorganization of school districts would be addressed is the fiscal disparity among the local school districts which has grown more serious as urban areas have developed more and more autonomous municipalities, each with its own property tax base. While suburban school districts do not necessarily follow municipal boundary lines, they have followed a similar pattern of proliferation.

FISCAL INEQUITIES AMONG SCHOOL DISTRICTS

Every state except Hawaii delegates public education to local school districts which depend for their support largely, and in some cases wholly, upon local property taxes. If a district happens to have a substantial amount of high value taxable property within its boundaries, a low tax rate can produce sufficient revenues for quality schools and fine educational programs. Districts that happen to be poor in taxable properties have the choice of high tax rates to support quality education or lower rates and correspondingly lower quality schools. Typically, localities across the nation pay more than half the cost of public schools out of the local property tax; the states pay on the average about 40 percent; and the federal government contributes about 10 percent. Hawaii has avoided this problem by creating one school district for the entire state and supporting all public schools from a common tax base. Other states have tried to "equalize" property taxation by requiring common assessment standards to all properties within their jurisdictions. Because tax-base disparities among districts are the result of residential and industrial development that bear little or no relationship to school district boundaries, most states have tried to equalize aid to education through proportionately higher state aid to districts with below average assessed value per pupil. It is also common practice for states to give basic grants to all local districts regardless of wealth. Except for the state-wide school district in Hawaii, none of the measures described above have effectively resolved disparities among the districts. (See Figure 12–1.)

Although innumerable studies of the inequities among districts have underscored the consequences of the situation, until recently, remedies were seldom taken seriously by state legislatures, and court actions failed to address the central issue. In *McInnis* v. *Shapiro* (1968) a three-judge federal court in Illinois rejected an appeal for statewide reapportionment of public school monies based upon educational needs.[16] That decision was upheld the following year by the U.S. Supreme Court in *McInnis* v. *Ogilvie*.[17] Subsequently, a Virginia suit against the state's school financing system was rejected on the basis of the *McInnis* decision (*Burrus* v. *Wilkerson*). In both cases the courts considered the "educational need" concept as vague and therefore nonjusticiable.

Then in quick succession over a six-month period in 1971 and 1972, the state courts of California and New Jersey and the federal courts in Minnesota and Texas ruled that the local property tax was in these cases shown to be discriminatory against the poor and therefore unconstitutional (under the Fourteenth Amendment clause requiring equal protection of the laws) as a method of financing public schools.[18]

The California Supreme Court in August, 1971, in a 6–1 decision in *Serrano*, ruled unconstitutional local property taxes which pro-

FIGURE 12–1   The Gap Between Rich and Poor Schools

State by State Ratio of Assessed Property Valuation per Pupil in School District with the Largest Figure to That in District with Smallest Figure, 1968–69.

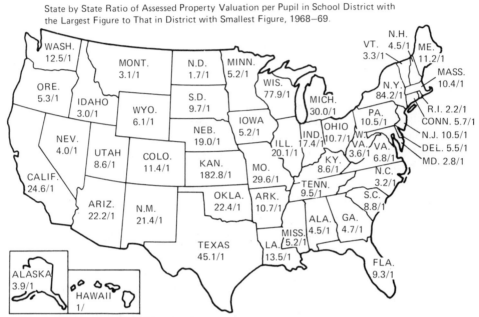

1/Property tax revenues not used to support education in Hawaii.

SOURCE: President's Commission on School Finance, Review of Existing State School Finance Programs, Vol. II, 1972.

duced wide disparities in per capita revenues among school districts. The court held that such disparities between rich and poor were unconstitutionally discriminatory and that the disparities rendered "the quality of a child's education a function of the wealth of his parents and neighbors." The California court noted that affluent districts are in a position to provide high-quality education while paying lower taxes than the poor districts. The court in this case was confronted with a comparison of two districts, one of which contained a high income population and high-value commercial properties and the other adjacent one populated by poor people with relatively low-value taxable property. The California case went to the heart of the matter of governmental intent. The defense argued *de facto* discrimination on the grounds of accidental distribution of residential and industrial development. The court disagreed:

> Indeed, we find the case unusual in the extent to which govern-
> mental action *is* the cause of the wealth classifications. The school
> funding scheme is mandated in every detail by the California Con-
> stitution and statutes. Although private residential and commercial
> patterns may be partly responsible for the distribution of assessed
> valuation throughout the State, such patterns are shaped and hard-
> ened by zoning ordinances and other governmental land-use controls
> which promote economic exclusivity. . . . Governmental action drew
> the school district boundary lines, thus determining how much local
> wealth each district would contain.[19]

Following the California example in *Serrano*, federal courts made
similar rulings in Minnesota in October, 1971, and in Texas in
December. A few weeks later, in 1972, a state court in New Jersey
held that the state's educational financing system was in violation of
both the state and national constitutions. New Jersey and a few other
states have clauses in their constitutions which guarantee the right of
an education to every citizen. By 1973 suits challenging the property
tax base for support of local schools were pending in thirty-one states.

The decision in the Minnesota case (*Van Dusartz* v. *Hatfield*) from
a federal court was based primarily on the *Serrano* ruling:

> Plainly put, the rule is that the level of spending for a child's edu-
> cation may not be a function of wealth other than the wealth of
> the State as a whole. For convenience we shall refer to this as the
> principle of 'fiscal neutrality,' a reference previously adopted in
> Serrano. . . . This is not a simple instance in which a poor man is
> inspired by his lack of funds. Here the property is that of a govern-
> mental unit that the state itself has defined and commissioned.[20]

Thus, "accidental" *de facto* discrimination was again rejected as a
defense, and Minnesota was held responsible for the fiscal disparities
among the school districts and municipalities it created.

The *Rodriguez* case in Texas showed a variation (in 1967–1968)
among seven San Antonio school districts ranging from an assessed
valuation of $5,429 per pupil in Alamo Heights to an assessed valu-
ation of $45,095 per pupil in Edgewood, while property taxes as
a percent of market value were highest in Edgewood and lowest in
Alamo Heights. Yet Alamo Heights could raise only $21 per pupil,
while Edgewood could raise $543. The decision of the federal
district court took note that the fiscal system supporting schools
subsidized the wealthy at the expense of the poor. In *Rodriguez*,
the defense argued that the state could discriminate so long as
the federal government made up the difference. The court re-
torted that federal aid did not compensate for state discrimination,

and in any event the court asked, why should the acts of other governmental units excuse local districts from the discriminatory consequences of state law?

The New Jersey case (*Robinson* v. *Cahill*) was decided by the state superior court (January, 1972) on grounds similar to the other three except in one important respect: it ruled that although the current state financing plan could provide nearly equal funding to local districts, it still failed to meet the constitutional test of equal protection because poor districts would have to levy higher taxes than would wealthy ones in order to raise the same revenues. The New Jersey court gave the legislature until January, 1973, to enact a non-discriminatory system of taxation, otherwise it would redistribute the state's minimum grants earmarked for wealthy districts to the poor districts. In April, 1973, the New Jersey Supreme Court upheld the decision of the lower state court.

Since all four court rulings based their decisions on the Fourteenth Amendment guarantee of the equal protection of the laws in the U.S. Constitution, they were subject to appeal to the U.S. Supreme Court. The decision of the U.S. Supreme Court was handed down in the *Rodriguez* case in March, 1973. In a 5–4 ruling, the Court decided that the equal protection clause did not extend to methods of financing local schools, that the complexity of the issue placed it beyond the competency of the judges to decide in substance, and that while "the need is apparent for reform in tax systems which may well have relied too long and too heavily on the local property tax," education is not among the fundamental rights guaranteed by the Constitution. Moreover, Justice Powell argued that the Constitution did not require "absolute equality or precisely equal advantages." The Court also noted that there was considerable dispute among educational experts and social scientists as to whether equal financial expenditure results in equal education, and that the Court lacked both the expertise and the familiarity with local problems that are necessary in making wise decisions with respect to the raising and disposition of public revenues. The Court argued that the object of the discrimination was not well enough defined, for example, poor families often live in both rich and poor districts. Echoing an article written by Daniel P. Moynihan in *The Public Interest* (1972),[21] Justice Powell observed that when the experts disagreed, "the judiciary is well advised to refrain from interposing on the states' inflexible constitutional restraints that could circumscribe or handicap . . . continued research and experimentation." However, Justice Stewart Potter, although voting with the majority, referred to the school finance system as "chaotic and unjust." The Court concluded that the issue of providing the fiscal basis for equality of educational opportunity lay entirely with the states and their localities. In reconciling *Rodriguez* with *Brown* v. *Board of Education* (which had held that "[t]he opportunity of an education must be made available to all on equal terms"), the court said in *Rodriguez* that this principle applied only to race, not to tax inequality.

The effect of the *Rodriguez* decision was to take the pressure off the states to reform fiscal inequities among school districts. The corollary effect was to place the responsibility for reform squarely on the states, and in doing so, the Court took care to declare that its action was not "to be viewed as placing its judicial imprimatur on the status quo."

Thus, shortly after the *Rodriguez* decision, the Court left standing the ruling of the New Jersey courts on the grounds that *Rodriguez* did not bar the lower federal courts or the state courts from contrary decisions that were based solely on state constitutions. The importance of the Court's refusal to review the New Jersey case was that it made explicit its admonition (in *Rodriguez*) that the states should move individually.

There is evidence of a growing recognition in the states of the injustices of the existing system of school financing. Although many studies of school finance systems which cropped up after 1971 were undertaken in anticipation of unfavorable court decisions, a momentum of reform seems to have built up that holds promise of outlasting the dampening effects the *Rodriguez* decision may have had. By 1973 nearly every state had one or more groups working on the problem, and there were fifty-two court cases pending in thirty-one states on the issue.

For example, the Minnesota legislature has revised its school formula to the satisfaction of plaintiffs in *Van Dusartz* who then dropped their suit. Ohio has made substantial changes in its state aid to schools, although according to Governor John J. Gilligan, the action did not go far enough. The Fleishman Commission in New York has recommended that the state assume the full costs of public education from a uniform statewide property tax. In 1972 a panel appointed by federal District Court Judge Roth in Detroit recommended that the state collect all school taxes in the city and suburban school districts as part of his metropolitan desegregation plan. Also in the same year, the Michigan Supreme Court ruled that the school finance system in the state was illegal and challenged the legislature to come up with a new plan. The following year, the legislature adopted a plan which limited state aid to wealthy districts and provided for proportionate increases to poorer ones. The Michigan plan was a compromise between the advocates of straight-out state support with state-levied taxes and those who feared that giving up the local property tax might lead to a loss of local control of schools. The desire to retain local control of the schools is one of the most often cited reasons for the widespread reluctance to give up the local property tax.

In Connecticut, a Governor's Commission on Tax Reform recommended that the state standardize assessments in all towns, establish a common tax formula which would apply to all localities, and provide a mechanism for equitable distribution of revenues among school districts. Although the governor supported the commission's recommendations, the legislature had not taken any action by 1974.

California, in the wake of *Serrano* (which like the New Jersey case was based on a provision in the state constitution for equal education), adopted a $1.1 billion tax reform school aid bill designed to increase the state's contribution to local school districts from 35 to 50 percent over a period of several years.

PROPOSALS AT THE NATIONAL LEVEL

President Nixon indicated in 1972 that his administration was studying alternative proposals for a national sales or "value-added" tax to provide new federal support for schools. Approximately two-thirds of the revenue from this source would be distributed to states on a one-for-two matching basis. The plan contained a condition that no local or state property be used to support the operating costs of public schools. The president submitted the plan to the Advisory Commission on Intergovernmental Relations for detailed study. The commission had recommended in 1969 that the states assume responsibility for financing schools.

In Congress, Senators Walter Mondale (Democrat-Minnesota) and Adlai Stevenson III (Democrat-Illinois) proposed that $5 billion be distributed annually among the states and school districts to reduce inequities and to relieve pressure on the local property tax. Senator Muskie proposed a federal subsidy to the states for property tax relief of the low-income elderly.

Most observers saw the U.S. Supreme Court's decision in the *Rodriguez* case as more of a setback than an end to reform. Still, it is impossible yet to foresee what effect it will have on the momentum that has built up for reform. The decision was an outright rejection of the notion that the national Constitution guarantees equality of educational opportunity. But the decision also recognized the injustices of the existing system. Thus, the decision may have avoided forcing a political decision upon the states, which many of them seemed ready to take, and placed the prestige of the Court behind the reform movement by *not* forcing the issue. What can be said is that many states are continuing to struggle with the issue, and several have developed politically acceptable solutions which begin to reduce inequities. Moreover, every state constitution provides for an educational system, and those that also contain an equal protection clause are likely to follow California and New Jersey in court challenges to flagrant inequities. In the long run, state-by-state political remedies adapted to local needs may proceed as rapidly (or slowly) as if the High Court had mandated the reform. In any event, the five justices who joined against *Rodriguez* can not be faulted for backing away from the issue when some of the nation's most influential social scientists were questioning the relationship between dollar resources and learning.

NOTES

1. *Brown* v. *Board of Education*, 347 U.S. 483 (1954).
2. *Racial Isolation in the Public Schools*, Summary of a Report by the U.S. Commission on Civil Rights, CCR Clearinghouse Publication No. 7 (Washington, D.C.: U.S. Government Printing Office, 1967).
3. Christopher Jencks, "A Reappraisal of the Most Controversial Educational Document of Our Time," *The New York Times Magazine* (August 10, 1969), pp. 12–13, 34–44.
4. Quoted in a *Christian Science Monitor* article of June 5, 1973.
5. *Green* v. *County School Board of New Kent County*, 391 U.S. 430 (1967).
6. *Beatrice Alexander, et. al.* v. *Holmes County Board of Education*, 396 U.S. 19 (1969).
7. The Commission's statement had no discernible impact on the President who was bent upon appeasing the South. (The political impact of busing in the North had not yet become fully apparent, although Boston and a few other cities use it to achieve racial balance in the schools.)
8. Statement of the U.S. Commission on Civil Rights concerning the "Statement by the President on Elementary and Secondary School Desegregation," April 12, 1970, p. 8.
9. *Swann* v. *Charlotte-Mecklenburg Board of Education*, 402 U.S. 1 (1971).
10. Quoted in *The New York Times*, March 19, 1972.
11. *School Board of Richmond* v. *State Board of Education*, No. 72–549,

decided May 21, 1973, preliminary slip opinion of the U.S. Supreme Court.

12. *Keyes* v. *School District No. 1, Denver, Colorado*, No. 71–507, decided June 21, 1973, preliminary slip opinion of the U.S. Supreme Court.
13. *The New York Times*, July 28, 1974, Sec. 4, p. 3, col. 3–5.
14. Stokely Carmichael and Charles V. Hamilton, *Black Power* (New York: Random House, Vintage Books, 1967), pp. 166–167.
15. Peter Schrag, *Village School Downtown* (Boston: Beacon Press, 1967), pp. 148–151, 181–182.
16. Cited in Advisory Commission on Intergovernmental Relations, *Financing Schools and Property Tax Relief—A State Responsibility* (Washington, D.C.: U.S. Government Printing Office, 1973), pp. 101–102.
17. *Ibid.*
18. *Serrano* v. *Priest*, the California decision, can be found in pp. 102–121 of Alan Shank, ed., *Political Power and the Urban Crisis*, 2nd ed. (Boston: Holbrook Press, 1973); the Minnesota (*Van Dusartz* v. *Hatfield*), Texas (*Rodriguez* v. *San Antonio Independent School District*), and New Jersey (*Robinson* v. *Cahill*) decisions are cited in ACIR, *Financing Schools and Property Tax Relief*, pp. 101–105.
19. Advisory Commission on Intergovernmental Relations, ACIR, *Financing Schools and Property Tax Relief*, p. 102.
20. Advisory Commission on Intergovernmental Relations, ACIR, *Information Bulletin No. 72–1* (March 8, 1972), pp. 4–6.
21. Daniel P. Moynihan, "Equalizing Education: In Whose Benefit?" *The Public Interest*, No. 29 (Fall 1972), pp. 69–8S.

SUGGESTIONS FOR FURTHER READING

Advisory Commission on Intergovernmental Relations. *Financing Schools and Property Tax Relief — A State Responsibility.* Washington, D.C.: U.S. Government Printing Office, January 1973.
Analysis of property tax burden, intrastate disparities in educational opportunity, capacity of states to alleviate problems, and role of federal government.

Armor, David J. "The Evidence on Busing," *The Public Interest*, No. 28 (Summer 1972).
Author reviews history of busing legislation and applications and concludes that busing has failed to accomplish aims of integration.

Bendiner, Robert. *The Politics of Schools: A Crisis in Self-Government.* New York: Harper & Row, 1969.
An explanation of school boards, concentrating on composition, relationships with other political actors and possible alternative means of public school governance.

Berube, Maurice R., and Marilyn Gittell, eds. *Confrontation at Ocean Hill–Brownsville.* New York: Praeger, 1969.
Collection of essays dealing with the New York City school strikes of 1968 over the issues of decentralization and community control.

Bolner, J., and R. Shanley. *Busing.* New York: Praeger, 1973.

Bowers, C. A. *Education and Social Policy: Local Control of Education.* New York: Random House, 1970.

"Community and the Schools," *Harvard Educational Review.* Reprint Series No. 3, 1969.
A collection of HER articles examining the link between the schools and the community in such diverse categories as curriculum and teacher training, with a concluding examination of relevance (or irrelevance) of education policies for community needs.

Conant, James B. *Slums and Suburbs.* New York: New American Library, Signet Books, 1964.
Analysis of unequal educational opportunity in the public schools.

Crain, Robert L. *The Politics of School Desegregation.* Garden City, N.Y.: Doubleday, 1969.
Case analysis of northern and southern city school desegregation.

Damerell, Reginald G. *Triumph in a White Suburb.* New York: William Morrow, 1968.
Interesting and informative case history of school and housing integration by voluntary community efforts in Teaneck, New Jersey.

Dentler, Robert A. "Barrier to Northern School Desegregation," *Daedalus,* Vol. 95, No. 1 (Winter 1966), pp. 45–63.
Finds that both larger and smaller northern communities remain segregated by tradition and population patterns and concludes that if education cannot evolve toward universality, it cannot be maintained as a general municipal service.

————, Bernard Mackler, and Mary Ellen Warshauer, eds. *The Urban R's.* New York: Praeger, 1967.
Eighteen essays examine the effects of racial, economic, and class segregation in the schools together with analyses of what happens when school desegregation is achieved.

"Education in the Ghetto," *Saturday Review.* Report and analysis presented with the Committee for Economic Development (January 11, 1969), p. 33 ff.

Educational Facilities Laboratories, Inc. *The Schoolhouse in the City.* New York: EFL, 1966.

Edwards, T. Bentley, and Frederick M. Wirt, eds. *School Desegregation in the North.* San Francisco: Chandler Publishing, 1967.
Case studies of the response to the challenge of *de facto* school segregation in four New York metropolitan area communities and six California communities.

"Equal Educational Opportunity," *The Harvard Educational Review.* Cambridge, Mass.: Harvard University Press, 1969.
An evaluation of the Coleman Report.

Equality of Educational Opportunity, Summary Report. U.S. Department of Health, Education, and Welfare. Office of Education. Washington, D.C.: U.S. Government Printing Office, 1966.

Summary findings of the landmark Coleman Report on the effects of unequal educational opportunity.

Fantini, Mario, Marilyn Gittell, and Richard Mazat. *Community Control and the Urban School.* New York: Praeger, 1970.
Study of the many problems facing urban schools in general, and New York City schools in particular, combined with an explanation of community control as a possible partial explanation.

Gittell, Marilyn, ed. *Educating an Urban Population.* Beverly Hills, Calif.: Sage Publications, 1967.
Gittell has selected studies which (1) establish the extent of urban education problems, (2) explore policy-making alternatives for adapting to new urban demands, and (3) recommend alternative policies based on newly generated knowledge about the urban setting.

Gittell, Marilyn and Alan G. Hevesi. *The Politics of Urban Education.* New York: Praeger, 1969.
This edited set of readings endeavors to chronicle the accelerated pace of urban growth and to explain the inability of schools and urban power structures to adapt to the transformed urban setting.

Kozol, Jonathan. *Death at an Early Age.* New York: Bantam Books, 1967.
Scathing attack on Boston public schools by a former teacher.

LaNoue, George R., and Bruce L. R. Smith. *The Politics of School Decentralization.* Lexington, Mass.: D. C. Heath, 1973.
Combines theoretical and historical treatment of the decentralization concept with case studies of several major cities. Of special interest is the conceptual differentiation between decentralization and community control.

Levin, Henry M. *Community Control of Schools.* Washington, D.C.: Brookings Institution, 1970.
A series of papers which grew out of a Brookings Institute Conference on the community school. These readings evaluate the utility of community control as a vehicle for redistribution of educational power and, ultimately, for a quality education program in our cities.

Levin, Melvin R., and Alan Shank, eds. *Educational Investment in an Urban Society.* New York: Teachers College Press, Columbia University, 1970.
Collection of articles and essays dealing with cost-benefit analysis of education, manpower, and public policy.

Marcus, Sheldon and Harry N. Rivlin, eds. *Conflicts in Urban Education.* New York: Basic Books, 1970.
A set of papers presented at a Fordham University conference on urban education. These readings are refreshing in that they offer a less theoretical and more practical orientation which reflects their authors' backgrounds as public school educators.

Mayer, Martin. *The Teachers Strike: New York, 1968.* New York: Harper & Row, 1969.
Brief and very critical account of school decentralization and community control issues in New York City.

McMurrin, Sterling M. *Resources for Urban Schools: Better Use and Balance.* New York: Committee for Economic Development, Supplementary Paper No. 33, 1971.
An edited series of proposed responses to the failure of urban schools to meet students' needs; proposals include radical changes in financing teacher training and recruitment and a radically different relationship between teacher and student. Of special interest is Leon Lessinger's selection on accountability.

Meranto, Philip. *School Politics in the Metropolis.* Columbus, Ohio: Charles E. Merrill, 1970.
Relationship of public school politics to cities, suburbs, states, and the federal government.

Mosteller, Frederick, and Daniel P. Moynihan, eds. *On Equality of Educational Opportunity.* New York: Random House, 1972.
Papers presented by distinguished scholars at a Harvard Conference to expand and further analyze the massive Coleman Report, with special emphasis on methodological and data analysis problems.

Pettigrew, Thomas F., Elizabeth L. Useem, Clarence Normand, and Marshall S. Smith. "Busing: A Review of the Evidence," *The Public Interest*, No. 30 (Winter 1973), pp. 88–118.
Authors criticize Armor for (1) setting unrealistically high standards for judging busing success, (2) a biased choice of examples, (3) unrepresentative control groups, and (4) a low response rate.

Roberts, Dennis L., II. *Planning Urban Education: New Ideas & Techniques to Transform Learning in the City.* Englewood Cliffs, N.J.: Educational Technology Publications, 1972.
A reform-oriented group of readings which share the assumptions that the urban setting is a detriment to human development which can only be overcome by a major overhaul of urban education.

Rogers, David. *110 Livingston Street.* New York: Random House, 1968.
Politics and bureaucracy in the New York City school system.

Rosenthal, Alan, ed. *Governing Education: A Reader of Politics, Power, and Public School Policy.* Garden City, N.Y.: Doubleday, 1969.
An edited volume of studies which examine systematically the relationships between participants in education policy formations.

Schrag, Peter. *Village School Downtown.* Boston: Beacon Press, 1967.
Critical attack on Boston public school system together with a useful proposal for a metropolitan school district.

Silberman, Charles E. *Crisis in the Classroom.* New York: Random House, 1970.

Accuses American educators of confusing purposes with process; calls for reforms of schools and teacher education.

Southern Regional Council Special Report. *School Desegregation in 1966: The Slow Undoing.* Atlanta, Ga., December 1966.
Strong argument that the Office of Education issued guidelines but no enforcement and that, as a result, southern schools remain segregated into grossly unequal facilities.

Toffler, Alvin, ed. *The Schoolhouse in the City.* New York: Praeger, 1968.
A set of papers presented at a Stanford University conference whose authors agree that cities can be made hospitable and that the education system is crucial in any such transition but disagree eloquently as to proper methods.

U.S. Commission on Civil Rights. *Racial Isolation in the Public Schools.* Washington, D.C.: U. S. Government Printing Office, 1967.

Wasserman, Miriam. *The School Fix, NYC, USA.* New York: Outerbridge Dienstfrey, 1970.
In an exhausting polemic directed at the New York City schools, Ms. Wasserman contends that the purpose of the schools' status perpetuation—and the educational needs of the students tend to be incompatible. Of special interest are sections on community control and student undergrounds as challenges to status quo.

Wirt, Frederick M., and Michael W. Kirst. *The Political Web of American Schools.* Boston: Little, Brown, 1972.
An insightful application of systems models to explain the current state of research into politics of education and to generate (topics for) future research.

Wise, Arthur E. "The California Doctrine," and Howe, Harold, II, "Anatomy of a Revolution," articles in *Saturday Review* (November 20, 1971) in a special section on education in America, financing public schools and whether the property tax is obsolete.

Wolff, Max, and Alan Rinzler. *The Educational Park: A Guide to its Implementation.* New York: Center for Urban Education, 1970.

Index